Front cover

Man has used light for communication from the earliest days. In recent times engineers and scientists have created materials and technology for guiding light in transmission lines: hair-thin silica glass fibers, which can be assembled to form cables of any size, act as the transmission medium for modulated light

About ten years ago it was decided to discontinue the development of millimeter waveguide transmission systems in the Federal Republic of Germany. These waveguides had been intended to extend the transmission capacity of the long-haul routes and take the place of coaxial cables, the transmission potential of which had already been largely exhausted. In the early 1970s, the results of research indicated that optical waveguides would offer greater potential for future developments in the long-haul network.

In the initial phase the optical waveguide gained entry worldwide into the junction and interoffice trunk cable network, mainly with transmission systems operating at 34 and 45 Mbit/s at an optical wavelength around 850 nm. The reason for this was that at that time neither the available fibers nor the transmitting and receiving components then obtainable were suitable for transmission at higher bit rates. From this beginning the extension of optical waveguide systems into the long-haul network and into the local network can now be discerned. It is probable that the penetration into the long-haul network, with single-mode fibers and transmission systems operating at 140, 274, 400, 565 Mbit/s and even higher bit rates, will proceed at a faster pace than in the case of the local network. Not only will the fibers have to be produced very economically for local network applications, but extensive development work will also have to be carried out on the transmission and switching systems, as well as on the terminal equipment.

From the present standpoint it is impossible to predict when widespread use of the new technology in subscriber line networks will occur. However, there is no doubt that the possibilities offered by optical wave-guides for wideband communication in the local network are so attractive that use should be made of them.

The development of optical waveguides provided a strong impetus for the development of the associated optical transmission systems and the components necessary for their realization. A worldwide trend toward longer wavelengths for optical transmission has since become discernible. The first systems employing a wavelength of 1300 nm are already in use. Some development work is now concerned with systems operating at 1500 to 1600 nm and beyond.

Optical communication technology is fascinating, even though the possibilities it offers have only been partly recognized so far. It is the technology of the future.

Dipl.-Ing. Bernd Zeitler
Head of Transmission Networks Division
Communications Group
Siemens AG, Munich

Heinrich Keil and Helmut Pascher

Communications Enter a New Era with Fiber Optics

For some 140 years Siemens has been involved in developing communications technology to its present state of maturity. The aim and object of this technology has always been firmly linked to the ability of communication to bring people and peoples closer together. For 100 years and more the telegraph and telephone, connected via copper cables and radio links, formed the unchanging basis for the now worldwide communication network. Although line transmission technology repeatedly underwent technical improvement, there were no revolutionary innovations. Only with the development of the semiconductor laser and optical fiber and the advance of digitalization in the last decade a radical change did appear in communication technology: electrical signals could be converted into optical signals and be conveyed over long distances in silica glass fibers no thicker than a human hair – optical communications was "born".

In view of the experience gained so far with this fledgling medium, we may turn with confidence to a new age of communications. In the field of communication cables, optical waveguides as an alternative to copper cable and optoelectronic transducers for connecting the various transmission systems will give fresh impetus to communication technology. Worldwide, many thousands of kilometers of fiber have already been successfully installed by Siemens. Transmission systems for PTT networks and for numerous industrial applications have already proved their worth even under adverse operating conditions. Furthermore, new fields of application are constantly being opened up in a great variety of experimental systems and pilot projects.

New technology for an old idea

From the dawn of history, man has been transmitting information by visual means and has constantly discovered new ways of doing this – from simple hand signals through beacons and smoke signals to semaphores and Aldis lamps. As early as 1880, Graham Bell experimented with the "photophone", but the most recent development is the modulated laser beam. At first this was confined to the propagation of light in air and, owing to the limited and very variable transparency of this medium (e.g. due to fog), only relatively short distances could be spanned. Only in 1970 did the possibility arise of optical line transmission (which would be unaffected by atmospheric conditions). The pioneering work on producing high-purity glasses (the prerequisite for light propagation with low attenuation and hence low transmission losses) was done in the USA. Newly developed methods made it possible to produce rods of synthetic silica glass and to draw hair-thin fibers about 0.1 mm thick in lengths up to several kilometers. Ingenious cable designs have been perfected to protect the thin fiber from stresses during installation and operation of the cables.

Optical line transmission

The principal elements of communications over a fiber-optic link, in which the light wave is conveyed in thin fibers, are shown in *Fig. 1* (transmission of a telephone call). As usual, the microphone in the telephone set converts the sound waves of the speech of one subscriber into electrical signals. At the point of reception, the earphone converts the electrical signals back into sound waves audible to the other subscriber (electroacoustic transducer). For transmission by means of light waves, the electrical signals must be converted into light signals and these converted back into electrical signals.

These tasks are performed by semiconductor components oper-

Dipl.-Ing. Heinrich Keil and
Dr.-techn. Helmut Pascher,
Siemens AG,
Public Communication Networks Division,
Munich

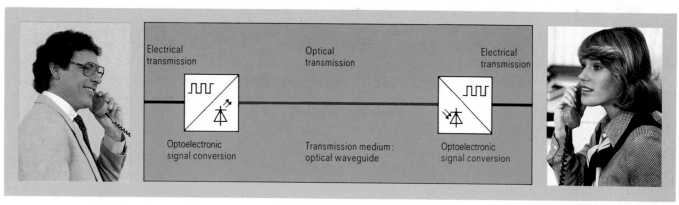

Fig. 1   Principle of optical communications

ating as optoelectronic transducers at both ends of the transmission route: certain crystals (e.g. gallium arsenide GaAs) emit light at a wavelength just above the visible spectrum when electric current is passed through them *(Fig. 2)*.
A thin fiber conveys this light with low losses to the receiver (also a semiconductor crystal) which reacts very sensitively to the light from the fiber by producing a corresponding current.

Advantages of fiber-optic technology

In optical fibers we now have an optical transmission medium which in important respects is superior to metallic conductors:

● *Very low line attenuation*

Whereas a high-frequency signal on a conventional coaxial cable will have lost half of its power after only a few hundred meters, the corresponding figure for optical power in particularly good optical waveguides is 15 km. In telecommunication systems this means that repeaters to refresh the signal are required only at far greater intervals than before, or not at all.

● *Significantly larger transmission capacity with certain types of fiber*

Transmission rates exceeding 10 Gbit/s are theoretically possible (by contrast, about 1 Gbit/s is now achieved with coaxial cables). This capacity can be multiplied by using several carrier waves with different optical wavelengths.

● *Considerable reduction in cable size and weight*

A very small fiber diameter (together with a protective plastic coating 0.25 to 0.5 mm compared with about 10 mm for copper coaxial tubes) and a correspondingly low cable weight with considerably greater mechanical flexibility provide a number of advantages as regards transport, installation and the space required in cable duct runs.

● *No electrical conductivity*

This means that the fibers do not have to be grounded or protected against lightning. An optical waveguide can bridge large differences in potential, for example when used as a control line in high-voltage switching stations.

● *No interaction between the light wave inside and electromagnetic waves and fields outside the fiber*

Transmission on optical fibers does not give rise to electromagnetic interference fields; conversely, transmission cannot be disturbed from outside by such fields. This means that transmission can be intercepted only with great difficulty by unauthorized persons.

New technology isn't a gift

Although quartz sand, the raw material used for producing optical waveguides, is available in unlimited quantities, far more energy than in metal smelting has to be used to obtain a glass with the required chemical purity (no more

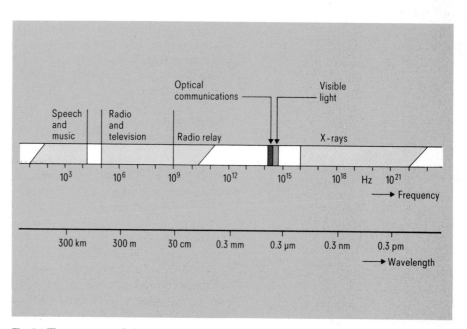

Fig. 2   The spectrum of electromagnetic waves and their applications

than one unwanted foreign atom for 10^7 to 10^9 silicon atoms). A further factor is that an extensive range of equipment is required in order to achieve the necessary high mechanical precision of the fiber. For this reason also, optical waveguides are still relatively expensive and are not (yet) able to replace all conventional cables.

Since the optical fiber is very fragile, it needs to be treated with special care when formed into a cable and also requires some special machinery. For joints also, whether permanent or nonpermanent (splices or connectors), new equipments of the greatest precision have been and are being developed. The same can be said for test procedures, some of which had to be supplemented by new processes.

On the basis of experimental and operational systems with fiber lengths up to several thousand kilometers, it has now been proved that all the associated technical problems can be overcome. Since 1976, Siemens has installed worldwide more than a hundred cable links with optical waveguides totalling more than 30,000 km, in some cases also equipped with transmission equipment *(Fig. 3)*. In

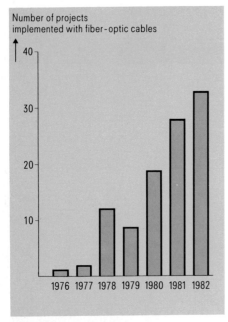

Number of projects implemented with fiber-optic cables

Fig. 3 Fiber-optic cable from Siemens – approximately 30,000 km of fiber installed in 13 countries

this way Siemens has played a considerable part in the development of such systems since they were first put to practical use.

Possible applications for optical waveguides

Transmission systems for the telephone network

From an economic standpoint optical waveguide systems are currently only to be preferred to systems with balanced copper lines if blocks of 120 voice channels or more (telephone calls on one cable) are to be transmitted. A development that is likely to bring benefits in the near future is the planned use of systems with 480 voice channels and more on trunks between the digital exchanges in large local networks and in the short-haul network. The repeater spacings that can at present be achieved in operational systems – about 10 to 30 km and more, depending on the optical wavelength and transmission capacity compared with 2 to 10 km in copper cable systems (e.g. PCM 30) – enable the distances between exchanges to be bridged in many cases without regenerative repeaters and hence without power feeding.

For long-distance links the single-mode fiber as it is known, featuring a particularly large transmission bandwidth and very low attenuation, has increasingly been attracting attention. Before the end of the eighties it will dominate this field of application.

Networks for new broadband services

In addition to its application in long-haul networks, the optical waveguide is of interest primarily in networks for new broadband services (cable television, videotex, videotelephony). Regarding the technology it should be noted that, compared with coaxial cable television networks able to transmit 12 to 30 television programs with a total bandwidth up to about 300 MHz and repeater spacings of

about 400 m, optical transmission systems require different solutions (e.g. switched communication and also a different network structure).

Since the optical fiber has a very much lower attenuation than the coaxial line, there are advantages in designing the subscriber network as a star configuration without regenerative repeaters between the central station and the subscribers. The star structure is necessary anyway for establishing a switched broadband communication network. Selection of the signals to be transmitted from and to the long-distance network would be made via the switching networks controlled by the subscriber, in other words the subscriber himself would be able to use a backward channel to switch the required services or programs to his line.

Connection of each individual subscriber will only make economic sense if the network does more than just distribute radio and television programs, in other words only when there is genuine broadband communication (e.g. videotelephony, cable text facilities). A comprehensive system of this kind will be implemented by the Deutsche Bundespost with its BIGFON field trial (broadband integrated glass fiber local communication network) in seven German cities. The BIGFON islands embracing a total of a few hundred subscribers are linked to each other by a long-haul network some sections of which are likewise routed over optical fibers. BIGFON and similar trial systems in other countries are useful in gathering technical experience and determining subscriber interest.

Transmission systems for industrial applications

There are doubtless a large number of industrial applications where fiber-optic technology should already be given consideration, and there are others where it has already proved itself in trials at least. The optical waveguide is an attractive proposition wherever it

Fig. 4 The optical waveguide, a hair-thin fiber of silica glass, is revolutionizing communication technology

switches. This would enable, for example, more telephone calls to be switched more quickly than ever before.

Another development concerns the transducer connected on the input, and output sides of the repeaters in the transmission link. At present, the light pulses must first be converted into electrical signals at the repeater input and these must then be converted back into light pulses. The rapid rate of innovation in semiconductor technology could one day make these transducers considerably cheaper or even unnecessary through direct regeneration of the light pulses.

Judging by the advances in electronics, we can also expect progress towards integration of optical components into initially separate passive and active modules.

The future looks bright for an economic breakthrough

Assuming that large-scale production and the experience gained in early development work lead to a corresponding reduction in the cost of fabrication, the optical waveguide will be able to replace conventional copper conductors in certain areas.

The subscriber area of the public telecommunication networks is, as we have said, particularly important, since it is here that the optical waveguide is superior to copper conductors, a single fiber being able to transmit all the telecommunication services to the subscriber *(Fig. 4)*. Besides the customary telephone service, optical waveguides will allow all subscribers to participate in person-to-person video communication (videotelephony) from the comfort of their own homes. This still leaves sufficient transmission capacity to provide the subscriber with a simultaneous selection of radio and television programs from a theoretically unlimited number of programs accessible in the exchange.

offers technical advantages over conventional transmission. It is, for example, immune to electromagnetic interference and can also provide isolation in monitoring the power network or save space and weight in aircraft, to name just two, quite different reasons for its use. Electrical protection and shielding for the line are not required. For transmission over short distances (e.g. between a computer and its peripherals) the cost of the fiber itself compared with the conventional equivalent is not of great importance, though the cost of the optoelectronic transducer is. These applications, therefore, operate the transmission path on a multiplex basis, suit-

able circuits being employed to process a number of signals so that they can be transmitted over a single fiber.

Opportunities for "integrated optics"

While the possibilities of the new technology are now being examined in practical applications, work is already being conducted in research laboratories into new technical solutions. At both the theoretical and practical level a method is being sought whereby switching operations will be triggered directly by light pulses. Researchers also hope to develop optical switches to replace both electromagnetic and electronic

Siegfried Geckeler

Physical Principles of Optical Waveguides

It has long been known that light can be guided in thin glass fibers along paths of virtually any curvature by means of total internal reflection. However, until a few years ago light losses in the available glasses were so high it was only possible to span distances of a few meters. Now, however, with the development of extremely low-loss glasses it has become possible to fabricate optical waveguides suitable for communication over distances of several kilometers. Such fibers, which are connectorized and embedded in plastic cable for mechanical protection and ease of handling, can be used to form the basis of highly efficient communication systems with light-emitting or laser diodes as the optical transmitters and semiconductor photodiodes as the receivers. What the fibers are primarily required to provide is good light guidance, low light losses and large transmission bandwidth. Starting with basic optical terms, the article goes on to describe how these requirements can be met.

Geometric optics of glass fibers

When light propagates in a glass of *refractive index n*, it moves by a factor of n more slowly than in free space, where the velocity of light c is known to be 300,000 km/s. In the glasses considered here with $n \approx 1.5$ the velocity of light is therefore

$$c_n = \frac{c}{n} \approx 200{,}000 \text{ km/s} = 200 \text{ m/}\mu\text{s}. \quad (1)$$

If light emerging from a glass with higher refractive index n_2 is incident on

Dipl.-Ing. Dr.-Ing. Siegfried Geckeler,
Siemens AG,
Research and Development Division,
Munich

◁ Optical waveguide fabrication is based on the production of the fiber preform from variously doped layers of silica glass. The resultant sequence of layers is retained in the subsequent fiber drawing process

a glass with lower refractive index n_1, it changes direction provided it strikes the interface at a steep angle. However, if the angle of incidence is shallower than the so-called critical angle γ_G, total internal reflection occurs (**Fig. 1**). This is expressed by the relation

$$\cos \gamma_G = \frac{n_1}{n_2}, \quad (2)$$

i.e. the critical angle is a function of the refractive index difference.

In the case of the simplest fiber, the *step-index fiber* (**Fig. 2**), a circular glass core 50 to 200 μm in diameter (depending on design) is surrounded by a glass cladding whose refractive index n_M is approximately 1% lower than the core refractive index n_K. All light coupled into the fiber such that its direction of propagation deviates from the axial direction of the fiber by no more than the critical angle γ_G is therefore guided along the fiber due to total internal reflection and will continue along the fiber even if the latter is bent. For this

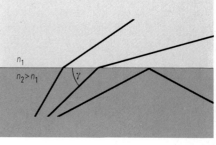

n_1, n_2 Refractive indices
γ Incidence angle at the interface

Fig. 1   Optical refraction and total reflection

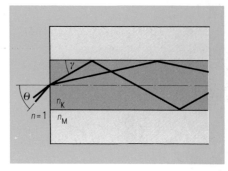

n_K Core refractive index
n_M Cladding refractive index
Θ Ray angle in free space
γ Ray angle inside fiber

Fig. 2   Ray diagram for a step-index fiber (not to scale)

to occur, the light must be launched to strike the end face of the fiber within the *acceptance angle* $\pm \Theta_A$. Owing to refraction at the end face as the light passes from $n = 1$ (air) to $n = n_K$ (core), the following applies:

$$\sin \Theta_A = n_K \cdot \sin \gamma_G$$
$$= \sqrt{n_K^2 - n_M^2} = A_N. \quad (3)$$

This sine of the acceptance angle is termed the *numerical aperture* A_N of the fiber.

As will be shown in greater detail later, the numerical aperture together with the diameter of the fiber core determines how much light from a given source can be coupled into the fiber. It would therefore appear desirable to make both values as large as possible. However, for various reasons this is only possible to a limited extent. For example, manufacturing costs increase with the core diameter and, in addition, extremely low-loss glasses yield numerical apertures of only about 0.2 ($\Theta_A \approx \pm 12°$), because large refractive index differences require higher-loss glasses. However, low fiber loss is even more important for a transmission system than a high launched power, since the optical power P decays along the length of the fiber according to the law

$$P(L) = P(0) \cdot 10^{-\frac{\alpha L}{10\,\text{dB}}}. \qquad (4)$$

The optical power $P(L)$ available to the photodetector at the end of fiber length L is therefore only a linear function of the launched power $P(0)$, but is an exponential function of the *attenuation coefficient* α of the fiber.

Fig. 3 shows the attenuation coefficients which can be achieved using modern fibers made of doped silica glass and how these values are a function of the optical wavelength λ. It is noticeable that there is a steep fall towards the longer wavelengths. This is because the light losses are largely due to light scattering (dashed curve). A second cause of light losses is the absorption of light by impurities in the glass; this effect only occurs at certain wavelengths, producing local attenuation peaks (note: whereas in a fiber with 10 dB attenuation only 10% of the launched power reaches the end of the fiber, this figure is 50% with 3 dB and 80% with 1 dB attenuation).

The lowest attenuation values are achieved at wavelengths around 1300 and 1600 nm which are therefore the most suitable for optical communication transmission over large distances. Although most transmitter and receiver devices currently available still operate at wavelengths of between 800 and 900 nm, components for the long wavelength range have been developed using new materials. These will assist in fully exploiting the capabilities of glass fibers.

A great disadvantage of the step-index fiber is its small transmission bandwith. The reason for this is that the

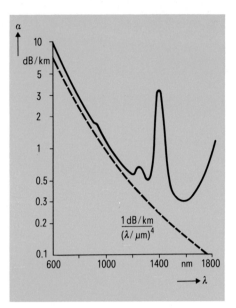

Fig. 3 Attenuation coefficient α of a silica glass fiber as a function of the optical wavelength λ

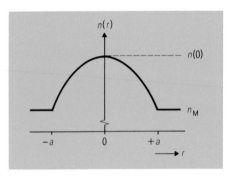

a	Fiber-core radius
$n(r)$	Radius-dependent refractive index
n_M	Cladding refractive index

Fig. 4 Refractive index profile of a graded-index fiber

light propagates in its core at various angles (between 0 and γ_G) relative to the fiber axis (**Fig. 2**) and these different angles result in varying optical path lengths. If a short light pulse is launched into the fiber, part of its optical power travels directly along the axis to the end of the fiber, while other parts follow zig-zag courses, arriving later due to the longer distances traveled (the ratio of maximum to minimum delay is the same as that of the core refractive index n_K to the cladding refractive index n_M; the difference is therefore around 1%). As a result, the width of the initially short light pulse steadily increases as it traverses the fiber and the pulse appearing at the end of the fiber becomes increasingly spread out the longer the fiber and the greater its refractive index difference.

This aspect of fiber behavior can be compared to a low-pass filter whose bandwith decreases the longer the fiber, thus restricting the transmission of wideband signals.

This disadvantage is largely avoided if the refractive index in the fiber core is made to decrease parabolically with radial distance from a maximum of $n(0)$ at the fiber axis to a value of n_M in the cladding (**Fig. 4**). In a *graded-index fiber* of this type the light, instead of zig-zagging, follows an undulating course (**Fig. 5**) with a period of a few millimeters. The greater length of the more devious trajectories is compensated by the light outside the fiber axis traveling faster due to the lower refractive index, so that all light components take virtually the same time to reach the end of the fiber. Graded-index fibers can now be fabricated whose *refractive index profile* comes so close to the ideal that for a transit time of 5 µs per km of fiber, as in equation (1), delay differences of only ± 0.1 ns/km arise.

The refractive index profile of the graded-index fiber makes the acceptance angle Θ_A a function of the distance r from the fiber axis. This angle decreases continuously from a maximum value on the axis ($r = 0$) until it reaches the value 0 at the core-cladding boundary ($r = a$). Instead of (3) the following then applies:

$$\sin \Theta_A(r) = \sqrt{n^2(r) - n_M^2} \leqq A_N. \qquad (5)$$

The magnitude of $\Theta_A(r)$ is thus determined by the difference between the local and cladding refractive indices, while the numerical aperture is understood to be the sine of the maximum acceptance angle. **Fig. 6** shows this for a graded-index fiber and a step-index fiber for comparison, using phase space diagrams which are also very useful for illustrating other fiber properties, as will be shown later. The coordinates r^2 and $\sin^2 \Theta$ of these diagrams are proportional to the area $A = \pi r^2$ of a circle of radius r concentric with the fiber axis, or the solid angle $\Omega = 2\pi \cdot (1 - \cos \Theta) \approx \pi \cdot \sin^2 \Theta$ of a circular cone about the fiber axis with vertex angle $\pm \Theta$ (the plotted limit curves show how the light must be distributed by position and direction through space for it to be guided in the fiber). In the case of the step-index fiber the refractive index n is constant over the entire fiber core, hence from (3) the acceptance angle Θ_A and the associated maximum solid angle are also constant. For the graded-index fiber the parabolic refractive index profile

$$n^2(r) = n^2(0) - A_N^2 \cdot \left(\frac{r}{a}\right)^2 \qquad (6)$$

or

$$n(r) \approx n(0) \cdot \left[1 - \frac{A_N^2}{2\,n^2(0)} \cdot \left(\frac{r}{a}\right)^2\right]$$

was adopted (**Fig. 4**); consequently the acceptance limit in **Fig. 6 a** is a sloping straight line due to (5). In actual fibers with profile irregularities it is necessary to replace $(r/a)^2$ in (6) by a corresponding profile function $f(r)$ with values between 0 and 1. The resultant acceptance limit curve is then a correspondingly irregular curved line.

An important application of the phase space diagram is in calculating the optical power P launched into the fiber from an optical source. If the distribution of the source radiance N – measured in W/cm²sr – over A and Ω is known, P can be calculated by integration over part of the phase space encompassed by the fiber:

$$P = \iint\limits_{\Omega A} N(A, \Omega)\,\mathrm{d}A\,\mathrm{d}\Omega. \qquad (7)$$

The simplest case is that of a constant radiance in the region $0 < r < a$, $0 < \sin\Theta < A_N$, which is approximated when the fiber is coupled to large-area LEDs. It then follows directly from **Fig. 6** that a *step-index* fiber accepts the power

$$P = N \cdot \pi a^2 \cdot \pi A_N^2 \qquad (8)$$

while the *graded-index* fiber with identical a and A_N accepts exactly half as much. The graded-index fiber is at less of a disadvantage when coupled to light sources with a small emitting area relative to the fiber core diameter or with a sharply focussed beam (small-area light-emitting diodes or laser diodes). Although in such cases the radiance is unevenly distributed in the phase space, the optical power P can still be calculated using (7), because the phase space diagram clearly shows which part of the power emitted by the light source lies within the acceptance area of the fiber and which does not. The same approach can be used to calculate connector and splice losses.

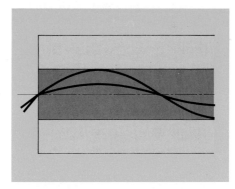

Fig. 5 Ray diagram for a graded-index fiber (not to scale)

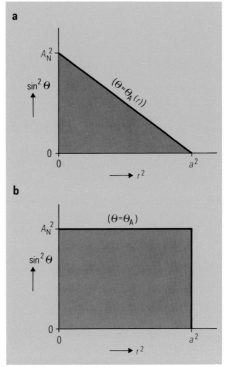

A_N Numerical aperture of the fiber
Θ Ray angle with fiber axis $(0 < \Theta < \Theta_A)$
r Distance from fiber axis $(0 < r < a)$

Fig. 6 Acceptance limits of a graded-index fiber (a) with parabolic refractive-index profile and of a step-index fiber (b), shown in the form of phase space diagrams

The glass fiber as an optical waveguide

Since the important characteristics of glass fibers cannot be explained entirely in terms of geometric optics as used so far, it is necessary to consider them also in terms of wave optics. A basic concept of physical optics is the interference of two light waves, i.e. the process of attenuation or extinction when the two waves are superimposed in antiphase, and of reinforcement when they are in phase. The implication of this for glass fibers is that light

cannot propagate in them at any angle, but only in those directions in which the light waves do not weaken each other. The number of permissible waveforms, also known as eigenwaves or modes of the fiber, while finite in normal fibers, is nevertheless very large (more than a thousand), because their core diameters of typically 50 to 200 µm are large compared with the optical wavelength λ. The previously described effect of delay differences between light components with different propagation paths controlling the transmission bandwidth of the fiber can be perceived more readily as delay differences between different modes.

The number of modes is on the order of the square of the characteristic fiber parameter

$$v = \frac{2\pi}{\lambda} \cdot a \cdot A_N \qquad (9)$$

and is proportional to the area under the acceptance limit curve of the fiber in **Fig. 6**. If v is reduced, e.g. by reducing the core diameter of the fiber, the number of propagating modes decreases until finally only a single mode is left at $v < 2.4$. A fiber of this type is termed a *single-mode fiber*, in contrast to the *multimode fiber* (v large). The main advantage of a single-mode fiber is its large transmission bandwidth, because no delay differences between different modes can occur in it – unlike in the multimode fiber. However, its disadvantage is its small core diameter of a few µm (microns) which makes splicing difficult and into which sufficient optical power can only be coupled using optical sources with very high radiance (e.g. laser diodes).

The bandwidth of single-mode fibers is essentially limited by an effect known as *material dispersion*: the refractive index n of glass is not constant but decreases gradually with increasing optical wavelength λ (**Fig. 7**). As a result the light velocity in the glass per (1) becomes wavelength-dependent and as the light from optical transmitters has a certain spectral width $\Delta\lambda$, delay differences occur even within a single mode. The controlling factor for the propagation velocity of light pulses is not n but the slightly higher *group index*

$$n_g = n - \lambda\frac{\mathrm{d}n}{\mathrm{d}\lambda} \qquad (10)$$

whose curve is also shown in **Fig. 7**. At $\lambda \approx 850$ nm, delay differences occur of approximately 0.1 ns per nanometer of spectral width and kilometer of fiber length. The delay differences are greatly reduced at $\lambda \approx 1300$ nm, where n_g is at a minimum. This wavelength range is therefore of interest not only because of the attenuation minimum shown in **Fig. 3**. The most commonly used measure of material dispersion is the parameter M obtained from the derivation of group index in terms of the wavelength:

$$M(\lambda) = \frac{-1}{c} \cdot \frac{dn_g}{d\lambda} = +\frac{\lambda}{c} \cdot \frac{d^2 n}{d\lambda^2} . \qquad (11)$$

Material dispersion is also a significant factor for graded-index fibers when operated with a light-emitting diode. The typical values $\lambda \approx 850$ nm and $\Delta\lambda \approx 40$ nm produce delay differences of around 4 ns per km which are much greater than the delay differences between the different modes (see above) and consequently reduce the usable transmission bandwidth. This problem can be overcome by using laser diodes ($\Delta\lambda < 5$ nm) or light-emitting diodes at $\lambda \approx 1300$ nm.

For a closer definition of the modes which can propagate in a fiber it is instructive to consider the wave vector k_n in **Fig. 8** which represents a locally plane light wave moving in the direction defined by angles γ and ψ at a distance r from the fiber axis. The magnitude of the wave vector is

$$k_n(r, \lambda) = \frac{2\pi}{\lambda} \cdot n(r, \lambda) , \qquad (12)$$

and is therefore a function of the local refractive index. The axial component of this vector is the *propagation constant* β which controls the propagation velocity of the mode and which, similar to (6), is expressed by

$$\beta^2 = \left(\frac{2\pi}{\lambda}\right)^2 \cdot (n^2(0) - A_N^2 \cdot D) \qquad (13)$$

where D, the normalized propagation constant, is between 0 and 1 for propagating modes. The two other components of the wave vector – radial component $q(\mu)$ and azimuthal component v/r – must be matched with β such that the wave vector points in one of the allowed directions. For complicated theoretical reasons it follows that, in the case of the parabolic refractive

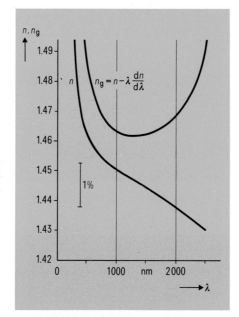

Fig. 7 Phase index n and group index n_g of silica glass as a function of the optical wavelength λ

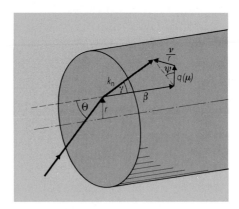

r	Distance from fiber axis
Θ	Ray angle with fiber axis
γ, ψ	Ray angles inside fiber
β	Propagation constant (axial component)
μ, v	Mode numbers

Fig. 8 Wave vector k_n and its components

index profile per (6), the two parameters μ and v of these components are linked to D by

$$D = \frac{2}{v}(2\mu - 1 + v) \geq \frac{2}{v} \qquad (14)$$

and that both must be integers ($\mu = 1$, $2, 3 \ldots$; $v = 0, 1, 2, 3, \ldots$). Each pair of numbers (μ, v) corresponds to a mode or more precisely a set of four modes which differ only in respect of polarization and orientation but are otherwise identical. Other refractive index profiles, i.e. $f(r) \neq r^2/a^2$, have more complicated expressions than (14) but even so the mode numbers μ and v are always integral.

The normalized propagation constant D is smallest for the fundamental mode ($\mu = 1$, $v = 0$) which is the only one which can propagate in a single-mode fiber. For higher-order modes D is larger, but these modes can only propagate if $D < 1$, i.e. modes with $D > 1$ are strongly attenuated. However, there is no abrupt attenuation increase in the range $D \approx 1$. There are therefore modes – so-called *leaky waves* – which, although their D is somewhat greater than 1, can nevertheless propagate to a limited extent. In fiber attenuation measurements the leaky waves constitute a source of error and must therefore be suppressed by suitable excitation conditions.

The geometric conditions necessary to excite particular modes can be obtained from **Fig. 8**: light striking the fiber end face at distance r from the fiber axis and at angle Θ with the axis excites modes with

$$D = f(r) + \frac{\sin^2 \Theta}{A_N^2} \qquad (15)$$

Mode number v is determined by rotation angle ψ as

$$v = v \cdot \frac{r}{a} \cdot \frac{\sin \Theta}{A_N} \cdot \sin \psi , \qquad (16)$$

and μ follows from this necessarily, e.g. for $f(r) = r^2/a^2$ by (14). Using (15) and (16) it is possible to locate each mode of the fiber in the phase space diagram, i.e. determine its propagation direction at each point in the fiber core. By integration in the phase space as in (7) it is possible, for example, to examine the effect of mode-dependent attenuations on the optical power guided in the fiber or on the near field and far field of the fiber.

Dispersion in optical waveguides

Dispersion is a collective term for all effects producing delay differences and thereby limiting the transmission bandwidth of a fiber. Two of these effects – the differing delays of different modes and the material dispersion – have already been described. This description can now be refined and amplified.

The group delay t_g of a mode, i.e. the delay of a signal modulated onto this mode, can be calculated in a fiber of length L from

$$t_g = L \frac{d\beta}{d\omega}$$
$$= \frac{L}{c}\left(n(0) - \lambda \frac{dn(0)}{d\lambda}\right) \cdot \frac{d\beta}{dk_0}, \qquad (17)$$

where $\omega = (2\pi/\lambda) \cdot c$
and $k_0 = (2\pi/\lambda) \cdot n(0)$.

In addition to the known group index (10) at $r = 0$, this equation contains a term $d\beta/dk_0$, which is influenced by the refractive index profile of the fiber. Although this term is virtually 1, it produces a slight additional wavelength dependence on t_g which is termed *waveguide dispersion*. In the case of single-mode fibers this results in t_g, like n_g, having a minimum at $\lambda \approx 1300$ nm (**Fig. 7**) where the transmission bandwidth of the fiber is at its maximum. However, this minimum is slightly shifted towards longer wavelengths.

In the case of multimode fibers the value of $d\beta/dk_0$ differs from mode to mode and determines the delay difference between the modes. It follows from theoretical considerations that

$$\frac{d\beta}{dk_0} = \frac{1 - 2\Delta \cdot D/C_P}{\sqrt{1 - 2\Delta \cdot D}}, \qquad (18)$$

where

$$\Delta = \frac{A_N^2}{2n^2(0)} \approx \frac{n(0) - n_M}{n(0)} \ll 1 \qquad (19)$$

is the relative refractive index difference of the fiber per (5) and (6). **Fig. 9** shows (18) for four different values of the parameter C_P which can be controlled by the choice of refractive index profile. It is shown that the best agreement in delay times among all the guided modes $(0 < D < 1)$ is obtained when $C_P \approx 2 - \Delta$. For the important class of refractive index profiles of the form $f(r) = (r/a)^g$, which includes the parabolic profile $(g = 2)$ and the step-index profile $(g \to \infty)$, the following applies

$$C_P = \frac{2 + g}{2 - P_0}, \qquad (20)$$

so that the optimum profile exponent

$$g_{opt} \approx (2 - \Delta) \cdot (2 - P_0) - 2$$
$$= 2 - 2P_0 - \Delta \cdot (2 - P_0) \qquad (21)$$

deviates slightly from $g = 2$. The magnitude of this deviation is influenced by

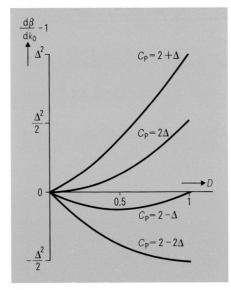

$\frac{d\beta}{dk_0} - 1$	Normalized group delay
Δ	Normalized index difference

Fig. 9 Dependence of the group delay of the modes of a graded-index fiber on the normalized propagation constant D and the profile parameter C_p

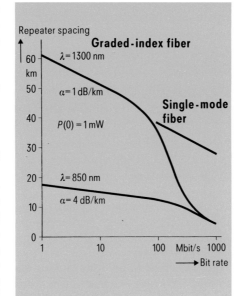

$P(0)$	Optical power of source (laser diode)
λ	Optical wavelength
α	Attenuation coefficient (fibers, splices, connectors)

Fig. 10 Theoretically possible repeater spacings and bit rates in fiberoptic transmission systems

the fact that the refractive indices in the core and cladding of the fiber do not vary by exactly the same amount with optical wavelength, so that the refractive index difference Δ becomes wavelength-dependent. This effect, known as *profile dispersion*, is taken into account in (21) by the parameter

$$P_0 = \frac{n}{n_g} \cdot \frac{\lambda}{\Delta} \cdot \frac{d\Delta}{d\lambda} = -\frac{k_0}{\Delta} \cdot \frac{d\Delta}{dk_0}. \qquad (22)$$

It is due to this effect that the refractive index profile of real graded-index fibers only approaches the ideal (21) in a limited wavelength range, and deviates from it at other wavelengths. The transmission bandwidth of such fibers therefore has a clearly defined maximum in this wavelength range. For wideband transmission it is advisable to locate this maximum in the region of the attenuation minimum around 1300 nm (see **Fig. 3**).

The common feature of all dispersion effects described thus far is that they increase the width of short light pulses launched into the fiber, this increase being proportional to the fiber length traversed. In a multimode fiber such a light pulse comprises several partial light pulses propagating in various modes. The width of the composite pulse grows, due partly to the individual partial pulses broadening and partly to the space between them increasing. However, the partial pulses do not move completely independently of each other, because, for various reasons, e.g. inhomogeneities of the fiber geometry, light guided in a particular mode may be gradually transferred into adjacent modes. As a result of this mode mixing the delay differences between the partial pulses is reduced, but their width increases. The two effects together cause the width of the composite pulse over long fiber lengths (above 2 to 5 km) to increase at a lower pace than proportionally to the fiber length, so that in the limiting case of very long lengths this increase becomes merely proportional to the square root of the fiber length. The transmission bandwidth of long fibers is therefore greater than the value linearly extrapolated from the bandwidth of short fibers.

In practice the fiber characteristics described here interact in a complex manner. This can best be shown by observing their effect on the capabilities of a transmission link. For this purpose **Fig. 10** shows the relationship between bit rate and possible span length, calculated from typical numerical data. At low bit rates the dispersion of the fiber is negligible and the span length is limited only by the optical power coupled in from the transmitter, the fiber attenuation and the optical power required by the receiver. Since the attenuation of the fibers decreases towards longer wavelengths (see **Fig. 3**), it is possible for the span length at $\lambda = 1300$ nm to be much greater than at $\lambda = 850$ nm. As the bit rate increases, the possible span length decreases slowly at first, because large bandwith photodetectors are noisier and therefore need more optical power. Above a certain bit rate the fiber dispersion then becomes apparent, resulting eventually in a considerable reduction in possible span length. For *graded-index fibers* operated with laser diodes this limit is on the order of 200 to 500 Mbit/s. For *single-mode fibers* it is considerably higher, especially if these fibers are operated at $\lambda \approx 1300$ nm, where material dispersion is extremely low.

Further details are provided in the ensuing papers in this issue.

References

Books

- Grau, G.: Optische Nachrichtentechnik. Berlin, Heidelberg, New York: Springer-Verlag 1981
- Kersten, R. Th.: Einführung in die optische Nachrichtentechnik. Berlin, Heidelberg, New York: Springer-Verlag 1983
- Midwinter, J. E.: Optical fibers for transmission. New York, Chichester, Toronto: John Wiley & Sons 1979
- Miller, S. E.; Chynoweth, A. G.: Optical fiber telecommunications. New York, San Francisco, London: Academic Press 1979
- Sandbank, C. P.: Optical fiber communication systems. New York, Chichester, Toronto: John Wiley & Sons 1980

Important journals with topical papers

- Applied Optics
- Electronics Letters
- Journal of Optical Communications
- Optical and Quantum Electronics

International conference publications

- European Conference on Optical Communication (ECOC): York 1980, Copenhagen 1981, Cannes 1982
- International Conference on Integrated Optics and Optical Fiber Communication (IOOC): Amsterdam 1979, San Francisco 1981, Tokyo 1983
- Topical Meeting on Optical Fiber Communication (OFC): Washington D.C. 1979, Phoenix 1982, New Orleans 1983

Claus Weyrich and Karl-Heinz Zschauer

Principles of Optoelectronic Signal Conversion

Optoelectronic semiconductor devices such as light-emitting diodes, laser diodes and photodiodes with their outstanding characteristics are key components for optical signal transmission. They are characterized by small size, ruggedness and long operating life, an important factor being that the optical transmitters can be directly modulated at high bit rates. The main semiconductor materials for the light sources are III-V compounds. Their properties can be engineered to a degree of perfection that allows complicated device structures to be realized which are optimally matched to the characteristics of the fiber-optic transmission medium. Striking examples are the double heterostructures of GaAlAs on GaAs and InGaAsP on InP whose dual functions of carrier confinement and waveguiding first made continuous operation of laser diodes at room temperature possible. Apart from the III-V semiconductors, the materials that have gained importance for photodiodes are Si and Ge.

Signal transmission over optical waveguides calls for optoelectronic transducers as sources and detectors whose characteristics are determined by the system requirements, i.e. primarily by the transmission length and transmission rate. Considering only systems employing intensity modulation – currently expected to predominate for the foreseeable future – the implications of this for *sources* are that

- the emission must occur in the spectral region of low absorption and/or dispersion determined by the characteristics of the optical waveguide, regard also being given to the permissible half-power width of the emission,

- the radiant power coupled into the optical waveguide must be as large as possible, which calls not only for a

high electrical/optical conversion efficiency but also for high efficiency in coupling the radiation into the fiber,

- the emission must be capable of simple modulation by the transmission signal,

- the life of the device must be comparable with those of the other components employed in the system,

- the fabrication technology finally must also be economical.

For the *detectors* the first three requirements are replaced by the following conditions:

- To achieve the minimum possible detectable radiant power for a given bit error rate, the sensitivity of the photodetectors in the required spectral region must be as high as possible and at the same time their noise characteristics must be favorable.

- The speed of response must be high enough for the particular transmission rate employed.

Dr. phil. Claus Weyrich and
Dipl.-Phys. Dr. rer. nat. Karl-Heinz Zschauer,
Siemens AG,
Research and Development Division,
Munich

Light-emitting and laser diodes made of III-V semiconductors as well as photodiodes made of III-V semiconductors and (with certain reservations) Si and Ge largely meet the stated requirements. They are additionally characterized by their small size, ruggedness, compatibility with other semiconductor components and low power consumption. The following paragraphs describe the principles of light generation and detection with semiconductors, the mode of operation and principal characteristics of light-emitting diodes, laser diodes and photodiodes as well as aspects of material selection. The explanations are provided purely in terms of the phenomena involved by reference to simple functional models.

Light generation and detection with semiconductors

Optical transitions in semiconductors

Semiconductors are characterized by having two energy bands for electrons, i.e. the *valence band* and *conduction band* separated from each other by the *band gap E*. The basic physical mechanism in sources and detectors is the interaction between electrons in the valence and conduction bands and photons. Photons are light particles defined by their photon energy $h\nu$ which is related to the wavelength λ of light as follows:

$$\frac{\lambda}{\mu m} = \frac{1.24}{h\nu/eV}. \qquad (1)$$

There are three simple interaction mechanisms which are shown schematically in **Fig. 1**.

In *absorption* (**Fig. 1a**), a photon radiated into the semiconductor is annihilated by lifting an electron out of the valence band into the conduction band, i.e. to a higher energy state, leaving a hole in the valence band.

Spontaneous emission (luminescence) occurs (**Fig. 1b**) when there are too many electrons in the conduction band so that they fall spontaneously into free energy states in the valence band (holes), each electron causing one photon to be emitted whose energy is equal to the band gap *E*. This process is termed the radiative recombination of

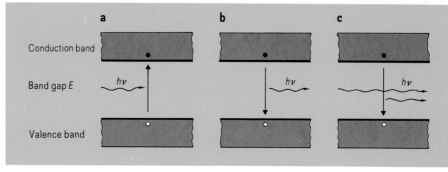

hv Photon   • Electron   ○ Hole

Fig. 1 Optoelectronic interactions at semiconductor junctions
a Absorption
b Spontaneous emission
c Stimulated emission

excess charge carriers (excess electrons and holes).

Stimulated emission (**Fig. 1c**) is referred to when photons in the semiconductor stimulate excess charge carriers to radiative recombination, i.e. additional photons are emitted. The light emitted is identical to the stimulating light in wavelength and phase.

The processes just described are direct optical transitions as opposed to indirect transitions which involve not only photons and electrons but also lattice vibrations or traps in the crystal lattice. Whether direct or indirect optical transitions dominate in a semiconductor depends on its band structure, i.e. on the relationship between the allowed energy states and the momentum of the electrons.

In optoelectronic devices absorption, spontaneous emission and stimulated emission always occur together. Essentially, however, only one mechanism dominates in a particular application. The devices corresponding to these three kinds of interaction are the *photodiode*, the *light-emitting diode* and the *laser diode*.

Materials selection

The main group of materials for the light sources used in fiber-optic systems are the III-V compound semiconductors. These are semiconductor compounds formed from elements of the third and fifth groups of the periodic system, e.g. GaAs, AlAs or InP. They generally have similar characteristics to elemental semiconductors like Si and Ge but, unlike these, some of them exhibit direct optical transitions. Both elemental and

III-V compound semiconductors are employed for detectors.

It is an important feature of the III-V semiconductors that they can form a wide range of solid solutions. The band gap of the solid solutions and hence the wavelength of the emitted light can thus be varied within certain limits. These solid solutions can be very easily produced by what are known as epitaxy techniques. Such techniques are used to deposit a new semiconductor layer on a substrate. The quality of the layers required for optoelectronic components (e.g. the absence of dislocations which would reduce the light output and cause aging effects) is achieved only if the layer and the substrate have the same lattice constant (lattice matching). Since only binary III-V semiconductors, such as GaAs and InP, are available as substrates the number of possible new semiconductors is severely restricted.

Two series of solid solutions have gained importance for optical communications, i.e. $Ga_{1-x}Al_xAs$ on GaAs and $Ga_x In_{1-x}As_yP_{1-y}$ on InP. The particularly simple series of form $Ga_{1-x}Al_xAs$ where $0 \leqq x \leqq 0.45$ – if the Al content is higher only indirect optical transitions are possible – is suitable for the wavelength range from about 670 to 880 nm. Since GaAs and AlAs have virtually the same lattice constant, no special action to match the lattice constants is required. Solid solutions of the form $Ga_x In_{1-x}As_yP_{1-y}$ on InP substrates are suitable for the wavelength range from 900 to 1700 nm. The correct composition for lattice matching is obtained when $x = 0.43y$. The **Fig. 2** shows the wavelength as a function of the composition for $Ga_{1-x}Al_xAs$ and $Ga_xIn_{1-x}As_yP_{1-y}$.

Of the two series of solid solutions the first has the simpler and more advanced technology, while the second covers the main wavelength range where the dispersion and absorption in silica optical waveguides is minimal.

Injection luminescence

In order to obtain the two emission effects the semiconductor has to be excited by introducing excess charge carriers. This is the purpose of the semiconductor p-n junction. In a forward-biased p-n junction, charge carriers are injected from one side of the junction to the other (the same effect is employed in the transistor) where, as minority carriers, they recombine with the majority carriers. The process of injecting charge carriers followed by emission of light is referred to as injection luminescence, an effect on which both light-emitting and laser diodes are based. This form of light generation lends itself to particularly simple intensity modulation of the emitted radiation directly via the diode current.

Light-emitting diodes

A light-emitting diode is basically a semiconductor diode in which the light generation is obtained by spontaneous emission. An important characteristic here is the efficiency with which electrical energy is converted into light.

Generally, the external power efficiency, i.e. the ratio of the externally available optical power to the electrical power consumed is considerably less than one. The losses are due to a number of possible effects. Excess charge carriers may recombine without the emission of light, an example of this being the so-called Auger effect in which an excess electron loses its energy on impact with another electron. Other losses occur on extracting the light generated in the semiconductor. At the semiconductor-air interface the light is refracted and partially reflected. Owing to the high refractive index of the semiconductors only a small fraction of the light reaches the outside, this being only 1.4% in the case of a flat GaAs-air interface. The rest is absorbed inside the semiconductor or at the contacts. Maximizing the external efficiency is a matter of mate-

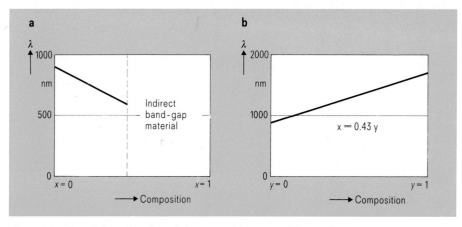

Fig. 2 Wavelength λ as a function of the composition (x, y) of $Ga_{1-x}Al_xAs$ (a) and $Ga_xIn_{1-x}As_yP_{1-y}$ (b)

rials selection and device structure optimization.

The band gap of the particular semiconductor determines the wavelength of the emitted light, so that the wavelength for GaAs with $E = 1.43$ eV at room temperature is $\lambda = 870$ nm. The spectral width of a spontaneous emission is approximately proportional to the so-called thermal voltage kT/e. At room temperature the following approximation holds:

$$\frac{\Delta\lambda}{\mu m} \lesssim 3.4 \cdot 10^{-2} \cdot \frac{\lambda^2}{\mu m^2}. \qquad (2)$$

It can be seen from this that the linewidth increases considerably at longer wavelengths. This is particularly important in connection with the dispersion of light in optical fibers.

Another important factor as regards optical communication is the limited modulation bandwidth of a light-emitting diode. The average lifetime of excess charge carriers sets a limit below which the emission of light ceases to follow temporal changes in the injected diode current. Minimum values for the life of radiative recombination in direct-gap semiconductors are in the order of a few nanoseconds, permitting modulation rates of up to a few hundred megabits per second only.

An important feature of light-emitting diodes for fiber-optic systems is their small area matched to the core diameter of the fiber to achieve high coupling efficiency of the light into the optical waveguide. As a result the current densities required to provide the necessary optical powers attain values which are far higher than those of ordinary

light-emitting diodes, placing stringent demands – as stated below – on diode design and technology.

Laser diodes

A laser diode is essentially a light-emitting diode with a wavelength-selective element – a Fabry-Perot cavity in the simplest case, consisting primarily of two plane-parallel semitransparent mirrors. This cavity causes the intensity of the light of identical wavelength and phase to become large even at low overall light intensity, so that the stimulated emission begins at low injection currents. The two mirror surfaces on the laser diode are natural crystal surfaces produced by cleaving the semiconductor crystal.

Fig. 3 shows the light/current characteristic of a laser diode. It comprises two regions: at low currents the laser diode acts as a light-emitting diode, while above the so-called threshold current the light emission increases much more steeply.

An important difference to the light-emitting diode is that the emission above the threshold ceases to be the typical broad spectral distribution and narrows to one or a few spectral lines (**Fig. 4**). The light produced in the laser diode by stimulated emission is spatially coherent and can therefore be effectively coupled into a single-mode fiber. By contrast, the emission of a light-emitting diode is incoherent and the optical power coupled into a single-mode fiber would be insignificant. Linked to this is a difference in the spatial radiation distribution – broad in the case of light-emitting diodes

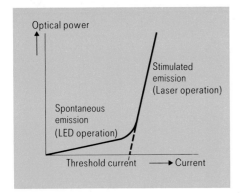

Fig. 3 Light-current characteristic
of a laser diode

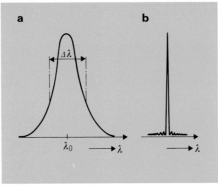

λ Optical wavelength

Fig. 4 Spectral distribution
of the emission from light-emitting diodes (a)
and laser diodes (b)

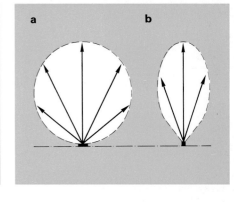

Fig. 5 Spatial distribution
of the emission from light-emitting diodes (a)
and laser diodes (b)

(Fig. 5 a) and significantly narrower in the case of laser diodes (Fig. 5 b).

The nonlinearity of the light/current characteristics shown in Fig. 3 also has an effect on the modulation characteristics of laser diodes. A rapid current rise produces stimulated emission only after a delay. If, however, the laser diode is operated with a dc bias current near the threshold this delay effect disappears. The modulation rates then achievable extend into the GHz range. On the other hand this means that at high transmission rates the laser diode is in effect operating continuously.

An intensive stimulated emission requires high densities of excess carriers and photons. However, charge carriers, such as electrons and holes, diffuse, i.e. concentration differences equalize and photons radiate in all directions unless they are prevented from doing so by suitable means. As a result of this, the threshold currents of early laser diodes with a single p-n junction were so high that continuous operation at room temperature was not possible.

An almost ideal solution to this problem is the so-called *double heterostructure*. This consists basically of an active semiconductor layer sandwiched between two confining layers of another semiconductor of wider band gap (Fig. 6). Carrier confinement is achieved by the wider band-gap confining layers forming barriers which prevent the electrons injected from the n-side and the holes injected from the p-side spreading outside the active region. The wider band gap of the confining layers is linked with a smaller

refractive index, producing a dielectric waveguide similar to the glass fiber waveguide: the double heterostructure thus concentrates the light.

It was the adoption of the double heterostructure that first made laser diodes capable of continuous operation at room temperature and hence suitable for a wide range of technical applications. The double heterostructure principle has also gained importance for light-emitting diodes. Common to both these emitter devices is that the maximum possible current densities are limited by heat dissipation. Light-emitting and laser diodes must therefore be designed with favorable thermal characteristics.

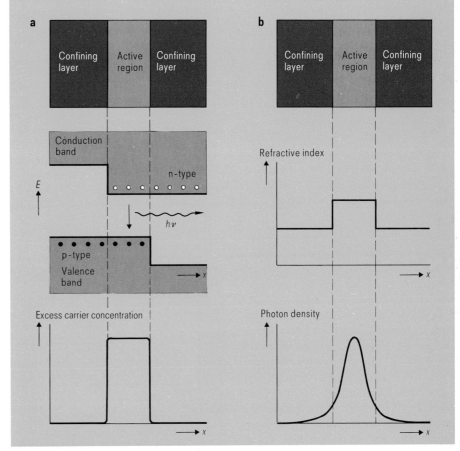

hv Photon ● Electron ○ Hole

Fig. 6 Dual function of the double heterostructure
a Electrical effect
b Optical effect

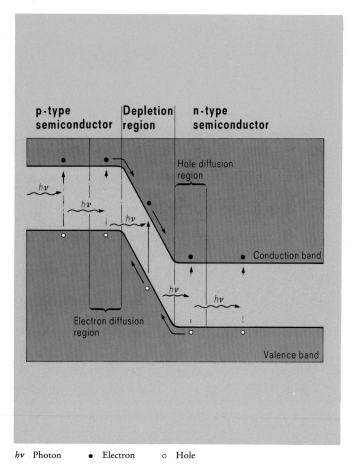

bv Photon   ● Electron   ○ Hole

Fig. 7   Operation of a reverse-biased photodiode

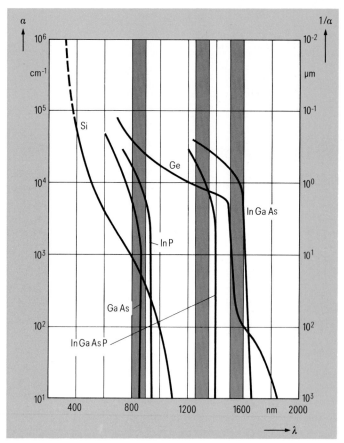

Fig. 8   Absorption coefficient α and penetration depth $d (= 1/\alpha)$
as a function of the wavelength λ for various semiconductor materials
(the three transmission windows are indicated by the colored bars)

Photodiodes

Semiconductor p-n junctions can be used not only for carrier excitation by injection but also for collecting optically excited carriers by separating them in the electric field of the depletion region, i.e. for radiation detection. **Fig. 7** illustrates the operation of a photodiode.

The carriers collected are those generated in the depletion region of the p-n junction and those generated no further away from the p-n junction than the diffusion length of electrons and holes, i.e. within the so-called diffusion region. Whereas in the first case the two generated carriers are separated immediately by the electric field in the depletion region, the minority carriers generated in the second case must first diffuse to the p-n junction before they can reach the field of the depletion region and be transported into the opposite neutral semiconductor region, causing a photocurrent to flow in the external circuit. With electric fields in excess of 10^4 V/cm the charge carriers

move at their saturation drift velocity of about 10^7 cm/s, whereas diffusing carriers only attain velocities up to 10^5 cm/s. Carriers generated outside the diffusion region disappear as a result of recombination and so do not contribute to the photocurrent, thus reducing the conversion efficiency.

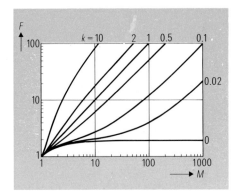

Fig. 9   Excess noise factor F as a function of carrier multiplication factor M (parameter is the ratio of the ionization coefficients of holes and electrons $k = \beta/\alpha$)

The **Fig. 8** shows a comparison of the absorption coefficients α of the available materials suitable for the wavelength range 850 to 1700 nm. For a photodiode to provide a high response speed, penetration depths $d = 1/\alpha$ not larger than 1 μm are desirable. Thus InGaAsP and Ge are favorable materials for the range 1300 to 1500 nm. The penetration depth in Si for the 850 nm range is about 10 μm. Efforts here are aimed at maximizing the contribution of carriers optically generated in the space charge region, e.g. by incorporating a high-resistivity region (i-region) between the n- and p-type semiconductors. This is referred to as a PIN photodiode whose low junction capacitance also favors a high speed of response. Photodiodes can also be operated in the avalanche breakdown mode (APD *a*valanche *p*hoto*d*iode), i.e. the carriers accelerated in the electric field reach such high velocities that further electron-hole pairs are generated by impact ionization. This internal amplification process provides a photocurrent increased by the multiplication factor of the carriers. The total transit time of the carriers also increases so the gain-bandwidth product remains virtually constant. However, it is generally large enough to detect signals at transmission rates up to 1 Gbit/s.

Photodiodes for optical communications must additionally be designed to detect the lowest possible signal powers at a given bit rate. The detection limit is determined by noise from the signal current, noise from the photodiode itself and from the following amplifier electronics as well as by the signal-to-noise ratio required for the specified bit error rate. On transmission systems with intensity modulation the signal noise at low power levels in the wavelength range 850 to 1700 nm is negligible compared with the shot noise of the photodiode dark currents and the amplifier noise.

In avalanche photodiodes the internal gain gives rise to an additional noise mechanism – referred to as excess noise – which increases with the multiplication. The excess noise factor F decreases with decreasing ratio of the ionization coefficients of the less easily and more easily ionizing carriers, the need being to inject almost exclusively the more easily ionizing charge carriers into the multiplication region of the diode. **Fig. 9** plots F as a function of gain M for various ratios k of the ionization coefficients of electrons α and holes β.

As a consequence of the excess noise, there is an optimum multiplication factor for avalanche photodiodes at which the noise of the multiplied signal and dark currents just equals the noise of the following amplifier electronics. The optimum multiplication factor assumes various values according to the particular application and the characteristics of the devices employed.

Further details are provided in the other papers on light-emitting, laser and photodiodes.

References

Books

- Panish, H. C.; Panish, Jr., M. B.: Heterostructure lasers. New York: Academic Press 1978
- Kressel, H.; Butter, J. K.: Semiconduction and heterojunction LEDs. New York: Academic Press 1977
- Yariv, A.: Introduction to optical electronics. New York: Holt, Rinehart and Winston 1977

- Winstel, G. H.1 Weyrich, C.: Optoelektronik I; Lumineszenz- und Laserdioden. Berlin: Springer Verlag 1980
- Grau, G.: Optische Nachrichtentechnik. Berlin: Springer Verlag 1981

General articles

- Botez, D.; Herskowitz, G. J.: Components for optical communications systems: a review. Proc. IEEE 68 (1980), pp. 689 to 731
- Müller, J.: Photodiodes for optical communication. Advances in Electronics and Electron Physics, Vol. 55, pp. 189 to 308, Academic Press, Inc. 1981

Jürgen Gier and Klaus Panzer

Principles of Optoelectronic Signal Transmission

Optoelectronic signal transmission in optical fibers provides technical and economic advantages for transmitting information, particularly in telecommunications networks. A transmission system of this type consists of an optical transmitter (light-emitting or laser diode), the optical waveguide transmission medium (multimode or single-mode fiber) and an optical receiver (photodiode). Compared with coaxial transmission systems, fiber-optic systems, especially those employing single-mode fibers and laser diodes, provide wide transmission bandwidth ($>500\,\text{MHz}$) over very long span lengths ($>20\,\text{km}$) while ensuring low loss ($<1\,\text{dB/km}$ at $\lambda = 1300\,\text{mm}$) across the entire frequency range. Owing to the nonlinear distortion of the optoelectronic system, it is better suited to digital transmission. For analog signal transmission, both the signal-to-noise ratio and the linearity of optoelectronic transmission can be improved by pre-processing the analog signal.

The two preceding articles dealt with the light-guiding properties of optical waveguides [1] as well as the design and performance of optical transmitters and receivers [2]. This article outlines the basic possibilities for signal transmission using these optical components, with particular attention to long-haul communication systems, i.e. systems of high capacity (bandwidth) and/or long span length.

Dipl.-Ing. Jürgen Gier,
Siemens AG,
Public Communication Networks Division,
Munich;
Dipl.-Ing. Dr.-Ing. Klaus Panzer,
Siemens AG,
Central Laboratories for
Communications Technology, Munich

Fig. 1 shows the principle of the optoelectronic transmission path in simplified form. Important characteristics for consideration from a communications point of view are:

- In what form is the information signal modulated onto the optical carrier signal?
- What usable bandwidth is provided by the transmission channel?
- How linear is the relationship between the transmit signal i_1 and the receive signal i_2?
- What factors determine the signal-to-noise ratio S_2/N_2 at the end of the transmission link?

These characteristics are not merely a function of the optical transmitter or the fiber alone, but are determined by the interaction of specific characteristics of the optical transmitter and the light-guiding properties of the particular fiber. This applies, for instance, to the usable bandwidth of the transmission channel which is affected by material dispersion [1]. It also applies to the receive-end signal-to-noise ratio which may be impaired not only by the noise characteristics of the optical receiver but also by so-called modal noise in multimode fibers resulting from unfavorable transmitter characteristics.

Communication aspects of the optoelectronic transmission path

Modulation of the optical carrier signal

Communication using electrical signals (e.g. on copper cables) relies on single-frequency oscillators whose output signals are virtually constant in frequency, phase and amplitude. These carriers can be variously modulated by the information signal in frequency, phase or amplitude. At the receive end, it is possible to employ highly sensitive

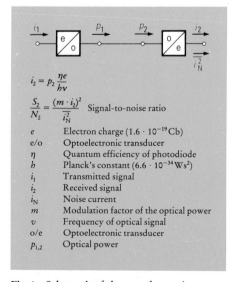

$$i_2 = p_2 \frac{\eta e}{h v}$$

$$\frac{S_2}{N_2} = \frac{(m \cdot i_2)^2}{\overline{i_N^2}} \quad \text{Signal-to-noise ratio}$$

e	Electron charge ($1.6 \cdot 10^{-19}\,\text{Cb}$)
e/o	Optoelectronic transducer
η	Quantum efficiency of photodiode
h	Planck's constant ($6.6 \cdot 10^{-34}\,\text{Ws}^2$)
i_1	Transmitted signal
i_2	Received signal
i_N	Noise current
m	Modulation factor of the optical power
v	Frequency of optical signal
o/e	Optoelectronic transducer
$p_{1,2}$	Optical power

Fig. 1 Schematic of the optoelectronic transmission path

detectors (demodulators) if the carrier can be regenerated there and used for signal demodulation.

With the optical components currently available, it is not possible to modulate or demodulate the optical signal in this way because the spectral width of the optical transmitters (the lasers and more especially the light-emitting diodes) is much too large and their frequency stability much too low for frequency or phase modulation to be practicable. In addition, all multimode fibers (step-index and graded-index fibers) greatly distort the transmitted signal due to their multimode transmission (multipath propagation). Therefore, the only type of modulation which can be and is used for practical application at present is intensity (power) modulation of the optical signal.

This simplifies transmitter and receiver designs since the optical source can be directly modulated by the drive current, and photodiodes convert the received optical power directly into an electrical current (photocurrent).

Research is in progress to stabilize the optical transmitters and to simulate in single-mode systems the modulation and demodulation processes (e.g. heterodyne reception) familiar to us from electrical systems. Theoretical calculations show that an increase in receiver sensitivity of some 10 to 15 dB is physically possible. As yet, it is uncertain when it will be possible to realize such designs in practical systems.

Usable bandwidth

The usable bandwidth of the optoelectronic transmission path for the power modulation method currently used is determined by the

- modulation bandwidth of the optical transmitter [2],
- dispersion effects in the fiber (e.g. modal, material and waveguide dispersion) [1],
- modulation bandwidth of the optical receiver [2].

Laser diodes can be modulated into the gigahertz range, light-emitting diodes, on the other hand, only to a few hundred MHz. The rise time of a light-emitting diode can be shortened only

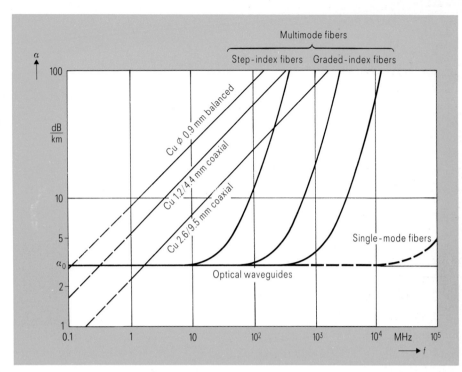

α_0 Basic attenuation of fibers as a function of wavelength (at $\lambda = 850$ nm it is around 3 dB/km, at $\lambda = 1300$ nm it is less than 1 dB/km)

Fig. 2 Transfer function of the optical waveguide (bandwidth) compared with copper lines

by reducing the available output power.

The response of the fiber to the information signal modulating the light intensity approximates to that of a Gaussian low-pass filter. Its cutoff frequency is determined not only by the fiber itself (mainly modal dispersion in the case of multimode fibers and waveguide dispersion in the case of single-mode fibers), but also in combination with material dispersion by the spectral width of the optical transmitter. **Fig. 2** shows the frequency-dependent responses of various fiber types (fiber length 1 km) due to modal dispersion compared with modern copper cables.

In addition, **Fig. 2** shows that, depending on its type, the fiber has a constant response over a wide frequency range; this is the preferred range for signal transmission. Distortion of the transmitted signal by the fiber link is then negligibly small, thus obviating the need for signal equalization in the receiver which, however, is essential in coaxial cable systems.

The transmission characteristics and cutoff frequencies reproduced in **Fig. 2** apply to a cable length of 1 km. A number of factors determine the length

dependence of the cutoff frequency in optical waveguides [3]. Modal dispersion in multimode fibers is largely determined by mode mixing in the fiber and thus by the fiber attenuation as well as the number of splices on the particular section. The cutoff frequency $f_c(L)$, determined by modal dispersion, for a fiber of length L is given approximately by:

$$f_c(L) \approx f_c(1\,\text{km}) \cdot L^{-\gamma}, \qquad (1)$$

where γ may lie between 0.5 and 1 (typically 0.75).

Material dispersion reduces the cutoff frequency proportionally to the fiber length.

At the receive end, photodiodes achieve rise and fall times $\leqq 0.2$ ns, enabling optical receivers to be realized with bandwidths in excess of 1 GHz.

Linearity

The linearity of the optoelectronic transmission system is mainly determined by the light/current characteristic of the transmitter. In general, the powers present at the detector diode are so low that nonlinear distortion caused by the receiver is negligible. This also applies to the transmission medium where nonlinear effects only occur at powers considerably higher than those currently employed.

Typical characteristics of the two optical transmitters considered here are shown in **Fig. 3**. Whereas the light-emitting diode shows signs of saturation at increased power levels, the linearity of the laser diode over a comparable power range tends to improve as the power increases. If the power increases further, it is largely a matter of laser design whether, and where kinks occur on the characteristic [4]. The order of magnitude of the achievable linearity may be illustrated numerically. With sinusoidal amplitude modulation of 70% and the operating point set at the maximum permissible CW optical power, it is possible to achieve 50 dB suppression of the second and third harmonics below the fundamental. However, this applies only to index guided lasers. Gain guided lasers ideally suitable for multimode fibers achieve 30 to 40 dB. These values are achieved directly from the laser mirror without a fiber coupled to the laser. Fiber coupling may reduce these values.

Signal-to-noise-ratio at the receive end

The signal-to-noise-ratio at the output of the optoelectronic transmission system is determined by the receive signal

$$i_2 = p_2 \frac{\eta e}{h \nu} \qquad (2)$$

(corresponding to **Fig. 1**) as well as by a number of noise sources which will be briefly described below.

Thermal noise of the optical receiver

The main thermal noise sources in an optical receiver are the resistance noise of load resistor R

$$\overline{i_R^2} = \frac{4 k T}{R} \cdot B \qquad (3)$$

(B noise bandwidth of the receiver) as well as the noise of the first amplifier stages ($\overline{i_v^2}$). **Fig. 5** shows circuit designs to minimize the effects of these noise sources on signal-to-noise ratio.

Quantum noise

After conversion to current i_2 the received signal is affected by quantum noise. The square of the rms value of the noise current is

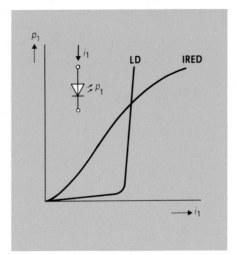

Fig. 3 Light-current characteristic of a laser diode (LD) and light-emitting diode (IRED)

$$\overline{i_Q^2} = 2 e i_2 B = 2 e p_2 \frac{\eta e}{h \nu} B. \qquad (4)$$

The noise power is proportional to the received optical power. The ratio of signal power to quantum noise power is

$$\frac{S_2}{N_Q} = \frac{i_2^2}{\overline{i_Q^2}} = \frac{i_2^2}{2 e i_2 B} = p_2 \cdot \frac{\eta}{2 h \nu B} . \qquad (5)$$

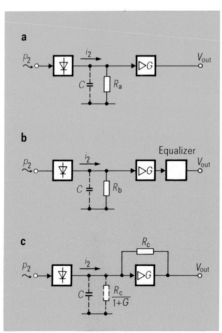

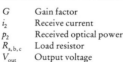

G	Gain factor
i_2	Receive current
p_2	Received optical power
$R_{a,b,c}$	Load resistor
V_{out}	Output voltage

Fig. 5 Circuit designs for optical receivers

a	Low-impedance amplifier	$R_a C \lesssim T$
b	High-impedance amplifier	$R_b C \gg T$
c	Transimpedance amplifier	$\dfrac{C R_c}{1 + G} \lesssim T$

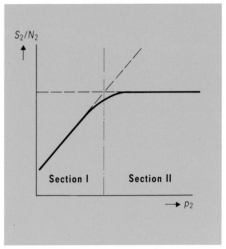

Fig. 4 Signal-to-noise ratio S_2/N_2 at the output of an optical receiver (in section I receiver noise predominates, in section II transmitter noise)

This ratio determines the physically achievable sensitivity of an ideal optical receiver. In electrical systems the quantum noise is negligible compared to the thermal noise sources.

Dark current noise

In semiconductor photodiodes a (reverse) current flows even when the diode is not illuminated. This dark current i_D produces a noise power proportional to

$$\overline{i_D^2} = 2 e \cdot I_D \cdot B. \qquad (6)$$

Avalanche noise

The multiplication process in avalanche photodiodes (APDs) results in a substantial increase in noise. The quantum noise of an APD is approximately

$$\overline{i_{Q(APD)}^2} \approx 2 e p_2 \frac{\eta e}{h \nu} M^2 F B. \qquad (7)$$

Where M is the valanche multiplication factor and $F \approx M^x$. For silicon APDs x is approximately 0.3, for germanium APDs about 1.0 and for APDs of In Ga As about 0.6.

In addition to these receiver noise sources, account must be taken of laser noise as well as noise caused by the interaction of laser and fiber. The following noise sources are particularly common:

Laser noise

The stability of the output power of a laser is subject to limitations. It is determined by the laser structure and the electrical and optical operating conditions (operating point and unwanted optical reflections from the fiber into the laser) [2].

Mode partition noise

Lasers generally operate at several optical wavelengths simultaneously – at least when modulated by the information signal [4]. Normally the individual spectral components or modes are very unstable, although the overall power of all the modes is virtually constant. Owing to material dispersion in the fiber, the individual laser modes may arrive at the receiver separated in time and produce an increase in noise, which has an undesirable effect mainly in high-bandwidth systems with large repeater spacings. This effect can be kept negligibly low if the laser is operated in an optical wavelength range in which the material dispersion is low or if the laser – even when modulated – oscillates at one wavelength only.

Modal noise in multimode fibers

If a multimode fiber, e.g. a graded-index fiber, is operated with a laser of very narrow spectral width, the superposition of all propagation modes guided in the fiber produces a very pronounced interference pattern, i.e. an uneven power distribution over the fiber core area. Owing to fiber effects and fluctuations in the optical wavelength, this pattern is generally very unstable and subject to constant variation. At discontinuities in the fiber (e.g. at splices and connectors) there is the danger of higher losses being present in certain regions of the fiber cross-section. The power components of the optical signal in these regions are then more heavily attenuated than other components. Consequently, additional noise effects may be produced [5]. The fiber is not itself the cause of the noise, which is in fact due to fluctuations in ambient conditions, such as temperature, vibrations etc. along the transmission path. Experience shows that these noise effects are less pronounced in a properly installed cable system than in loose reels of fiber kept in the laboratory. These effects are negligible if the optical transmitter used is not monochromatic but provides a wide spectrum with several modes, because then the superposition of interference patterns of several

wavelengths results in a time-averaged virtually constant power distribution over the fiber cross-section. Optical transmitters for multimode fibers must therefore have a sufficiently wide spectrum. This consideration is of particular importance for the transmission of analog signals.

The signal-to-noise-ratio S_2/N_2 at the output of the optical receiver due to the noise sources previously described can be expressed qualitatively in simplified form as follows:

$$\frac{S_2}{N_2} = \frac{a^2 p_2^2}{b + c p_2 + d p_2^2}. \tag{8}$$

Here, p_2 is the average optical power at the receiver. The factor a contains the efficiency with which optical power is converted into electrical power, and the light modulation factor determining the magnitude of the electrical signal. The denominator of the equation (8) contains three kinds of noise power which differ only in respect of their dependence on the optical power p_2. The thermal noise powers independent of the optical power are included with the dark current noise in quantity b. The noise power $c p_2$ represents mainly the noise power produced by the quantum noise of the light. The third term $(d p_2^2)$ combines the noise powers already in the light at the transmit end (laser noise, modal noise of the laser and modal noise in the multimode fiber).

Fig. 4 shows the generalized curve of the signal-to-noise-ratio as a function of the optical power at the receiver. The curve can be divided into two sections. In the region of low receive power (section I) the signal-to-noise ratio improves with increasing optical power, the noise power $(b + c \cdot p_2)$ in this section being greater than $(d \cdot p_2^2)$ as in (8). In the region of high receive power (section II) the signal-to-noise ratio remains constant, because here $d p_2^2$ is the dominant noise power.

With gain guided laser diodes, signal-to-noise ratios of around 40 dB can be achieved (the light modulation factor is 70% and the noise is considered in a bandwidth of 5 MHz). Like the linearity, this maximum signal-to-noise ratio is similarly subject to large variations which in the nature of modal noise are determined by the type of laser, the

fiber coupling to the laser as well as the connectors and splices in the cable system.

Design principles of transmitter and receiver circuits

Transmitter circuits

The design of an optical transmitter incorporating a light-emitting diode involves relatively little technical complexity. It mainly comprises a driver stage for modulating the diode. The light/current characteristic of these diodes is only slightly dependent on temperature and aging, so that in general the output power does not require regulation.

A laser transmitter, however, is more complex to design because the magnitude of the threshold current is a function both of the temperature and of aging. Regulation of the drive currents is therefore essential to provide a constant output power. For this purpose light from the back mirror of the laser is applied to a photodiode whose output signal regulates the drive currents. Criteria for laser regulation can be obtained from a wide range of parameters of the optical signal, e.g. the mean optical output power (well suited to analog transmission) or the peak optical signal power (suitable for digital transmission).

Receiver circuits

As the system span length is heavily dependent on the sensitivity of the receiver, it is necessary to optimize the receiver as regards its noise sources. Digital systems require relatively low signal-to-noise ratios; in the curve shown in **Fig. 4** these are always in section I where the receiver noise dominates the signal-to-noise ratio of the receiver. It is therefore worthwhile using complex circuitry to minimize those noise power components b in (8) which are independent of the optical power, in order to approach as closely as possible the theoretically achievable limit of sensitivity. This can be achieved by means of the receiver designs shown in **Fig. 5**. An optical receiver is usually designed as shown in **Fig. 5a**. The current furnished by the photodiode produces a voltage across

Bit rate Mbit/s	Wave-length nm	Fiber type	Transmitter			Receiver		
			Type	Material	Δλ nm	Type	Material	Pre-amplifier
34	850	Graded index	LD	GaAlAs	2 to 10	APD	Si	TI
			IRED	GaAlAs	50			
	1300	Graded index	LD	InGaAsP	2 to 10	PIN	InGaAsP	HI
			IRED	InGaAsP	120			
140	1300	Graded index	LD	InGaAsP	2 to 10	PIN	InGaAsP	HI
			IRED	InGaAsP	120			
		Single mode	LD	InGaAsP	2 to 10	(APD	InGaAs	TI)*
565	1300	Single mode	LD	InGaAsP	2 to 10	APD	Ge; (InGaAs)*	TI

APD   Avalanche photodiode
HI   High Impedance
TI   Transimpedance
IRED   Infrared-emitting diode
LD   Laser diode

* Under development

Table   Optical transmitters and receivers for digital transmission

R_a which is then amplified. Resistor R_a should be as large as possible in order to minimize the resistance noise per (3). The capacitance C formed by the photodiode capacitance and the amplifier input capacitance in conjunction with R_a form a low-pass filter whose cutoff frequency must not exceed the required system bandwidth. However, if the value of R_a is increased beyond that point, equalization is required following amplification (**Fig. 5 b**). Another way of increasing R_a without losing bandwidth is shown in **Fig. 5 c** where the load resistor is located in the negative feedback path of the amplifier.

The effect of noise sources b in (8) can also be reduced by using an avalanche photodiode. Its internal gain has the effect of reducing the influence of noise component b (excluding the dark current noise). However, this gain based on the avalanche effect introduces excess noise per (7), so that there is an optimum gain factor M and therefore a maximum signal-to-noise ratio.

System design and span length

Digital transmission

Of the previously described characteristics of the optoelectronic transmission path, the only ones affecting span length for digital transmission are the bandwidth and the signal-to-noise ratio or permissible attenuation between optical transmitter and optical receiver. The criterion for receiver sensitivity used here is not the signal-to-noise ratio of the optical receiver but the average received optical power necessary to achieve a certain bit error rate. Detailed consideration of the theoretically achievable receiver sensitivity shows that binary optical transmission (only two optical levels are transmitted) provides receiver sensitivity several decibels higher than multi-level optical transmission [6], provided the system is not bandwith limited. Optical transmission systems for long span lengths therefore employ exclusively binary optical signals.

Fig. 6 summarizes the currently achievable receiver sensitivities, disregarding impairment of the bit error rate due to any bandwidth limiting in the transmission system. Suitable optical system configurations for digital transmission are given in the **table**.

For systems up to 140 Mbit/s it is possible to use *graded-index fibers* at both wavelengths of 850 nm and 1300 nm (1600 nm). As the material dispersion at 850 nm is a factor of more than 10 higher than at 1300 nm, systems operating above 100 Mbit/s at 850 nm are limited primarily by the bandwidth (material dispersion). At 1300 nm a 140 Mbit/s system is limited both by attenuation and bandwidth. Whatever the wavelength, it is advisable to use optical sources which have a sufficiently wide emission spectrum to avoid modal noise in the graded-index fibers.

Systems operating at bit rates above 140 Mbit/s in long-haul applications require *single-mode fibers,* as only they provide the bandwidth at the large repeater spacings required. Systems of this type place stringent requirements on optical transmitters whose spectral bandwidth must be low in order to prevent the bandwidth being limited

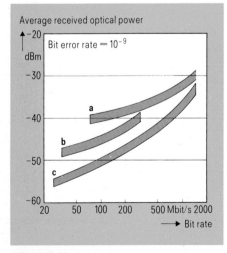

Fig. 6   Required average receive power of optical receivers as a function of the bit rate

a Germanium avalanche photodiode for 1300 nm

b InGaAs-PIN photodiode with high-impedance FET amplifier for 1300 nm

c Silicon avalanche photodiode for 850 nm

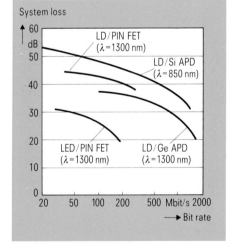

APD   Avalanche photodiode
λ   Optical wavelength
LD   Laser diode
LED   Light-emitting diode
PIN FET   PIN field-effect transistor

Fig. 7   System loss (difference between optical transmit and receive powers) as a function of the bit rate and optical wavelength at a bit error rate of 10^{-9}

by material dispersion at high bit rates. This is particularly necessary for systems operating at 1550 nm, as the material dispersion at this wavelength is markedly higher than at 1300 nm. Lasers of this type react relatively sensitively to optical reflections from the fiber. Possible methods of avoiding these reflections or rendering the optical transmitter insensitive to reflections are currently under research and development.

Fig. 7 summarizes the currently achievable system losses of the optoelectronic transmission path. Together with the cable loss and the achievable bandwidth, the system loss determines the physical system span length. In order to determine the repeater spacings nowadays physically achievable on practical transmission systems, it is additionally necessary to allow loss margins both for the equipment and for the cable (e.g. for repairs and rerouting), which may result in significant reductions [7].

Analog transmission

An important factor in analog transmission apart from bandwidth and attenuation is the linearity of the optoelectronic transmission path. Compared with electrical transmission systems both the linearity and the

achievable signal-to-noise ratios on multimode fibers are significantly worse in optoelectronic systems. This is due primarily to the characteristics of the optical transmitters. Although the linearity can be improved by restricting the drive to a small section of the light/current characteristic, a reduction in modulation factor will further reduce the already mediocre signal-to-noise ratio of the system. Negative feedback circuits, which improve the linearity of electrical amplifiers, are barely feasible here – especially in the case of wideband systems – as the inclusion of the optical section in the negative feedback loop introduces excessive attenuation. Suitable nonlinear pre-equalization could also be used to improve linearity. This approach is only slightly successful, however, due to the spread of the diode characteristics.

Even restricting the span length brings no improvement as a higher optical power at the receiver does not improve the signal-to-noise ratio above the value of the transmitter noise (a^2/d), as shown in **Fig. 4**. Hence in optical systems, direct analog transmission is possible only where quality requirements are modest.

If the bandwidth of the optoelectronic transmission path is substantially greater than that of the signal to be

transmitted, the transmission characteristics can be substantially improved compared with direct analog transmission with the aid of a suitably modulated electrical subcarrier. Angle modulation methods, such as frequency modulation, are particularly suitable for modulating this subcarrier, which is subsequently used for intensity modulation of the light [8]. These provide both immunity to nonlinear distortion and a considerable improvement in the signal-to-noise ratio. Modulation of a subcarrier thus makes it possible to create an "analog" transmission channel suitable for transmitting video signals, FDM signals, as well as digital signals [9, 10, 11].

If several analog signals (e.g. four video signals) are to be transmitted simultaneously via a fiber, two transmission methods are possible. Firstly, the four video signals can be combined to form an FDM signal which then frequency modulates the electrical subcarrier.

However, by multiplexing the four TV signals in this way, so much of the dynamic range is lost as to be uneconomic. It is better to modulate each of the TV signals onto a separate carrier, e.g. FM, and then to transmit these carriers over the optoelectronic link multiplexed on a frequency-division basis [12, 13].

References

[1] Geckeler, S.: Physical Principles of Optical Waveguides.
telcom report 6 (1983) Special Issue "Optical Communications", pp. 9 to 14

[2] Weyrich, C.; Zschauer, K.-H.: Principles of Optoelectronic Signal Conversion.
telcom report 6 (1983) Special Issue "Optical Communications", pp. 14 to 19

[3] Zeidler, G.: Designing Fiber-Optic Cable Systems.
telcom report 6 (1983) Special Issue "Optical Communications", pp. 41 to 45

[4] Amann, M.-C.; Mettler, K.; Wolf, H. D.: Laser Diodes – High-Power Light Sources for Optical Communications.
telcom report 6 (1983) Special Issue "Optical Communications", pp. 79 to 84

[5] Epworth, R. E.: The phenomenon of modal noise in analogue and digital optical fibre systems.
Proc. ECOC, Sept. 1978, Genoa

[6] Rocks, M.: Optimierung von digitalen Mehrstufen-Lichtleiterübertragungssystemen.
Frequenz 33 (1979), pp. 290 to 298

[7] Braun, E.; Keil, H.: Optical Waveguide Transmission Systems.
telcom report 6 (1983) Special Issue "Optical Communications", pp. 113 to 118

[8] Gier, J.; Kügler, E.; Seiffert, W.-D.: Fiber-Optic Communications.
telcom report 1 (1978), pp. 34 to 39

[9] Pichlmayer, E.; Stegmeier, A.: A Fiber-Optic Transmission System for Signal Bandwidths up to 7.5 MHz.
telcom report 6 (1983) Special Issue "Optical Communications", pp. 151 to 155

[10] Aichholz, E.; Tilly, B.: A Fiber-Optic System for FM Radio Relay Feeder Links and High-Quality TV Transmission.
telcom report 6 (1983) Special Issue "Optical Communications", pp. 147 to 150

[11] Anders, A.: A Fiber-Optic Analog System for Application in Electric Utilities.
telcom report 6 (1983) Special Issue "Optical Communications", pp. 156 to 160

[12] Braun, E.: BIGFON Brings the Optical Waveguide into the Subscriber Area.
telcom report 6 (1983) Special Issue "Optical Communications", pp. 136 to 139

[13] Bauch, H.; Weinhardt, K.: Communication in the Subscriber Area of Optical Broadband Networks.
telcom report 6 (1983) Special Issue "Optical Communications", pp. 140 to 146

Hartmut Schneider and Günter Zeidler

Manufacturing Processes and Designs of Optical Waveguides

It is more than ten years since Corning Glass Works in the USA first produced an optical fiber with an attenuation of about 16 dB/km. This figure was substantially lower than the optical attenuation commonly encountered in glass fibers at that time [1]. This event, now seen as something of a landmark, triggered extensive research and development activity worldwide and finally resulted in fibers with attenuations as low as 0.16 dB/km.

Preparation of silica glasses by gas phase deposition

Optical waveguides for communications consist mainly of silica glass (silicon dioxide SiO_2), with the light-guiding fiber core doped by additions of germanium and phosphorus to increase the refractive index and possibly boron or fluorine to reduce the index. The outstanding suitability of SiO_2 for preparing high-purity, ultratransparent glasses is due not only to the low intrinsic absorption (which can also be obtained from common multicomponent silicate glasses) but more especially to the fact that silica glass – doped or undoped – can be obtained by deposition from a pure and homogeneously mixed gas phase.

Dipl.-Chem. Dr. rer. nat. Hartmut Schneider,
Siemens AG,
Research and Development Division,
Munich;
Dipl.-Ing. Dr. phil. Günter Zeidler,
Siemens AG,
Public Communication Networks Division,
Munich

◁ Optical cables from Siemens, based on the crush resistant and antibuckling filled, loose buffer tube design, have been adopted in communication networks worldwide. The fiber counts of these cables range up to a few thousand

Natural silicon dioxide – obtained in the form of crystalline quartz or silica sand – cannot be used directly for glass fiber manufacture due to its metallic oxide content [2]. It therefore has to be processed via the readily vaporizable liquid silicon tetrachloride ($SiCl_4$) which can be produced from silica by reduction with carbon and reaction with chlorine (reaction 1 in **Fig. 1**). Fractional distillation ensures that the silicon chlorides resulting from the chlorination are obtained in ultrapure form, leaving the metallic chlorides such as iron chloride behind as a residue. Silicon chlorides are used, for instance, in silicone chemistry and the manufacture of high-purity silicon for semiconductors.

The pure silicon dioxide required is then recovered from the silicon tetrachloride by gas phase deposition and the relevant chlorides ($GeCl_4$, $POCl_3$ etc.) are added to the silicon tetrachloride for doping the SiO_2 glasses. The chloride or chloride mixture is either hydrolyzed in a gas flame (reaction 2 in **Fig. 1**) or oxidized in the oxygen-gas stream by a thermal reaction initiated at around 1300 °C (reaction 3 in **Fig. 1**) [3], where upon the fine-grained SiO_2 powder condenses out, growing in highly porous form on a suitable substrate.

Residual water (e.g. from the flame gases) can be effectively removed from the resultant silicon dioxide with chlorine gas, since water and chlorine form volatile hydrogen chloride at temperatures of around 1000 °C (reaction 4 in **Fig. 1**) [4]. This drying process considerably increases light transmission through the glass.

The porous silicon dioxide is sintered at temperatures in excess of 1200 °C to form solid, bubble-free glass, the driving force for this consolidation process resulting from the reduction in surface energy on transition from particulate to consolidated glass [5].

Fiber preform preparation processes

The following three methods are available depending on the shape of the substrate for deposition [6].
● *Inside vapor deposition* on the inner surface of a silica tube
● *Outside vapor deposition* on the outer surface of a rod
● *Vapor axial deposition* on the end face of a rod.

The *inside vapor deposition* (IVD) process was first reported by the research laboratories of Corning Glass Works [7] and Bell Telephone (MCVD modified chemical vapor deposition) [8]. In this process the doped SiO_2 powder is deposited in layers – beginning with the cladding-glass layers and ending with the innermost core-glass layer – on the inner wall of a rotating tube (**Fig. 2a**) which is locally heated to around 1600 °C by an external burner. As each discrete layer is deposited it is simultaneously sintered to form solid glass. This is done by moving the burner along the tube in the direction of the gas flow to fuse the powder deposited ahead of the burner.

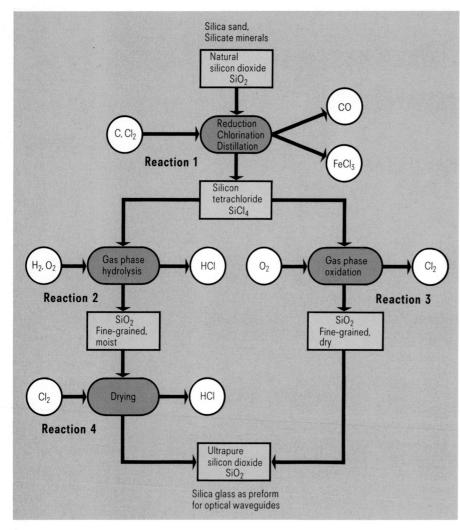

Fig. 1   Purification of natural silica sand by conversion to the vapor phase and deposition of high-purity silica glass by gas phase hydrolysis or oxidation

refractive index of the layers. **Figs. 4** and **5** show sections through preforms for multimode and single-mode fibers, the ring structure being a characteristic result of the deposition and fusion process.

The size of the preform used in production is generally equivalent to a fiber length of around 10 km. The achievable attenuation values of 1 dB/km at $\lambda = 1300$ nm can nowadays be brought as low as 0.5 dB/km in high-grade fibers [9]. The reason for this, apart from the inherent advantages of vapor phase deposition, is that inside the tube all contact by the synthetic glass with dusty or moist air is prevented [10].

The oxidation of the silicon and germanium chlorides can also be initiated by a plasma, and a *plasma chemical vapor deposition* (PCVD) process has been developed by Philips [11]. As the gas discharge zone can be rapidly moved along the tube, a comparatively large number of thin layers can be deposited in a short time by this method, producing particularly smooth profiles with no detectable ring structure.

In the *outside vapor deposition* (OVD) process developed and employed by Corning Glass Works, the vaporized starting chlorides are introduced to a gas-burner flame from which the oxides then condense out [12]. The flame burns radially onto a ceramic substrate rod which is moved relative to the burner (**Fig. 6**). Once again several hundred layers are deposited, the core glass composition being deposited first, followed by the entire cladding glass; no outside tube is used in this

After deposition, the tube is collapsed to form a cylindrical rod by further heating with the burner at elevated temperature, i.e. the tube progressively shrinks down (**Fig. 3**). The result is a solid preform the inside of which consists of pure synthetic material forming

the fiber core and inner fiber cladding, while the outer cladding region is the material of the commercial silica glass tube used. Preforms can be prepared by this method for various fiber types in accordance with the selected thickness, number and composition or

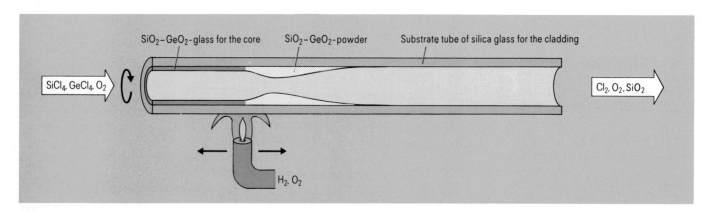

Fig. 2   Preparation of a fiber preform by the inside vapor deposition process with subsequent collapse of the glass tube to form a glass rod

Fig. 3 The MCVD-processed glass tube being collapsed to form a glass rod, the preform

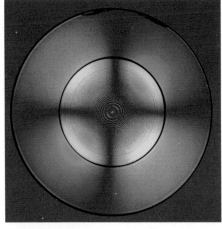

Fig. 4 Preform cross-section of a graded-index fiber

Fig. 5 Preform cross-section of a single-mode fiber

case. After the deposition process and removal of the substrate rod, drying is effected in a separate furnace using chlorine gas (reaction in **Fig. 1**) and then the porous body is sintered to form a solid rod. As the "deposition", "drying" and "sintering" steps occur sequentially allowing each step to be optimized separately, it is possible to achieve particularly high powder deposition rates with this process. Moreover, the deposition rate increases since the substrate surface becomes larger with successive layers [13], which is a helpful factor in scaling up the process. High glass deposition rates of 4.3 g/min corresponding to a fiber production rate of 5 km/h (including preform losses) have been achieved. With optimized drying this process can also be used to produce low-loss fibers of comparable quality to those obtained by inside tube deposition.

The *vapor axial deposition* (VAD) process developed in Japan also employs flame hydrolysis [14]. The gas flow is directed along or slightly inclined to the rod axis (**Fig. 7**), so that the porous blank grows in a longitudinal direction. In this process, the profile is formed by depositing variously doped SiO_2 powders next to each other rather than after each other as is the case with the outside process. Care must be taken to ensure that comparatively more germanium dioxide is deposited in the axial region than at the periphery, a requirement that can be met by precise control of a number of process parameter in a defined manner. The porous glass body is drawn off as it grows and

then passed through in-line drying and sintering zones so that comparatively long rods can be drawn. In this process it is not necessary to remove the sub-

strate rod. Less advantageous is that the deposition area on the end face is comparatively small, limiting the growth rate.

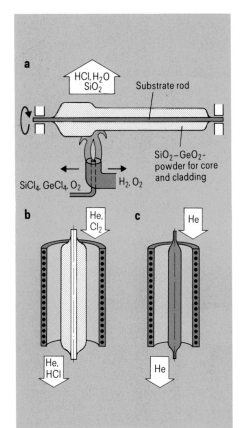

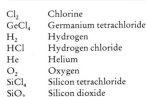

Cl_2	Chlorine
$GeCl_4$	Germanium tetrachloride
H_2	Hydrogen
HCl	Hydrogen chloride
He	Helium
O_2	Oxygen
$SiCl_4$	Silicon tetrachloride
SiO_2	Silicon dioxide

Fig. 6 Preparation of a fiber preform by the outside vapor deposition process (a) with subsequent drying (b) and sintering (c)

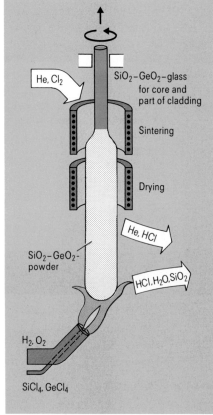

Cl_2	Chlorine
$GeCl_4$	Germanium tetrachloride
H_2	Hydrogen
HCl	Hydrogen chloride
He	Helium
O_2	Oxygen
$SiCL_4$	Silicon tetrachloride

Fig. 7 Preparation of a fiber preform by the vapor axial deposition process

Fiber drawing

The preform undergoes non-contact drawing in a high-temperature tube furnace at 2000°C to produce a fiber with similar geometry and essentially the same optical properties as the preform (**Fig. 8** and **Fig. 9** and **plate** on **page 8**). The main requirement is for the thin fiber to be drawn at a steady rate in a low-convection furnace atmosphere in order to minimize diameter variations in the fiber. In addition, care must be taken to prevent particles of the heating element (graphite or zirconium oxide) from contaminating the surface of the glass, as any foreign substances present on the hot fiber surface generally produce microcracks causing breaks in the fiber [15].

Before the fiber is taken up by the winder it is given a primary plastic coating to protect the fiber surface from mechanical damage and also to cushion the fiber to prevent microbending. Application of the viscous prepolymer requires suitable coating processes to ensure that the coating is evenly centered and bubble-free even at high drawing rates (about 1 to 4 m/s). Curing to an elastic polymer layer is sometimes thermally activated, but is now more usually initiated by a photochemical reaction (UV radiation).

Fig. 8   Start of fiber drawing process

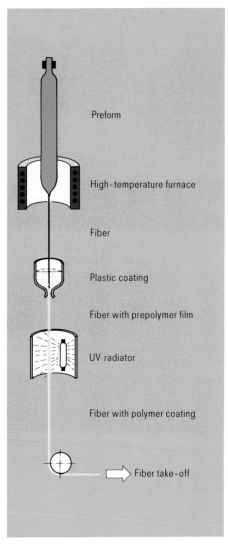

Preform

High-temperature furnace

Fiber

Plastic coating

Fiber with prepolymer film

UV radiator

Fiber with polymer coating

Fiber take-off

Fig. 9   Schematic of fiber drawing process

Design and properties of optical waveguides for communications applications

Communications applications in existing and future communications networks are determined principally by the transmission characteristics of the fibers, especially by attenuation and bandwith.

Graded-index fibers

Fig. 10 shows the main characteristics of a currently common type of graded-index fiber. Suitable doping causes the refractive index to decrease parabolically with radial distance from the fiber axis. The core diameter is 50 µm, the cladding diameter 125 µm (CCITT Recommendation G.651). The optical fiber is protected by a two-layer cushion coating of urethane acrylates. The

refractive index $n = 1.52$ of this plastic material is much greater than that of the cladding glass ($n \approx 1.45$), so that cladding light is stripped off and is absorbed in the plastic after a few meters.

The plastic coating (cushion coating) has the additional purpose of absorbing lateral pressure which causes microbending of the optical fiber axis and hence increased attenuation. The cushion coating consists of a very soft inner layer protected by an abrasion-resistant outer layer. The outside diameter of the entire coating is generally 250 µm. This makes the optical fiber easier to handle and provides good cross-sectional utilization in cables of loose-tube design. In special cases (e.g. in tight-buffer cables), the primary coating can have an outside diameter of 500 µm.

The core doping is selected such that the refractive index in the center of the fiber is around 0.9% higher than in the cladding glass; this corresponds to a numerical aperture [16] of 0.2 and an acceptance angle of 11.5° in air (and a propagation angle of 8° maximum in the fiber core).

Fig. 11 shows the typical attenuation curve of a graded-index fiber as a function of the optical wavelength. The attenuation falls steadily from 800 nm towards longer wavelengths, reaching minimum values around 1550 nm. The declining attenuation to around 1300 nm is due mainly to Rayleigh scattering from the thermodynamically related density fluctuations in the glass.

In addition to the Rayleigh scattering, there are also water absorption bands. The attenuation peaks associated with the individual resonance wavelengths for hydroxyl groups (−OH) forming 1 ppm by weight of the glass [17] are given in the following table:

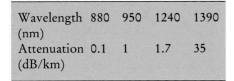

Wavelength (nm)	880	950	1240	1390
Attenuation (dB/km)	0.1	1	1.7	35

In the attenuation curve in **Fig. 11** these bands can be seen at 1390 nm, their magnitude corresponding to water content of around 10 ppb. During production the water content may vary by as much as 50 ppb, producing corresponding variations in the attenuation peaks.

In addition to the wavelength-dependent attenuation components due to Rayleigh scattering and water absorption, actual optical waveguides additionally exhibit wavelength-independent attenuation on the order of 0.1 to 0.5 dB/km which is the result of microscopic waveguide discontinuities (diameter variations, doping variations, inclusions, e.g. in the form of gas bub-

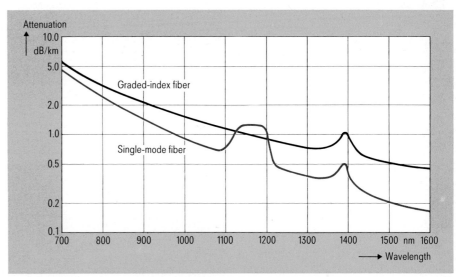

Fig. 11 Attenuation spectrum for multimode and single-mode fibers

bles, etc.). These effects combine during manufacture to produce a spread of attenuation values. For this reason optical waveguides are divided into various attenuation categories depending on application, e.g. for:
$\lambda = 1300$ nm,
$\alpha \le 1.5$ dB/km or
$\alpha \le 1.0$ dB/km or
$\alpha \le 0.7$ dB/km.

Another important parameter of the graded-index fiber, apart from attenuation and numerical aperture, is bandwidth. The power modulation of an optical transmitter is influenced by a graded-index fiber as if it were a low-pass filter. The magnitude of the transfer function decreases steadily with the modulation frequency, while the phase distortion in all specimens tested remains very small. For system calculations this response can be assumed to a first approximation to be equivalent to a Gaussian low-pass filter. The numerical value of the low-pass cutoff frequency is a function of the wavelength of the light due to the particular glass composition used and the profile shape. The maximum bandwidth can only occur for a single wavelength; for all other wavelengths the low-pass frequency decreases similarly to a band-pass filter characteristic.

Fig. 12 shows the bandwidth-length product as a function of the wavelength for two fiber designs currently in use. The first-window fiber A has its optimum bandwidth in the 850 nm wavelength range, while the second-

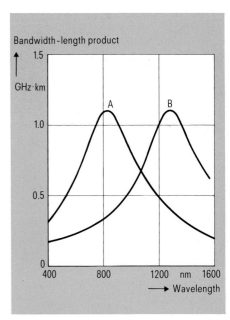

A First-window fiber
B Second-window fiber

Fig. 12 Bandwidth-length product of various graded-index fibers

window fiber B has its optimum bandwidth at 1300 nm.

Single-mode fibers

If core diameter and refractive index difference are selected small enough, only a single mode – the so-called fundamental mode – is propagated in the fiber [16]. In this single-mode fiber, bandwith ceases to be dominated by the difference in delays of the individual modes and is limited merely by such lesser effects as material and waveguide dispersion. In the 1300 nm wavelength range it is therefore pos-

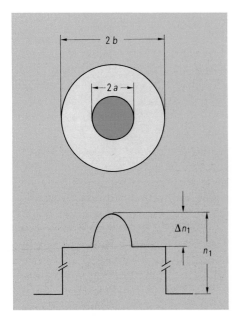

Core diameter $2a = 50$ μm
Cladding diameter $2b = 125$ μm
Core refractive index $n_1 \approx 1.45$
Maximum refractive index difference between core and cladding glass $\Delta n_1 = 0.014$
Numerical aperture $A_N = 0.2$

Fig. 10 Cross section and graded-index profile of an uncoated multimode fiber. The real fiber always has a plastic coating with an outside diameter of 250 μm and a refractive index of about 1.52

sible to expect specific bandwidth-length products in excess of 20 GHz·km. This high bandwidth makes the single-mode fiber particularly suitable for long-haul systems.

Although the dimensions of a future single-mode fiber have not yet been standardized, a particularly favorable size for operation at 1300 nm is given here (**Fig. 13**). In a core of about 9 μm diameter (see **Fig. 3 b**) the refractive index is raised as a step function by 0.3%; the outside dimensions are similar to the graded-index fiber. The only mode which can propagate in the wavelength range above the so-called cutoff wavelength λ_c is the fundamental mode with its bell-shaped field distribution. The next higher-order mode with a field zero occurs only at wavelengths shorter than the cutoff wavelength λ_c. For the given dimensions λ_c lies between 1100 and 1270 nm.

As shown in **Fig. 14** the intensity distribution of the fundamental mode extends outside the core region by varying amounts. For values $\lambda \gg \lambda_c$ the light penetrates increasingly deeply into the cladding region, resulting in radiation losses at fiber bends. The fiber is therefore usually operated at $1.0 < \lambda/\lambda_c < 1.3$. This corresponds to an interval of 2.4 to 1.8 for the structural parameter v of the fiber [17].

Owing to the reduced core doping and the consequently reduced scattering losses, the single-mode fiber exhibits lower overall loss than the graded-index fiber (**Fig. 11**); a loss of less than 0.5 dB/km at $\lambda = 1300$ nm can be assumed. (Best values at 1300 nm and 1600 nm are 0.32 and 0.16 dB/km respectively.) Apart from the water band at 1390 nm the spectrum exhibits another apparent attenuation peak caused by radiation of the light guided in the higher mode. The point at which the long-wavelength edge of this peak intersects the pedestal attenuation at 1200 nm marks the effective cutoff wavelength of this fiber.

A common method of measuring the effective cutoff wavelength is the so-called bending method. In this method, the attenuation of a short piece of fiber (e.g. 1 m) is measured in a straight and in a curved condition (winding the fiber loosely around a cylinder of about 20 mm diameter). The excess

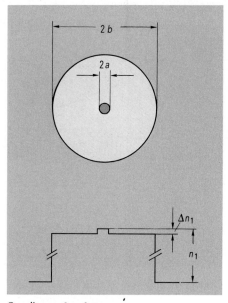

Core diameter $2a = 9$ μm
Cladding diameter $2b = 125$ μm
Core refractive index $n_1 \approx 1.45$
Maximum refractive index difference between core and
 cladding glass $\Delta n_1 = 0.0044$
Cutoff wavelength $\lambda_c = 1150$ nm

Fig. 13   Cross section and step-index profile of an uncoated single-mode fiber. The real fiber always has a concentric plastic coating with an outer diameter of 250 μm and a refractive index of about 1.52

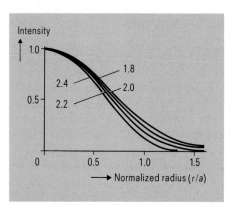

Fig. 14   Intensity distribution of the fundamental mode for various v values

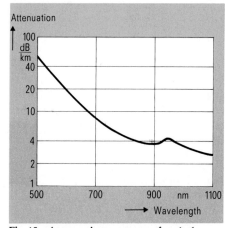

Fig. 15   Attenuation spectrum of optical waveguides (100/140 μm fiber) for industrial applications

attenuation due to the bending is calculated. The effective cutoff wavelength is defined as that wavelength, at which this excess attenuation is 0.1 dB.

Another important parameter of a single mode fiber is the mode field diameter, sometimes referred to as "spot size". For Gaussian fields it is the diameter at the $1/e$ point of the optical amplitude distribution, which is equivalent to the $1/e^2$-point of the optical power distribution (**Fig. 14**). A typical value for the mode field diameter is 10 ± 1 μm. A suitable measurement result is provided by the transverse offset method measuring the power coupling between two fiber pieces being moved transversely past one another by means of micropositioners. The mode field diameter is defined as the transverse offset between the two points at $1/e$-intensity. In fact, the most important parameters of single mode fibers are the attenuation at 1300 nm, the cutoff wavelength and the mode field diameter.

Optical waveguides for industrial applications

Links for industrial applications range in length from meters to several kilometers. They employ mainly LED transmitters which have a relatively large emitting area to provide relatively simple coupling. The optical fiber should collect as much of the emitted light as possible, i.e. core diameters and numerical apartures must be relatively large.

A *silica fiber* (outside diameter 140 μm, core diameter 100 μm) is produced for these applications by using the outside vapor deposition process previously described. **Fig. 15** shows the typical attenuation characteristic of this fiber. The core region is relatively highly doped, giving a numerical aperture of 0.29 (corresponding to an angle of 17.5°). The graded index and doping are such that a bandwidth-length product of over 100 MHz·km is obtained for a wavelength at 850 nm and at 1300 nm.

References

[1] Kapron, F.P.; Keck, D.B.; Maurer, R.D.: Radiation losses in glass optical waveguides. Appl. Phys. Let. 10 (1970), p. 423

[2] Brückner, R.: Properties and structure of vitreous silica (Part I). J. Non-Cryst. Solids 5 (1970), pp. 123 to 175

[3] Powers, D.R.: Kinetics of SiCl₄ Oxidation. J. of the Amer. Ceramic Soc. 61 (1978), pp. 295 to 297

[4] Elmer, T.H.: Dehydroxylation of Porous Glass by Means of Chlorine. J. of the Amer. Ceramic Soc. 64 (1981), pp. 150 to 154

[5] Scherer, G.W.: Sintering inhomogeneous glasses: application to optical waveguides. J. Non-Cryst. Solids 34 (1979), pp. 239 to 256

[6] Schultz, P.C.: Progress in optical waveguide process and materials. Appl. Opt. 18 (1979), pp. 3684 to 3693

[7] U.S. Patent 3, 711, 262 of 16.1.1973, (D.B. Keck; P.C. Schultz): Method of producing optical waveguide fibers

[8] MacChesney, J.B.; O'Connor, P.B.; Di Marcello, F.V.; Simpson, J.P.; Lazay, P.D.: Preparation of low-loss optical fibers using simultaneous vapor phase deposition and fusion. Proc. of 10th Int. Congr. Glass, Kyoto, 1974, pp. 6–40 to 6–44

[9] Jablonowski, P.D.; Padgette, D.D.; Merten, J.R.: Performance of the MCVD preform process in mass production conditions. Proc. Topical Meet. on Opt. Fiber Commun. 1982, Phoenix, Arizona, p. 18

[10] Schneider, H.; Deserno, U.; Lebetzki, E.; Meyer, A.: A new method to reduce the central dip and the OH⁻ content in MCVD preforms. 8th Europ. Conf. Opt. Commun., Cannes, September 1982, Conf. Proc., pp. 36 to 40

[11] Geittner, P.; Küppers, D.; Lydtin, H.: Low-loss optical fibers prepared by plasmaactivated chemical vapor deposition (CVD). Appl. Phys. Let. 28 (1976), pp. 645 and 646

[12] Schultz, P.C.: Fabrication of optical waveguides by the outside vapor deposition process. Proc. of the IEEE 68 (1980), pp. 1187 to 1190

[13] Blankenship, M.G.; Morrow, A.J.; Silverman, L.A.: Large GRIN preforms deposited at high rate using OVD. Proc. of Topical Meet. Opt. Fiber Commun. 1982, Phoenix, Arizona, p. 18

[14] Izawa, I.; Kobayashi, S.; Sudo, J.; Hanawa, F.: Continuous fabrication of high silica fiber preform. Int. Conf. Integrated Optics & Opt. Fiber Commun., Tokyo, 1977, pp. 375 to 378

[15] Maurer, R.D.: Effect of dust on glass fiber strength. Appl. Phys. Let. 30 (1977), pp. 82 to 84

[16] Geckeler, S.: Physical Principles of optical Waveguides. telcom report 6 (1983) Special Issue "Optical Communications", pp. 9 to 14

[17] Keck, D.B.; Maurer, R.D.; Schultz, P.C.: On the ultimate lower limit of attenuation in glass optical waveguides. Appl. Phys. Let. 22 (1973), pp. 307 to 309

Ulrich Oestreich

Fiber-Optic Cables for Long-Haul Communication Links

New information services and the transition to digital transmission techniques are making further cable network expansion necessary for long-haul links also. Optical fibers of very low loss and suitable bandwidth provide such favorable combinations of repeater spacing and channel capacity that there was never any doubt about their economic viability, as soon as their reliability and life equalled that of established transmission media. The reliability and life of a complete transmission system depend, however, to a large extent on the characteristics of the cable employed. Yet, a cable's reduced reliability and end of life do not depend merely on the cable or individual fibers being damaged or destroyed. A serious change in attenuation on the route could be enough to exceed the system performance range and reduce the transmission bandwidth.

Cable design

Experience to date has shown that cable designs, causing individual fibers to exhibit a distinct change in attenuation compared with the original condition or producing perceptible mechanical responses to permitted changes in temperature or other conditions, must be regarded as unsuited for long-term service. Such changes in effect mean that the fibers are being excessively deformed with long-term consequences which can be judged merely in a probabilistic way [1, 2]. In view of this the only appropriate cable design is one which under all permitted conditions keeps the fibers in a state of minimum mechanical stress, minimizing local deviations from a tolerable mean bending stress. This eliminates any design which does not provide the fibers with sufficient radial clearance for the inevitable changes in length, bending

or twisting of the cable (e.g. tightly buffered fibers in a tightly stranded cable core).

In meeting this requirement, it is possible to arrive at widely differing results. One of the earliest solutions, which has been readopted in recent years, is the slotted core cable in which the rugged core is provided with helical grooves accommodating one or several fibers. The problems with this design become apparent only on closer examination. Firstly, it is not easy to insert the fibers in such a way as to give them a satisfactory bilateral length margin adequate for all situations, and secondly, it is necessary to provide sufficient protection for fibers or groups of fibers at branching points. The adaptability of this system to widely differing fiber counts and operating conditions is moderate.

Other solutions, emphasizing the identification and easy handling of the individual fiber, provide it first with a strong, tightly-fitting buffer and then enclose it in the core structure with a relatively large cross section. This often

Dipl.-Ing. Ulrich Oestreich,
Siemens AG,
Public Communication Networks Division,
Munich

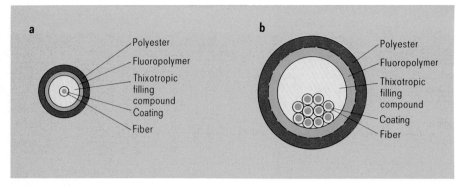

Fig. 1 Configuration of the basic modules (scale 10 : 1) for single fiber (a) and multifiber unit (b)

results in loose, very bulky and relatively heavy designs lacking variability and arising mainly out of a desire to utilize capacity on machines making conventional cables. The conclusion is rapidly reached that the smallest cross-section and materials usage are achieved when the required radial clearance is located directly around the fiber which should be coated as thinly as possible.

Cable configuration

Buffered fiber

In realizing a protective buffer with adequate resistance to deformation and optimally suited to the fiber, the natural solution is a precision-made circular plastic tube which can be treated like a quad or coaxial pair and hence exhibits all the advantages of a general-purpose cable module (**Fig. 1**). This

module provides the basis (with a few exceptions relating to highly specialized cables with low fiber counts for industrial or military applications) for calculating precisely the best configuration for any particular application. Various materials and combinations of materials for the buffer tube can be used to suit a wide range of environmental conditions. The tubes can be filled with gases, pasty or gel-like compounds and can be made non-hosing, water and gas blocking and as crush resistant as required. The special manufacturing equipment employed is justified by the advantages which the resultant basic module confers in both technical and economic terms.

The cable design envisaged by the Deutsche Bundespost in preliminary technical supply specifications is the result of the knowledge and experience described.

First, the fibers are given a double coating of UV cross-linked acrylate about

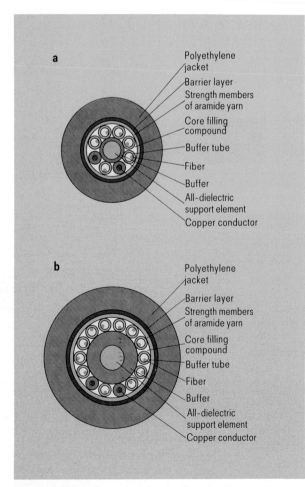

Fig. 2 Cable configurations for the short-haul network including two copper conductors (scale 2.5 : 1); six fiber (a), twelve fiber (b)

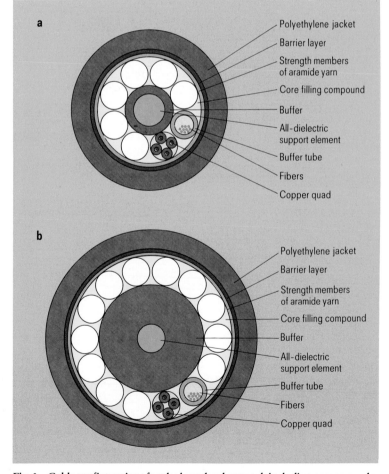

Fig. 3 Cable configurations for the long-haul network including copper quads (scale 2.5 : 1); 60 fiber (a), 120 fiber (b)

60 μm thick. The inner coating is extremely soft, thereby preventing microbending at points of contact, and can be easily removed leaving no residue. The outer coating is a first mechanical protection layer with a moderate coefficient of friction, but to which suitable inks will adhere. Fibers can be produced and processed in lengths of several kilometers.

The loose buffer tubes generally consist of a double layer with a wall thickness about 15% of the overall buffer diameter. The materials have been chosen to minimize expansion and contraction while optimizing aging behavior and inertness to inner and outer filling compounds. Since the buffer tubes are smooth inside and outside, they offer minimum resistance to the movement of the fibers inside and to the movement of other buffers outside.

The outside diameter chosen for single-fiber buffers (**Fig. 2**) is 1.4 mm while for 10-fiber buffers (**Fig. 3**) it is 3 mm. These two values do not represent the minimum dimensions achievable with the technology, but have proven to be suitable in the field.

The buffer filling compound is partially thixotropic and consists mainly of chemically inert oil which in the temperature range of interest from −30 to +70°C neither freezes nor runs and neither attacks nor swells the fibers' protective coating. The compound can be easily stripped and washed off, leaving no residue to hinder the jointing of the fibers. Moreover, it contains no easily flammable constituents.

The double buffer tube is produced and combined with the filling compound and fiber in one operation. This enables the most important properties of the buffer tube (long-term dimensional stability, low defined coefficient of expansion, high degree of flexibility with a high Young's modulus together with toughness and inertness to inner and outer filling compounds) to be optimized. Whereas the buffer filling compound should hinder fiber movement as little as possible without actually running and dripping, the filling compound for the interstices between the buffers, i.e. the voids in the cable core, should be somewhat more viscous.

Fig. 4 View of the cable production facility

The main task of the fiber buffering process is to co-ordinate the tube and fiber length to a tolerance of ±2 · 10⁻⁴. This in turn depends not only on the tube materials, but also on the process speed, the cooling, the braking of the fiber and the guiding of the buffer. **Fig. 4** shows a typical production machine.

Cable core and jacket

The length-defining, all-dielectric central support member consists of high-tensile glass filaments bonded with a resin highly resistant to aging and thermal effects. Since the support member is required to absorb not only the contractions due to cooling but also some of the tensile forces, it merits particular attention to quality and inspection. Wherever space permits, the support member is provided with an adhering protective polyethylene (PE) overcoat to ensure that the end of the cable is securely anchored for splicing or distribution.

The buffered fibers are stranded onto the support member at defined retention forces to suit the buffer tube. The stranding lay length S and the pitch radius R are calculated so that the bilateral longitudinal movement of the fi-

bers inside the buffers with radial clearance ΔR

$$\frac{\Delta l}{l} \approx \pm 4\pi^2 \cdot \frac{R \cdot \Delta R}{S^2} \qquad (1)$$

and the stranding bend radius

$$\varrho = R\left(1 + \frac{S^2}{4\pi^2 R^2}\right) \qquad (2)$$

permit tensile strain on the cable up to the rated force and cooling down to the rated lower temperature limit without affecting the fiber, i.e. its attenuation and life (smallest stranding bend radius used: 65 mm).

Fig. 5 SZ-stranding

Fig. 6 Jacketing an optical cable

Fig. 7 72-fiber cable

The stranding with alternating direction of lay (SZ) used (**Fig. 5**) facilitates branching and permits cable cores to be produced in lengths limited only by the length of the fibers used and the capacity of the cable reel. This stranding technique can be employed without modification to include current-carrying metallic elements in the form of individual conductors or quads for use as order wires or to facilitate fault location. However, to take full advantage of the inherent EMI immunity of optical fibers, it is preferable to provide for these classic ancillary functions in such a way as to enable cables to be of nonmetallic design.

The central support member can, of course, also be used to take up tensile forces, but it is not the only supporting element. Aramid yarns or rovings are stranded onto the cable core in such a proportion as to produce, with the central member, the required tensile strength (**Fig. 6**). Distributing the strength members between the center and periphery of the cable core reduces lateral stress on the buffered fibers in

cable bends. This approach also has the advantage that, since the jacket is bonded to the aramid yarn covering, it is possible to use cable pulling grips without high-tensile cable end sealing in spite of the core being filled with a waterblocking compound.

Experience to date indicates that it is advisible to use a poly-isobutylene based filling compound for the cable core. This has a number of advantages, including a lower coefficient of expansion and less action on the polyethylene jacket than other petroleum jellies used. To exclude all influences, the jacket is provided on the inside with a barrier in the form of an extruded polyamide adhesive layer. This layer enables the jacket to maintain its mechanical quality throughout its life even without the aluminium foil and to provide full tensile strength without impairing flexibility.

Cable jacket

Jacket thickness and markings conform to the existing requirements.

The design principle described can be adapted to suit all types of fiber (including single-mode fibers) and all applications (e.g. submarine cables).

Cable types

Cables supplied to the Deutsche Bundespost are shown in **Figs. 2** and **3**. **Fig. 7** shows cable of the type already installed on a large scale in the USA. All together, some 30,000 kilometers of cabled fiber have been supplied in the Federal Republic of Germany and abroad, predominantly in configurations for long-haul applications. The reliability of these configurations is due to the use of the "filled, loose tube" principle. This is confirmed by the fact that so far not a single fiber break has been reported that was not attributable to violent damage. The number of cases of such damage are, moreover, very few. A case of damage caused by rodents (American gophers), which was not repeated after repair, raises the question of the need and economic justification for protection against rodent attack. A reliable solution would be a longitudinally applied or possibly wrapped covering of steel tape over the cable core. Apart from the increased cost and weight of the cables, however, this type of protection runs counter to the all-dielectric design desired for fiber-optic cables. The objective can be achieved, for instance, by using an extremely tough jacketing material, but this significantly increases the flex resistance and also raises the cost. The most rigid, most expensive and, of course, most secure protection is a jacket made of resin-impregnated glass. Special polyamides also produce a sufficiently secure and flexible non-conducting jacket.

While in Europe and other areas with high population density the usual way of installing long distance cables is pulling the cables in ducts or ploughing them in, crossing of vast areas with low population densities points to the use of existing high voltage overhead lines as an economic way of installation. For this purpose rugged reliable easily installable cables are needed which must be selfsupporting and fully dielectric in order to be installed as independently as possible on power leads. The loose tube design together with a sufficiently strong Aramide yarn reinforcement enables us to design light and strong cables which even under very high ice and wind loads represent reliable connections [3].

References

[1] Oestreich, U.; Aulich, H. A.: Tensile Strength and Static Fatigue of Optical Glass Fibers. Siemens Forsch.- u. Entwickl.-Ber. 9 (1980) pp. 123 to 127

[2] Bark, P. R.; Oestreich, U.; Zeidler, G.: Stress – Strain Behaviour of Optical Fiber Cables. 28th Int. Wire & Cable Symp., Cherry Hill, November 1979, pp. 385 to 390

[3] Oestreich, U. H. P.: Fiber Optic Aerial Cables. Fiber and Integrated Optics, Vol. 4, No. 1 (1982) pp. 95 to 106

Ernst Mayr, Herwig Schinko and Gernot Schöber

Fiber-Optic Unit-Based Cables in the Local Network

Optical fibers have opened up new possibilities for communications. Apart from the various advantages they have over conventional communication paths it is primarily their high transmission bandwidth together with a relatively small physical size that enables new information and communication services to be provided in the local network. These services include videoconferencing, videotelephony, multichannel television programs as well as facilities for banks, businesses and companies to communicate with each other and with any other subscriber. This paper highlights the currently available cable facilities, enabling the capacity of local networks to be expanded.

A suitable cable design has been developed to take account of the various applications and expansion stages in the local network.

Employing the multifiber unit as the basic module (a loose buffer tube containing several fibers), this cable design is characterized primarily by ruggedness, high packing density, flexibility and obsolescence-proof versatility.

Cable design

Leaving aside cables in the outlying distribution network and subscriber drops, the multifiber unit forms the basic module in fiber-optic cables for the local network. This unit is a loose tube in which are grouped up to ten optical fibers (**Fig. 1**) [1]. Assuming two-way traffic via a single fiber, this unit is equivalent to the conventional basic ten-pair unit. Several of these units are stranded around a central antibuckling and support member to

Dipl.-Ing. (FH) Ernst Mayr,
Dipl.-Ing. (FH) Herwig Schinko and
Dipl.-Ing. (FH) Gernot Schöber,
Siemens AG,
Public Communication Networks Division,
Munich

form the cable core which is secured by a binder or core whipping. After strength members have been applied and a moisture-resistant filling introduced, the cable cores are enclosed in a jacket of the kind found in conventional cable designs. In the peripheral distribution network, the number of fibers can be reduced to one per tube so that the tube diameter decreases from 3.0 to 1.4 mm.

Multifiber unit

The multifiber unit comprises a rugged, flexible, aging-resistant round plastic tube which is inert to filling compounds and moisture. It has a relatively low coefficient of expansion over a wide temperature range.

Its inside diameter of 1.8 mm provides generous space for up to ten 0.25 mm diameter fibers. The void is filled with a soft, slightly thixotropic compound which does not drip or freeze between -30 and $+70\,°C$. The tube and filling compound allow the core and fibers to relax and adjust to a wide range of tensions. When completely filled with this compound and securely laid up, the tube is not only laterally rugged but also as impact-resistant as can be expected. All this also applies to the 1.4 mm single-fiber unit.

In order to distinguish the individual fibers from each other, they are colored and, if necessary, ring-marked. The color coatings of about 2 μm applied for this purpose have no effect on the optical properties of the fiber. Similarly, the filling compound in the unit does not affect the fiber colors or the ring identification. **Table 1** shows an example of color coding as already envisaged in a draft standard.

Cable core

Several units, stranded together around a central member, form the cable core. It is mainly this stranding which provides the optical fibers with a defined range of longitudinal movement inside the unit so that tensile, compressive and, of course, bending stresses up to specified limits do not affect the optical transmission properties. To identify the individual units, the tube of one unit per layer is colored as a so-called tracer. The number of single or multifiber units to be stranded is determined by the requirements, but can be easily adapted to any application. When there are up to 250 or even 300 optical fibers per cable, the units are stranded around a central element in one or two layers to form the cable core.

To ease identification of the individual units when there are more than 300 fibers per cable it is advisable to form the core from main units containing 50 or 100 fibers stranded in layers like the units described above. Each individual main unit can be easily identified by designating one per layer as the tracer unit with a colored binder.

Fig. 2 shows how a fiber-optic cable for 50 fibers is made up from five units

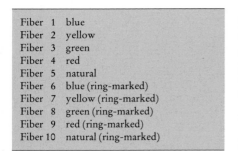

Fiber 1	blue
Fiber 2	yellow
Fiber 3	green
Fiber 4	red
Fiber 5	natural
Fiber 6	blue (ring-marked)
Fiber 7	yellow (ring-marked)
Fiber 8	green (ring-marked)
Fiber 9	red (ring-marked)
Fiber 10	natural (ring-marked)

Table 1   Example of the colored coatings of fibers (rings marked black)

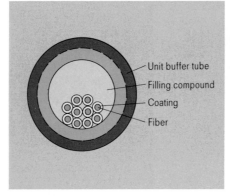

Fig. 1   Unit with ten fibers

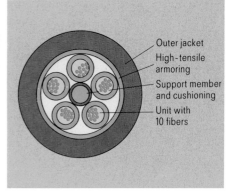

Fig. 2   Unit-based cable with 50 fibers, formed from one main unit containing five units

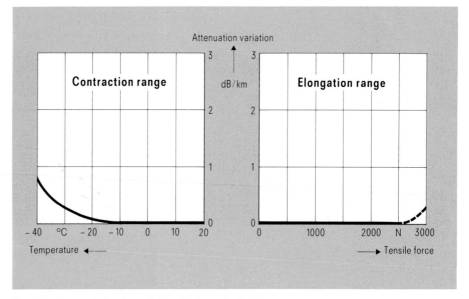

Fig. 3   Characteristics of a unit-based cable as in Fig. 2

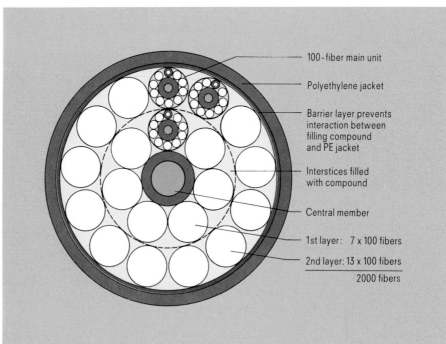

Fig. 4   Unit-based cable with a total of 2000 fibers

to form a core corresponding to a 50-fiber main unit. The behavior of this cable in relation to tensile stress and temperature fluctuations is shown by the characteristics in **Fig. 3**. **Fig. 4** illustrates the possible design of a 2000-fiber main cable with its core formed from main units of 100 fibers each. The single main unit detailed in **Fig. 4** has, itself, the same design as the core of a 100-fiber cable.

To prevent hosing in the event of water ingress, the cable core contains a special filling compound which can be easily removed for installation work. The formulation of the compound, the configuration of the units and the provision of a barrier between core and jacket prevent any detectable interaction between the filling compound and the cable components. The compound also meets drip test requirements.

Cable sheath

If the filled core is surrounded by a high-tensile covering of glass or aramid yarns and a plastic sheath, the saturated yarn covering must have a barrier between it and the jacket to prevent the compound coming directly into contact with the jacket. The widely proven material generally used for the jacket is polyethylene which, if unprotected, is softened by petroleum jelly or similar filling compounds. The barrier layer can be composed of any resistant plastic (extruded or wrapped) or the aluminum foil of the laminated jacket. The cable, designed to withstand all the usual stresses, can be provided with a high-tensile capping (connected to the strength members) and can be placed or pulled in the usual way.

Since high-tensile capping is expensive and at variance with cutting sections of cable as required from maximum factory lengths, there is an increasing demand for a so-called "high-tensile" jacket. This jacket must be strong enough to allow lengths over 1000 m to be pulled in with a cable sock without slipping over the cable core [2]. Jackets incorporating strength members are certainly one solution. They are, however, usually flex resistant and, when bent, there is a risk of the core buckling due to shifting of the elastic axis. There

Fig. 5   Fiber-optic cable with 800 fibers grouped in units

is a simple and technically satisfactory solution to this problem. If the filled core with its covering of strength members is coated with a petrolatum-resistant and relaxing thermoplastic adhesive, this will produce a barrier layer to support the jacket.

This also enables the jacket to utilize the cable strength members without the risk of buckling the core, since the relaxation times of the thermoplastic adhesives are short enough even at low temperatures. The adhesive allows strength members to move slowly without losing its effectiveness.

For special applications, e.g. when particularly high flame resistance is required, there are other special jacket materials available besides polyethylene, the preferred materials being special PUR (*polyu*rethane *r*ubber) or FRNC compounds (*f*lame *r*etardent *n*on-corrosive).

The present state of the art provides for fiber-optic cables with between 10 and 2000 fibers in the local network. **Fig. 5** shows a typical example of such cable. The main advantages of the loose tube unit-based design are:

● sufficient space for the fiber to move when cable length changes, e.g. in response to temperature fluctuations or

tensile stresses, so that within specified limits there is no increase in attenuation or mechanical strain,

● grouping of up to ten fibers in one tube, enabling a high packing density to be achieved,

● use of splicing modules for each unit, thereby facilitating jointing and branching operations,

● makes possible small cable diameter and low cable weight,

● non-metallic cable design,

● non-hosing unit and cable,

● negligible attenuation variation under design conditions [3].

When configuring complete cables, the design engineer needs to know all the related conditions. Of primary interest to him are:

● required number of fibers and their transmission properties,

● particular application (indoor, ducted, buried, aerial or submarine cable),

● climatic and geographic environmental stresses (e.g. temperature, tension, pressure, ice or wind loading).

Any of the problems likely to occur can be solved by supplementary provision without fundamentally altering the unit-based design.

By varying the size of the loose tube and the lay length in stranding the core, or by varying the strength and anti-buckling elements, it is possible to extend the mechanical application range of the cable, while by the choice of different materials the thermal range can be extended. Special nonflammable plastics or rodent-resistant outer jackets can be employed to produce flame-retardant and rodent-proof cables.

Cable installation and network structure

As regards installation, "light weight" fiber-optic cables have advantages over copper cables. Multi-pair copper cables, for instance, can still only be pulled in using standard 330 m lengths because of their weight and size. The diameters of these cables have hitherto also determined the maximum duct diameter. A comparison of the dimensions, weights and factory lengths of fiber-optic and copper cables is given in **Table 2**. This assumes that the subscriber line employs wavelength-division multiplexing to allow transmission in both directions on one fiber.

The introduction of fiber optics will mean rethinking the local network layout. In view of the possible additional attenuation at splices, it is necessary to reduce the number of joints by minimizing in-line and branch closures and by avoiding jumpering operations in the cable distribution cabinet. The number of joints can be reduced as follows:

● lay several cables in parallel to cover the maximum length (fewer branch closures),

● fan cables out inside the exchange without using closures,

● forward-backward distribution in the branch cable closures.

An example of a Deutsche Bundespost local network as in **Fig. 6** illustrates how joints can be reduced by adopting this strategy.

Experience with unit-based cables

In North America extensive routes have already been realized using unit-based cables with non-metallic jackets [4]. Although these cables are mainly in the long-haul and short-haul networks, the experience gained is relevant to all fiber-optic unit-based cables, including local cables. Since units with six or twelve fibers are preferred in North America, Siemens has produced standard cables with 66 fibers for several large projects. These cables are pro-

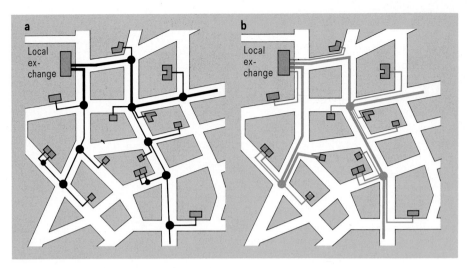

Fig. 6 Layout of a local network
a Installation with copper cables and ten closures
b Installation with fiber-optic cables and three closures

vided with a cushioned support member, around which eleven units are stranded with six colored fibers in each unit. The cable core is filled with a moisture-resistant compound, the cable jacket (outside diameter about 18 mm) consisting of polyethylene.

Some of the data obtained on one of these projects, where approximately 4000 km of fibers were installed on a cable route of about 70 km, are useful in illustrating the main properties of the cable lengths supplied.

● As regards their tensile characteristic, the cables showed no significant increase in attenuation ($\Delta\alpha < 0.1$ dB/km at $\lambda = 850$ nm) in response to a tensile force of 2500 N and elongation of 0.5%.

● In the temperature range from -30 to $+60\,°$C the attenuation variations were always less than 0.8 dB/km at $\lambda = 850$ nm.

● The water-blocking properties under 1 m of water were proved over three days on a test piece 3 m long.

It is now eighteen months since this system went into service and the transmission properties have so far remained unchanged.

Fiber/conductor count		Diameter		Weight		Factory length	
Opt.	Cu pairs	Opt. mm	Cu mm	Opt. kg/km	Cu kg/km	Opt. m	Cu m
Main cable							
50	50	13.5	17.0	100	295	2000	1000
100	100	17	21.5	190	495	2000	1000
500	500	38	40.0	1055	1985	1000	1000
1000	1000	45	56.0	1850	3865	1000	750
2000	2000	66	76.5	2750	7395	1000	333
Distribution cable							
2, 4, 6	6	10	11.0	95	120	2000	1000
10	10	11	12.5	95	165	2000	1000
40	40	13.5	21.0	100	500	2000	1000
100	100	17	30.5	190	1125	2000	1000
200	200	24	41.5	295	2120	2000	1000

Table 2 Technical data of fiber-optic and copper (Cu) cables

References

[1] Oestreich, U.: Fiber-Optic Cables for Long-Haul Communication Links.
telcom report 6 (1983) Special Issue "Optical Communications", pp. 33 to 37

[2] Goldmann, H.: Installation of Fiber-Optic Cables.
telcom report 6 (1983) Special Issue "Optical Communications", pp. 46 to 49

[3] Sutor, N.: Testing the Mechanical and Thermal Characteristics of Optical Cables.
telcom report 6 (1983) Special Issue "Optical Communications", pp. 183 to 187

[4] Bark, P. R.; Szentesi, O. I.: Fiber-Optic Projects in the USA.
telcom report 6 (1983) Special Issue "Optical Communications", pp. 66 to 71

Günter Zeidler

Designing Fiber-Optic Cable Systems

Recent years have seen great advances in optical communications. Initial operating data on communication over the new optical fiber medium is already to hand and a large number of fiber-optic cable systems have already proven their worth in the field. The primary considerations in designing such systems are the loss and bandwidth of the fibers used and of the associated joints.

Transmission characteristics of an optical waveguide

Loss and bandwidth are the most important parameters in designing fiber-optic cable systems. Both parameters are generally referred to the optical power which the optical waveguide or the fiber-optic device is required to transmit under specified operating conditions. If the input and output powers are designated p_{in} and p_{out} respectively, the loss a (in dB) can be calculated as follows:

$$a = -10 \log (P_{out}/P_{in}) \qquad (1)$$

Assuming a homogeneous transmission line (i.e. a homogeneous optical waveguide), the loss a can be referred to the length L (in km) using the attenuation coefficient (in dB/km) derived as follows:

$$\alpha = a/L. \qquad (2)$$

α is a function of the optical wavelength. The attenuation coefficients of currently available graded-index fibers at 850 nm are between 2.5 and 3 dB/km. At 1300 nm the corresponding values are around 1.5 dB/km lower (i.e. around 1.0 to 1.5 dB/km). Typical attenuation curves are given in [1].

Dipl.-Ing. Dr. phil. Günter Zeidler,
Siemens AG,
Public Communication Networks Division,
Munich

Fiber-optic transmission links exhibit a pronounced low-pass filter response. If the optical input power is sinusoidally modulated, the amplitude of this modulated power at the output decreases with increasing modulating frequency. The transfer function is similar to a Gaussian low-pass filter. The modulating frequency at which the amplitude of the optical power modulation has decreased by 3 dB (i.e. the signal attenuation has increased by 3 dB) is known as the low-pass cutoff frequency or, more commonly, as bandwidth B. This low-pass response is shown in **Fig. 1**.

The bandwidth required for a transmission link is determined by the signal to be transmitted. For example, 50 MHz is envisaged for a 34 Mbit/s system and 120 MHz for a 140 Mbit/s system. The bandwidth requirement of a cable system can be established by tracing the bandwidth B along the cable system or by suitably aggregating the additional loss at a given frequency (e.g. Δa at 120 MHz).

With all these definitions referred to the optical power, it must be remembered that in currently available receivers the optical power undergoes linear conversion to current. The electrical power appearing in a load resistor therefore varies as the square of the optical power P_{out}; the defined 3 dB cutoff frequency on the optical side is

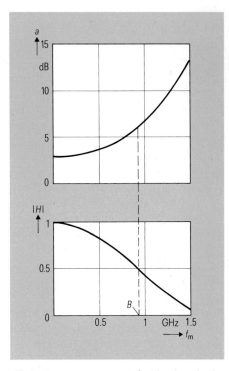

Fig. 1 Low-pass response of a 1 km length of optical fiber with $b_1 = 800$ MHz · km showing loss a and magnitude of the transfer function $|H|$ as a function of modulating frequency f_m

therefore equivalent to a 6 dB roll-off in the baseband. The term "6 dB bandwidth" therefore sometimes occurs in the literature, but is synonymous with bandwidth B described above.

Attenuation and level data

In accordance with electromagnetic theory, optical fibers are open, dielectric waveguides. As well as the guided modes (as specified) there are in addition a large number of more or less radiating modes (leaky waves) whose effect must be taken into account in all measurements and definitions, as they may produce transient characteristics not only at the point of launch but also at each splice. A system can be designed only if all level and attenuation data are referred to a field condition which varies as little as possible along the line (steady-state condition).

When measuring loss in a *single-mode fiber*, for instance, care must be taken to ensure that light is launched only into the core region (diameter typically 10 μm, refractive index difference 0.3%) with the appropriate numerical aperture. If the waveguide is overfilled, the interfering leaky waves and cladding modes must first be carefully stripped (either by means of a fiber coating whose refractive index is higher than that of the cladding glass or by the immersion of an uncoated section of fiber in a fluid of higher refractive index).

The situation is even more complex with graded-index *multimode fibers* (50 μm core), in which the possible angles of the guided modes decrease outwards from the axis to the periphery [2, 3]. This characteristic must be taken into account in loss measurements and only test sources providing defined optical distribution may be used.

Various methods of measuring loss on graded-index fibers

Although loss measurement has not yet been standardized, two principal methods have emerged [4]:

In the *launching-fiber method* the transmitter output is itself a graded-index fiber, whose light distribution is made to approach the defined state by the use of a long fiber (e.g. 300 to 500 m) or statistical bending in a short fiber (mode mixer).

In the *restricted launch method* a suitable combination of lenses and aperture stops is used to form a ray of light filling approximately 70% of the core diameter and 70% of the numerical aperture.

In order to determine whether a particular launch method approaches the steady-state condition, a near-field and far-field measurement can be performed using a short length of fiber. For a 50 μm graded-index fiber with a maximum numerical aperture of 0.2, an approximation to the steady-state condition is achieved if, after 2 m, the bell-shaped radial light distribution (near-

field) has a half-power diameter of around 26 μm and the associated, similarly bell-shaped light distribution as a function of the angle (far-field) has half-power points equivalent to a numerical aperture of 0.11.

At the joints (connectors, splices) it is advisable to use an input and an output fiber (also, if necessary, a receiver with aperture stop/lens combination) in order to be sure of eliminating leaky waves produced at the joint.

The measurements can be carried out using either the equipment required in (1) to measure the input and output powers separately (insertion loss method, cut-back method [4, 5]), or optical time-domain reflectometers (OTDR) [6].

Detailed regulations for unambiguous attenuation measurements on cables and splices are currently being drafted by Technical Committee 46 of the IEC and the relevant sub-committees 412.6 of the German Electrotechnical Commission (DKE). It can be assumed that following publication of these draft standards it will become a relatively simple matter to measure the attenuation of the individual components of a cable system (connectors, splices, cables) in a defined manner.

As these measurements are each referred to the same field pattern at the input and output (steady-state condition), the individual loss contributions of concatenated fiber lengths, splices and connectors can be added together directly.

System parameters

Following on from the above discussion, it is useful to state the transmit level with reference to the steady-state condition. Level measurements are best performed by coupling the transmitter to a comparatively long optical fiber cable (1 to 2 km) of known attenuation, measuring the level at the end of this cable and then working back to obtain the transmit level. If the minimum receive level required to achieve a defined bit error rate is subtracted from this steady-state value, the result is the maximum permissible system loss, which is actually more of theoretical interest. In practical transmission systems allowance must also be made for the usual ratios and margins for aging,

temperature effects and tolerances. In addition, any branches, couplers, connectors, distribution panels etc., must be taken into account. Finally, the remaining factor to be taken into consideration when designing the cable system is the permissible regenerator section loss a_R.

Transmission plan of a fiber-optic cable system for multimode and single-mode fibers

A fiber-optic cable system consists of the installed and spliced cable sections and extends to the first demountable connector at each end. For system acceptance testing it is advisable to demount this connector and insert the line-side half in the receptacle of the link tester. Since connector loss is not included in this measurement, it must be taken into account in the equipment transmission plan.

Providing the previously described measurement technique is employed, it is possible to add the individual loss contributions (cable sections l_i with attenuation coefficient α_i splices of loss s_j) to give:

$$a_K = \Sigma \, a_i + \Sigma \, s_j \quad \text{with} \quad a_i = l_i \, \alpha_i. \qquad (3)$$

This equation expresses the loss a_K of the cable system when all the individual loss contributions are known. In particular, the losses α_i of the cable sections must take account of all sources of increased attenuation (e.g. due to installation stress or temperature effects). Siemens' experience of installing over 30,000 km of fibers has revealed no attenuation increases where correctly dimensioned loose-tube cables are used [5 to 10]. This being so, it is merely a matter of inserting in (3) the losses measured on factory lengths during quality control by the cable manufacturer.

Various design approaches

The addition method per (3) can be used in various ways for planning proposed cable systems. When *designing by averages,* the averages for splice loss $\bar{s}$ and cable loss $\bar{\alpha}$ are known. If j is the number of splices, the following expresses the average loss of a cable system of length L:

$$\bar{a}_K = \bar{\alpha} \, L + j \, \bar{s}. \qquad (4)$$

The average cable loss is a function of the wavelength and of the quality of cable employed; depending on the jointing technique, the average splice loss is in the range 0.05 to 0.2 dB. The attenuation values of the cable systems actually installed may vary around this figure. These variations are most conveniently allowed for as standard deviations of the individual distributions.

When *designing by standard deviations* it is assumed that the variances of the individual distributions can be added, hence the standard deviation σ_a of the system loss is:

$$\sigma_a = \sqrt{j\sigma_s^2 + i\sigma_K^2}. \qquad (5)$$

Where σ_s and σ_K are the standard deviations of the splice and cable losses, j is the number of splices and i the number of factory lengths of cable (e.g. in km). Statistical measurements provide the following numerical values: σ_s about 0.05 to 0.15 dB and σ_K about 0.2 to 0.3 dB/km. The spread can be taken into account by adding k times the standard deviation ($k = 2$ or 3) to the average value $\bar{a}_K$:

$$a_K \lesssim \bar{a}_K + k\,\sigma_a, \qquad (6)$$

This provides an indication of the maximum system loss to be expected.

When *designing to clearly defined limits* it is assumed that each cable length is precisely measured in the factory and that only those lengths are used whose attenuation is below a specified limit value α_g. It is also assumed that each joint will be measured again in the field and will remain unchanged only if the attenuation is below the limit value s_g. From (3) it then follows that:

$$a_K < L\alpha_g + js_g. \qquad (7)$$

If the splices are not to be checked in the field, it is advisable to adopt a *mixed design* approach. The cable loss is taken as the limit value α_g per (7) as agreed with the supplier, while the splice loss is treated statistically per (5) and (6):

$$a_K \lesssim L\alpha_g + j\bar{s} + k\,\sigma_s\sqrt{j}. \qquad (8)$$

Either (6), (7) or (8) can be used to calculated the maximum predicted link loss.

Allowances

When designing a practical cable system, however, certain additional factors must be borne in mind. It is, for example, necessary to design cable installations to provide a long operating life. Account must therefore be taken of the fact that, during the lifetime of the system, new cable sections will have to be spliced in as a result of construction and excavation work, cable rerouting etc. [7]. The size of the margin required to cover this depends on local conditions and is best selected on the basis of statistical data from existing older cable systems. Owing to its statistical nature the value is assumed to be proportional to the length L of the cable system, giving the following planning formula for the required repeater section loss a_R:

$$a_R = a_K + rL. \qquad (9)$$

a_K can be derived optionally from (6), (7) or (8); numerically, the margin r lies between 0.1 and 0.6 dB/km depending on conditions.

An example of link design for the 34 Mbit/s system using the mixed approach as in (8) is provided on the basis of the following data (L_s average splice distance);

$L_s = 0.7$ km; $\bar{s} = 0.2$ dB,
$\sigma_s = 0.15$ dB; $r = 0.3$ dB/km,
$\alpha_g = 3.0$ dB/km at 850 nm,
$\alpha_g = 1.0$ dB/km at 1300 nm.

The **table** shows the individual planning stages.

Bandwidth of cable systems employing graded-index fibers

The low-pass response of graded-index fibers is due mainly to two effects, namely modal and material dispersion. The delays of the individual modes are never fully equalized (modal dispersion), thus giving rise to pulse spreading in the time domain and a low-pass response of given cutoff frequency (B_1) in the baseband.

Optical transmitters always emit in a particular wavelength band around a given center wavelength. Light components of different wavelengths, moreover, propagate in the fiber at different rates (material dispersion), similarly giving rise to pulse spreading and a low-pass response with the cutoff frequency (B_2).

The two effects can be combined by connecting in series the two equivalent low-pass filters with cutoff frequencies B_1 and B_2:

$$B^{-2} = B_1^{-2} + B_2^{-2}. \qquad (10)$$

Modal dispersion

Modal dispersion is taken into account by characterizing factory lengths of graded index fiber-optic cables according to their specific bandwidth-length product b_1 (e.g. in MHz·km). The numerical value of b_1 is a function of the optical wavelength and depends on the particular glass composition employed and the type of profile. The maximum bandwidth can occur at only one wavelength. At all other wavelengths b_1 decreases similarly to a bandpass filter characteristic [1].

Converting the normalized bandwidth b_1 of the factory lengths to the link bandwidth B_1 is extremely complex in theory [11] and is still not fully understood. However, a few approximations will be given here which have already been proven in practice.

The bandwidth of the long link initially decreases in inverse proportion to the length. However, on sections longer

Wavelength	(nm)	850	1300
Length	(km)	10.7	20.8
No. of splices		17	31
Average attenuation of all splices	(dB)	3.4	6.2
σ-spread of the splice loss	(dB)	1.3	1.7
Margin for rerouting etc.	(dB)	3.2	6.3
Cable loss	(dB)	32.0	20.8
Planned repeater section loss	(dB)	39.9	35.0

Table   Example of link design (mixed) for a 34 Mbit/s system

than the coupling length L_K the bandwidth is predicted as the square root of the length owing to the effects of mode mixing at discontinuities (splices, bends) and the statistical distribution of slight profile variations between concatenated factory lengths.

This length dependence can be expressed in unified form per [12]:

$$B_1 = b_1 \left[L \cdot L_K + \frac{L_K^2}{2} \left(e^{-\frac{2L}{L_K}} - 1 \right) \right]^{-\frac{1}{2}}. \quad (11)$$

Approximations to this equation can be derived for each section as follows:

$$B_1 \approx b_1 \cdot \frac{1}{L} \quad \text{when} \quad L < L_K, \quad (12)$$

$$B_1 \approx b_1 \left(\frac{1}{L} + \frac{1}{3 L_K} \right)$$

when $0 < L < 3 L_K$, $\quad (13)$

$$B_1 \approx b_1 \left(L \cdot L_K - \frac{L_K^2}{2} \right)^{-\frac{1}{2}}$$

when $L > L_K$. $\quad (14)$

An approximation for the section $L > L_K$ can also be made using the relationship:

$$B_1 \approx b_1 (L_K + \sqrt{L - L_K})^{-1} \quad (15)$$

(where L and L_K are in km).

The numerical value of L_K is a function of:

- the additional attenuation coefficient of the cable system (due to splices etc.) compared with the theoretically possible minimum attenuation coefficient (L_K is approximately inversely proportion to this additional loss),

- the statistical deviations in the wavelength at which the fiber profile provides maximum bandwidth [1] and of the wavelength of the transmitter.

Actual values obtained for L_K are in the region of 2 to 8 km. When designing shorter lengths (normal cable quality, average splices) $L_K = 2$ km is the recommended figure, while values of between 4 and 8 km are suitable for high-grade long-haul cable links.

Material dispersion

Bandwidth limiting due to material dispersion is expressed as:

$$B_2 = b_2 \cdot L^{-1}. \quad (16)$$

The normalized bandwidth b_2 in MHz · km is also a function of the

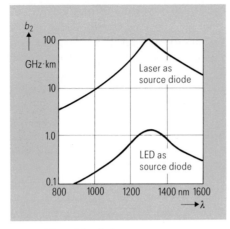

LED Light-emitting diode

Fig. 2 Cutoff frequency b_2 (material dispersion) as a function of the wavelength λ referred to a laser spectrum 1 nm wide

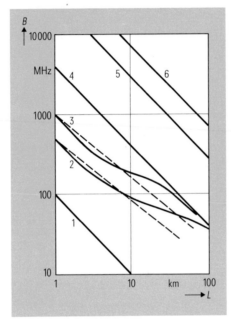

1 Light-emitting diode at 850 nm
2 Laser diode at 850 nm;
  $b_1 = 500$ MHz · km
3 Laser diode at 850 nm;
  $b_1 = 1000$ MHz · km
  (dashed curve with $\gamma = 0.8$)
4 Limit due to material dispersion for laser diode at 850 nm
5 Range of a single-mode fiber ($\lambda \approx 1300$ nm)
6 Limit due to material dispersion for laser diode capable of emitting in the wavelength range $\lambda = 1270$ to 1330 nm

Fig. 3 Bandwidth B as a function of span length L for various systems

wavelength, reaching a maximum for silica glass fibers at 1300 nm. **Fig. 2** shows b_2 for a laser diode with an optical linewidth of 1 nm – typical value for a good laser diode. For a laser diode with a broader emission spectrum b_2 is to be devided by the specific

optical linewidth. For a light-emitting diode (LED) the optical linewidth is considerably greater (e.g. 40 nm at 850 nm carrier wavelength), so that b_2 has to be reduced in proportion to the linewidth, which for a diode of this type operating at 850 nm produces approximately 100 MHz · km. The lower curve in **Fig. 2** gives b_2 for LED transmitters operating at different wavelengths. At 1300 nm LEDs also achieve their maximum of around 1 GHz · km at 1300 nm, which explains the growing interest in this wavelength range.

Length dependence of the bandwidth

Fig. 3 shows the relationship between bandwidth B and link length L on a logarithmic scale. The examples selected assume a laser diode operating at 850 nm ($b_2 = 4000$ MHz · km). Assuming a fiber of $b_1 = 1000$ MHz · km, the general relationship of (11) becomes clear. After B has decreased in inverse proportion to the length up to the coupling length, it describes an S until it finally reaches the material dispersion limit and then again decreases in inverse proportion. This relationship is expressed mathematically by (10) with (11) and (16). Another way of approximating this is empirically possible using the power law:

$$B = b_1 \cdot L^{-\gamma} \quad (17)$$

This approximation is plotted in **Fig. 3** as a dashed line for an exponent $\gamma = 0.8$. Highly dispersive values of γ have appeared in the literature; on the basis of information currently available it is recommended that values between 0.7 and 0.9 be used to provide a rough estimate.

When fibers of differing bandwidths B_i are concatenated, the link bandwidth B is given by:

$$B = \left[\sum_{(i)} B_i^{-\frac{1}{\gamma}} \right]^{-\gamma}. \quad (18)$$

When designing LED systems (850 nm) it should be remembered that material dispersion predominates and that from (10) and (11) $B \approx B_2 = b_2 / L$. On the other hand, in laser diode systems (850 and 1300 nm, medium values of b_1) modal dispersion predominates in accordance with (11) or (15). By way of example **Fig. 3** shows the bandwidth as a function of length, as predicted for a 34 Mbit/s system with a bandwidth-length product of $b_1 = 500$ MHz · km.

Planning the additional loss Δa for a given modulating frequency

Whereas in single-mode transmission systems the additional losses occurring at a modulation frequency f_m (see **Fig. 1**) can merely be added, this is unfortunately not possible in optical transmission systems using multimode graded-index fibers. Linear addition of the loss contributions of individual sections would be possible if the field distribution at the output of a fiber section were completely independent of the field distribution at the input. In graded-index fibers this is the case only when mode coupling is extreme ($L \gg L_K, \gamma = 0.5$).

Using the approximations previously referred to it is possible to calculate the overall additional loss Δa for a modulating frequency f from the additional attenuation coefficient of the individual factory lengths ($\Delta\alpha(f)$) as follows:

$$\Delta a \approx \Delta\alpha(f)\, L^{2\gamma}. \tag{19}$$

The additional loss increases linearly with length only if there is strong mode coupling ($\gamma = 0.5$); for normal graded-index fibers a superlinear increase ($\gamma = 0.8$) must be assumed.

Bandwith of cable systems employing single-mode fibers

The main consideration in establishing the bandwidth requirement on single-mode cable systems is material dispersion. As shown in **Fig. 2**, a bandwidth-length product of around 100 GHz · km is predicted at 1300 nm, while at 1600 nm on simple step-index single-mode fibers, this value reduces to 20 GHz · km. These figures are referred to a laser spectral width of 1 nm. For greater linewidths, e.g. due to the dynamic broadening of the spectrum, the bandwidth-length product is divided by the specified linewidth.

The transfer function of single-mode links can be expected to be similar to a Gaussian low-pass filter characteristics. This is caused by the fact that most optical transmitters show Gaussian line shapes, which are transferred by dispersion effects into the frequency domain.

In the more distant future, applications in the 1600 nm wavelength range will achieve a similarly high bandwidth-length product as a result of the material dispersion being compensated by waveguide dispersion [13].

In addition to material and waveguide dispersion, account must also be taken of the different delays of the two polarizations possible in the circular-symmetric single-mode fibers. However, this effect is negligible if fibers with a good core circularity and incoherent detectors are used. The length dependence of the bandwidth can therefore be planned on the basis of a linear correlation per (16).

References

[1] Schneider, H.; Zeidler, G.: Manufacturing Processes and Designs of Optical Waveguides.
telcom report 6 (1983) Special Issue "Optical Communications", pp. 27 to 33

[2] Geckeler, S.: Physical Principles of Optical Waveguides.
telcom report 6 (1983) Special Issue "Optical Communications", pp. 9 to 14

[3] Geckeler, S.: Das Phasenraumdiagramm, ein vielseitiges Hilfsmittel zur Beschreibung der Lichtausbreitung in Lichtwellenleitern.
Siemens Forsch.- u. Entwickl.-Ber. 10 (1981), pp. 162 to 171

[4] Klement, E.; Rössner, K.: Principles of Optical Measurements for Communication Systems.
telcom report 6 (1983) Special Issue "Optical Communications", pp. 167 to 171

[5] Eibl-Vogt, A.; Permien, J.: System Test Equipment for Optical Waveguides and Optical Cable Links.
telcom report 6 (1983) Special Issue "Optical Communications", pp. 171 to 175

[6] Schicketanz, D.; Schulze, J.: Test Equipment for Fiber-Optic Cable Facilities.
telcom report 5 (1982), pp. 33 to 35

[7] Zeidler, G.H.; Bark, P.R.; Lawrence, D.O.; Szentesi, O.I.: Reliability of fiber optic cable systems. Int. Conf. Commun., Seattle 1980, Conf. Rec. 10.3

[8] Bark, P.R.; Oestreich, U.; Zeidler, G.: Fiber optic cable design, testing and installation experiences. Proc. 27th Int. Wire and Cable Symp., Cherry Hill, 1978, pp. 379 to 384

[9] Bark, P.R.; Oestreich, U.; Zeidler, G.: Stress-strain behaviour of optical fiber cables. Proc. 28th Int. Wire and Cable Symp., Cherry Hill, 1979, pp. 385 to 390

[10] Oestreich, U.; Zeidler, G.; Bark, P.R.; Lawrence, D.O.: Fiber optic cables for aerial applications. Proc. of the Int. Wire and Cable Symp., Cherry Hill 1980, pp. 394 to 401

[11] Geckeler, S.: Pulse broadening in optical fibers with mode mixing.
Appl. Opt. 18 (1979), pp. 2192 to 2198

[12] Personick, S.D.: Time dispersion in dielectric waveguides. Bell Syst. Techn. Journ. 50 (1971), pp. 843 to 859

[13] Oestreich, U.; Zeidler, G.: Development Trends in Fiber and Cable.
telcom report 6 (1983) Special Issue "Optical Communications", pp. 198 to 201

Horst Goldmann

Installation of Fiber-Optic Cables

Fiber-optic cables do not in themselves require any special installation techniques. Owing to their low weight compared with metallic-conductor cables, their high flexibility and their hitherto small diameter with relatively high tensile strength, they do not present significant installation problems by conventional standards. This article, therefore, will concentrate less on general or familiar placement techniques, and more on projects recently completed by Siemens and the experience gained from them. Some modified and new equipment and techniques used in these projects are also introduced.

The use of fiber-optic cables should provide the means for meeting some new installation requirements, for example, to

● pull cables into ducts and duct bores in longer sections than before and hence reduce the number of joints,

● use existing bores more efficiently by installing several cables,

● use high-voltage open-wire lines as a means of supporting fiber-optic cables.

Owing to their mechanical strength, fiber-optic cables can be easily installed using all known methods, provided that their specific characteristics and permissible temperature range are taken into account. Such methods include:

● pulling them into a duct, conduit or trench by power winch or hand,

● placing them into the cable trench from a dolly,

● plowing them in,

Dipl.-Ing. Horst Goldmann,
Siemens AG,
Public Communication Networks Division,
Munich

● clipping them to walls for indoor installation, and also in vertical runs over 1000 m and more (mining),

● placing them on cable trays, planar shelves or in PVC conduit,

● installing them aerially and attaching them to supporting wires,

● placing them in rivers or in the sea.

All these methods have been satisfactorily proven by Siemens in the field with fiber-optic cable installations to date totalling some 1000 km.

Fiber-optic cable designs and specifications for cable installation

There are two approaches to fiber-optic cable design which may cause the cables to exhibit entirely different installation characteristics. The first approach provides for *all-dielectric (non-metallic) cables* which can be bent easily to small diameters. Pulling forces are taken up by means of high-tensile, low-elongation elements usually of Aramid yarn. The second approach involves the use of *cables with metallic elements* and may employ, for instance, wire armoring or an aluminium laminated sheath and copper conductors. These cables, however, can have less

favorable bending properties, i.e. permissible bending and deflecting diameters* may be larger than for the first type of cable.

Fiber-optic cables are designed to ensure that a permissible installation stress does not have a damaging effect on the individual optical fiber. With a tensile strength approximately equal to twice the kilometric cable weight, 1000 m lengths can be easily installed in most cases (urban area, cable conduit or duct, pulled in by winch). For all cables up to an outside diameter of 30 mm, the recommended loaded bending diameter for practical reasons is 400 mm (only *one* size of guide element required).

Cap-sealing of fiber-optic cables

Fiber-optic cables are usually capped at both ends in the factory in such a way as to allow their rated pulling tension to be applied (generally via a cable sock). When there are no factory-fitted caps (e.g. on the cable sections cut on site), an eye about 300 mm long can be formed as in **Fig. 1** at the pulling end of the cable to enable it to be drawn in.

If required, fiber-optic cables with a low fiber count can be provided with a transparent, high-tensile cap to enable the optical fibers to be illuminated after installation (testing for fiber breaks). The pulling tension is then applied using a special pulling head with integrated twist compensator (**Fig. 2**).

---

* The *bending diameter* is the minimum permissible diameter for bending and forming a cable during installation when subjected to little or no tensile force. The *deflecting diameter* is the minimum permissible diameter over which the cable can be guided during installation when subjected to the permissible tensile force

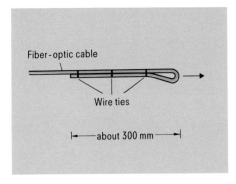

Fig. 1 Hand-formed eye for pulling the cable

Installation of fiber-optic cables in the cable conduit or duct system

Aids

Cable installation is greatly assisted by low-friction guides for manhole installation, e.g. cable roller guides (**Fig. 3**) and sheaves.

These devices enable both the power winch rope and subsequently the fiber-optic cable to be drawn over long sections with minimum effort. There is no objection to sparing application of a pulling lubricant.

Manual installation

The insertion of a winch rope into a duct system is usually a manual operation involving the use of an auxiliary rope and the same effort as pulling in a light fiber-optic cable by hand. If a record of the pulling tension applied during installation (route pulling tension diagram) is not required, manual installation of light-weight cables is an economic alternative even for long lengths (access about every 100 m, one craftsman ≙ 200 N pulling tension).

"Injecting" cables

The "injection" of auxiliary ropes (for subsequently pulling in a winch rope) into dense duct systems using compressed air is a well established practice.

In one trial, where a winch failed to pull a cable into a closed, tortuous 1000 m long duct because of excessive friction, a fiber-optic cable was successfully injected using compressed air (duct bore 50 mm, cable diameter 9 mm, cable weight 50 g/m). The running time was somewhat less than

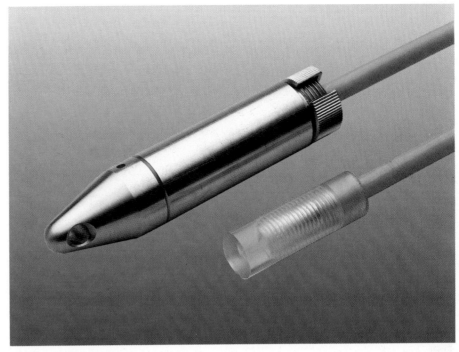

Fig. 2 Transparent cap with pulling head

60 min, the speed dropping from about 100 initially to 5 m/min accompanied by a change in air inlet pressure from 1 to 5 bar. The pulling seal was subjected to a maximum tension of about 1000 N. Using this method the extra drag on the cable due to the duct bends was not as great as it normally is.

Installing long lengths in one section

For installing fiber-optic cables in long lengths (e.g. 3 km and more in one sec-

tion and in one direction), an intermediate take-up unit has been developed (**Fig. 4**). This powered unit deployed in sufficient numbers to suit cable weight, installation length and routing, permits economic installation especially in cable duct systems.

With these units, the installation proceeds as follows. The first section is installed from the slightly braked cable reel by being pulled off manually (with an auxiliary rope or grip fixed to one end) by two craftsmen, for instance. If

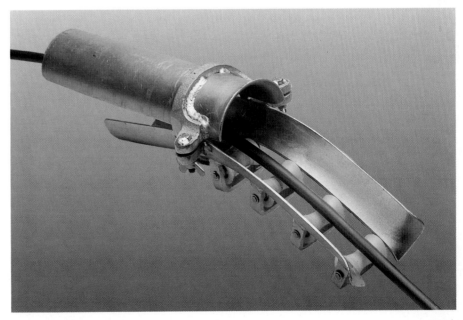

Fig. 3 Cable roller guide

Fig. 4   Intermediate take-up unit, cable guide and drive (direction of operation reversible) in a manhole

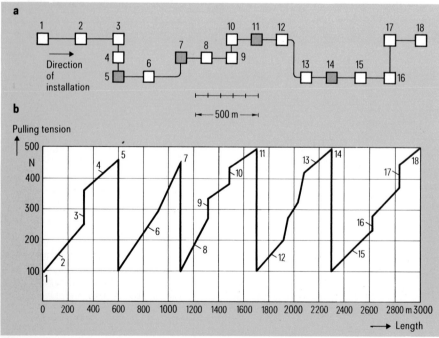

☐ Intermediate take-up unit installed in manhole   Manholes numbered 1 to 18

Fig. 5   Route pulling tension diagram for a 3 km placement section
a   Cable duct route with 18 manholes   b   Pulling tension – length diagram

the pulling tension begins to approach the limit for this method (e.g. 400 N), an intermediate take-up unit is installed in the last manhole passed by the cable tip and this moves the cable through the section of the route already installed. The next section of the route can then be installed using the previously described method until it becomes necessary to install the next take-up unit, etc.

*Mode of operation
of the intermediate take-up unit*

The cable to be installed is fed over a wheel driven by an electrohydraulic motor (angle of contact greater than 180°), the pulling tension being applied through friction on the cable sheath. Units connected in tandem operate automatically without supervision, controlled only by the passing cable. They thus adjust automatically to the movement of the cable, i.e. the required pulling tension is applied only in response to a small pilot pulling tension. The speed of pulling-in is controlled in the range between 0 and 30 m/min by the cable tip. The system operates without oscillation or slippage. When a motor fails, the unit is allowed to freewheel.

Depending on the nature of the route, the route pulling tension diagram may have the characteristic shown in **Fig. 5**. No provision is made, however, for recording this.

At bends in the cable route the intermediate take-up unit can also be used as a powered guide. The additional use of low-friction guides (as already described) increases the spacing and reduces the required number of intermediate take-up units.

The excess cable required for storage in the manholes is obtained when removing the cable from the unit or can be adjusted manually with little effort using the unit (direction reversible).

Multiple utilization of ducts

For improved utilization of bores already installed in the duct system (e.g. the Deutsche Bundespost's 100 mm duct bore), it has frequently been the practice recently to insert three corrugated plastic subducts with a bore diameter of about 30 mm. These

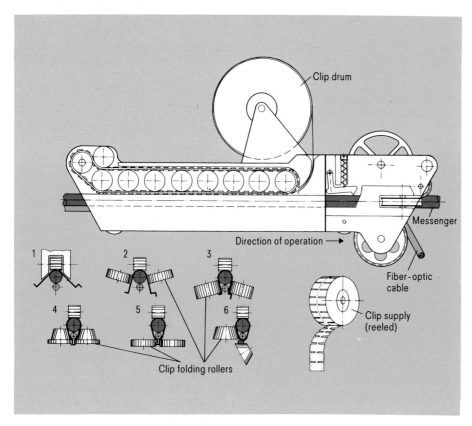

Fig. 6　Mode of operation of the clip-fitting device (folding sequence 1 to 6)

subducts enable three cables with outside diameters of up to 23 mm to be installed and if necessary replaced independently of each other. This advantage, however, is offset by a certain installation difficulty. This arises from the fact that the subducts, having a high degree of longitudinal elasticity and being anchored at the duct openings, pucker in the direction of installation and thus increase the friction. Non-corrugated plastic subducts provide better installation performance.

There is no practical objection to installing small diameter (fiber-optic) cables one after another in non-subsectioned ducts. The maximum difference in outside diameter of cables installed in this way should, however, be no greater than 5 mm to avoid the possibility of wedging or jamming. This approach improves the utilization of the particular duct-bore considerably compared with the method previously mentioned.

There is, however, a disadvantage in that, if the cables have to be removed, this can only be done in the reverse order to that in which they were originally installed.

Fiber-optic cables in the power network

The installation of optical fibers on overhead power lines provides considerable advantages for various types of engineering traffic (speech, remote supervision and control) within energy supply areas [1].

Owing to the low weight of fiber-optic cables, the existing overhead power line route can be used without the masts being subjected to considerable additional stress. The problem of inductive interference is also eliminated and the transmission capacity is many times higher than with conventional communication links.

Two approaches are currently under discussion for this application:

● The principle of the self-supporting aerial cable as used in conventional designs, but completely non-metallic for this application. The installation techniques and equipment are as normally employed in overhead construction.

● Lashing light-weight and again non-metallic standard fiber-optic cables to

phase conductors (if single conductors) or ground wires.

Following a project in which a cable of this type was secured along a section of ground conductor about 6 km long using preformed wire helices [2], a device was developed and tested to facilitate "lashing" a fiber-optic cable to an existing messenger by the following procedure. The device (**Fig. 6**) is placed onto the phase or ground conductor in close proximity to the mast. The cable is fed through the device from below in the direction of installation, and anchored to the mast with sufficient excess for bending and closure installation. The device can be pulled in the direction of installation by hand or winch.

As the device is drawn along, a roller mechanism driven by the friction places prefabricated clips from an accompanying magazine over the messenger and fiber-optic cable at adjustable intervals (e.g. 500 mm) and folds the clips to produce a form fit. The speed is determined here by the draw-rope, with the device following it smoothly (it does not stop when folding the clips). If a blockage occurs, the mechanism can be released. The device can be pulled forwards or backwards to the next mast and, after the blockage has been removed, can continue working at any point. There are plans for a powered version.

Unlike conventional lashing (winding a wire continuously around messenger and cable), this method uses individual fasteners. The loss or ineffectiveness of an individual fastener of this type produces no consequential faults.

References

[1] VDI-Nachr. of 28.11.80

[2] Fischer, K.; Möller, W.; Rüger, W.; Tannhäuser, A.: Ein neues Lichtwellenleiter-Übertragungssystem für Nachrichtennetze von Energieversorgungsunternehmen. Österr. Z. f. Elektr.-Wirtsch. 34 (1981), pp. 1 to 5

Norbert Odemar and Peter Steinmann

Jointing Techniques for Fiber-Optic Cables

When fiber-optic cables of relatively low fiber-count were used commercially for the first time, specially developed units employing bonding and fusion splicing techniques were already available for joining the individual fibers. In addition, rugged connectors enabled optical fibers to be connected to transmitters, receivers, regenerators and distribution frames. The initial pilot projects undertaken by the Deutsche Bundespost have also employed these jointing methods. However, when the main cable of the Berlin project (comprising 19 basic units of six fibers each, i.e. 114 fibers in all) was being installed, a six-fiber splicer was employed experimentally in order to reduce installation times.

● The BIGFON project (broadband integrated glass-fiber local telecommunication network) will require multifiber-cables where all fibers have to be joined. The multifiber unit design has already become established for manufacturing cables of high fiber-count [1]. The jointing of these cables involves various approaches using largely automatic equipment to produce quick single-fiber splices, multifiber splices, as well as demountable or permanent multifiber connectors.

For future projects the jointing techniques must meet two requirements:

● In the long-haul network the requirement is to maximize regenerator spacings on high bandwidth fiber-optic cables, every tenth of a decibel being critical. However, since the trend is towards single-mode fibers for this application, requirements will become even more stringent. The increased cost of an individual joint is certainly justified if one considers that a splice loss of 0.3 dB is approximately equivalent to the loss due to 1 km of single-mode fiber.

Fig. 1 The mechanical splicer in use

Ing. (grad.) Norbert Odemar and
Dipl.-Ing. Peter Steinmann,
Siemens AG,
Public Communication Networks Division,
Munich

Mechanical splicing of single fibers

The mechanical splicer shown in **Fig. 1** is used for splicing individually-buffered graded-index fibers in the field. As this method involves no naked flames, the splicer is particularly suitable for use in hazardous areas. The unit is supplied packed in a shock-proof aluminium case containing all the tools and aids required for splicing.

The splicing principle employed is based on self-alignment of the two fibers in a V-groove splice connector. The buffer tubes and optical fibers are held in position by two pivoted arms.

After the fibers have been cut precisely to length, they are moved to the splicing position and pressed together in the V-groove of the splice connector. The fiber ends are permanently fixed by a rapid-curing index-matching adhesive and a hold-down acting on the joint under spring pressure. The U-shaped splice connector is crimped onto the

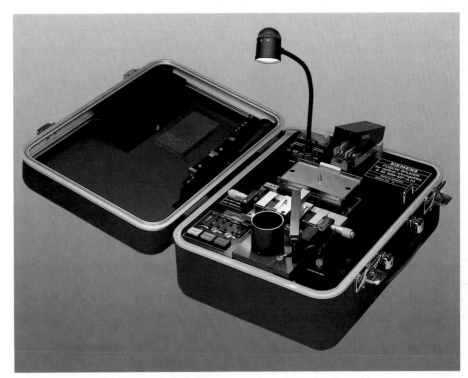

Fig. 3 Fusion splicer for graded-index fibers

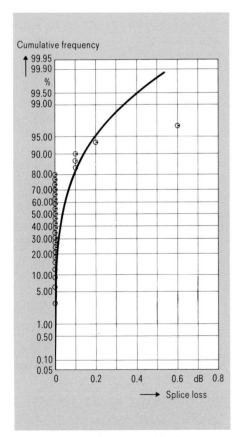

Fig. 2 Loss of splices produced mechanically under laboratory conditions (graded-index fiber: 50/125 μm; test method: OTDR/850 nm)

two buffer tubes to provide stress relief.

The single-fiber mechanical splice with its ease of handling has already proved its worth in many cable installations. The index-matching adhesive employed was carefully chosen to ensure that no appreciable additional attenuation would occur on aerial cables in response to seasonal temperature variations. The index matching adhesive used is therefore aging-resistant.

Provided the fibers spliced together are identical, the mechanical splicer will normally achieve splice losses of less than 0.1 dB. However, the use of a V-groove to align the fibers may result in higher losses due to diameter variations. **Fig. 2** shows typical splice loss values obtained using the mechanical splicer under laboratory conditions.

Fusion splicing of single fibers

For fusion splicing of single optical fibers made of silica or multicomponent glass Siemens has developed a new fusion splicer (**Fig. 3**) of ergonomic design for particularly easy operation. The entire mechanical and electrical system together with the tools and aids

required for operating the machine are housed in a handy, extremely rugged aluminum case.

Power is supplied by an easily replaceable, maintenance-free lead-acid battery. When fully charged more than 150 splices can be performed. Continuous operation is possible with the aid of an integral charger for 110 and 220 Vac or 12 Vdc supplies. On-charge and state-of-charge indications are provided by light-emitting diodes.

A 20 kHz supply produces the electric arc required for splicing. The arc produces a high surface tension on the molten glass and consequently precise self-alignment of the fibers to be joined. Fiber misalignment of up to 10 μm is automatically compensated without significantly adding to the attenuation. The currents for prefusion (for cleaning and rounding off the ends) and for fusion can be set independently. The two processes are controlled by separate timers.

The unit incorporates a fiber cutting tool employing the well-known stress, bend and score technique. After cutting with a carbide tip for clean mirror-zone fractures with perpendicularity deviations of no more than 3°, the optical fibers are placed in guides where they are automatically aligned. Given the high precision of the guides and the good self-aligning properties of the electric arc, it is now only necessary to adjust the fibers axially. Both the right and the left-hand fiber guides can be adjusted independently via separate micropositioners.

The process can be observed through a "projection microscope" with 50× magnification, using alignment marks on the microscope screen for easy positioning of the fiber ends. A special, high-efficiency light source has been developed for the microscope. It was possible to minimize its drain on the battery by using only a 10 W halogen lamp whose on-time, moreover, is controlled by a timer.

The electrode spacing can be adjusted, if necessary, with the aid of two marks on the microscope screen. The microscope magnification is reduced during this operation to 10× by throwing a lever.

Splicing can be greatly facilitated with the aid of an optional automatic fiber feed attachment. The splicer is already equipped for retrofitting this device. After the two fiber ends have been aligned to the marks previously mentioned, pressing a button initiates operation in an automatic sequence of prefusion, fiber end feeding and fusion. The feed distance is adjustable and must be matched to the particular fiber type being used.

Figs. 4 and **5** show the low splice losses which can be achieved with the splicer on optical fibers with low geometric tolerances. The superiority of the automatic fiber feed can be clearly seen.

As the splicer can be operated either manually or automatically, the experienced jointer can easily solve even the most difficult splicing problems.

After splicing, the fibers are protected in the usual way with a metal splice connector which is crimped over the two buffer tubes. An air-curing silicone rubber is then poured completely over the splice connector to recoat the joint.

The unit incorporates a splice-mount support which can accommodate various splice mounts. A special support for up to five multifiber splice modules is optionally available.

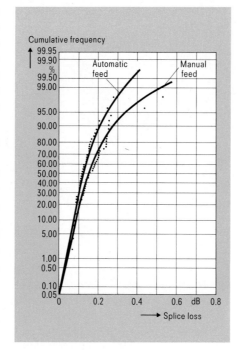

Fig. 4 Fusion splicer, splice loss (graded-index fiber: 50/125 µm; number of splices: 50; test method: OTDR/850 nm)

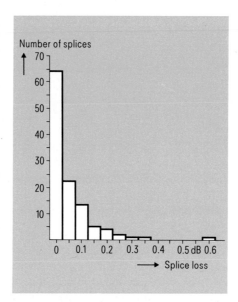

Fig. 5 Splice loss using the fusion splicer with automatic fiber feed (graded-index fiber: 50/125 µm; number of splices: 113; test method: OTDR/850 nm)

All mechanical and electrical elements of the thermal splicer are of modular design. In the event of a fault it is merely necessary to change the defective module and send it to the workshop for repair, which makes for highly convenient servicing.

To supplement the virtually automatic splicer another fusion splicer is being developed to splice twelve optical fibers simultaneously. This is intended to increase the splicing rate further, although these multifiber splicing techniques may entail somewhat higher splice losses.

Fusion splicing of single-mode fibers

Long-haul cable in the future will make increasing use of single-mode fibers. However, the small core diameters of around 10 µm require a level of precision and care in splicing that outstrips the accuracy of the ordinary splicers developed for graded-index fibers. A fusion splicer has therefore been developed especially for single-mode fibers (**Fig. 6**).

In order to minimize the splice losses, the fibers are aligned with the aid of three extremely stiff manipulators fitted with differential screws, allowing minimum adjustments to a tenth of a micron in all three space coordinates. Any concentricity errors between core and cladding are equalized using the fiber rotator additionally provided.

The self-centering effect required for graded-index fibers, i.e. automatic equalization of the fiber outside diameters to minimum misalignment, is not required when splicing single-mode fibers. Since the core diameters must not move relative to each other after alignment, splicing is effected using a specially adapted fusion technique and quite short feed distances (less than 5 µm). Clearly, the fiber cutting tools must also meet stringent requirements. The deviations of the fiber ends from perpendicularity must not exceed 0.5°. In addition, the endfaces must be completely clean. This is essential to ensure serviceable splices. The fiber cutters used are therefore more sophisticated and have cutting characteristics specially adapted to suit single-mode fibers.

Multifiber connectors for permanent or separable fiber joints

The methods of joining by means of bonding and fusion described so far assume that the fiber ends are smooth and perpendicular to the fiber axis, with fusion additionally requiring that

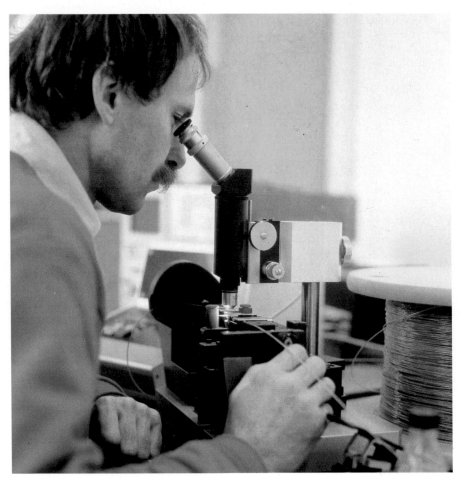

Fig. 6   Fusion splicer for single-mode fibers

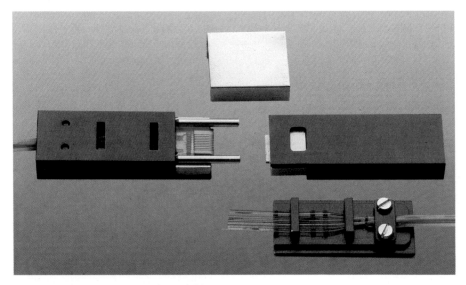

Fig. 7   Precision components of a multifiber connector

the fibers to be joined have similar glass properties. To supplement these processes, investigations are therefore being conducted into various demountable multifiber connectors. Although a fiber cutter is not required, assembly does involve grinding and polishing in the field (however, complete or partial preassembly in the factory might be possible). Jointing techniques of this kind offer the prospect of space savings, relatively inexpensive connector parts and short assembly times.

The completely flat surface of a substrate has (usually V-shaped) grooves arranged precisely parallel to the abutting surfaces, holes or grooves for the shaped alignment parts (e.g. pins) which are subsequently used for precise alignment of the two substrate halves. As initial experiments showed that the lowest losses are obtained when alignment grooves are fabricated with the fiber grooves in a single operation, discussion here will be restricted to this design (**Fig. 7**).

If two substrate halves are fabricated jointly and then separated, it is relatively easy to meet the tolerances on the substrate pair. The disadvantage is that it is not possible to combine any two substrate halves indiscriminately. In order to avoid this disadvantage the dimensional variations, especially the groove pitch, should be within only a few microns.

Assembly itself proceeds in the following stages:

- Remove cable or buffer tube.

- Arrange fibers in the spreader in the specified color sequence.

- Remove fiber coating.

- Place prepared fibers together in the grooves.

- Place cover plate on the fibers, then bond fibers, substrate and cover plate together.

- Grind and polish endfaces of both connector halves after curing.

All the stages described here can easily be carried out using simple equipment (**Fig. 8**). After grinding and polishing, the two connector halves are brought together in a coupling consisting of a spring clip and two shaped alignment parts (e.g. pins).

In laboratory experiments these connectors achieved loss values of less than 0.5 dB. As with mechanical splicing, the result is affected not only by variations in core diameter and numerical aperture, but also to a large extent by variations in fiber outside diameter.

These connectors are being considered primarily for cable-to-cable jointing in a closure. In this application two connector halves are bonded permanently together with the coupling. Another

Fig. 8 Jig for assembling a multifiber connector

in several national and international draft standards. There will therefore be various ferrule diameters and various quality grades in each diameter group.

The most stringent requirements will call for a connector capable of aligning the center of the fiber core precisely to the axis of the cylindrical ferrule. However, connectors employing this method of alignment can only be assembled in the factory, so for field applications they would need to have suitable fiber pigtails already attached.

A large number of the connectors on the market only enable the outer fiber contour to be centered on the cylindrical ferrule, e.g. by inserting the fibers in concentric bores or capillary tubes. Connectors of this type can generally be assembled by the customer himself.

Siemens offers a large number of different connectors for telecommunications and industrial applications [2, 3]. Connector losses are around 1 dB on average including intrinsic fiber loss components (e.g. due to variations in the fiber and core diameters and the numerical aperture).

These connectors have passed their severest practical test on aerial cables linking a number of remote mountain huts to their local networks [4]. The connectors joining the individual factory lengths are housed in enclosures mounted on the poles. After two years' continuous operation there have been no failures either in the cables or the connectors.

logical application is provided by the equipment units in exchanges where, for instance, units each containing several optical transmitters and receivers need a similar number of optical fibers to be connected. In this instance the coupling can be screwed onto the circuit board, allowing the unit to be demountably connected to the fiber-optic cable coming from the main distribution frame.

Single-fiber connectors

The requirements placed on fiber-optic connectors have already been specified

References

[1] Mayr, E.; Schöber, G.; Sutor, N.: Properties of Fiber-Optic Cables.
telcom report 4 (1981), No. 4, pp. 236 to 240

[2] Odemar, N.; Steinmann, P.: Optical Fiber Jointing Techniques.
telcom report 4 (1981), No. 4, pp. 241 to 245

[3] Knoblauch, G.; Toussaint, H.-N.: Connectors for Fiber-Optic Components and Systems.
telcom report 6 (1983) Special Issue "Optical Communications", pp. 96 to 101

[4] Köstler, G.: Fiber-Optic Projects for the Deutsche Bundespost and other Users in Europe.
telcom report 6 (1983) Special Issue "Optical Communications", pp. 59 to 65

Gerd Witt

Closures and Containers for Fiber-Optic Cables

The purpose of a closure in communication cable systems, whether employing copper or fiber-optic cables, is to enclose and protect the splices and all other components of a cable at a jointing or branch point or, indeed, to act as the jointing element itself. It was therefore logical to utilize the long experience with plastic closures in conventional systems by adapting the universal closures with their proven craftibility and performance in the arduous conditions of underground, buried and aerial cable installations to the special requirements of the new transmission medium. A family of closures to meet field requirements was already in existence and left little to be desired in terms of either diameter or length.

To connect the transmission elements there are single, multiple or modular splices both for copper conductors and glass fibers. However, the optical fiber requires significantly more care in handling, which means that the splices must be neatly arranged in the closures. In addition, the single-fiber or multifiber unit must have sufficient slack to enable the jointer to make or renew the splice in the jig outside the closure. The space inside the closure for the splices must always be sufficient to ensure that any bends in single-fiber or multifiber units are not tighter than the minimum permissible bending radii.

Any conventional interstitial elements (e.g. service wires) must, of course, be connected in the closures in the usual way. In certain applications additional space is required for loading coils. Cable sheaths and shields must be joined, where necessary, as must also the special strength elements of steel or high-tensile plastic.

Straight and branch closures

Siemens' universal closures (UC) comprise basically a closure body of a highly stable polypropylene copolymer, a sealing system with a resilient, corrosion-resistant sealing compound and an inner metallic frame for mechanical cable sheath jointing and electrical shield connection [1]. The small-capacity closures consist of half shells closed by means of bolts or clamping bands. The larger closures have split end caps squeezed onto the cables by clamping bands and a slit tube closed by wedge-shaped clamping bars. All the closures can be fitted on uncut cables and be placed in the ground or in a manhole without further protection.

The basic approach was to retain all the main components of the internationally adopted and proven UC closures. A few "O packs", (optical *packs*), are all the user additionally requires to convert the UC closures for equally convenient jointing of fiber-optic cables. This not only makes inventory holding easier but also has the advantage that the jointers are already familiar with most aspects of the closure design.

For fiber-optic cables with single-fiber units there is a splice mount holding 24 single fusion splices or 18 single bonded splices. This splice mount fits into UC closure 4–6 (**Fig.1**) and, in slightly modified form, into the TSK A-6 closure (**table**) adopted by the Deutsche Bundespost. Both closures accommodate sufficient slack to allow the splices to be conveniently performed outside the closures on jigs, then placed in the closure and subsequently removed for further cutting

Dipl.-Ing. Gerd Witt,
Siemens AG,
Public Communication Networks Division,
Munich

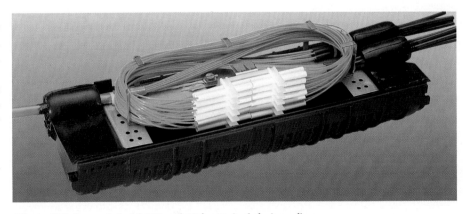

Fig. 1   UC closure 4–6 with "O pack 1" for 24 single fusion splices

Fig. 2   Jointing the optical waveguides using the fusion splicer on a UC closure 10–20

and resplicing, if necessary. The splice mount also provides simple facilities for rapidly and securely clamping the whole cable or individual parts of it to provide stress relief.

Fiber-optic cables with multifiber units (each unit normally contains ten individual fibers in a common filled plastic tube) are interconnected by splicing modules [2]. A suitable range of closures for these cables has been selected from the large family of UC closures and includes end caps, closure tube and clamping bars (**Fig.2**). They are supplied with "O packs" containing components for holding the splicing modules and for clamping the cable or strength member. These components are secured to the inner metallic frame of the standard UC closure without the need for additional fittings. On completion of the splice the closure is assembled in the usual way.

Closure UC 6–9 can accommodate up to twelve splicing modules for 120 individual fibers. A UC closure of the same diameter but longer (**Fig. 3**) accommodates up to 24 modules or 240 fiber splices. The modules have a cen-

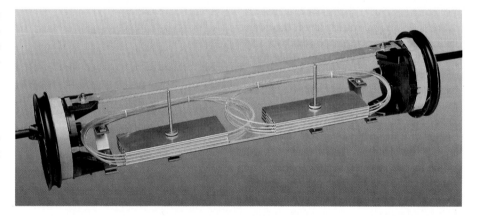

Fig. 3   UC closure 6–18 with 8 splicing modules or 80 fiber splices

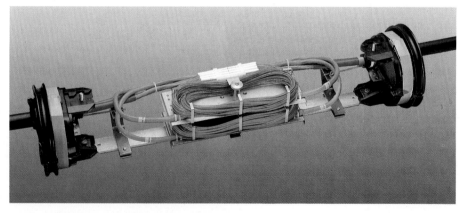

Fig. 4   UC closure 6–18 with two splice mounts and altogether 48 single splices (two "O packs 1" and one "O pack 2")

tral hole by which they are easily and neatly mounted on a stud.

For cables with very high fiber counts, e.g. for fully served areas in the local PTT network, the UC closure 10–40 is particularly suitable as it can accommodate up to 2000 fiber splices of modular design. The intermediate closure sizes and their capacities are shown in the **table**.

For fiber-optic cables with a high count of single-fiber units, the holder for splice modules can be fitted with two splice mounts for single-fiber splices (**Fig 4**).

The result is a practical and economical range of closures based on the UC family of closures with a few additional components which meets all use and network security requirements.

Vault closures

At distribution points high-count fiber-optic cables are connected to several low fiber-count cables. This situation generally arises at the transition from buried or underground cables to special-purpose tip cables inside buildings. Closures are available for these applications which outwardly resemble the proven UC type vault closures.

Here again, closure assembly is the same as established UC practice. Tip cables are inserted through the special endcaps and the unused openings are sealed with plugs. The "innards" of the vault closures are basically the same as those of the straight and branch closures.

Repeater containers

The use of underground containers of corrosion-resistant steel which has been proven over many years in numerous coaxial cable installations both at home and abroad has been continued for long-haul fiber-optic cables. The containers are made of welded steel plate, hot galvanized inside and out. They are given a plastic-based multilayer anticorrosion coating. Buried in the soil, these containers are subject to only slight external temperature variations and are difficult to access by unauthorized persons. The rubber-gasketed lid bolted firmly down onto the container flange sec-

Fig. 5 Unterground container housing all the transmission equipment for 60-fiber cables

Closure type	Module count	Splice count	Design
UC 4–6	–	18/24**	Half shells
UCS A–6 TSK A–6*	–	18/24**	
UCS 4–8 TSK 200–4*	8	80	
UC 6–9 TK 95–64*	12	120	Slit closure tube with clamping bars and endcaps
UC 6–18 TK 95–64L*	24	240	
UC 6–18 TK 95–64L*	–	36/48**	
UC 8–18 TK 155–100*	50	500	
UC 8–28 TK 155–100L*	75	750	
UC 10–20 TK 216–100*	100	1000	
UC 10–30	150	1500	
UC 10–40	200	2000	

* Closure adopted by Deutsche Bundespost (O packs already used in trial projects)
** Single bonded or fused splices

Table   Capacity of closures for single or modular splices in optical waveguides

Fig. 6   Man-accessible underground container prepared for 30 systems

Fig. 7   Plastic container for the short-haul network

urely seals the interior while providing good access when opened. The largest container with capacity for 30 regenerative repeaters and the associated equipment provides easy man access.

At the present state of the art, regenerative repeaters for wideband, long-range optical communication systems have relatively high dissipations. The dissipated energy in underground repeaters must be transferred through the container wall to the surrounding soil to prevent a specified maximum temperature inside the container being exceeded.

Two unterground containers were selected from the existing range to provide neat and easily accessible mounting of regenerative repeaters and to take into account the special characteristics of optical fibers. One is 850 mm, the other 1050 mm in diameter, accommodating five and ten regenerators respectively together with the associated power-feeding equipment.

For up to 30 regenerative repeaters (go and return) dissipating approximately 600 W, a man-accessible underground container is available providing all necessary safety precautions for the maintenance personnel (**Fig. 5**). Rack mounting style 7R has been incorporated in a successful application of a proven system to a new technology. This container is supplied to the site fully wired (**Fig. 6**), thus requiring only the incoming and outgoing cables to be spliced in and the transmission equipment to be installed.

For transmission systems of lesser span length and bandwidth and correspondingly lower dissipation (e.g. in the short-haul network), plastic containers are available in various sizes (**Fig. 7**). They provide a practical solution to complete the range of containers for fiber-optic cable installations.

References

[1] Giebel, W.; Kunze, D.: Plastic Clamping Sleeves, a Standard Accessory for Communications Cables. Siemens Rev. XLIV (1977), No. 3, pp. 132 to 137

[2] Odemar, N.; Steinmann, P.: Optical Fiber Jointing Techniques. telcom report 4 (1981), No. 4, pp. 241 to 245

Günter Köstler

Fiber-Optic Projects for the Deutsche Bundespost and other Users in Europe

The aim of this article is to provide an overview of the fiber-optic cable systems installed by Siemens in Europe. Particular reference is made to the Deutsche Bundespost projects – and for two reasons: firstly, the plans of the Deutsche Bundespost to transmit future new services on optical fibers are of far-reaching importance for the entire communications industry; secondly, by introducing new technology the Deutsche Bundespost is paving the way for other users. Fiber-optic cable systems of "other users" – categorized according to PTT and industry – are described with the aid of selected typical examples. As implied by the term "overview", a detailed report is not given, merely a brief account of objectives and recent experience.

Fiber-optic cable systems for the Deutsche Bundespost

For the initial projects the shared aim of the Deutsche Bundespost and industry was to investigate fiber-optic technology as comprehensively as possible under operating conditions. They wanted the empirical data thus obtained to reflect not only "feasibility", in other words the technology and economics involved, but also such important operating parameters as

- reliability,

- installation by
Deutsche Bundespost personnel, and

- the introduction of this new technology into the existing infrastructure and the individual network levels.

This last point was particularly important for formulating objectives. An attempt is made to illustrate this aspect in the schematic diagram of the structure of the Deutsche Bundespost telephone network (**Fig. 1**).

The telephone network is divided into local and long-distance levels. In the *local network* the subscriber is connected to the local or terminating exchanges via distribution and main cables – known collectively as local cables. Local exchanges in turn are interconnected via local interexchange trunks. The cables used in the local network are of balanced design and nowadays mainly comprise plastic-insulated copper conductors; they contain 6 to 200 wire pairs, depending on the hierarchy level.

In the *long-distance network* a distinction is drawn between the regional and national levels. The regional network begins at the terminating exchange and extends via the nodal exchanges to the

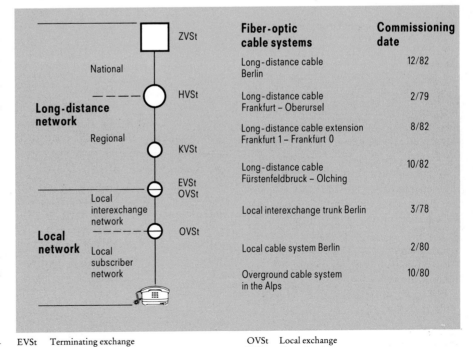

Fiber-optic cable systems	Commissioning date
Long-distance cable Berlin	12/82
Long-distance cable Frankfurt – Oberursel	2/79
Long-distance cable extension Frankfurt 1 – Frankfurt 0	8/82
Long-distance cable Fürstenfeldbruck – Olching	10/82
Local interexchange trunk Berlin	3/78
Local cable system Berlin	2/80
Overground cable system in the Alps	10/80

EVSt	Terminating exchange	OVSt	Local exchange
HVSt	Main exchange	ZVSt	Central exchange
KVSt	Nodal exchange		

Fig. 1 Structure of the Deutsche Bundespost telephone network and of the fiber-optic projects implemented by Siemens

Dipl.-Ing. (FH) Günter Köstler,
Siemens AG,
Public Communication Networks Division,
Munich

main exchange. The trunks to the central exchange are part of the national long-distance network.

Whereas both coaxial cables and cables with balanced copper conductors are used in the regional network, only coaxial cables are used in the national long-distance network. Depending on the method of transmission, these cables are designated VF or FDM long-distance cables for analog operation, and PCM long-distance cables for digital transmission.

Cable type 32c, with twelve 2.6/9.5 mm coaxial elements, may be regarded as typical of the various cable designs.

Fiber-optic systems have undergone trials at all four levels of the Deutsche Bundespost telephone network. The projects were completed by the firms involved within approximately five years [1].

The systems built by Siemens (see **table**) will now be briefly described in chronological order, and the author will attempt to evaluate, in the light of the present state of the art, the technical concepts which at the time represented the correct approach. The intention is not to criticize the earlier solutions, but to highlight the individual steps on the way to the present state of fiber-optic cable engineering.

Fig. 2   First fiber-optic cable in the Deutsche Bundespost telephone network, installed on September 1, 1977 in West Berlin as an interexchange trunk

Local interexchange trunk Berlin

On September 1, 1977 the first fiber-optic cable was installed in the telephone network of the Deutsche Bundespost (**Fig. 2**). It is customary at historic events of this nature to look for an historical link, and one such was found: almost exactly 100 years ago the General Postmaster, Heinrich von Stephan, held the first public telephone conversation in Germany. In the intervening years much has changed, not least in communications, but we had to wait until that September day for this momentous innovation to the Deutsche Bundespost network. The fiber-optic cable route has yet to carry telephone conversations, as it is being used initially to investigate the long-term performance of cables and transmission systems under actual environmental conditions [2]. The optical link, incorporating a 34 Mbit/s digital transmission system, was given a favorable

reception in the final report of the Deutsche Bundespost Research Institute [3].

Today this cable would have a central member of glass-fiber reinforced plastic instead of steel wire for protection against buckling. This would make it all-dielectric and immune to electromagnetic interference, without impairing the mechanical properties of the cable. In addition, the entire cable cross-section would be of waterblocking design, as with distribution cables containing metal conductors.

Long-distance cable Frankfurt 1 – Oberursel

The Deutsche Bundespost's first operational fiber-optic route, 15.4 km long [4], has been transmitting up to 480 telephone conversations simulta-

neously for more than three years (**Fig. 3**). Apart from two short interruptions, this optical link has provided trouble-free service [5]. On one occasion some of the light-emitting diodes on the operating and standby systems had to be changed owing to an inadmissible drop in optical power; in addition, the cable was damaged at several places during roadworks, so that about 20 m of new cable had to be spliced on.

In this connection, it must be mentioned that an adequate loss margin is provided when planning fiber-optic cable systems to allow for such repairs or cable rerouting. The link contains two regenerative repeaters, resulting in a repeater spacing of around 5 km.

In line with the current state of the art, laser diodes would be used instead of the light-emitting diodes, as they launch a considerably higher optical power into the fiber; the 15.4 km link could then be spanned with only one regenerative repeater. With more advanced optical semiconductors and using the fibers already available for operation at 1300 nm, it will soon be possible to install a link of this type without regenerative repeaters.

Local cable system Berlin

The main purpose of this system is to test the new cable technology in the local network [6]. This step, extending optical fibers into the subscriber's home, gave rise to the following requirements:

- design of waterblocking cables with 114 or 42 fibers,
- pulling-in of indoor cable into ducts already occupied by copper wiring,
- installation of the cables and
- on-site connector assembly.

In order to waste no time in putting the entire system into operation, pulse code modulation was chosen as the transmission method. This enabled the optical transmission route to be set up without modification to the EMD exchange or to the analog telephone set.

In simple terms, the copper pair in the local exchange was cut at the splitting strip and at the subscriber's telephone set and replaced by two optical fibers. At these interfaces the transducers convert all voice frequencies, dial pulses, busy signals and metering pulses into optical signals (**Fig. 4**).

In order to feed power to these transducers from the exchange battery, the transducer at the subscriber terminal is connected to the battery via a copper cable running parallel to the fiber-optic cable. The same copper wires provide a standby system should the optical transmission link fail; switching at the two interfaces is initiated from the exchange.

This first step – the introduction of fiber-optic technology into the local network – has enabled valuable experience to be acquired. An important point for further planning is that the fiber-optic cable could be drawn into and installed in the cable ducts and building wiring ducts without difficulty.

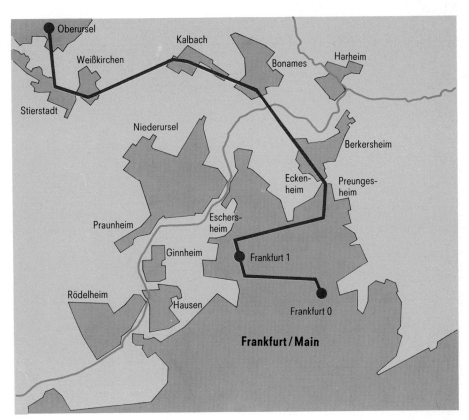

Fig. 3   Routing of the 15.4 km fiber-optic link (long-distance cable) from Oberursel to Frankfurt 1 and its extension to Frankfurt 0

Today the outdoor fiber-optic cable would be made up of multifiber and not single-fiber units, in which case the diameter of an outdoor cable with 114 fibers would be 23 mm instead of 32 mm.

For three years 76 telephone subscribers in the West Berlin local network have been making telephone calls via optical fibers. The number of faults is on the whole lower than for comparable conventional connections.

Aerial cable installations in the Alps

Ten mountain huts in the Alps have been connected to the local network via fiber-optic cables in lengths of between 1.2 and 5.6 km (**Fig. 5**). This trial project [7] highlights a further advan-

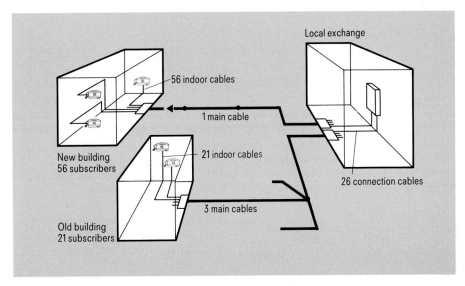

Fig. 4   Network plan of the fiber-optic local cable system in West Berlin

Fiber-optic cable system	Cable length	Cable design							
		Fiber count	Fiber properties				Cable structure		Features
			Diameter core/ cladding	Atten- uation (at λ = 850 nm)	Bandwith (at λ = 850 nm)	Suitable for operation at 1300 nm	Central member	Buffer tube and cable core filled?	
	km		μm	dB/km	MHz · km				
Local interexchange cable Berlin	4.3	8	62.5/125	5	400	no	Steel wire	no	
Long-distance cable Frankfurt 1 – Oberursel	15.4	6	62.5/125	5	300	no	Glass-fiber reinforced plastic	no	
Local cable system Berlin: Main cable Switchboard cable	2.2 1.3	42/114 6					Glass-fiber reinforced plastic	yes no	Unit stranding
Installation cable	4.7	2	50/125	6	300	no	No central member	no	Two copper conductors in cable
Aerial cable systems in the Alps	20	4	50/125	4	300	yes	Glass-fiber reinforced plastic	yes	Aerial cable with integral aramid fiber messenger
Long-distance cable Frankfurt 1 – Frankfurt 0	4.5	12	50/125	4	300	yes	Glass-fiber reinforced plastic	yes	
Long-distance cable Fürstenfeldbruck – Olching	8.7	2	50/125	3	300	yes	Glass-fiber reinforced plastic	yes	
Long-distance cable Berlin	9	4	50/125	0.8 (at λ = 1300 nm)	1300 (at λ = 1300 nm)	yes	Glass-fiber reinforced plastic	yes	Laminated sheath cable, two copper conductors in cable

Table   Typical properties of the fiber-optic cables supplied by Siemens for Deutsche Bundespost projects

tage of fiber-optic cables – not only do they have low attenuation and high transmission capacity, they are immune to atmospheric interference thanks to their metal-free design. Previously the telephones, some of which are emergency sets for the mountain rescue services, were often out of action as a result of lightning strikes or cables being broken by ice loading or by falling trees.

In view of this extreme mechanical stress, the cable is in the form of a figure 8 aerial cable. Instead of the conventional steel messenger, aramid fibers have been used for stress relief. In addition, the cables are suspended from the poles on suspension clips, each of which has a rupture joint. As the two previous winters have shown, this protects the cables and poles from breaking on overload. By comparison, some sections of the copper cables laid in parallel have been broken in several places (Fig. 6).

The transmission principle employed is basically the same as that of the local cable system Berlin. However, two fundamental modifications had to be made in order to adapt the transmission system to local conditions:

Firstly, the transducer at the subscriber end had to be powered by a solar bat- tery. As the available power supplies were not sufficiently reliable, self-contained solar power plants were installed at the huts. These comprised a solar panel with a maximum output of 12 W, a regulator and a floating battery providing 65 Ah at 12 V. Substantial reserve capacity was intentionally provided. Measurements on a single subscriber terminal over approximately four months showed that the actual reserve capacity is considerably greater than the calculated margin of 100 hours continuous telephone operation.

The second important modification to the transmission system is that the fiber-optic cable does not start from

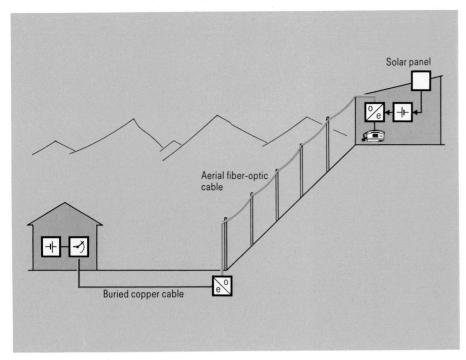

Fig. 5 Design of the fiber-optic aerial cable systems in the Alps

the exchange but up to ten kilometers away at the transition from buried cable to aerial cable. For this reason, the exchange-end transducer with its feeder unit and changeover equipment for standby operation via copper cable had to be designed for installation underground in a protective closure.

Extension of the long-distance cable in Frankfurt

A fiber-optic cable comprising twelve graded-index fibers connects Frankfurt 1 and Frankfurt 0, with four fibers through-connected to Oberursel (**Fig. 3**). The utilized transmission capacity of the cable corresponds to that of type 24f coaxial cable (with twelve 1.2/4.4 mm coaxial elements). When the two cables are compared, one of the advantages of the optical fiber becomes apparent immediately. Whereas the coaxial cable has an external diameter of 45.0 mm and a weight of 2170 kg/km, the corresponding figures for the fiber-optic cable are 10.4 mm and 95 kg/km respectively.

Owing to the low weight of fiber-optic cables, their pull-in lengths are considerably greater than those for copper cables; for example, while the permissible pull-in length for the comparable 24f coaxial cable is only 425 m, in six of the seven projects fiber-optic cables

were pulled using lengths of 1000 m. In the first system in West Berlin, the pull-in lengths were shorter, as in this case splices at mandatory locations were prescribed.

Modern fiber-optic cable design would allow even greater lengths. The upper limit will become clear in future projects, though what is certain is that the pull-in length must be specified for each application on the basis of local conditions. This subject is dealt with in greater detail in [8].

Long-distance cable from Fürstenfeldbruck to Olching

To gain the experience necessary to standardize designs for future operational systems, the Deutsche Bundespost selected four further projects in the regional long-distance network level for introducing fiber-optic systems. As a result, Siemens was awarded the contract for the Fürstenfeldbruck–Olching link. A regenerative repeater was not necessary for transmitting the 34 Mbit/s signal on the 9 km route, as the optical source used is a laser diode [9].

For the first time, the fiber-optic cable was plowed in on a section some 4 km long together with corouted cables (**Fig. 7**), and no problems were encountered.

Long-distance cable Berlin

For fiber-optic trials in the national network the Deutsche Bundespost selected a 9 km cable route between telecommunication center 1 and local exchange 451 in West Berlin. As a result of the four optical waveguides in the cable being looped in pairs at an end point, the link transmits 140 Mbit/s signals over a total distance of 18 km.

The fiber-optic cable and line terminating unit in the optical transmission system installed by Siemens already meets many of the requirements in the Deutsche Bundespost's Technical Conditions of Supply.

The 18 km link length corresponds to the nominal repeater spacing in a future long-distance network and is spanned by using powerful laser diodes and graded-index fibers providing very low attenuation and high bandwidth in the 1300 nm wavelength region.

Although the attenuation of an optical waveguide joint spliced with the newly developed fusion splicer [10] is very low (average value less than 0.2 dB), the number of splices on a link of this length begins to have a significant impact on the overall attenuation. It was for this reason that, in West Berlin, cables were pulled into the duct system in 2000 m lengths for the first time.

Experience with fiber-optic cable systems

In any attempt to draw conclusion from the projects implemented by Siemens for the Deutsche Bundespost, a distinction must be made between operational and technical aspects.

From the operational point of view, the project provided the following information:

The new transmission medium has been proved in operation and can now, without any great difficulty,

• be incorporated at the network level and into the existing infrastructure (fiber-optic cable can be installed as duct, buried or aerial cable) and

• be handled by Deutsche Bundespost personnel (cable was installed successfully by PTT personnel after thorough training by Siemens).

These results will certainly have a positive effect on any decision by the Deutsche Bundespost to introduce fiber-optic technology on a wide scale. The preliminary requirements for a standard fiber-optic design were drawn up by the FTZ (Central Bureau for Telecommunications) together with technical specifications for the cable and transmission systems at the regional and national long-distance network levels. Several projects covering both network levels are planned for the next few years.

In 1983, in addition to the projects already planned, Siemens will be involved in two comparatively large projects: the Bonn government buildings network and BIGFON [10].

Today, fiber-optic cable technology is already highly advanced. The prime reason for this is that experience has been gained not on laboratory models but on systems constructed and operated under field conditions, and it is the Deutsche Bundespost, with the projects described above, that has made this possible.

Application of fiber-optic technology in other PTTs and Research Institutes in Europe

The *Heinrich Hertz Institute for Telecommunications in West Berlin* has been involved in optical communication from a very early stage. In a large-scale model experiment they investigated possible PCM hierarchies and network configurations for fiber-optic systems. Among other things, Siemens supplied cables for two 3 km links. The 560 Mbit/s systems for one of the links were also provided by Siemens.

The 1120 Mbit/s system was developed by the Heinrich Hertz Institute itself. Delivery and construction of the experimental systems began in 1977; the project was completed in 1981 [11].

The first fiber-optic link for the *Greek Post Office OTE* was installed at the beginning of 1981. The 11.3 km cable, comprising six graded-index fibers and linking two exchanges in Athens, is protected against rodent attack by additional steel-wire armoring. Since

Fig. 6 Figure 8 aerial cable in the Alps showing the ice loading on the cable

Fig. 7 Plowing in the long-distance fiber-optic cable with corouted cables between Fürstenfeldbruck and Olching

being put into service the 34 Mbit/s systems have been operating faultlessly.

The 4 km fiber-optic link in *Riihimäki (Finland)* is also equipped with a 34 Mbit/s system; the cable itself has two graded-index fibers. The system was put into service in the middle of 1982 by the Riihimäen Puhelin OY Telephone Company.

Fiber-optic systems for industrial applications in Europe

Fiber-optic technology is also being increasingly used in areas not covered by PTTs. This is due less to the high transmission capacity of the optical fiber than to the advantages of zero-potential transmission and immunity to electromagnetic interference. It is in applications where induced interference voltages are becoming more of a problem (due to high switching currents and concentration of power lines) and in which communications receiver circuits are becoming increasingly sensitive that optical communication provides a more promising alternative to other solutions, such as costly potential equalization circuits.

Below are just some of the many systems planned and installed by Siemens. In 1980 a fiber-optic link 5 km long was installed for the *CERN Synchronotron in Geneva;* the cable, which contains two graded-index fibers, is used for transmitting synchronizing pulses [12]. The system has so far provided trouble-free operation.

A further interesting application is the transmission of data via optical fibers for electric utilities. The first system of this kind installed by Siemens has been operated since 1980 by the *Austrian Power Authority,* again with no trouble. A cable, comprising four graded-index fibers, was lashed to the ground conductor of a 5.1 km 110 kV power line from St. Peter to Ranshofen [13]. As the ground conductor was suspended from the tower tops, the fiber-optic cable had to be installed at heights of up to 73 m above the ground.

Cables incorporating two to ten fibers and totalling 9 km in length have been installed for the *Duisburg railroad and port authority.* The railroad signals are controlled and monitored via these cables from a switch tower.

Optical transmission on the graded-index fibers has been troublefree since the system went into service in 1982 despite the high induction currents.

Conclusion

This survey of the fiber-optic cable systems installed by Siemens for the Deutsche Bundespost and the examples of other users in Europe attempt to show how important optical communication has become today. The speed with which optical waveguides have developed into a viable transmission medium for use in operational systems has been impressive. The positive experience gained so far is bound to lead to a more extensive application of fiber-optic cable technology.

References

[1] Theml, D.: Der Einsatz der Glasfaser im Netz der Deutschen Bundespost. Z. f. d. Post- u. Fernmeldewes. 33 (1981) No. 8, pp. 16 to 21

[2] Graßl, F.; Krägenow, H.: Die Lichtwellenleiter-Kabelstrecke Berlin, ein Projekt von grundsätzlicher Bedeutung. telcom report 1 (1978), pp. 40 to 45

[3] Deutsche Bundespost: Jahresbericht des Forschungsinstituts der DBP (1980)

[4] Kahl, P.; Köstler, G.; Laufer, A.; Wartmann, H.: First Optical Cable Link of the Deutsche Bundespost. telcom report 2 (1979) No. 3, pp. 169 to 173

[5] Müller, K.; Unterlaß, W.; Weber, W.: Two Years' Experience with the First Operational Fiber-Optic Route in the Deutsche Bundespost Network. telcom report 4 (1981) No. 4, pp. 246 to 249

[6] Krägenow, H. et al.: Die erste LWL-Ortskabelanlage für die Deutsche Bundespost. Nachr.-tech. Z. 33 (1980), pp. 608 to 610

[7] Nußbaum, J.: Telefonieren mit Licht und Sonne. telepost (1981) H. 2, pp. 30 and 31

[8] Goldmann, H.: Installation of Fiber-Optic Cables. telcom report 6 (1983) Special Issue "Optical Communications", pp. 46 to 49

[9] Heister, G.; Knop, W.; Unterlaß, W.: Auf neuer Welle. Funkschau, Heft 8/1983

[10] Odemar, N.; Steinmann, P.: Jointing Techniques for Fiber-Optic Cables. telcom report 6 (1983) Special Issue "Optical Communications", pp. 50 to 54

[11] Braun, E.: BIGFON Brings the Optical Waveguide into the Subscriber Area. telcom report 6 (1983) Special Issue "Optical Communications" pp. 136 to 139

[12] Heinrich-Hertz-Institut: Zukünftige Übertragungstechnik. Bericht über Forschungsvorhaben der optischen Nachrichtenübertragung. Hannover-Messe 1979

[13] Beger, H.; Bosser, J.; Burnod, L. C.; Rossi, V.; Liertz, H.; Pichlmayer, E.: Beam Observation via an Optical Transmission System in the CERN Super Proton Synchrotron. telcom report 2 (1979), No. 3, pp. 164 to 168

[14] Fischer, K.; Möller, W.; Rüger, W.; Tannhäuser, A.: Ein neues Lichtwellenleiter-Übertragungssystem für Nachrichtennetze von Energieversorgungsunternehmen. Österr. Z. f. Elektr.-Wirtsch. 34 (1981) No. 1, pp. 1 to 5

Peter Rudolf Bark and Otto Istvan Szentesi

Fiber-Optic Projects in the USA

Siecor Optical Cable was founded five years ago as a joint venture between Siemens Corporation and Corning Glass Works. Since then, intensive work has been carried out in the field of fiber-optic technology – the fact that around 25,000 kilometers of cabled fiber have already been installed speaks for itself. The main demand was for outdoor installations involving duct, aerial or buried cables, while cable trays or special duct systems were used for indoor installations.

This article discusses typical cable plant and the installation techniques usually employed in the USA. For all installed cable systems a total of 34 million fiber kilometer-hours and the same number of fiber splice-hours were recorded and evaluated. In most cases, the operating data resulting from this analysis showed improvements over comparable copper cable plant.

Siecor Optical Cable, now a division of the Siecor Corporation, was founded in 1977 at a time when the use of fiber-optic cables was still in its infancy. This fact, coupled with a customer network spread over a wide area, called for a special business strategy for this field. The key to this strategy is that the transmission properties of the entire passive *cable system*, defined as the fully installed, spliced cable between end connectors, are guaranteed. The hardware and services product line includes cable, jointing material for connectors, splices and installation, auxiliary equipment (splicing tools and test equipment) and technical support and backup services.

In order to achieve guaranteed operation in this new technical field with the installed equipment, Siecor Optical Cable has attached special importance

Dipl.-Ing. Dr.-Ing. Peter Rudolf Bark and
Dr. (Ph. D.) Otto Istvan Szentesi,
Siecor Optical Cable,
Hickory, North Carolina, USA

to "program management" which acts as the technical interface between the customer and the system suppliers. Activities include

- planning,
- developing procedures and training programs,
- instructing the customer in cable installation and splicing techniques,
- supervising installation work and
- testing and troubleshooting.

The success of this approach is confirmed by the large number of reliable operating cable systems which have already been installed by Siecor Optical Cable.

Specific types of cable had to be developed for the various applications and environmental conditions and these are described in greater detail in [1, 2]. The aim of this article is primarily to give information on customary American installation and splicing techniques, field testing, reliability and repairs, and to illustrate these points by reference to typical cable systems.

Typical cable systems

Fig. 1 gives some idea of the number and geographic distribution of fiber-optic cable systems for communication routes supplied so far by Siecor Optical Cable (systems for industrial applications are not included). Many of the early systems were significant first steps in the development of the necessary technology and some of these will now be considered more closely.

Joplin (Missouri)

Although optical fibers are used less frequently in CATV networks than in telephony, a few systems have been installed. One of the first typical video systems for analog transmission over optical fibers was installed in the fall of 1978 [3, 4] by Cablecom General. The electronics was supplied by Siemens Corporation and cable and system integration was carried out by Siecor Optical Cable.

The system at Joplin transmits three video signals from the local origination studio (LOS) to the headend and one video signal in the opposite direction from the headend to the local origination studio. The two sites, approximately 6 km apart, are interconnected by a lashed 4-fiber aerial cable with one repeater. The 4-fiber cable (produced in two continuous lengths of 3 km and preconnectorized) was installed in two days using conventional equipment and methods.

Aerial cable installation has proved itself in practice to be a very quick and effective method. The preferred technique is to lash the fiber-optic cable to a steel messenger suspended from the cable poles. The messenger does not require special treatment, and the reels of optical cable are far smaller and

Fig. 1 Number and geographical location of fiber-optic cables
installed by Siecor Optical Cable in the USA for telecommunication systems (as of July 1982)

Customer	Location	Fiber count/ length in km	Customer	Location	Fiber count/ length in km
1. Cablecom-General	Joplin	4/6.0	28. Port Authority of NY	New York	6/3.1
2. Western Telecommunications	Colorado Springs	16/1.2	29. General Telephone of Hawaii #4	Alakea-Kalihi	36/3.9
3. General Telephone of Indiana	Fort Wayne	10/4.5	(Expansion of #1)		
		6/4.5	30. General Telephone of Hawaii #5	Alakea-Pinahua	10/10.0
4. United Telephone of Pennsylvania	Carlisle	6/13.0	(Expansion of #2)		
5. Western Union	New York City	10/7.0	31. General Telephone of Florida	Clearwater	12/17.6
6. Mountain Bell Telephone Co.	Phoenix	6/3.0			8/10.1
7. General Telephone of Pennsylvania	Oil City	4/10.0	32. Anchorage Telephone Utilities	Anchorage	6/4.6
8. General Telephone of Florida	Tampa	8/6.7	33. General Telephone of Hawaii #6	Kalihi-Moanalua	20/3.7
		2/2.5	34. General Telephone of Hawaii #7	Moanalua-Aiea	20/6.7
9. General Telephone of Hawaii	Honolulu	10/4.0	35. General Telephone of Hawaii #8	Aiea-Pearl City	20/4.2
10. Continental Telephone of Virginia #1	Woodbridge	6/8.0	36. General Telephone of Hawaii #9	Pearl City-Mililani	10/10.5
11. Southwest Bell Telephone Co.	Greenville	12/4.6	37. New England Telephone Co.	White River	12/4.0
12. General Telephone of California	Beaumont	10/4.1	38. New England Telephone Co.	Manchester	16/13.0
13. Mountain Bell Telephone Co.	Colorado Springs	8/30.3	39. Southwestern Bell Telephone Co.	Conway	8/8.4
14. Niagara Mohawk	Syracuse	8/13.3	40. U.S. Government	Fort Monmouth	12/3.8
15. Continental Telephone-Gulf Division	Atlanta	6/5.8	41. Southwestern Bell Telephone Co.	Padre Island	20/8.7
16. General Telephone of Florida	Sarasota	8/9.5	42. Continental Telephone of Indiana	Seymour	4/32.0
17. Continental Telephone of Arkansas	Russellville	6/7.1			6/42.0
18. Continental Telephone of California	San Bernardino	12/2.4	43. New York Telephone Co. #1	Long Island	36/6.4
19. Continental Telephone of California	Taft	6/2.6			66/64.4
20. General Telephone of the Southeast	Ozark	6/1.3			24/47.0
21. Continental Telephone of Missouri	Wentzville	10/23.0	44. New York Telephone Co. #2	Saratoga	16/32.0
22. Continental Telephone of Virginia #2	Triangle	6/16.8	45. AT & LL, Pa.	Troy Hill	8/10.0
23. Telephone Utilities	Cheney	6/25.0	46. MCI	New York	10/10.0
24. United Telephone of Pennsylvania	Carlisle	12/4.2	47. Citibank	New York	30/12.0
25. Telephone Utilities	Kalispell	6/16.1	48. General Telephone of Hawaii #10	Mililani-Wahiawa	10/6.4
26. General Telephone of Indiana	Ft. Wayne Extension	6/5.0	49. General Telephone of Hawaii #11	Pearl City-Waipahu	12/7.5
27. Pacific Northwest Bell Telephone Co.	Lake Washington	35/6.7			
		70/6.5			

more manageable than in the case of self-supporting cable (**Fig. 2**).

Furthermore, the cable and messenger can be designed independently to suit the relevant installation requirements. The messenger consists of stranded, high-tensile steel wire which is attached to the poles by means of conventional bolts and clamps. The tension for each span and the environmental conditions to be expected are calculated beforehand.

Carlisle (Pennsylvania)

In the fall of 1978 and spring of 1979, independent telephone companies installed a number of digital transmission systems for 45 Mbit/s signals.

Carlisle was the location chosen by United Telephone System for field trials [5, 6]. The 12 km long system with one repeater (the first of this kind in a rural area) was supplied by Harris Corporation and Siecor Optical Cable. A variety of installation techniques was employed for the all-dielectric 6-fiber cable: some was laid in trenches, some plowed in, some suspended on poles and some pulled into ducts. Initially there were no problems; seven months later, however, the all-dielectric buried cable was gnawed through by an unknown animal. After a short section of cable had been replaced and protected by a conduit, no further problems occurred.

Phoenix (Arizona)

In February 1979 Mountain Bell installed a 3 km all-dielectric cable route between the West Central Office and a substation of a power plant in Phoenix. The cable was pulled manually into 25 mm diameter subducts with the cable reel located at a manhole about halfway along the route. It was initially pulled in through the first six manholes; the remaining 1.5 km of cable was then de-reeled and laid out in a figure eight (**Fig. 3**). In the second pass, the cable was pulled in through a further six manholes.

The entire installation took six hours.

Owing to the long cable lengths, pulling-in from the middle of the route is often the preferred method of installation. Its advantage over other methods is that it requires fewer craftspeople and less equipment (compressor, trans-

Fig. 2 Installation of an aerial fiber-optic cable which is first pulled along the messenger on rollers and then lashed

Fig. 3 Laying out the cable in a figure eight for pulling into the cable duct system

portation vehicles, etc.). Lengths up to 3 km have already been routinely installed in this way.

It is often necessary to pull cable slack out of a manhole. If the radius of the winch capstan is greater than the minimum bending radius of the cable, it is safe to feed the cable over the capstan. If the cable is exposed, in a manhole or cable vault for example, some protection is recommended. A preferred method involves installing an additional flexible conduit into one of the existing cable duct runs. The fiber-optic cable can then be pulled into this

conduit which then provides the cable with adequate mechanical protection.

Colorado Springs (Colorado)

When it was put into service in September 1980, the 31 km 8-fiber cable system installed by Mountain Bell was the longest in North America for a 45 Mbit/s system. It links the North American air defence headquarters to Peterson Air Force Base in Colorado Springs.

The system is of interest for its three regenerative repeaters located in manholes. In addition, fusion splicing was used by Mountain Bell for the first time in the field. Training, cable installation, field splicing and end-to-end testing of the four sections were completed within two months.

Woodbridge (Virginia)

In September 1981, the first 45 Mbit/s system for the 1300 nm wavelength range was put into service by Continental Telephone Company of Virginia between Woodbridge and Triangle [7]. The 17 km cable system installed between the two offices is designed with no regenerators outside the offices. The fiber-optic cable has six double-window fibers with an extended spectral transmission range which are suitable for operating at both short (about 850 nm) and long (about 1300 nm) wavelengths.

In long-wavelength systems, cable maintainability becomes a significant factor. Since OTDRs (Optical time domain reflectometers) for long wavelengths were not commercially available at the time of the early installations, users had to rely on short-wavelength OTDRs for fault location purposes. Unfortunately, the range for short wavelengths is limited by the attenuation, so that in long-wavelength systems it is necessary to provide midspan fiber access. Operational experience so far indicates that long-wavelength technology is at least of equal quality in terms of reliability and operability [8].

Splicing of optical fibers can be performed in the manhole itself or on the messenger. In the USA splicing is very often carried out in a splicing van. The necessary cable slack and splicing closures are accommodated in a protective enclosure in the manhole. A splicing crew normally consists of two people: the splicer and the OTDR operator who monitors splice quality.

World Trade Center (New York City, N.Y.)

The system installed in the World Trade Center in New York is an example of an in-building fiber-optic system. In August and September 1981, six reels of 6-fiber cable were installed and connected vertically from floor B1 to the 7th, 41st, 74th, 75th, 108th and 110th floors (**Fig. 4**). Installation of the cable took about a week. All the cables

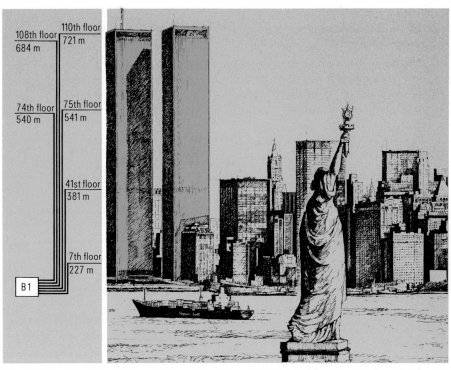

Fig. 4 In-building installation of fiber-optic cables in the World Trade Center in New York (the figures refer to the length in meters of the fiber-optic cables installed)

were pulled by hand into a common 100 mm duct which also housed a number of conventional copper cables. Pull-in boxes were provided approximately every fifth floor for cable access.

The cables were pulled in by stages, as follows:

- The reels for the 74th, 75th, 108th and 110th floors were set up on the 74th floor and the cable pulled in the direction of floor B1.

- The reel intended for the 41st floor was set up on that floor and the cable from this reel was added to the cable bundle when it reached this level. The cables were then pulled together towards B1.

- The reel intended for the 7th floor was set up on that floor and the cable from this reel was added to the cable bundle when it reached this level. The cables were then pulled further towards B1.

- Once all the cables had reached floor B1, the control center, sufficient slack was provided. The cables on the 74th floor intended for the 75th, 108th and 110th floors were de-reeled and coiled into figure eights so that the cable ends were accessible. The cables were then fed back into the duct and pulled up to their final positions.

Seattle (Washington)

In the fall of 1981 Pacific Northwest Bell Telephone Company installed a 9.6 km long 70-fiber 45 Mbit/s cable system [9, 10]. The route includes a 3.4 km submarine section on the bottom of the 60 m deep Lake Washington. For reliability two 3.4 km long 35-fiber Minibundle submarine cables were placed parallel, 150 m apart. The submarine cables were joined to 70-fiber all-dielectric duct cables on both shores.

The installation, which was delayed for one week by high winds, commenced on the eastern shore of Lake Washington with the placement of the first 3.4 km long fiber-optic underwater cable. The reel containing the heavily armored 18.5 mm diameter 35-fiber underwater cable was mounted securely to a "Hogg-Davis" cable reel unit positioned on the deck of the placing barge. The cable end was fed by divers into the 150 mm steel pipe extending into the lake and pulled through the on-shore duct system. When an adequate length had been pulled, the cable was secured and left for future splicing. The placing barge, towed by a small tug, began to move slowly westward across the lake. The speed of the barge was limited to 1 to 2 knots to ensure that minimal strain was exerted on the cable as it was fed from the power-driven reel.

The placing angle from the barge was maintained at approximately 45° resulting in the cable touching bottom approximately 140 m behind the tug. In order to maintain the correct course during the placing operation, both visual sighting of on-shore targets and electronic surveying equipment were used to keep the placing crew constantly in touch with their position along the route.

When the tugs reached the lake's western shore, they were secured to a moored barge. The remaining cable was then de-reeled and coiled into a figure eight to access the bottom end of the cable. The cable was then pulled through the on-shore duct system and secured. Anchoring was accomplished with special split finger trap grips secured to the manhole wall. This completed the installation of the first underwater fiber-optic cable.

The procedure was repeated two days later with the second 35-fiber underwater cable. Installation of the 70-fiber duct cables began shortly after these initial placements, using a conventional winch and standard cable placing techniques, with the exception that cable tension was constantly monitored to ensure that the maximum tensile load did not exceed the nominal value of 2500 N. The cables were installed in plastic subducts (inner diameter 25 mm) placed in the existing duct system allowing for efficient duct utilization. To further assist the pulling of the cable and limit cable tension, craftsmen were located at each intermediate manhole. Communications among all parties involved in the placing effort was maintained via two-way radio. The placement of two 1 km reels per day proved to be a realistic and attainable goal.

For all of the field splices, the fusion method was used. After an initial period of introduction to this new technology, the splicing crews completed an average of one 70-fiber splice in three shifts ($3 \times 8 \times 2 = 48$ man-hours) including set-up, sealing and placement of the splice closure. Actual splicing times of 5 to 10 minutes per fiber were typical. The crews worked around the clock, eliminating the need

Route	Distance km	Fiber count	Total number of cables on each route
Garden City – Levittown	9.5	66	10
Levittown – Farmingdale	7.1	66	7
Farmingdale – Deer Park	10.9	66	11
Deer Park – Bay Shore	8.9	66	5
Bay Shore – CEV	8.3	66	7
CEV – Sayville	8.3	66	6
Sayville – Patchogue	9.2	66	6
Patchogue – Selden	13.0	24	7
Garden City – Mineola	5.8	36	5
Mineola – Roslyn	8.0	24	5
Huntington – Syosset	9.0	24	5
Huntington – Farmingdale	15.8	24	9

Table   Data for the system installed on Long Island by the New York Telephone Co.

for numerous set-up times. The measured average for splice losses was 0.29 dB.

At the end-points the cables were terminated in an array format to interface with Western Electric *Lightguide Cable Interconnect Equipment* (LCIE). To accomplish this, the inner seven fibers of a short length of 12-fiber Western Electric "ribbon" were removed and replaced with the seven fibers of the Minibundle. The fibers were secured with mylar tape and an epoxy plug was then cast at the Minibundle/ribbon interface. The cable could then be terminated in accordance with standard Western Electric procedures. This process posed no major craft difficulties and, on the basis of subsequent measurement, proved to be successful. Upon completion of this procedure, the cable was spliced to the LCIE with WE fan-out cable providing access to the cable system via 70 single-fiber connectors.

Long Island

The New York Telephone Company's system on Long Island is noteworthy for its size (**Table**). About 64 km of 66-fiber cable, 6 km of 36-fiber cable and 47 km of 24-fiber cable have been installed for 90 Mbit/s operation (1344 telephone channels). The 14 repeater sections cover distances from 2.9 to 11 km for short wavelengths and up to 16 km for long wavelengths. Several 2 km lengths of 66-fiber Minibundle cable have been installed without any special problems.

The cables were installed in ducts with an internal diameter of 25 mm. With an outer diameter of 18.5 mm, some of the

66-fiber cables proved very difficult to pull in. The standard lubricants failed to improve the sliding resistance. Use of an aerosol lubricant, however, did reduce the resistance. In general, the cables were intended for pulling in from a midpoint. Since with the 66-fiber cable the pulling tension reached its maximum value (2600 N) after a pulling length of about 650 m, the 2 km cable lengths were installed in several stages. The cable reel was set up at the midpoint of the route and the cable was pulled in one direction. The remaining cable was de-reeled using a large capstan winch and laid out in a figure eight to access the free cable end. The cable was then fed back into the duct system and pulled to the end-point. During haul-off, the pulling tension at the pulling eye was constantly monitored by means of a remote detector. In this way, two kilometers of cable were routinely installed per day.

Reliability

The record for reliability of installed fiber-optic systems is excellent although some failures have been reported. Data on the reliability of 35 cable systems installed by Siecor Optical Cable have already been published [11]. These systems include a total of 289 kilometers of cable, over 34 million fiber kilometer hours and over 34 million fiber splice hours. A distinction has been made here between intrinsic and extrinsic failures.

Extrinsic failures include uncontrollable breaks such as those due to dig-ups, breaking poles and collapsing ducts. All cable types, fiber or copper, are subject to such failures. Avoidable failures of this type are those caused by improper installation. Fiber failures are recorded as intrinsic if they occur in spite of the specifications being met during installation and operation.

The majority of fiber failures fall into the category of uncontrollable, extrinsic failures which are usually the result of complete cable cuts (by excavators). In the more important category of intrinsic failures, there was only one occurrence of fiber failure. The cause was a failed repair splice that had been carried out in the factory. Interestingly, another avoidable fiber failure occurred seven months later. Subsequent scrutiny of the recordings made by the OTDR revealed that the damage occurred while the cable was handled and the failure could have been avoided.

The OTDR is an important aid that is always employed during cable production and installation to increase the reliability of the cable system.

Out of 2893 splices, there were three failures, two of which were avoidable. This extraordinarily low failure rate is particularly commendable in view of the fact that experienced splicers were employed on only six of the systems installed. The remaining craftsmen received on average three days of training followed by three days of field supervision.

Restoration of service in emergencies

In order to ensure continuity of service in fiber-optic cable systems, procedures have been developed for troubleshooting and service restoration, since most failures in such systems cannot be controlled. Two typical cases are:

● **Complete cable cut with slack available**

In this case, the slack must be retrieved and the cable spliced. To speed service restoration, it is recommended that a few fibers (25 to 98%, depending on traffic) be spliced as soon as possible without regard to splice quality and the remainder according to established procedures. The first 25 to 98% are then verified with the OTDR and respliced if necessary.

● **Complete cable cut with no slack**

The procedure is the same as that described above; however, it is necessary to insert an additional length of cable. This requires two splices and therefore two splicers with OTDR support. The result is a shorter repair time.

A further reduction in down time can be achieved by using an emergency restoration kit developed for quick, easy and convenient restoration followed by final repair of severed or damaged fiber-optic cable.

This kit meets the two most important requirements for restoration in an emergency, namely

● rapid temporary repair and
● transition to final repair without interruption to fibers except those affected.

The restoration kit contains all the materials required for service restoration in the field. The standard version includes 30 m of preconnectorized cable, quick connectors (bare fiber adapters), patch panels and splice inserts which allow easy transition to permanent repair. After service is restored, the system can then be per-manently repaired using the usual splicing techniques.

The estimated restoration times for a completely severed 70-fiber cable are shown in **Fig. 5**. The times given start when the seven men restoration splicing crew arrives on site and the cable ends are exposed. Four fusion splicers and two OTDRs are required for the "quick" splicing technique. If the emergency restoration kit is used, one fusion splicer can effect the permanent repair.

References

[1] Oestreich, U.: Fiber-Optic Cables for Long-Haul Communication Links. telcom report 6 (1983) Special Issue "Optical Communications", pp. 33 to 37

[2] Mayr, E.; Schinko, H.; Schöber, G.: Fiber-Optic Unit-Based Cables in the Local Network. telcom report 6 (1983) Special Issue "Optical Communications", pp. 37 to 40

[3] Szentesi, O. I.; Kügler, E.; Petty, W. D.: A fiber optic trunk system for analog video transmission. Proc. o. the Intern. Telecommunication Exposition. Dallas, Texas, 26. February to 2. March 1979, pp. 142 to 145

[4] Szentesi, O. I.: Fiber optic analog video transmission. Proc. o. the Fiber Optics and Communications Exposition. Chicago, 5. to 7. September 1979, pp. 144 to 148

[5] Forbrich, W. E.: Aerial, buried and duct fiber optic cable go into the field. Telephony, 25. December 1978, pp. 35 to 41

[6] Golob, J. E.; Midgley, H. S.; Shealer, R. C.: Fiber optic activity in the United Telephone system. Intern. Conference on Communications. Boston, June 1979, p. 19.2.1

[7] Cotten, W.; Dewitt, R.; Fergusson, C.; Hwang, C. J.; Gibbons, G.: America's first 1300 nm long-wavelength laser telephone transmission system. International Conference on Integrated Optics and Optical Fiber Communications. San Francisco, 27. April 1981

[8] Dewitt, R. G.; Cotton, W.: Field experience with long-wavelength optical fiber cable systems at Continental Telephone. Proc. IEEE International Conference on Communications. Philadelphia, 13. to 17. June 1982, p. 5D.3.1

[9] Greulich, R. A.; Lux, R. K.: PNB installs underwater FO links – a landmark job. Telephony, 22. February 1982

[10] Bark, P. R.; Lux, R. K.; Szentesi, O. I.: Design, testing and installation experiences of a 35-fiber minibundle submarine cable. Proc. IEEE International Conference on Communications. Philadelphia, 13. to 17. June 1982, p. 7D.2.1

[11] Zeidler, G. H.; Bark, P. R.; Lawrence, D. O.; Szentesi, O. I.: Reliability of fiber optic cable system. Int. Conf. Commun., Seattle 1980, Conf. Rec. 10.3

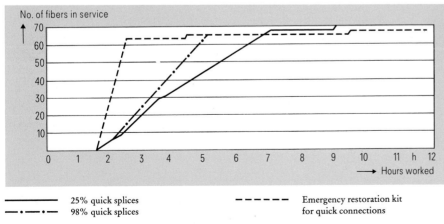

Fig. 5   Estimated restoration times for a 70-fiber cable using various approaches

—————— 25% quick splices
—·—·—·— 98% quick splices

------ Emergency restoration kit for quick connections

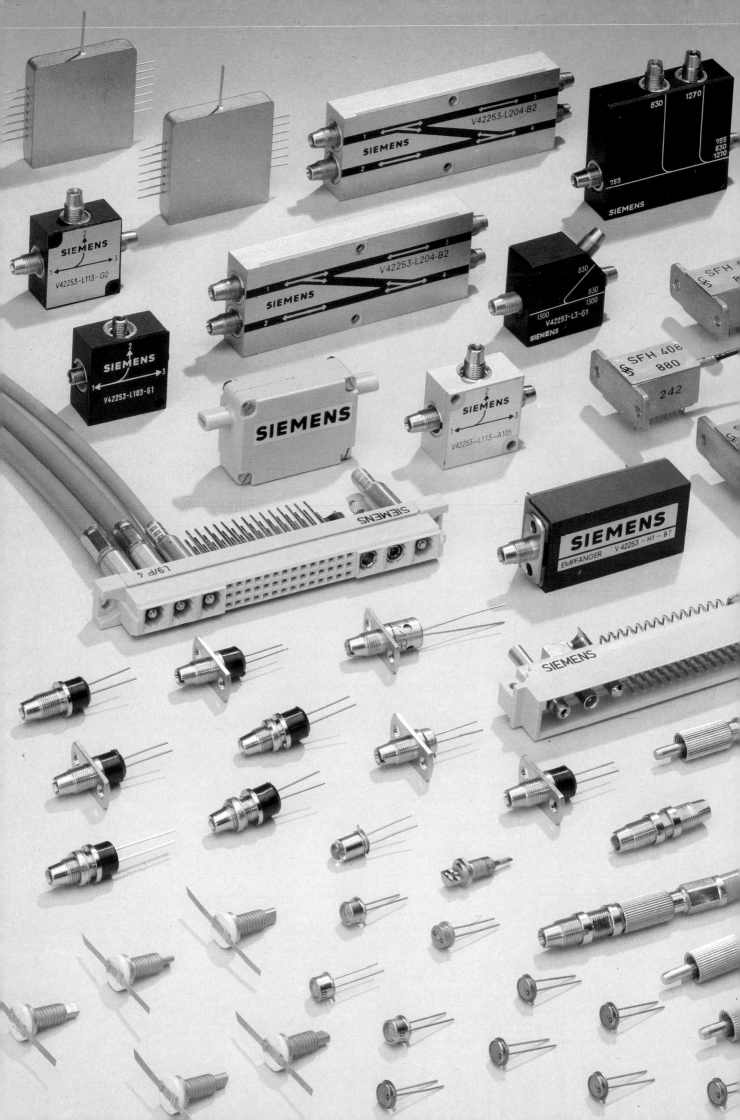

Christian Clemen, Jochen Heinen and Manfred Plihal

High-Radiance Light-Emitting Diodes for Optical Transmitters

Suitable sources for optical communication with multimode fibers over a wide range of repeater spacings and transmission rates are available in the form of simple, low-cost light-emitting diodes (LEDs), characterized by ruggedness and longevity. The simplest systems can be operated with ordinary diodes emitting in the visible red region of the spectrum. For more stringent requirements, e.g. on systems operating at transmission rates in the Mbit/s range over repeater distances in the km range, special infrared-emitting diodes have been developed for use in fiber-optic systems and optimized for the favorable transmission windows at wavelengths of 800 to 900 nm and 1300 nm.

This paper presents a GaAs LED operating at a wavelength of 900 nm for simple applications. In addition AlGaAs/GaAs and InGaAsP/InP double-heterostructure high-radiance LEDs emitting at 830 and 1300 nm are presented for system applications covering transmission rates from a few Mbit/s to more than 100 Mbit/s and span lengths from a few meters to more than 10 km.

Light-emitting diodes for fiber-optic transmission systems are adapted to the requirements by

● setting the emission wavelength to regions of low fiber attenuation and dispersion,

Dipl.-Phys. Dr. rer. nat. Christian Clemen,
Siemens AG,
Components Division, Munich;
Dipl.-Ing. Dr.-Ing. Jochen Heinen and
Dipl.-Phys. Dr. rer. nat. Manfred Plihal,
Siemens AG,
Research and Development Division,
Munich

◁ Active and passive optical waveguide components – key elements in optical communications. The applications range from simple transmission requirements under harsh industrial conditions to broadband communication

● making rise and fall times in the infrared emission short enough for the specified bandwidth or transmission rate, but particularly by

● designing the diodes in such a way that the infrared light of a very small active region is emitted perpendicular to the p-n junction from the surface layer of the semiconductor crystal (surface emitter). This, combined with a low thermal resistance permitting high drive currents, produces high radiance and hence a high launched radiant power on coupling the diode to the fiber.

The high radiance LEDs additionally exploit the advantages of double-heterostructure design, particularly the high quantum efficiency [1].

Diffused GaAs LED emitting at 900 nm

Probably the simplest LED for fiber-optic systems from the design point of view is a diffused GaAs LED, SFH 407, which is shown in **Fig. 1**. **Fig. 2** shows a cross section through the diode body, which is 400 μm on a side and 240 μm high. The diode body contains a p-region of 200 μm diameter on the top, where the infrared radiation is generated. Radiation emerging from the p-surface can be coupled into the fiber.

The diode is fabricated in planar technology starting with n-doped GaAs wafers of about 10 cm^2 and low dislocation density ($< 4000/cm^2$) to minimize losses due to nonradiative recombination [1] at crystal defects. Next an Al_2O_3 layer, which serves as a diffusion mask, is sputtered onto the wafers and the diffusion windows are opened. The Zn diffusion is carried out in a closed ampule to avoid erosion of the semiconductor surface due to the volatility of the group V element. Together with a zinc diffusion source, the wafers are sealed under vacuum in a quartz ampule and are placed in a diffusion furnace (**Fig. 3**).

By employing suitable diffusion conditions [2] it is possible to diffuse a 10 μm thick p-region with relatively low p-doping and hence low self-absorption. As regards to radiant power output, this has to be a compromise between increasing self-absorption with layer thickness and decreasing nonradiative recombination at the surface. In addition, the p-n junction is graded, which reduces lattice strains and additional losses due to nonradiative recombination.

After lapping the wafers to the final thickness, the contact metallization is evaporated onto both sides of the wafers. **Fig. 4** shows an opened deposition system employed for this purpose. The wafers can be seen on holders. The p-contact geometry is formed by a conventional photolitography and etching process; only fingershaped contact-stripes protrude into the p-region. Finally, the p-surfaces are coated with an anti-reflection layer of Si_3N_4 which improves the radiation output of the

Fig. 1   LED SFH 407
in front of a finished GaAs crystal wafer

Fig. 2   Schematic of the diffused GaAs LED SFH 407

Antireflection coating
p-contact
Al_2O_3 insulation
p-GaAs (diffused)
200 µm
n-GaAs (substrate)
n-contact

epoxy encapsulated diodes by about 17%. After the wafer has been separated into individual diodes, these are soldered onto headers (**Fig. 1**) and provided with a very thin flat encapsulation of epoxy.

Because of the Zn-doping of the GaAs the emission wavelength of this LED is set to 900 nm and the spectral linewidth to 40 nm. The radiant power of the LED rises approximately proportional to the forward current. At 100 mA the radiant power output is typically 3 mW, the angular distribution of the intensity obeying a cosine law (Lambertian source). With its relatively large emitting area the LED SFH 407 is particularly suitable for large-core fibers. The radiant power coupled into fibers with 200 µm core diameter, with step-index profile and a numerical aperture $A_N = 0.4$ is typically 120 µW at 100 mA. **Fig. 5** shows the decrease in radiant power coupled into the fiber, when the fiber is offset axially and laterally relative to the diode. In either case a misorientation of 50 µm merely produces a relative reduction in the launched radiant power of less than 15%. When the diodes are mounted in special connectors [3], similar tolerances of ±50 µm are maintained, enabling easily separable interfaces to be realized with low insertion losses.

Owing to the thick GaAs substrate and the simple package, the thermal resistance between junction and air is high; on assembly in connectors it is still 400 K/W. As a result the forward current is restricted to 100 mA, because the maximum permissible temperature

at the p-n junction is 80 °C. Diodes operated at room temperature are expected to have an average life (time until the radiant power falls to 50%) of 10^5 h [4].

The relatively long rise and fall times of 40 to 50 ns of radiance output are due to the long lifetimes of the minority carriers in the lightly doped p-region. The LED SFH 407 is therefore suitable for signal transmission up to about 5 Mbit/s and span lengths of a few hundred meters. Higher doping levels would enable larger modulation bandwidths to be obtained with the same diode geometry but only by sacrificing power, primarily due to the previously mentioned increase in self-absorption.

AlGaAs/GaAs high-radiance LEDs emitting at 830 nm

More stringent requirements are met by AlGaAs/GaAs high-radiance LEDs

Fig. 3   Sealed quartz ampule with GaAs wafers being inserted into the diffusion furnace

[5, 6]. LED SFH 404 (**Figs. 6** and **7**) consists of a semiconductor crystal 70 µm high and 400 µm on a side. A double heterostructure, comprising three AlGaAs layers of varying thickness and doping levels, is epitaxially grown on an n-doped GaAs substrate 60 µm thick. With the epitaxial layers pointing downwards ("upside down" configuration) the diode is soldered via a 10 µm thick gold heat sink onto a silicon chip with conductor track and SiO_2 insulation. An Al_2O_3 insulation layer on the bottom of the diode crystal confines the current flow to the small-area p-contact 40 µm in diameter. The thickness and in particular the doping level of the AlGaAs capping layer above it are selected to prevent any significant current spreading in this layer. The result is that the active AlGaAs layer is excited to emission within an area of only slightly larger diameter (about 45 µm) than that of the p-contact, thus providing the desired small emitting area.

The two AlGaAs layers with the higher aluminum content form potential barriers for the electrons and holes entering the active layer in between when current is applied and confine radiative recombination vertically onto the active AlGaAs layer [1]. The nonradiative recombination of electrons and holes at the interface between the AlGaAs layers is significantly lower than at AlGaAs surfaces. Even with the thickness of the active layer set at 1 µm the possible reduction in quantum efficiency due to nonradiative recombination at the layer interfaces is accordingly negligible.

74

The quantum efficiency depends not only on the crystalline quality but also to a significant degree on the doping and the composition of the active layer. Optimum values are achieved with compounds for wavelengths between 800 and 880 nm and doping levels around $2 \cdot 10^{18}/cm^3$, such diodes exhibiting a rise time of about 15 ns.

The infrared light radiated upwards in the direction of the GaAs substrate is used for launching into the fiber. This radiation is subject to negligible self-absorption in the active layer, due to the small layer thickness, and emerges through the AlGaAs layer above without being absorbed, although it would be totally absorbed within a few micrometers in the GaAs substrate. For this reason, the GaAs above the emitting area is etched away concentrically to the p-contact and the n-contact is applied to the remaining GaAs material. The "upside down" configuration thus has the advantage that a suitably small emitting area can be defined with the aid of the small area p-contact without the contact causing an obstruction. In addition, the dissipative diode regions, i.e. the the p-contact and the p-n junction, are located near the heat sink, bringing the thermal resistance below 50 K/W.

These diodes are fabricated by first depositing the three layers of the double heterostructure onto an n-doped GaAs substrate about 3 cm² in area and of low dislocation density (<3000/cm²) by means of liquid phase epitaxy, cooling gallium-rich melts saturated with Al and As down from 800 °C [7]. A final Zn diffusion increases the carrier concentration at the surface of the p-doped AlGaAs capping layer and provides p-contacts of adequately low resistance. The capping layer then has Al_2O_3 sputtered onto it for insulation. Windows 40 µm in diameter are opened and the p-contacts are applied. After the epitaxial wafer has been etch-polished to an end thickness of 70 µm the n-contacts are fabricated and the gold heat sinks electrodeposited onto the p-side. The GaAs is removed from above the p-contacts by selective etching.

After scribing and breaking the wafer the individual diodes are soldered onto the silicon chips with SiO_2 insulation.

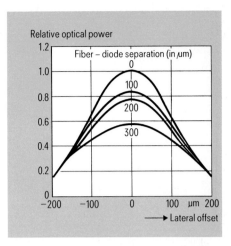

Fig. 5 Relative optical power launched with axial and lateral offset between LED SFH 407 and a large-core fiber ($d_c = 200$ µm, $A_N = 0.4$)

For type SFH 404, such a device is mounted into a header (**Fig. 6**) with insulated feedthroughs on a floating basis in such a way that the emitting area of the diode is centered on the header axis with a maximum deviation of ± 20 µm. The diode is then encapsulated similar to LED SFH 407. The header used here differs from the header for type SFH 407 by greater precision in the specified dimensions and by having a thicker base plate. These headers – like those for type SFH 407 – are particularly suitable for assembly in connectors [3], providing a demountable optical interface requiring no further alignment even on links employing graded-index fibers.

Diode type SFH 404 described here produces peak emission at 830 nm with a spectral bandwidth of 45 nm. As the temperature rises the emission peak is displaced to longer wavelengths at the rate of 0.3 to 0.4 nm/K. The diodes have a series resistance of 5 Ω primarily due to the small-area p-contact. The voltage requirement for 100 mA is about 1.9 V. Under reverse bias the diodes exhibit a soft breakdown. Typically 10 µA reverse current is measured at voltages of 4 to 6 V.

To achieve a rise time of 15 ns requires special operating conditions (**Fig. 8**). In the absence of dc bias the rise time is reached only with pulse currents around 100 mA. The decrease in rise time with higher pulse currents is due to carrier lifetimes shortening with increasing carrier density in the active layer [8]. The rise time is extended at low pulse currents by the junction

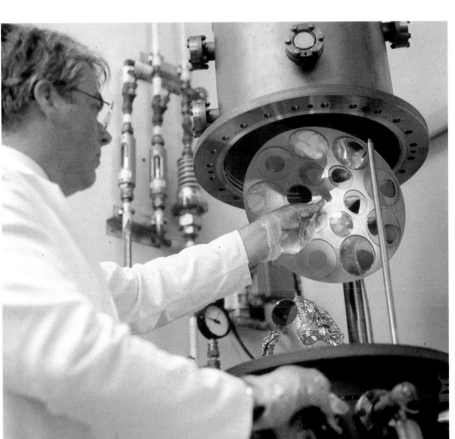

Fig. 4 Open chamber of a deposition system for metallizing the semiconductor wafers

Fig. 6   AlGaAs/GaAs
high-radiance LED SFH 404
emitting at 830 nm

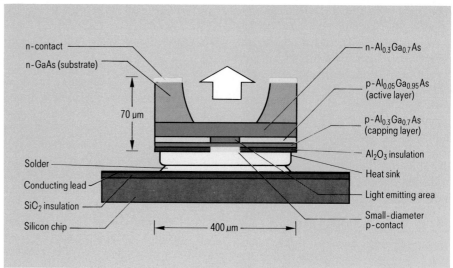

Fig. 7   Schematic of AlGaAs/GaAs high-radiance LED SFH 404

capacitance of the diodes of about 400 pF (at 0 V). However, this can be largely suppressed by dc biasing. Leaving aside type SFH 404, shorter rise times down to about 4 ns are easily realizable but only with a disproportionate decrease in optical power, if the active layer doping is increased to levels around $10^{19}/cm^3$.

For diodes SFH 404 the optical power is approximately proportional to the forward current as long as the temperature of the diodes is not increased by internal heating. At 100 mA, a total optical power of about 4 mW is achieved, 60 µW of optical power being launched in graded-index fibers (core diameter 63 µm, $A_N = 0.2$) and 700 µW into large-core fibers (core diameter 100 µm, $A_N = 0.4$) at this current. If the temperature rises, the powers decrease by 0.3 to 0.4% per Kelvin. If lenses matched to diode and fiber are employed or the end face of the fiber is spherically shaped, the launched power can be increased provided that the diameter of the diode emitting area is smaller than the fiber core diameter [9]. This is the approach adopted on high – radiance LEDs operating at 1300 nm.

The operating lifetime can be determined from the enhanced rate at which the optical power of the diodes decreases at p-n junction operating temperatures up to 200 °C. For defect-free diodes with uniformly decreasing optical power and absence of "dark line" defects [10] the resultant average

life extrapolated to room temperature is in excess of 10^6 h, which is in agreement with the data from other manufacturers [11]. However, to achieve this life it is necessary to screen the diodes by a burn-in test after fabrication and to ensure that during operation the p-n junction temperature does not significantly exceed room temperature. The thermal resistance of the diode crystal to the insulation is 50 K/W, the thermal resistance of packaged diodes to air is 400 to 500 K/W. Full utilization of the capabilities provided by LED SFH 404 therefore requires packaging with adequate heat sinking.

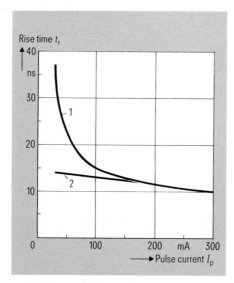

Fig. 8   Rise time of AlGaAs/GaAs LED SFH 404 (time between 10% and 90% optical power) as a function of pulse current (curve 1 without bias; curve 2 with bias)

LED SFH 404 extends the possible applications for light-emitting diodes in transmission systems beyond those for LED SFH 407 to include typically repeater spacings around 6 km at a transmission rate of 34 Mbit/s.

InGaAsP/InP high-radiance LEDs emitting at 1300 nm

The latest development in infrared-emitting diodes for fiber-optic applications are diodes for the 1300 nm wavelength range [12, 13], the transmission window of modern multimode fibers providing minimum loss and material dispersion. The change from the 800 to 900 nm wavelength range to values around 1300 nm requires a change in materials from the ternary AlGaAs to the quaternary semiconductor InGaAsP and to InP substrate crystals [1]. The design of quaternary high-radiance LEDs (**Figs. 9** and **10**) is basically the same as that of the GaAlAs/GaAs diodes. A crystal layer composed of $In_{0.72}Ga_{0.28}As_{0.61}P_{0.39}$ emits at the 1300 nm wavelength and is lattice-matched to InP. Thus, the effective double-heterostructure design can again be used with the InP now assuming the role of barrier. In this type, a p-doped InGaAsP layer is added to ensure low-resistance p-contacts which are difficult to fabricate on InP.

The external dimensions of the LED are approximately the same as those of

Fig. 9 InGaAsP/InP high-radiance LED
emitting at 1300 nm
in front of a semiconductor wafer
with integral lens structure

Fig. 10 Schematic of the InGaAsP/InP high-radiance LED structure

LED SFH 404. However, the p-side contact dot – and hence the emission spot – is typically only 25 to 30 μm in diameter, facilitating power launching into optical fibers. The InP substrate is transparent to 1300 nm radiation, so there is no need for the hole etching required on GaAs and it is also possible to form the substrate material into an integral lens to improve the coupling. A good lens effect is achieved with a surface radius of curvature of about 80 μm, the active layer of the structure lying in the focal plane of the lens. The efficiency of the diode is additionally enhanced by the anti-reflection coating of silicon nitride.

The starting material for diode fabrication is typically a 1 cm × 1 cm sized InP substrate on which a sequence of layers as shown in **Fig. 10** is grown by liquid phase epitaxy. The epitaxy is performed from about 650°C with indium-rich melts, using Sn and Zn additions to produce an n or p-type semiconductor [14]. **Fig. 11** shows a disassembled graphite boat in front of the opened epitaxy tube on completion of layer growth, with the solidified melts visible on the boat.

The emission wavelength and the exact matching of the heterostructure crystal lattices are strongly dependent on the melt composition and on the selected growth temperature. Hence, even a slight lattice mismatch reduces the efficiency. The fabrication processes sub-

sequent to the epitaxy are similar to those employed in fabricating the AlGaAs diode. In a two-step etching process the lens is formed from the substrate material concentric to the emitting area. The LEDs fabricated hitherto as laboratory specimens are mounted electrically floating on a header of good thermal conductivity (**Fig. 9**). It is, however, advisable to mount these high-power diodes

directly in a module with a connecting fiber aligned to the diode.

Although the spectral bandwidth of InGaAsP diodes of 100 nm is considerably higher than that of AlGaAs diodes, this is not harmful because the effect of the fiber dispersion on the pulse spreading at 1300 nm is slight. The wavelength can be set in the range from about 1200 to 1310 nm with no loss of power. Typical for the quater-

Fig. 11 Disassembled graphite boat with solidified melts on completion of epitaxy

nary diodes is the nonlinear optical powercurrent characteristic shown in **Fig. 12**, which suggests that there are current-dependent loss mechanisms which are not yet properly understood [13]. This saturation behavior makes these diodes more suitable for digital transmission techniques. Another effect of the internal losses is the differing time responses with pulse modulation, where the fall time is typically about twice the rise time. For optimum use of the available bandwidth it is therefore advisable to employ a modified modulation current in which the fall time at the end of the pulse is shortened by changing the polarity of the current.

When the infrared-emitting layer has standard doping in the region $10^{18}/cm^3$, the LEDs have a rise time of 8 ns and a fall time of 18 ns and are thus suitable for transmission rates of 34 Mbit/s. With a higher doping level – but with a halving of the radiated power – the rise and fall times are shortened to 3 and 6 ns respectively, thus making transmission rates of 140 Mbit/s possible. The lens employed doubles the optical power coupled into standard graded-

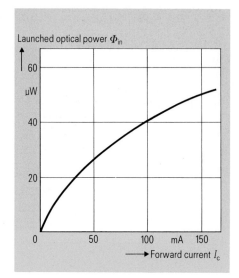

Fig. 12   Optical power launched by an InGaAsP/InP high-radiance LED into a standard fiber ($d_c = 50$ μm, $A_N = 0.2$) as a function of the drive current

index fibers (core diameter 50 μm, $A_N = 0.2$) compared with flat-surface diodes. Typical values for 100 mA forward current are 40 and 20 μW for the differently doped diodes. InGaAsP-LEDs have a greater temperature-

dependence of 0.7% per Kelvin than AlGaAs-LEDs, but they are characterized by an extremely low aging rate [13, 15]. Even at the high ambient temperature of 70°C lifetimes in excess of 10^6h can still be expected. Failures due to "dark line" defects, as in GaAlAs diodes, do not occur.

In order to assess the capabilities of a transmission system with quaternary source diodes, the mean power available in the optical fiber is assumed to be about -17 dBm for transmission rates of 34 Mbit/s and about -20 dBm for 140 Mbit/s. Receivers combining InGaAs photodiodes with field-effect transistor preamplifiers operating at these transmission rates achieve sensitivities of about -47 and -42 dBm at the commonly specified bit error rate of 10^{-9}. Accordingly, a transmission system assembled from these components provides a margin of 30 or 22 dB. Assuming a safety margin of 6 dB and a fiber loss of 1.5 dB/km including the splices, this means that quaternary LEDs can transmit 34 Mbit/s signals over a distance of at least 15 km and 140 Mbit/s signals up to 10 km without a repeater.

References

[1] Weyrich, C.; Zschauer, K.H.: Principles of Optoelectronic Signal Conversion. telcom report 6 (1983) Special Issue "Optical Communications", pp. 14 to 19

[2] Herzog, A.H.; Keune, D.L.; Craford, M.G.: High-efficiency Zn-diffused GaAs electroluminescent diodes. J. of Appl. Phys. 43 (1972), pp. 600 to 608

[3] Knoblauch, G.: Fiber-Optic Components and Systems for Industrial Applications. telcom report 6 (1983) Special Issue "Optical Communications", pp. 161 to 165

[4] Völkel, G.; Wallner, E.: Quality Assurance Methods for Optoelectronic Semiconductors. telcom report 6 (1983) Special Issue "Optical Communications", pp. 188 to 193

[5] Burrus, C.A.; Miller, B.I.: Small-area double heterostructure Aluminium-Gallium-Arsenid electroluminescent diode sources for optical-fiber transmission lines. Opt. Commun. 4 (1971), pp. 307 to 309

[6] Plihal, M.; Kunkel, W.: (Al,Ga)As-Dioden hoher Strahldichte für die optische Nachrichtenübertragung mit Glasfasern im Wellenlängenbereich um 850 nm. Siemens Forsch.- u. Entwickl.-Ber. 10 (1981), pp. 37 to 43

[7] Dawson, L.R.: Near-equilibrium LPE growth of GaAs-Ga$_{1-x}$Al$_x$As double heterostructures. J. of Cryst. Growth 27 (1974), pp. 86 to 96

[8] Ikeda, K.; Horiuchi, S.; Tanaka, T.; Susaki, W.: Design parameters of frequency response of GaAs-(Ga,Al)As double heterostructure LED's for optical communications. IEEE Trans. on Electron. Devices 24 (1977), pp. 1001 to 1005

[9] Plihal, M.: Improvement of launching efficiency of high-radiance surface-emitting IREDs with hybrid or integrated spherical lenses into step-index and graded-index fibers. Siemens Forsch.- u. Entwickl.-Ber. 11 (1982), pp. 221 to 226

[10] Ueda, O.; Isozumi, S.; Yamakoshi, S.; Kotani, T.: Defect structure of degraded Ga$_{1-x}$Al$_x$As double heterostructure light-emitting diodes. J. of Appl. Phys. 50 (1979), pp. 765 to 772

[11] Yamakoshi, S.; Hasegawa, O.; Hamaguchi, H.; Abe, M.; Yamasaka, T.: Degradation of high-radiance Ga$_{1-x}$Al$_x$As LED's. Appl. Phys. Let. 31 (1971), pp. 627 to 629

[12] Dentai, A.G.; Lee, T.P.; Burrus, C.A.; Buehler, E.: Small-area, high-radiance CW InGaAsP LEDs emitting at 1.2 to 1.3 μm. Electron. Let. 13 (1977), pp. 484 and 485

[13] Heinen, J.; Lauterbach, Ch.: High-radiance surface-emitting (In,Ga)(As,P)/InP IREDs with an emission wavelength of 1.3 μm for transmission rates of 34 Mbit/s and 140 Mbit/s. Siemens Forsch.- u. Entwickl.-Ber. 11 (1982), pp. 209 to 215

[14] Trommer, R.; Heinen, J.: Liquid-phase epitaxy of (In,Ga)(As,P) and (In,Ga)As on InP for 1.3 μm high-radiance IREDs and for photodiodes in the 1.3 μm to 1.65 μm wavelength range. Siemens Forsch.- u. Entwickl.-Ber. 11 (1982), pp. 204 to 208

[15] Yamakoshi, S.; Abe, M.; Wada, O.; Komiya, S.; Sakurai, T.: Reliability of high radiance InGaAsP/InP LED's operating in the 1.2–1.3 μm wavelength. IEEE J. of Quantum Electron 17 (1981), pp. 167 to 172

Markus-Christian Amann, Klaus Mettler and Hans Dietrich Wolf

Laser Diodes – High-Power Light Sources for Optical Communications

Laser diodes – long regarded as particularly critical components in fiber-optic communication systems – are the only light sources currently available for long haul systems operating at high bit rates. For the wavelength range 820 to 880 nm there is the GaAlAs oxide-stripe laser, a fully developed rugged laser diode of user-oriented design [1], featuring stable operating characteristics up to high temperatures (100 °C) and extrapolated operating lifetimes well above 100,000 h at 25 °C.

GaInAsP/InP laser diodes for 1300 to 1600 nm are under development in many laboratories in view of the much lower fiber attenuation in this wavelength range. Laser diodes currently in the forefront of practical interest are those operating at 1300 nm because here the fiber dispersion approaches zero, rendering the dynamic spectrum broadening of ordinary Fabry-Perot lasers largely ineffective. Characteristic features of the lasers in this wavelength range are the pronounced temperature dependence of the lasing threshold and the restricted CW temperature range compared with GaAlAs lasers. Thus the emphasis has shifted towards laser structures having a low threshold current; however, this is achieved only at the expense of a high optical feedback sensitivity. Hence it follows that the laser diode characteristics affecting transmission performance are fundamentally interlinked and cannot be varied or assessed independently.

Laser diodes are small, rugged, coherent optical radiation sources of high intensity which require only a low supply voltage and which can be modulated directly at high speed. The uniqueness of the devices due to these characteristics was recognized early on. However, for subsequent applications in fiber-optic communication systems

Dipl.-Ing. Dr.-Ing. Markus-Christian Amann,
Dipl.-Phys. Klaus Mettler and
Dipl.-Ing. Dr. techn. Hans Dietrich Wolf,
Siemens AG,
Research and Development Division,
Munich

a number of additional requirements had to be met. Laser diodes are therefore nowadays required to provide

● spectral characteristics matching the fiber characteristics,

● continuous operation up to the temperatures occurring in the transmitter and at the specified optical output powers (typically 5 to 10 mW),

● stability in the spatial and spectral distribution of the laser emission,

● adequate stability of the principal laser characteristics over long periods of operation,

● a sufficiently simple, i.e. economical, fabrication method.

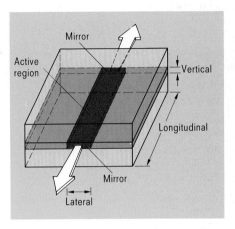

Fig. 1 Spatial confinement of the active region of a laser diode: longitudinally by the cavity mirrors, vertically by the heterostructure and laterally by the additional internal structuring

These requirements, which are highly complex in some respects, can nowadays be met. An important measure in this connection is the internal structuring of the laser in addition to the external confinement by the two mirror surfaces (**Fig. 1**). This serves to confine the electrically pumped region around the p-n junction and the optical cavity to a small region in the laser crystal. An essential prerequisite for continuous operation at and above room temperature is the vertical confinement of the charge carriers and the optical wave by the double heterostructure [2] to an active region usually only 0.1 to 0.2 μm thick.

An important factor as regards the characteristics of laser diodes for optical communications – particularly as regards their stability – is the lateral confinement. Lateral confinement of the active region to a few microns or less compels the laser to oscillate in the fundamental transverse mode only and prevents higher-order modes from propagating. This avoids such instability effects as kinks in the characteristic, laser emission noise and the possibility of the far field fluctuating as a result of competing modes. It also prevents deformation of the lateral gain profile by the stimulated emission itself.

Two structure families

Different technological possibilities for implementing lateral confinement of the active region have led to a large variety of laser structures. However, present-day laser diode structures can generally be assigned to two structure families, characterized by the type of lateral *waveguide* in the laser.

Laser diodes with current-induced waveguide

In these lasers, the current path and thus the injected charge carriers are laterally confined by technological means. In the *oxide-stripe laser* [3, 4], for instance, this is achieved by an electrically insulating masking layer with the current applied via a stripe-shaped contact window (**Fig. 2 a**). Concentrating the injected carriers onto the active stripe causes the imaginary refractive index n_i to assume a lateral profile which, for very narrow stripe widths, provides stable guidance of the fundamental transverse mode. Since this index profile corresponds to an optical *gain* profile, the lasers of this family, which includes other well-known types such as the *proton-isolated laser* [5] and the *V-groove laser* [6], are therefore also referred to as *gain-guided laser diodes (GLD)*.

Laser diodes with built-in waveguide

Laser structures of this group have both lateral current confinement as well as a "built in" lateral refractive index profile realized during fabrication, e.g. in the form of a step on each side of the active laser region either in the real part (as in the vertical double heterostructure) or in the imaginary part of the refractive index. The best known examples of this type of waveguiding are the so-called *BH laser* (*b*uried *h*eterostructure [7]) and the *CSP laser* (*c*hanneled *s*ubstrate *p*lanar [8]) where the dominant guidance is by a profile in the real or imaginary part of

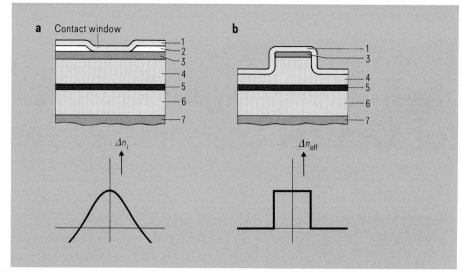

1 Metallization (TiPtAu)
2 Oxide mask (Al$_2$O$_3$)
3 Capping layer (p-GaAs)
4 Confining layer (p-GaAlAs)
5 Active layer (GaAs)
6 Confining layer (n-GaAlAs)
7 Substrate (n-GaAs)

Above: Cross-sections parallel to the mirror plane;
Below: Lateral profile of the imaginary refractive index n_i in the oxide-stripe laser and of the effective refractive index n_{eff} in the MCRW laser

Fig. 2 Structure and waveguiding mechanisms of oxide-stripe lasers (a) and MCRW lasers (b)

the refractive index. A laser from this family providing special fabrication advantages is the so-called *MCRW laser* (*m*etal *c*lad *r*idge *w*aveguide [9]), shown in **Fig. 2 b**.

With this laser structure, lateral current confinement and waveguiding are achieved in only one process step. The confinement of the diode current to the lasing stripe is due to blocking by the metal contact on the lightly doped layer in the region outside the stripe. At the same time, the increased reflection of the optical wave from the metallization on both sides of the mesa stripe produces a profile of the effective refractive index n_{eff} and hence an optical waveguide.

Since all these lasers have a permanent refractive index profile they are also known as *index-guided laser diodes (ILD)*.

Structure-related characteristics

The described differences in the structures are so fundamental that they produce widely differing application-specific laser characteristics (**Fig. 3**).

As regards *threshold current*, index-guided laser diodes are superior to gain-guided diodes in having values about a factor of 5 smaller. The heating in the former is therefore correspond-

ingly lower at the dc bias level required for high-bit-rate modulation.

The *spectrum* of ordinary Fabry-Perot lasers with dominant gain guidance consists of a greater or lesser number of spectral lines, decreasing with increasing optical power, the spacing between two longitudinal modes being given by the cavity length L, the refractive index n and its dependence on wavelength λ.

$$\Delta \lambda = \frac{\lambda^2}{2L\left(n - \lambda \dfrac{\mathrm{d}n}{\mathrm{d}\lambda}\right)} \qquad (1)$$

ILDs operating continuously tend to emit only one dominant spectral line at the peak of the gain curve. This characteristic is not, however, retained at high modulation rates. Since the spectral position of maximum gain varies with modulation, the dynamic spectrum broadens and the number of oscillating modes rises with the transmission rate. An increase in temperature causes the spectrum of both laser structure families to shift to longer wavelengths by a few tenths of a nanometer per K. In GLDs this merely produces a shift in the envelope, but in ILDs it may produce mode jumping.

The *far field* of the semiconductor laser, i.e. the spatial radiation distribution measured at a large distance from the laser mirror, is as a result of the small cavity dimensions (diffraction effect) inevitably wider than the radiation characteristic of conventional gas and solid-state lasers. It is also generally asymmetrical due to the differing longitudinal and lateral dimensions of the emitting area. The vertical dimensions of the dielectric waveguide in ILDs and GLDs are comparable, both producing the same half-power widths of about 40 to 60° for the radiation characteristic perpendicular to the p-n plane. In contrast, the lateral far fields of ILDs and GLDs with their differing waveguiding mechanisms produce differing half-power widths of typically 5 to 15° and 25 to 35° as well as different imaging characteristics. GLDs, in particular, with dominant gain guiding exhibit astigmatism due to the curved wave fronts for light propagating parallel to the p-n junction and this can adversely affect the launching of light into fibers.

The *launching* of laser beams into the optical waveguide poses some problems. At first sight it appears to be determined by the far field and astigmatism of the beam. However, maximum launching efficiency is not the sole objective, since it is also necessary to minimize the *feedback* of reflected light from the fiber system into the laser. The *optical feedback sensitivity* of laser diodes differs widely between the two laser families. In GLDs the optical feedback sensitivity is low, but in ILDs it is high due to their higher cavity Q factor. The benefit of an ILD with its narrow far field is lost, therefore, as a result of this effect under normal launching conditions.

Fig. 4   GaAlAs/GaAs oxide-stripe laser on Si substrate and metal heat sink

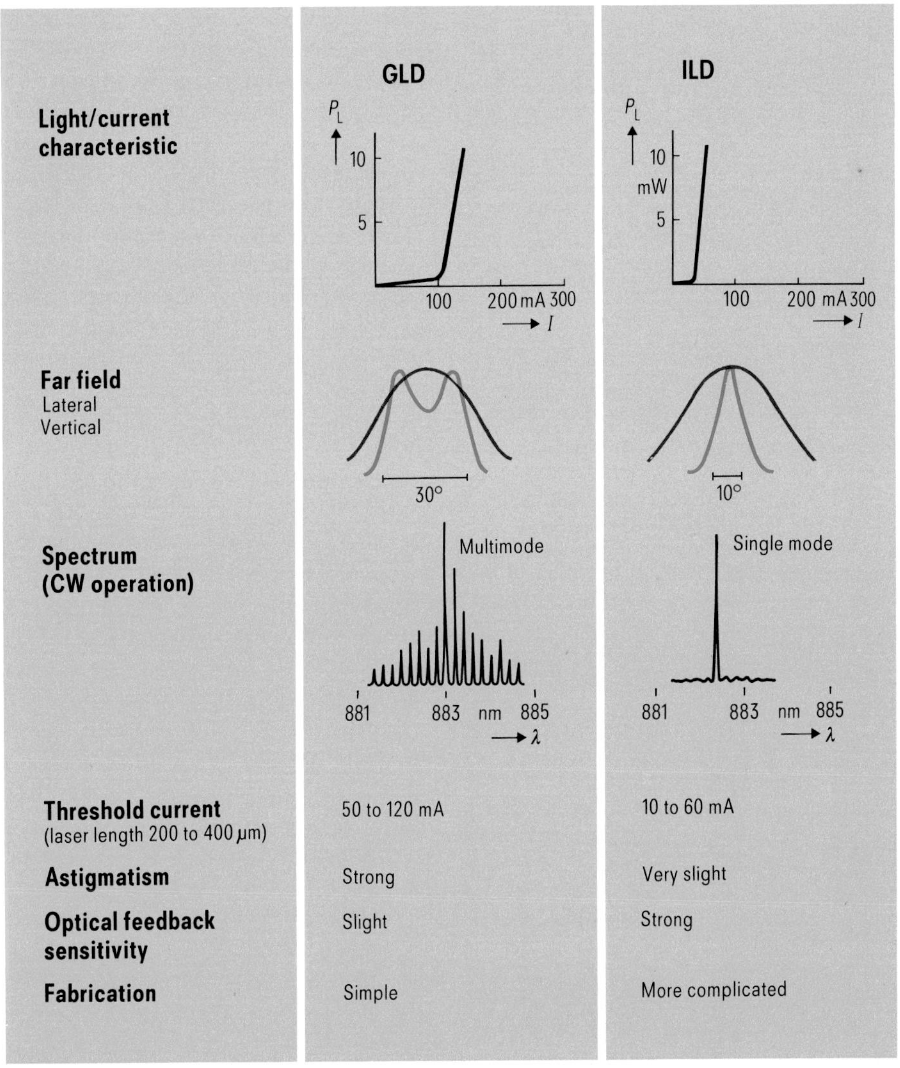

ILDs are generally also more demanding than GLDs as regards *fabrication technology*. The oxide-stripe laser is particularly simple in this respect.
This analysis shows how the choice of laser structure influences the system characteristics and links them with aspects of manufacture, leaving only a little room for optimization. Moreover, individual laser characteristics cannot be varied independently of other features.

Laser diodes for the first transmission window (800 to 900 nm)

The furthest advanced technically are lasers based on the GaAlAs material system for the wavelength range 820 to 880 nm. The long-wavelength limit is determined by the GaAs band gap. The short-wavelength limit can be moved to about 700 nm by increasing the Al content, without significantly affecting the laser characteristics.
Typical of the advanced state of development is the 880 nm GaAlAs/GaAs oxide-stripe laser (**Fig. 4**) [4] designed to a high degree of perfection for use in optical multimode systems. In this type of laser the high optical and electrical power densities typically occurring at the semiconductor laser mirrors (up to 10^6 W/cm^2) and contacts (around $5 \cdot 10^3$ W/cm^2) are now reproducibly and reliably controlled. In particular, the longstanding problem of *aging* has

	GLD	ILD
Light/current characteristic	P_L (mW), 10, 5 / 100 200 mA 300 → I	P_L (mW), 10, 5 / 100 200 mA 300 → I
Far field Lateral Vertical	30°	10°
Spectrum (CW operation)	Multimode / 881 883 nm 885 → λ	Single mode / 881 883 nm 885 → λ
Threshold current (laser length 200 to 400 µm)	50 to 120 mA	10 to 60 mA
Astigmatism	Strong	Very slight
Optical feedback sensitivity	Slight	Strong
Fabrication	Simple	More complicated

I Diode current   λ   Optical wavelength P_L Optical power

Fig. 3   Features of the two structure families GLD (gain-guided laser diode) and ILD (index-guided laser diode) exemplified by the GaAlAs/GaAs laser

been resolved to a point where the aging rates for principal operating parameters in laser diodes are as low as those of the best IREDs (infrared-emitting diodes [2]). This means that it has been possible to render specifically laser aging processes (e.g. mirror and contact aging) largely ineffective. Any remaining effects of residual aging are so slight that they can hardly be detected even with severe thermal loading on the laser, e.g. 100 °C over almost 10,000 h of operation (**Fig. 5**). This yields extrapolated room temperature operating lifetimes well above 100,000 h during which, for instance, the operating current required to maintain 5 mW optical power does not vary by more than 10 %.

The oxide-stripe laser is also characterized by the following features:

- relatively low sensitivity of the threshold current to temperature variations of up to 100 °C, i.e. the laser can be employed without a Peltier cooler,

- stable laser emission and no self-pulsing up to high temperatures,

- high stability up to high pulse powers (**Fig. 6**) and hence reduced sensitivity to spikes, e.g. from electronic supply and regulating circuits.

This laser is therefore particularly suitable for reliable transmission of large volumes of data over shorter routes of a few kilometers. The design and practical realization of a transmitter incorporating a GaAlAs oxide-stripe laser are described in [1].

Laser diodes for the second transmission window (1300 to 1600 nm)

Whereas in the first transmission window (800 to 900 nm) the achievable repeater spans are limited primarily by attenuation, in the second window (1300 to 1600 nm) the attenuation is lower making the dispersion characteristics of the fiber an important factor. As a result, the previously mentioned dynamic spectrum broadening of Fabry-Perot lasers becomes a limiting factor for transmission over long spans. However, a feature of the transmission band between 1300 and 1600 nm is that the overall dispersion of a single-mode fiber can be made to disappear almost completely at a par-

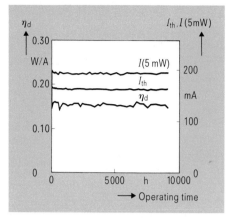

Fig. 5   880 nm GaAlAs oxide-stripe laser: operating current I for 5 mW per mirror, threshold current I_{th} and differential efficiency η_d as a function of operating time at a case temperature of 100 °C and an optical CW power of 5 mW per mirror

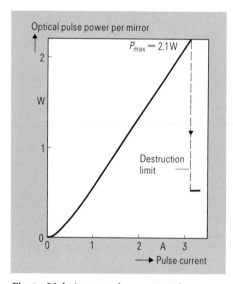

Fig. 6   Light/current characteristic for pulsed operation (pulse width 18 ns, repetition rate 100 kHz) up to the mirror power density limit P_{max} for a GaAlAs oxide-stripe laser (wavelength λ = 880 nm, contact stripe width 3 µm, cavity length 400 µm, case temperature 25 °C)

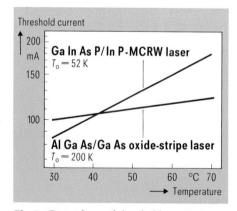

Fig. 7   Dependence of threshold current on temperature exemplified by a GaInAsP/InP MCRW laser compared with an AlGaAs/GaAs oxide-stripe laser

ticular wavelength [10], thus negating the effect of the dynamic broadening. This is most easily achieved at wavelengths around 1300 nm and explains the preference for this transmission wavelength in current practical systems.

Laser diodes for the long-wavelength range are fabricated predominantly from GaInAsP/InP. Principally, this system can cover the wavelength range from 900 to 1700 nm. In fact, owing to the minimum height required for the potential barrier at the heterojunctions on each side of the active region and the need for lattice matching to the InP substrate [2], the lower wavelength limit for GaInAsP/InP lasers suitable for CW operation lies at about 1200 nm. The GaInAsP/InP material system has essentially the same basic characteristics as the GaAlAs/GaAs systems but with one important difference: GaInAsP/InP laser diodes exhibit the "T_o problem". This is the growth of nonradiative recombination [2] with increasing wavelength which makes the realization of longer wavelength laser diodes increasingly difficult. The practical implications of this effect are the high temperature sensitivity of the threshold current I_{th} which is related to the characteristic temperature T_o via an exponential function

$$I_{th} \approx \exp{(T/T_o)} \qquad (2)$$

(T temperature in K).

In **Fig. 7** the high temperature sensitivity of the threshold current of the GaInAsP/InP laser diodes is clearly indicated by the greater slope in the threshold-temperature diagram compared with GaAlAs lasers. This unfavorable temperature response reduces the temperature range for CW operation of the 1300 nm laser diodes decisively. Since these restrictions partially negate the advantage of the GLD family due to their higher threshold currents, the balance in this transmission band shifts to the ILDs with their lower threshold currents.

Even in the 1300 nm wavelength range the MCRW laser is a particularly easy ILD to fabricate. **Fig. 8** shows one of these lasers mounted on a heat sink. In spite of the high temperature sensitivity of the quaternary lasers, the low threshold current of this particular

Fig. 8   GaInAsP/InP MCRW laser (1300 nm) mounted on heat sink (laboratory model)

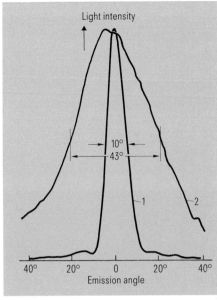

1 Lateral   2 Vertical

Fig. 10   Far-field distribution
of a GaInAsP/InP MCRW laser

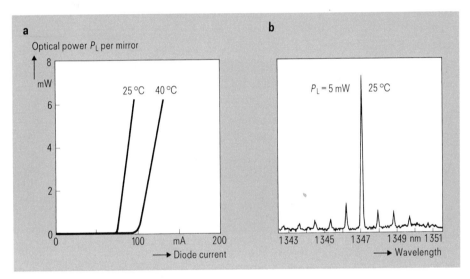

Fig. 9   Light/current characteristics (a) and spectrum (b) for CW operation
of a GaInAsP/InP MCRW laser

ILD enables the laser crystal to be mounted on copper heat sinks substrate down, i.e. using a relatively straightforward mounting technique. The light/current characteristics of such lasers plotted in CW operation are given in **Fig. 9 a** with a typical spectrum in **Fig. 9 b**. **Fig. 10** shows the long-wavelength MCRW laser field distributions controlling the launch into optical waveguide. The half-power width perpendicular to the p-n junction is defined, as for the oxide-stripe lasers, by the heterostructure and is typically between 40 and 50°. However, due to the index guiding, the MCRW structure has an emission angle parallel to the p-n junction which is a factor of 3 smaller than that of the oxide-stripe laser and thus facilitates launching, albeit at the cost of increased optical feedback sensitivity.

By exploiting the minimal dispersion of SiO_2-based optical waveguides at 1300 nm, it is possible to achieve repeater spacings exceeding 40 km at transmission rates up to 2 Gbit/s, as demonstrated in the laboratory by various working groups [11]. The achievable repeater spacing at this wavelength is predominantly attenuation-limited up to about 1 Gbit/s. Longer repeater spacings than those at 1300 nm are possible in the region of minimum

attenuation at about 1500 nm, providing that the strong material dispersion there in these fibers can be negated. This requires special measures to be adopted either at the fiber or at the transmitter. One measure is for the fiber to be suitably dimensioned (e.g. smaller core diameters, special refractive index profile) to compensate for the material dispersion and thus shift the overall dispersion minimum into the region around 1500 nm [10]. If, however, the price of this is an excessive attenuation increase (e.g. due to splices) or if the tighter tolerances due to the reduced fiber core diameter cannot be justified, there is still a possible solution in narrowing the dynamic laser diode spectrum to a dominant longitudinal mode. However, this can only be achieved by one of the following complicated approaches:

● Instead of using laser diodes with a Fabry-Perot cavity, distributed feedback lasers are employed [12]. It has so far only been possible to fabricate these devices with considerable technological complexity.

● The laser diode to be modulated is stabilized with a second laser diode which operates CW in a single mode ("injection locking").

● The single-mode dynamic spectrum is compelled by an external cavity or a double cavity.

• The optical power of a CW operating single-mode laser diode is modulated externally.

It is not yet clear which of these solutions is best suited to technical applications. In any event, the additional measures discussed make solutions for the region around 1500 nm far more complex than those for 1300 nm.

References

[1] Althaus, H. L.; Kuhn, G.: Modular Laser Source. telcom report 6 (1983) Special Issue "Optical Communications", pp. 84 to 90

[2] Weyrich, C.; Zschauer, K.-H.: Principles of Optoelectronic Signal Conversion. telcom report 6 (1983) Special Issue "Optical Communications", pp. 14 to 19

[3] Ripper, J. E.; Dyment, J. C.; D'Asaro, L. A.; Paoli, T. L.: Stripe-geometry double heterostructure junction lasers: Mode structure and CW operation above room temperature. Appl. Phys. Let., Vol. 18, pp. 155 to 157, February 1971

[4] Wolf, H. D.; Mettler, K.; Zschauer, K.-H.: High Performance 880 nm (Ga, Al) As/GaAs oxide stripe lasers with very low degradation rates at temperatures up to 120°C. Jpn. Journ. of Appl. Phys., Vol. 20, pp. L693 to L696, September 1981

[5] Dyment, J. C.; D'Asaro, L. A.; North, J.; Miller, B.; Ripper, J. E.: Proton-bombardment formation of stripe-geometry heterostructure lasers for 300 K CW operation. Proc. IEEE 60, 726 (1972)

[6] Marschall, P.; Schlosser, E.; Wölk, C.: New diffusion-type stripe-geometry injection laser. Electron. Let. 15, 38 (1979)

[7] Tsukada, T.: GaAs-Ga$_{1-x}$Al$_x$As buried-heterostructure injection lasers. J. Appl. Phys. 45 (1974), p. 4899

[8] Aiki, K.; Nakamura, M.; Kuroda, T.; Umeda, J.: Channeled-substrate planar structure (AlGa) As injection lasers. Appl. Phys. Let., Vol. 30, No. 12, 15. Juni 1977

[9] Amann, M.-C.: New contacting system for low-expense GaAs-AlGaAs light sources. Frequenz 34 (1980), pp. 343 to 346

[10] Tsuchiya, H.; Imoto, N.: Dispersion-free single-mode fiber in 1,5 µm wavelength region. Electron. Let. 15 (1979), pp. 476 to 478

[11] Yamada, J. Y.; Machida, S.; Kimura, T.: 2 Gbit/s optical transmission experiments at 1.3 µm with 44 km single mode fibre. Electron. Let. 17 (1981), pp. 479 to 480

[12] Ikegami, K.; Kuroiwa, K.; Itaya, Y.; Shinohara, S.; Hagimoto, K.; Inagaki, N.: 1.5 µm transmission experiment with distributed feedback laser. European Conference on Optical Communication, Cannes, September 1982

Hans Ludwig Althaus and Gerhard Kuhn

Modular Laser Source

The optoelectronic transducers in the transmitting and receiving equipment perform a key function in optical communications, since they have a decisive influence on the transmission quality of the entire system. In the selection of these components, maximum possible operating life as well as simplicity in operation are among the most important criteria, in addition to the performance of the optical transmitter and the sensitivity of the optical receiver. The laser module presented here is a particularly high-performance optical source which is suitable for universal application. Its modular design takes into account the special characteristics of the laser diode and the optical fiber.

Demands placed on an optical source

Particularly high demands are placed on optoelectronic transducers at the beginning and end of an optical fiber link, since they represent additional elements compared with a conventional transmission facility. Their behavior in the transmission system must be such that they introduce the minimum of restriction and complexity into the overall system. The demands with regard to long life and simplicity in operation must always be met. Operation under the normal environmental conditions and stresses must always be guaranteed. In addition, the transducer must not impair the high transmission quality of the optical fiber.

Particular importance attaches to the linearity of the optoelectronic conversion in the case of analog transmission.

Whereas detectors were available as ultralinear receiving elements for optical signals before the development of optical communications, suitable transmitters have only been developed in recent times. Due to their physical characteristics [1], the transmitters – above all the laser transmitters – are not easy components to deal with. Modular design has made a decisive contribution to converting the discrete laser source into a reliable and rugged component.

Characteristics of the discrete laser diode

The high transmission capacity and range of optical communications can only be fully exploited if laser diodes are used as optical sources [2, 3]. However, in order to be able to make optimum use of the principal advantages of this diode compared with other optical sources, such as light-emitting diodes (LED and IRED), a more elaborate arrangement is necessary to ensure stable operation and to protect the laser diode.

Fig. 1 shows typical light/current characteristics of light-emitting diodes and laser diodes at two different

Dipl.-Phys. Dr. rer. nat. Hans Ludwig Althaus and Dipl.-Phys. Dr. rer. nat. Gerhard Kuhn, Siemens AG, Components Division, Regensburg

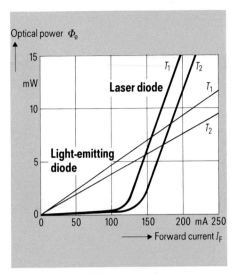

Fig. 1 **Light/current characteristics of laser and light-emitting diodes at $T_1 = 25°C$ and $T_2 = 60°C$**

operating temperatures. The fundamental differences can be clearly seen. Whereas the light-emitting diode emits significant optical power at very low currents ($I < 50$ mA), the optical power from the laser diode is very low and incoherent until a minimum current (threshold current) is reached, but then a coherent optical power rises very rapidly for a modest increase in current [2, 4].

The substantial advantages of the laser diode, but also its critical operating characteristic, are clearly evident from the characteristic curve:

• When lasing at currents above the threshold value it emits coherent radiation. The increase in useful power for

increasing current (e.g. differential efficiency $\eta \approx 0.2$ W/A) is orders of magnitude greater than that of the light-emitting diode, which above all affects the ability to modulate the radiation.

• It is clear that it is almost impossible to control the optical power by means of the current, since modest current variations result in huge changes in the optical power. Consequently, operation with constant light output is possible only by measuring the optical power.

• The thermal characteristic of the laser diode represents a further problem. Whereas the optical power from the light-emitting diode at constant current decreases by about 0.7% per Kelvin increase in temperature, the laser diode displays a parallel displacement of the characteristic towards higher currents. This means that a temperature increase of only a few Kelvin can result in the diode ceasing lasing action and emitting only incoherent radiation at low power level.

Good heat extraction and temperature stabilization of the laser diode are thus of fundamental importance for a constant optical power output [5].

Since the dimensions of the emitting aperture for the optical radiation in the plane of the mirror of the laser diode are of the same order of magnitude as the light wavelength [4], the radiated light is subject to diffraction effects and consequently the beam divergence is greater than in the case of gas lasers, for

instance. In addition, there is the astigmatism of the radiation field which results from a longitudinal displacement of the apparent emitting area from the lateral and transverse far field (**Fig. 2**).

Fig. 3 shows the light coupled into a typical graded-index fiber ($d_c = 50$ μm) for displacement of the fiber in the plane of the mirror and at right angles to it. The curves clearly indicate the accuracy with which the fiber must be aligned to the diode in order to make optimum use of the laser diode's high optical power. In spite of the divergence of the diode beam, up to 70% of the total radiation emitted by one mirror of the laser diode can be coupled into the fiber with good optical matching. Such values are unattainable with light-emitting diodes and infrared light emitting diodes [6, 7].

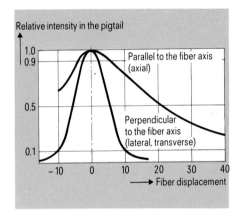

Fig. 3 **Light coupled from an oxide-stripe laser into a graded-index fiber with $d_c = 50$ μm**

The differing values for the light coupling into optical fibers can be attributed to the difference in optical power density and to the differing radiation patterns of the optical sources. Whereas infrared light-emitting diodes, e.g., produce typical optical power densities of about 4 W/cm² in the case of isotropic radiation, the optical power density at the emitting aperture of a laser diode is typically 1 MW/cm². For this reason the mirror facet of an operating laser diode is very sensitive to all environmental factors, such as dust, humidity and organic vapors, which would immediately burn into the emitting window region. The laser diode must be provided with effective protection against this danger.

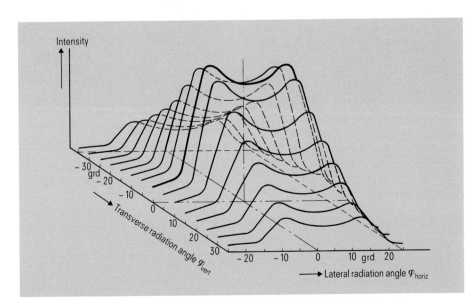

Fig. 2 **Far field of the oxide-stripe laser**

Function of the module

The purpose of the laser diode's modular design must be to eliminate the difficulties associated with the use of laser diodes in optical communications. The module is intended to be easy and reliable in application. The modular design principle is shown in **Fig. 4**. The central position is occupied by the laser diode which, with the aid of the modular design, is matched to the environment and to the fiber optic link. As can be seen in **Fig. 1**, regulation of the laser diode to produce a constant radiant power can be effected satisfactorily only by direct measurement of a quantity proportional to the emitted radiation. For this purpose, use is made in the laser module of the fact peculiar to laser diodes that mutually proportional radiation components are emitted from both mirrors in opposite directions. With suitable mounting of the diode chip on its carrier (primary heat sink), only the front laser mirror can emit radiation into the optical fiber. The rear mirror is used for radiant power measurement, a monitor diode receiving the emitted light and converting it into a proportional photocurrent which can be fed to an external control circuit.

The modular assembly in a hermetically sealed enclosure of the measurement, control and matching components necessary for laser operation is of great importance for optimum utilization of the specific characteristics of a laser diode. All demands made on a modern laser source for applications in optical fiber link systems are met by the Siemens laser module SFH 408 (**Fig. 5**).

Temperature control

The constant operating temperature in the module necessary for a constant radiant power is obtained by heat extraction via the primary heat sink and via suitable internal heat transfer to the external module wall, the secondary heat sink. In the case of passive heat transfer via the secondary heat sink, the temperature of the laser diode is principally dependent upon the temperature of this heat sink, and consequently assumes a temperature determined by it after a certain transient period. In

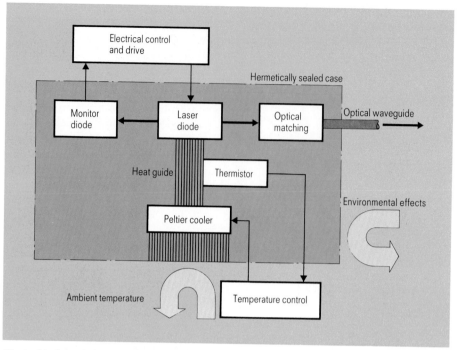

Fig. 4   Modular design principle of the laser source

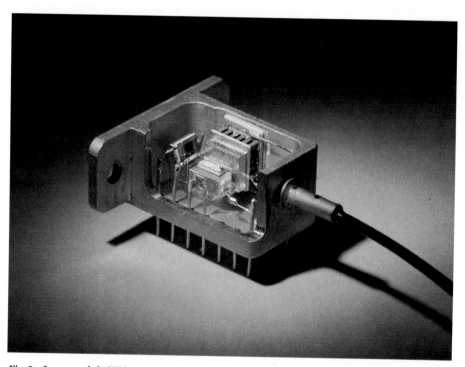

Fig. 5   Laser module SFH 408 with monitor diode, laser diode, connected pigtail and thermistor, as well as Peltier cooler (in background)

this case the laser diode is dependent upon the ambient temperature.

In the case of active heat transfer, the temperature of the laser diode can be set within certain limits ($\Delta T \approx 40$ K) by means of a Peltier cooler irrespective of the ambient temperature. For this purpose the cold side of the cooler incorporated in the module is con-

nected directly to the primary heat sink of the laser diode. The warm side of the cooler then transfers the heat via the wall of the enclosure to the secondary heat sink.

The temperature measurement necessary for temperature control is effected by means of a thermistor mounted on the primary heat sink [8]. With this

86

arrangement a temperature control circuit connected externally to the module can hold the temperature of the laser diode constant to within $< \pm 0.5\,\mathrm{K}$, regardless of the ambient temperature and the set laser power.

Optical matching

In order to couple a maximum possible linear proportion of the laser emission into the fiber, special attention must be paid to matching the diode to the optical fiber [2, 9 to 12]. In this modular design the laser diode/optical fiber interface is transferred into the module and a short pigtail is fed out. As a result, the coupling problem for the user is restricted to joining the pigtail to the optical fiber link.

The matching of the laser diode to the pigtail is effected inside the module. This makes it possible to couple various types of laser source to an optical fiber link to suit differing requirements:

● *Multimode laser diode and multimode optical fiber at a wavelength of $\lambda = 880\,nm$*

The light from the oxide stripe-laser is coupled into the pigtail by means of optically matching the end of the fiber in the vicinity of the laser facet. With suitable tapered fiber ends and attached spherical lenses, a coupling efficiency between 60% and 70% is possible (graded-index fiber, $d_c = 50$ μm and $A_N = 0.21$) [6, 9, 11].

The fiber can be aligned to the diode and fixed during laser operation, so that coupling of optimum laser power is possible (**Fig. 6**). With this type of coupling, the optical power level can be measured and controlled via the monitor diode (Si-PIN photodiode). A particularly fast regulation, comparable with the lasing delay, is possible with a monitor fiber arrangement via the laser rear mirror feeding the laser radiation directly to a detector (e.g. APD) outside the module.

● *Multimode laser diode and multimode optical fiber at a wavelength of $\lambda = 1300\,nm$*

Satisfactory operation of laser diodes for this wavelength region has been

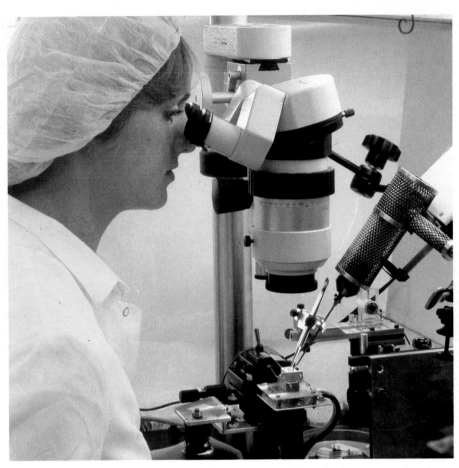

Fig. 6   Adjusting the pigtail in the module for optimum coupling to the laser

possible hitherto only with an active cooler, due to the diode's high temperature sensitivity [13]; a suitable arrangement is provided in the module. The light is coupled into the pigtail as previously described, regulation of the optical power level being possible via a photodiode with high sensitivity at $\lambda = 1300$ nm (e.g. GaInAs). In this case also, it is possible to measure the laser power outside the module via a monitor fiber.

● *Single-mode laser diode and single-mode optical fiber at a wavelength of $\lambda = 1300\,nm$*

Due to the very high demands made on the accuracy of the fiber-to-diode alignment in the case of single-mode operation (alignment accuracy < 0.2 μm at $d_c < 10$ μm), optimum light coupling into the fiber is only possible with a modular design [14, 15].

In all the cases mentioned above, the modular design serves to match the particular laser diode to the optical waveguide link.

Hermetic seal

The sensitivity of the highly stressed laser mirrors as well as the gap between the laser diode and the end of the pigtail (generally about 10 μm) necessitate absolute cleanness, in order to ensure constant light coupling. It is thus necessary to ensure that under normal operating conditions dust or dirt particles are not deposited and that condensation – possibly from organic solutions or humid air – do not effect the laser mirror and the optical fiber. The modular design meets these requirements by means of a hermetically sealed case. The sealing of all feedthrough connections and, above all, the pigtail also prevent any type of environmental effect on the laser diode and optical fiber.

Due to the use of only solder for attaching and fixing the individual components in the interior of the module, outgassing of organic solvents or constituents (e.g. from adhesives) is completely excluded even during extended operation.

Qualification and test methods

Measurements and inspections are repeatedly performed during the fabrication and assembly of laser diodes and modules, in order to assure quality. Every individual diode is accompanied by a record form on which all test results and characteristics observed during the course of the manufacturing process are recorded. Some of the more important checks and measurements are described in more detail below.

Testing the laser diode chip

Before the diodes are separated, i.e. when they are still joined together in a strip, they are subjected to the first test for laser operation. In order to assess the optical characteristic, a pulsed measurement is made up to an optical power of 10 mW at each laser mirror. The optical power radiation pattern can be measured in two spatial directions before the chips are separated from the strip. The measured half-power width of the optical power in both spatial directions is one of the criteria used for deciding whether the diode is suitable for incorporation in a module.

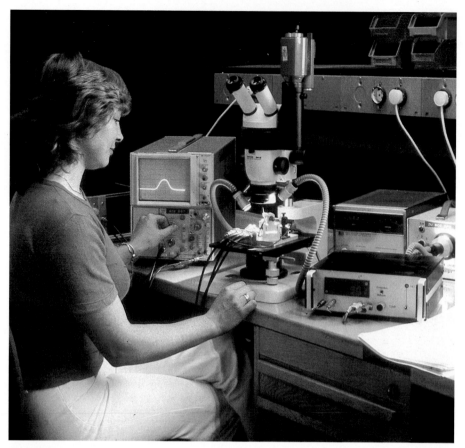

Fig. 7   Measurement of the characteristics

Measuring the characteristics

After the laser diode chips have been separated, they are mounted on separate copper blocks (primary heat sink) and a series of measurements is performed on these components to determine their characteristics (**Fig. 7**). The optical power is measured as a function of the forward current during CW operation, pulsed operation and pulsed operation with forward bias at various temperatures. The thermal resistance between the active region and the heat sink is determined from the difference between the threshold currents during CW and pulsed operation. Pulsed operation with forward bias results in a temperature increase in the active region. Variation of the heat sink temperature up to $T = 90\,°C$ yields the quantity T_0, which characterizes the temperature dependence of the laser threshold current. Similarly, the slope of the characteristic (differential efficiency η) can be checked and evaluated with the aid of the temperature. After a final visual inspection, the diodes are

Fig. 8   Measuring the lasing spectrum

checked with regard to lasing spectrum before they are subjected to a severe continuous test.

Life test

In order to detect any possible aging, each laser diode is operated under extreme conditions over a period of 14 days, during which it is continuously monitored. The burn-in process takes place at an ambient temperature of 90°C with the laser diode operated to produce an optical power of 5 mW at each mirror [5]. The set-up is so arranged that the entire light from one mirror is detected by a large-area photodiode. A control circuit sets the forward current of each laser diode so that an optical power of 5 mW is continuously received by the photodiode.

The aging of a laser diode is compensated by the control circuit by means of an increase in current, which in turn accelerates the aging process. This procedure permits prematurely degrading laser diodes to be detected with great certainty and subsequently rejected [16]. Following on the burn-in process, measurement of the entire range of characteristics as previously described is repeated.

Measuring the lasing spectrum

Measurement of the lasing spectrum supplies important information on the quality of the resonator and about the condition of the laser mirrors in the vicinity of the active region. A typical lasing spectrum for a laser diode with a resonator length of 400 µm can be seen in **Fig. 8**. The individual spectral lines correspond to the longitudinal modes of the laser resonator, the distance between two modes being $\Delta\lambda \approx 0.2$ nm and the half-power width of the envelope lying between one and a few nanometers. The powers in the individual modes of a laser are connected with the gain mechanism and are liable to exhibit small variations although the agregate power is constant (mode partition noise). However, a minimum number of modes is desirable, since this minimizes the effect of reflections on laser operation. Nevertheless, the envelope of the lasing spectrum must not become so wide that the possible transmission rate of about 1 Gbit/s is reduced [2]. Finally, a measured lasing spectrum yields information on self-

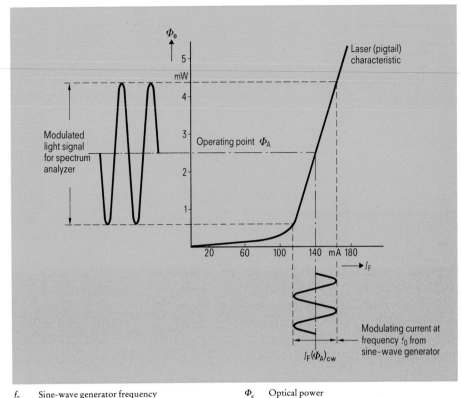

| f_0 | Sine-wave generator frequency | Φ_e | Optical power |
| Φ_A | Operating point | I_F | Forward current |

Fig. 9 Principle of the linearity measurement

pulsation of the laser diode, which manifests itself as a broadening, splitting or asymmetry of the individual modes. The half-power width of a single mode of a good laser diode is about 0.01 nm.

Coupling to the pigtail

The radiation pattern of the laser diode is measured at various optical powers before it is mounted in the module package. In addition, the possible coupling into the pigtail employed is

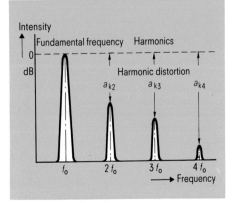

| a_k | Harmonic distortion |
| f_0 | Sine-wave generator frequency |

Fig. 10 Linearity measurement by means of spectrum analysis

determined with the aid of a laser with standardized far-field. These data permit the coupling efficiency attainable in the module and the linearity of the light in the fiber as a function of the laser diode forward current to be calculated in advance.

Module final test

Measurements are performed on the completed module which facilitate

- the assignment of the module to particular requirements,

- the acquisition of the data for the record accompanying each module, and

- quality control and inspection.

If, for instance, a module is required for analog data transmission, the user is interested in the linearity of the optical power at the operating point; typical test conditions are 2.5 mW CW optical power and 70% modulation factor. For this purpose a sinusoidal signal of suitable amplitude is superimposed on a constant laser diode forward current (**Fig. 9**). The light in the fiber is detected by a photodiode, the electrical signal from which is resolved into spectral components by a spectrum analyzer (**Fig. 10**).

Typical values for the harmonic distortion are $a_{k2} > 25$ to 35 dB and $a_{k3} > 35$ to 45 dB. Further measurements to determine the limiting frequency, the noise and the crosstalk coupling are important for wavelength division multiplex operation.

The final test begins with 75 h storage at $T = 70°C$ then follows 75 h operation of all components incorporated in the module. The Peltier cooler and the thermistor are so driven by their control circuit that a temperature of $T = 60°C$ results at the primary heat sink. A further control circuit drives the laser diode and the monitor diode such that the monitor diode detects an opti-

cal power of 5 mW. An optical power of about 2.5 mW is then coupled into the pigtail. None of the measured variables is allowed to go outside the permissible tolerances during the test.

The following are required for producing the final test record:

- curves of the optical power as a function of the forward current at various temperatures,

- forward voltage of the laser diode,

- the linearity of the light in the fiber as a function of the monitor diode current,

- lasing spectrum.

Each module is supplied with such a test record.

Future developments

Further development of the laser module will concentrate primarily on a reduction in size by using a monolithic internal structure with a cooler incorporated in the case, or without a cooler. The level of integration can certainly be raised in this way; for instance, the drive, control and protection circuits could be incorporated in the module package. In addition to extending the wavelength region into the visible spectral region (laser printing element, audio disc), laser diodes radiating at 1300 nm will also be incorporated in the SFH 408 module package in the near future. Further development of the module will proceed in close contact with the users.

References

[1] Panish, M. P.: Heterostructure injection lasers. Proc. of the IEEE 64 (1976), pp. 1512 to 1540

[2] Grau, G.: Optische Nachrichtentechnik. Berlin–Heidelberg–New York: Springer-Verlag 1981

[3] Geckeler, S.: Einführung in die Glasfaser-Nachrichtenübertragung: Grundlagen. Siemens AG, München 1980

[4] Mettler, K.: Planarer (GaAl)As-Oxid-streifenlaser für die optische Nachrichtentechnik. Siemens AG, München 1982

[5] Mettler, K.; Wolf, H. D.; Zschauer, K. H.: Calculation of the homogeneous degradation of injection laser parameters from initial degradation rates. IEEE, J. QE-14, 1978, No. 11, pp. 819 to 826

[6] Brackett, C. A.: On the efficiency of coupling light from stripe-geometry GaAs lasers into multimode optical fibers. J. Appl. Phys. 45 (1974), pp. 2636 and 2637

[7] Joyce, W. B.; Sachrach, R. Z.; Dixon, R. W.; Sealer, D. A.: Geometrical properties of random particles and the extraction of photons from electroluminescent diodes. J. Appl. Phys. 45 (1974), pp. 2229 to 2253

[8] Siemens Datenbuch: Heißleiter. Siemens AG, München 1982

[9] Kuwahara, H.; Furuta, H.: Efficient light coupling from semiconductor lasers into tapered hemispherical end fibers. Proc. IEEE 67 (1979), pp. 1456 and 1457

[10] Timmermann, C. C.: Highly efficient light coupling from GaAlAs lasers into optical fibers. Appl. Opt. 15 (1976), pp. 2432 to 2433

[11] Kato, D.: Light coupling from a stripe geometry GaAs diode laser into an optical fiber with spherical end. J. Appl. Phys. (1973), pp. 2756 to 2758

[12] Benson, W. W.; Pinnow, D. A.; Rich, T. C.: Coupling efficiency between GaAlAs lasers and low loss optical fibers. Appl. Opt. 14 (1975), pp. 2815 and 2816

[13] Arai, S.; Itaya, Y.; Kishino, K.; Suematsu, Y.; Moriki, K.; Wakao, K.; Iga, K.: 1.1 long wavelength semiconductor lasers. Jap. Ann. Rev. in Electr., Comp., and Telecom., Opt. Dev., and Fibers, Editor Y. Suematsu, 1982, pp. 1 to 19

[14] Kuwahara, H.; Sasaki, M.; Tohoyo, N.: Efficient coupling from semiconductor lasers into single-mode fibers with tapered hemispherical ends. Appl. Opt. (1980), pp. 2578 to 2583

[15] Weidel, E.: Light coupling from a junction laser into a monomode fibre with a glass cylindrical lens on the fibre end. Opt. Comm. 12 (1974), pp. 93 to 97

[16] Völkel, G.; Wallner, E.: Quality Assurance Methods for Optoelectronic Semiconductors. telcom report 6 (1983) Special Issue "Optical Communications", pp. 188 to 193

Manfred Plihal, Werner Späth and Reiner Trommer

Photodiodes as Detectors for Optical Fiber Transmission Systems

Whereas silicon photodiodes and silicon avalanche photodiodes are used for the transmission window of optical fibers in the wavelength region from 800 to 900 nm, germanium avalanche photodiodes are used for the transmission windows around 1300 and 1500 nm. Recent developments have been concentrated on realizing more sensitive receivers for the two longwave transmission windows than is possible with germanium avalanche photodiodes. In a development similar to that employed for optical sources, the photodiodes and avalance photodiodes for this purpose are being fabricated from III–V compound semiconductors and, in particular, from the material system InGaAsP/InP. The most sensitive receivers currently available for the longwave region and for bit rates up to 565 Mbit/s incorporate InGaAs/InP photodiodes with low-noise GaAs field-effect transistors as preamplifiers. Even greater sensitivities can be anticipated from receivers incorporating avalanche photodiodes fabricated from III–V compound semiconductors. However, in spite of very promising individual results the incorporation of such diodes into practical systems cannot yet be anticipated.

Photodiodes for wavelengths up to 1100 nm

Silicon photodiodes are particularly suitable for the optical fiber transmission window in the wavelength region from 800 to 900 nm. Their spectral responsivity ranges from the near ultraviolet into the infrared spectral region, with the long wavelength cutoff at about 1100 nm due to the silicon

Dipl.-Phys. Dr. rer. nat. Manfred Plihal,
Siemens AG,
Research and Development Division,
Munich;
Dipl.-Phys. Werner Späth,
Siemens AG,
Components Division, Munich;
Dipl.-Phys. Dr. rer. nat. Reiner Trommer,
Siemens AG,
Research and Development Division,
Munich

band gap. In [1] it is shown that infrared light in the wavelength region of the first transmission window has a very high penetration depth in silicon. Consequently, in order to realize more sensitive and simultaneously faster photodiodes, the charge carriers must be generated by the light, as far as possible, in a relatively thick depletion layer (about 10 µm). This boundary condition applies to both silicon photodiodes with internal gain as well as those without gain.

A highly developed silicon technology makes possible the production of photodiodes which are optimally adapted to the specific application with regard to spectral responsivity, speed of response and dark current. These diodes are currently fabricated almost exclusively by means of the planar technique.

PIN photodiodes

In the case of PIN photodiodes without gain the aforementioned requirement is met by separating the heavily doped n-layer from the heavily doped p-layer by means of a wide high resistance i-region. Even for small reverse voltages the depletion layer, and thus also the electrical field, extends over the entire i-region.

Fig. 1 shows schematically the construction of a diode with $p^+ \nu n^+$ structure, were ν indicates that the i-region is n-type. The infrared light passes through the p^+-layer into the diode; in order to prevent reflection losses the surface is coated with an Si_3N_4 layer. In contrast to the ν-region, the p^+ and the n^+ regions are kept very thin, so that the majority of the light is absorbed in the ν-region and long diffusion times of carriers from these neutral regions are prevented. The generated carrier pairs are separated in the depletion layer field in the ν-region, the electron drifting to the n^+ side and the hole to the p^+ side. For an electric field of 2 V/µm the carriers attain their saturation velocities, which for electrons amounts to 84 µm/ns and for holes 44 µm/ns. With a depletion layer width of 20 µm this velocity is reached for a reverse bias of 40 V and an electron then drifts through this distance in only 250 ps, while a hole takes about 500 ps. Since the majority of the light is absorbed in the vicinity of the $p^+\nu$ junction, this structure offers the advantage that, on average, the holes have to travel shorter distances than the electrons.

The quantum efficiency of such $p^+\nu n^+$ diodes is typically about 80%; the junction capacitance of a diode designed for optical fiber applications

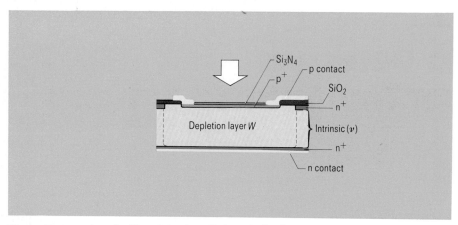

Fig. 1 Construction of a silicon PIN photodiode with $p^+\nu n^+$ structure

Fig. 2 PIN photodiode SHF 202

with an active area of 200 μm diameter amounts to 0.2 pF. The n^+-layers lying outside the light sensitive area on the top of the diode are intended to suppress surface leakage currents. The dark current then lies in the picoampere range. **Fig. 2** shows a diode type SFH 202.

Avalanche photodiodes

Due to the favorable characteristics of these silicon photodiodes without internal gain (low dark-current shot noise, small capacitance), amplifier noise generally predominates in optical receivers employing such diodes. Consequently, the receiver sensitivity can be substantially increased if photodiodes are employed in which internal current gain, resulting from avalanche multiplication of the generated charge carriers, is possible. Silicon is particularly favorably endowed in this con-

nection, since the ionization rates of the electrons (α) are very much greater than those of the holes (β) ($k = \beta/\alpha$ = 0.01 to 0.1). As a result, the excess noise resulting from the avalanche process and depicted by the excess noise factor F is very low ($F < 10$) [1].

In principle the PIN photodiodes described above can also be operated as avalanche photodiodes. However, they then have the following disadvantages:

● The voltage required to achieve the high field strength for avalanche multiplication in the ν-layer of the diodes is very high (≈ 1000 V).

● The total drift time of the charge carriers is increased by the avalanche built-up process. Since the multiplication region extends over a large part of the ν-layer, the diodes have only a very modest gain-bandwidth product. It is thus necessary to restrict the multiplication to a very narrow region of about 1 μm thickness.

The requirements for minimum possible voltage, high gain-bandwidth product and, in addition, high quantum efficiency are met by photodiode structures in which the electrical field shown in **Fig. 3** is established when an external voltage is applied. The high-field region with a maximum field strength E_m limits the multiplication to the narrow region W_L; this is followed by a wide region with a relatively low field E_d for charge carrier collection. For technological reasons such diodes are nowadays fabricated almost exclusively with an $n^+ p\pi p^+$ structure.

The diode has a guard ring to prevent edge breakdown and a channel stop to limit possible inversion layers on the surface. In order to reduce reflection losses at the receiving aperture, an anti-reflection coating of Si_3N_4 is applied.

As in the case of the PIN diode, the absorption of the infrared light and associated generation of carrier pairs takes place principally in the π-region, the holes being swept into the p^+-region while the electrons are injected into the p-layer in which avalanche multiplication takes place.

Such diodes, in which the depletion layer extends over the p and π-regions to the p^+-layer, are referred to as reach-through APDs (RAPD). The doping and geometric dimensions of the p and π-regions are, as far as possible, chosen such that, during operation of the diode, the saturation field strength for the generated carriers exists in the π-region.

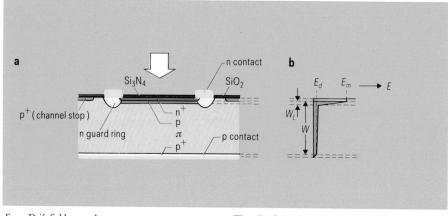

E_d	Drift field strength	W Depletion layer
E_m	Maximum field strength	W_L Avalanche region

Fig. 3 Construction (a) and electric field (b) of a silicon avalanche photodiode

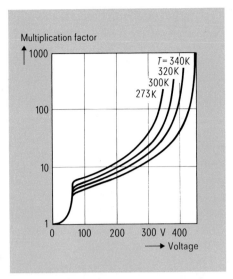

Fig. 4 Multiplication factor *M* of a silicon avalanche photodiode after [2] as a function of the voltage (temperature *T* as parameter)

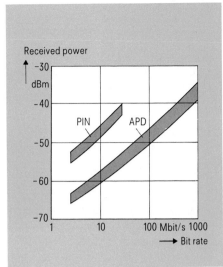

Fig. 5 Sensitivity of receivers with silicon PIN and avalanche photodiodes (APD) for the transmission window 800 to 900 nm at a bit error rate of 10^{-9}

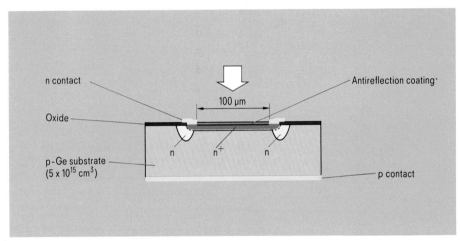

Fig. 6 Construction of a germanium avalanche photodiode with n⁺p structure

set between 930 and 1650 nm [1]. The physical characteristics of the compound semiconductor system InGaAsP/InP result in more favorable photodiode parameters than in the case of germanium; above all photodiodes with lower dark currents can be realized. However the problem lies in the fabrication of avalanche photodiodes, since

● these diodes with a pn-junction in InGaAsP exhibit tunneling without carrier multiplication, which is why it is necessary to resort to complicated structures with the high-field region of the pn-junction in InP and with an absorption layer of InGaAsP [1],

● in addition, the ratio of the ionization coefficients *k* of holes and electrons in germanium and indium phosphide attains values from 2 to 3, which is why avalanche photodiodes fabricated from these materials exhibit a substantially higher excess noise than silicon diodes [1].

Consequently, for high sensitivity receivers in the two longwave transmission windows the following photodiodes are currently available or under development:

● photodiodes with low dark current fabricated from InGaAsP,

● avalanche photodiodes fabricated from germanium, and

● avalanche photodiodes fabricated from III–V alloys, mainly InGaAsP/InP, but whose development is not yet completed.

Germanium photodiodes

Fig. 6 shows a structure for germanium avalanche photodiodes [3] for 1300 nm which makes minimum demands on technology and is consequently one of the most frequently used. The diode consists of a lightly doped p-type germanium substrate ($p \approx 5 \cdot 10^{15}$ cm⁻³) with an n⁺p-junction produced on the surface by diffusion or ion implantation. To prevent edge breakdown the n⁺-layer is surrounded by a lightly n-doped guard ring. The infrared-light sensitive area typically has a diameter of 100 μm and, due to the shading by the ring-shaped p contact, is smaller than the area of the n⁺p-junction. The surface of the diode is passivated by an

Fig. 4 shows typical curves of the multiplication factor *M* of a RAPD as a function of the applied voltage with temperature as the parameter. At low values of *M* only the p-region is depleted and *M* rises steeply. Subsequently the π-region is depleted; the maximum field strength E_m increases only slightly until finally the breakdown voltage of the diode is reached.

In optical fiber transmission systems the diodes are usually operated with gains less than 100 at reverse voltages between 100 and 400 V. As in the case of the PIN diode, the rise time at such gains is determined by the carrier drift time in the π-region, if no limitation is imposed by the RC time constant. The receiver sensitivities attained using PIN and avalanche photodiodes in

the transmission window from 800 to 900 nm are shown in **Fig. 5**.

Photodiodes for wavelengths from 1100 to 1600 nm

Due to the declining absorption above 1100 nm, silicon photodiodes and avalanche photodiodes cannot be employed for the two optical fiber transmission windows at 1300 and 1500 nm. Germanium and alloys of various III–V compound semiconductors are available as alternative semiconductor materials with adequately high absorption coefficients. As in the case of the optical sources, the preferred material system of the III–V alloys is InGaAsP/InP, with which cutoff wavelengths of the responsivity corresponding to the band gaps can be

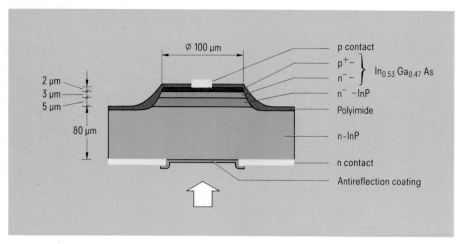

Fig. 7 Construction of an $In_{0.53}Ga_{0.47}As/InP$ photodiode without gain

$M = 10$ can be attained with technically more difficult to realize p^+n and n^+np doping sequences [5, 6], in which predominantly holes from the n-layer initiate the avalanche multiplication.

The diode structures described above are not suitable for wavelengths above 1500 nm, due to the fact that the absorption coefficients are substantially lower than for 1300 nm. Germanium photodiodes optimized for this wavelength region should be structured simular to the silicon photodiodes. Diodes with a p^+nn^- doping sequence have already been fabricated [7].

oxide (e.g. SiO_2). An anti-reflection coating increases the quantum efficiency of this diode.

The absorption coefficient of germanium for wavelengths shorter than 1500 nm lies in the vicinity of $10^4/cm$ [1]. On absorption of infrared light with a wavelength of 1300 nm all electron-hole pairs are thus generated within a layer 1 to 2 μm thick beneath the surface. As a consequence, the thickness of the n^+-region of the diode determines whether the absorption takes place predominantly in the n^+ or the p-layer, and whether, as a result, holes from the n^+-layer or electrons from the p-layer reach the high-field region and there contribute to the current gain by carrier multiplication. In this way the thickness of the n^+-region likewise influences the important diode characteristics quantum efficiency and excess noise from the avalanche process, as well as the rise time, for which optimum values are obtained for an n^+-region width of 400 nm. With an anti-reflection coating such diodes have a quantum efficiency of 80%; at a current gain of $M = 10$ the excess noise factor $F = 11$. At room temperature and voltages below the breakdown value of about 25 V, the photodiodes exhibit a dark current of 0.1 μA, and this increases by an order of magnitude for a temperature increase of 20 K. Receivers equipped with these diodes attain sensitivities of -46, -40 and -35 dBm for bit rates of 34, 140 and 565 Mbit/s at bit error rates of 10^{-9} [4].

Somewhat more favorable excess noise factors (e.g. $F = 7$) at a current gain of

Fig. 8 $In_{0.53}Ga_{0.47}As/InP$ photodiode in which the pigtail is threaded through the ceramic substrate on to the light sensitive anti-reflection coating of the diode

$In_{0.53}Ga_{0.47}As/InP$ photodiodes with low dark current

Fig. 7 shows the structure of a photodiode without internal gain with low dark current for which n^-- and p^+-$In_{0.53}$-$Ga_{0.47}As$ layers were grown on an InP substrate by liquid phase epitaxy [8, 9]. The mesa diode is illuminated through the substrate, which is transparent for wavelengths above 950 nm. This procedure avoids surface recombination of the charge carriers generated by the photons, and results in the attainment of high quantum efficiency.

In addition, the active area is not shaded by contacts, and capacitance and dark current can be kept low. Fig. 8 shows a diode fabricated in this way on a ceramic substrate.

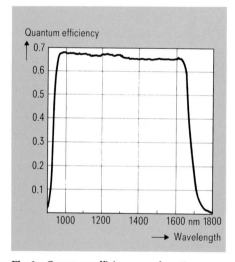

Fig. 9 Quantum efficiency as a function of wavelength for an $In_{0.53}Ga_{0.47}As/InP$ photodiode

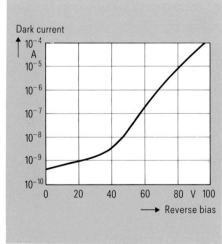

Fig. 10 Reserve-bias characteristic of an $In_{0.53}Ga_{0.47}As/InP$ photodiode

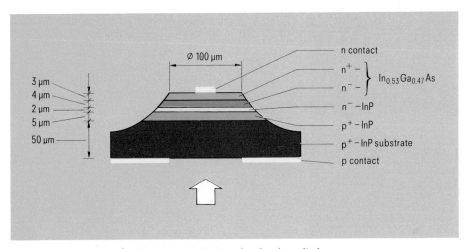

Fig. 11 Construction of an $In_{0.53}Ga_{0.47}As/InP$ avalanche photodiode with the pn junction in the InP region

The quantum efficiency of these diodes without an anti-reflection coating amounts to 65 to 70% for wavelengths between 950 and 1650 nm (**Fig. 9**). By deposition of a suitable Si_3N_4 coating, the quantum efficiency can be increased to about 90% for the desired wavelength region around 1300 or 1500 nm. The characteristic in **Fig. 10** rises slowly up to reverse voltages around 40 V; thereafter the dark current rises almost exponentially with the voltage. This behavior has been identified as tunneling; the avalanche breakdown and associated high multiplication of the photocurrent cannot be reached. At an operating reverse voltage of 10 V, state-of-the-art diodes exhibit junction capacitances below 0.5 pF, dark currents of about 1 nA, quantum efficiencies of about 90%, as well as rise and fall times of about 200 ps. When used in hybrid PIN-FET receivers, these diodes permit the attainment of receiver sensitivities of −51, −46 and −38 dBm for bit rates of 34, 140 and 565 Mbit/s [4].

$In_{0.53}Ga_{0.47}As/InP$ avalanche photodiodes

The problem of tunneling can be resolved by a special diode structure; a suitable heterojunction diode, whose structure is shown in **Fig. 11**, is currently being developed [9]. As in the case of the PIN diode, illumination takes place through the substrate, however, the pn-junction is not located in the absorbing $In_{0.53}Ga_{0.47}As$-layer but in the InP-layer. As a result, a region of high electrical field strength is formed

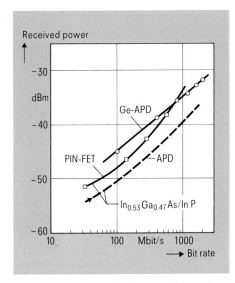

Fig. 12 Sensitivity of receivers with InGaAs photodiodes (PIN-FET combination), germanium and InGaAs avalanche photodiodes for wavelengths around 1300 nm at a bit error rate of 10^{-9}

in the n^--InP-layer where avalanche breakdown can be more readily achieved. In order to collect the holes generated by the photons, it is only necessary to establish a low field in the $In_{0.53}Ga_{0.47}As$-layer. Current gains M up to 50 have already been achieved with these diodes with dark currents of a few microamperes at $M = 10$.

The other characteristics of this type of diode – capacitances of about 0.3 pF, an internal quantum efficiency of over 90%, as well as rise and fall times less than 300 ps – make it appear very promising. An increase in the receiver sensitivity of 4.8 dB over that attainable with a photodiode without internal gain has been measured at a bit rate of

45 Mbit/s [10]. Due to the sharply rising amplifier noise, a corresponding improvement should be possible for higher bit rates also.

The attainable sensitivities of receivers with InGaAs photodiodes (PIN-FET combinations) as well as with germanium and InGaAs avalanche photodiodes at wavelengths around 1300 nm are shown in **Fig. 12**.

References

[1] Weyrich, C.; Zschauer, K.-H.: Principles of Optoelectronic Signal Conversion. telcom report 6 (1983) Special Issue "Optical Communications", pp. 14 to 19

[2] Müller, J.: Advances in electronics and electron. devices. New York: Pergamon Press 1980

[3] Ando, H.; Kanbe, H.; Kimura, T.; Yamaoka, T.; Kaneda, T.: Characteristics of germanium avalanche photodiodes in the wavelength region of 1–1.6 μm. IEEE J. of Quantum Electron. 14 (1978), pp. 804 to 809

[4] Smith, D. R.; Hopper, R. C.; Smyth, P. P.; Wake, D.: Experimental comparison of a germanium avalanche photodiode and an InGaAs PINFET receiver for longer wavelength optical communication systems. Electron. Let. 18 (1982), pp. 453 and 454

[5] Kaneda, T.; Fukuda, H.; Mikawa, T.; Banba, Y.; Tayama, Y.: Shallow junction p^+-n germanium avalanche photodiodes (APD's). Appl. Phys. Let. 34 (1979), pp. 866 to 868

[6] Kaneda, T.; Kagawa, S.; Mikawa, T,; Toyama, Y.: An n^+-n-p germanium avalanche photodiode. Appl. Phys. Let. 36 (1980), pp. 572 to 574

[7] Yamada, J.; Kawana, A.; Nagai, H.; Kimura, T.: 1.55 μm optical transmission experiments at 2 Gbit/s using 51.5 km dispersion-free fibre. Electron. Let. 18 (1982), pp. 98 to 100

[8] Trommer, R.; Heinen, J.: Liquid-phase epitaxy of (In,Ga) (As,P) and (In,Ga) As on InP for 1.3 μm high radiance IREDs and for photodiodes in the 1.3 μm to 1.65 μm wavelength range. Siemens Forsch.- u. Entwickl.-Ber. 11 (1982), pp. 204 to 208

[9] Trommer, R.; Kunkel, W.: $In_{0.53}Ga_{0.47}As/$ InP PIN and avalanche photodiodes for the 1 μm to 1.6 μm wavelength range. Siemens Forsch.- u. Entwickl.-Ber. 11 (1982), pp. 216 to 220

[10] Forrest, S. R.; Williams, G. F.; Kim, O. K.; Smith, R. G.: Excess noise and receiver sensitivity measurements of $In_{0.53}Ga_{0.47}$ As/InP avalanche photodiodes. Electron. Let. 17 (1981), pp. 917 to 919

Günter Knoblauch and Hans-Norbert Toussaint

Connectors for Fiber-Optic Components and Systems

Connectors in optical transmission paths provide a simple and reproducible means by which two fiber-optic components can be coupled together with minimum loss and, if required, easy demountability. Components in this sense include not only lines, filters and optical couplers but also the optoelectronic transducers at the transmit and receive ends. Differing requirements are placed on the mechanical tolerances of the connector parts depending on the core diameter of the fiber used and the specified connector insertion loss. On a connector designed, for example, for graded-index fibers with a core diameter of 50 µm the tolerances on the critical dimensions of the connector parts must not exceed approximately 1 µm. The resulting connector insertion loss is, however, also largely a function of the fiber tolerances.

Principles of demountable connectors

Connectors for optical signal transmission can be divided into two groups according to function. The first group is based on the principle of *end-fire coupling* (**Fig. 1**), the second on *lens coupling* (**Fig. 2**). A feature of the former is that the optical exit and entrance faces are arranged parallel and in close proximity to one another. From a functional point of view it is unimportant whether the exit face is the end of a fiber or the window of an emitting diode or whether the entrance face is the end of a fiber or the silicon surface of a photodiode.

Fig. 1a shows the coupling of a large exit face to a small entrance face. This case arises in practice when, for example, the radiation from a large-area emitting diode is to be launched into a thin fiber. It is evident that high losses will occur in this situation.

Fig. 1b shows the case in which the exit and entrance faces are of equal size. In practice this condition is fulfilled (at least theoretically) when two fibers with identical core diameters are coupled together in a connector. If the two fibers additionally have identical numerical apertures, this is referred to as *symmetrical end-fire coupling*. This has a "reciprocal" transmission characteristic, i.e. insertion loss is equal in both transmission directions.

Lastly **Fig. 1c** shows how a large entrance face is coupled to a small exit face. In this case virtually the entire radiation emerging through the exit face is accepted by the entrance face and the insertion loss is low. This is equivalent in practice to coupling a large-area photodiode to a (relatively) thin fiber.

Lens coupling (**Fig. 2**) employs lenses or other optical imaging systems for coupling the exit face to the entrance face.

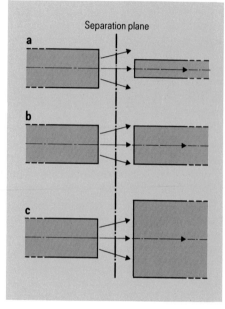

Fig. 1   End-fire coupling
a   Exit face larger than entrance face
b   Exit face and entrance face of equal size
c   Exit face smaller than entrance face

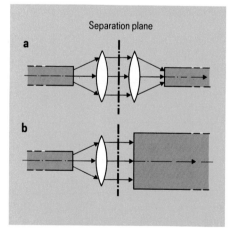

Fig. 2   Lens coupling
a   Symmetrical arrangement with identical imaging systems and equally sized exit and entrance faces
b   Asymmetrical arrangement with dissimilar imaging systems and differently sized exit and entrance faces

Dipl.-Ing. Günter Knoblauch and
Dipl.-Ing. Dr.-Ing. Hans-Norbert Toussaint,
Siemens AG,
Safety and Security Systems Division,
Munich

Fig. 2 a illustrates a symmetrically designed connector with lens coupling. This employs identical imaging systems, with the exit and entrance faces of equal size. The practical advantage of connectors employing this principle is that they permit greater mechanical tolerances at the junction (symbolically represented in **Fig. 2 a** by the "separation plane"). However, this advantage brings penalties which will be considered later.

In the asymmetrical lens-coupling configuration (**Fig. 2 b**) the imaging systems on either side of the separation plane are not identical and the exit and entrance faces are also of different size. This is equivalent in practice to coupling a fiber to the relatively small exit face of a Burrus diode with a spherical lens.

The following designs rely exclusively on the end-fire coupling principle. There are two main reasons for this:

● Apart from special situations such as semiconductor diodes being coupled to optical fibers with spherical lenses, it is preferable in practice to use connectors with end-fire coupling.

● For coupling two precisely aligned fibers of identical diameter a connector based on the lens-coupling principle basically provides no better results (i.e. lower insertion losses) than a connector employing end-fire coupling. On the contrary, due to additional losses introduced by the imaging system and reflections at the individual boundary layers of different refractive index, the losses of a lens-coupling connector are in general markedly higher than those of a connector employing end-fire coupling.

The following considerations apply only to connections between two identical fibers per **Fig. 1**; this case is the most important in practice. However, a detailed analysis of this case will provide information which is also applicable to the two special cases (exit face much larger or smaller than the entrance face).

Connector insertion loss

Test method

The transmission quality of a connector is evaluated by considering its insertion loss, i.e. calculating the amount by which the loss of an optical

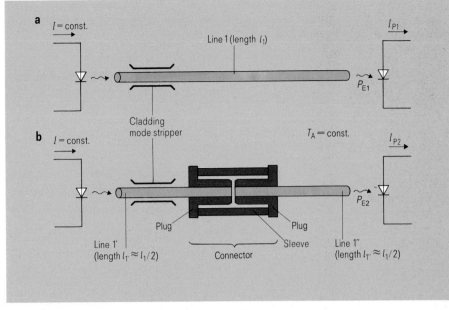

| I_P | Photocurrent | | P_E | Receive power |
| l | Line length | | T_A | Ambient temperature |

Fig. 3 Test method to determine the insertion loss of a connector using identical fibers on both sides of the connection
a Power measurement without connector (reference measurement)
b Power measurement with connector inserted

transmission link increases when an additional connector is inserted.

It is evident that connector insertion loss is not only a function of the tolerances on the connector parts but also of the fiber tolerances. In order to identify just the effects of the connector tolerances, the connector manufacturer is therefore interested in a test method in which identical fibers are employed on both sides of the connector (**Fig. 3**).

Initially a reference measurement is performed (**Fig. 3 a**). For this purpose the input endface of line 1 is optimally aligned to the source diode in all three axes using a micromanipulator. The output endface is similarly aligned to the detector diode. The photocurrent furnished by the detector diode is proportional to the received power P_{E1}. Line 1 is next cut through approximately in the center with the input and output coupling conditions unchanged, then a plug is mounted on each free line end (**Fig. 3 b**). These two plugs are mechanically mated in a sleeve to form the connector whose insertion loss is to be measured. After insertion of the connector the detector diode photocurrent decreases to a value proportional to power P_{E2}. The connector insertion loss can now be

calculated according to the relationship

$$a_c = 10 \log (P_{E1}/P_{E2}).$$

In this test method the effects due to the fiber are largely eliminated; core eccentricity and ellipticity are the only sources of measurement error. The disadvantage of this method is that

● mounting plugs on lines whose ends must remain aligned in micromanipulators is very involved and

● the end user is ultimately interested in the attenuation of connectorized fiber optic cables and not in the insertion loss of a single connector.

A test method more closely related to practical requirements is shown in **Fig. 4**. In **Fig. 4 a** a connection is initially established between the optoelectronic transducers (source and detector diodes) via a connectorized reference line L_B. The detector diode furnishes a current proportional to reference power P'_{E1}. The line to be measured L_M is then inserted (**Fig. 4 b**); the detector diode now furnishes a photocurrent corresponding to the reduced power P'_{E2}. The insertion loss of the connector set St 2/St 3 can now be calculated from the relationship

$$a_c = 10 \log (P'_{E1}/P'_{E2}),$$

provided the following conditions are fulfilled:

- The loss of the fiber being measured is either known or negligible compared with the connector insertion loss.
- The effect of plug St4 on signal coupling to the transducer at the receive end is the same as that of St2 (if plug St2 were to cause additional losses e.g. due to dirt on the endface, it would automatically be attributed to connector St2/St3 in view of the approach adopted).

The advantage of a measurement meeting practical needs by enabling connectorized fiber optic cables to be tested, is balanced by the serious disadvantage that the measured insertion loss can be considerably affected by fiber tolerances.

For the test methods shown in **Figs. 3** and **4** care must naturally be taken to ensure defined and reproducible launch conditions, without which no comparable attenuation measurements can be performed [3]. Thus, in the case of graded-index fibers, the length of lines L_B and L_M in Fig. 4 should be at least 500 m in order to permit establishment of a stable mode distribution.

Before going into further detail on the specific features of the two test methods considered, an analysis is provided of the elements contributing to the insertion loss [4].

General factors

The following relationships are directly applicable only to step-index fibers,

but may also be regarded as having qualitative relevance to graded-index fibers.

Axial fiber misalignment is the most critical tolerance factor (**Fig. 5a**). For example, an axial (transverse) offset of around 30% (equivalent to 30 μm for a fiber with core diameter of 100 μm) is sufficient in itself to introduce a loss of approximately 2 dB.

Fig. 5b shows the effect of *angular misalignment* between the two fiber axes. The smaller the numerical aperture of the two fibers (the more collimated therefore the radiation), the greater the loss produced by a given angular misalignment.

Fig. 5c shows attenuation as a function of the *separation* between the two fiber endfaces. The essential factor here is that the resultant attenuation is largely a function of the numerical aperture. As the latter is not a constant for any given fiber but is affected by the launch conditions, this loss component can be manipulated within certain limits. If, for instance, line 1 (**Fig. 3**) or line L_B (**Fig. 4**) is selected sufficiently long (e.g. 1 km for a 50 μm fiber), the higher-order modes are virtually eliminated due to absorption. The resultant, effectively smaller numerical aperture A_N produces a lower loss value a_d.

A generally applicable factor to bear in mind are the "Fresnel losses" due to reflection at the glass-air interfaces.

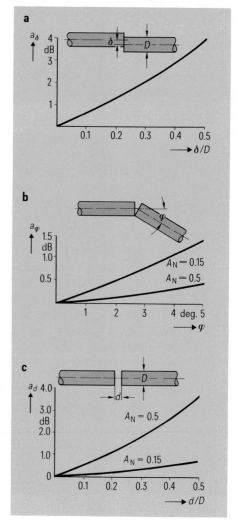

Fig. 5   General factors

a   Loss a_δ due to axial fiber misalignment δ/D

b   Loss a_φ due to angular misalignment φ between the fiber axes (parameter illustrated: numerical aperture A_N)

c   Loss a_d due to fiber end separation d/D (parameter illustrated: numerical aperture A_N)

These losses for the fiber end – air – fiber end combination are 0.35 dB and must always be included if there is an air gap between the endfaces (see **Figs. 5b** and **5c**). The Fresnel losses can be reduced by applying a dielectric coating and/or index-matching liquid. However, as a film of water between the fiber ends also reduces the losses due to reflections, the endfaces must be thoroughly cleaned and dried prior to measurement (without damaging the fiber faces).

Clearly, the surface finish of the endface will also affect the insertion loss. *Endface roughness* per **Fig. 6a** not only produces absorption centers but

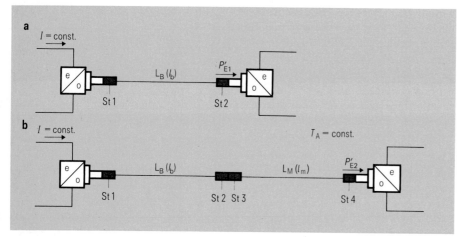

e/o	Optoelectronic transducer	P_E	Receive power
I	Photocurrent	St	Connector
o/e	Optoelectronic transducer	T_A	Ambient temperature

Fig. 4   Test method to determine the insertion loss of a connector on a short, preconnectorized line

a   Power measurement on reference line L_B (reference measurement)

b   Power measurement with line under test L_M inserted

also causes increased light scattering. It may be assumed to a first approximation that a fiber endface with a peak-to-valley height of 10 µm introduces a loss of around 0.5 dB. Nonperpendicular endfaces as in **Fig. 6b** have an effect akin to angular misalignment of the fiber axes. The effect of such nonperpendicularity can be estimated from **Fig. 5b** by substituting the nonperpendicular angle Θ for the angular misalignment φ.

The above factors relate primarily to tolerances occurring in a connector and to poorly finished fiber endfaces. In this context it is worth mentioning that a clearance of as little as 2 µm between plug and sleeve (see schematic connector diagram in **Fig. 3b**) is sufficient, under otherwise ideal conditions, to introduce a loss of 0.2 dB in a mated connector inserted into a 50 µm graded-index fiber.

The insertion loss of a connector for fiber bundle lines is determined – ignoring other factors – by the degree of overlapping between several opposing individual fiber ends. Practical fiber bundle connector insertion losses are between 0.5 and 3.5 dB.

Fiber-related factors

The following paragraphs analyze those connector losses attributable to fiber tolerances.

One factor is due to tolerances on the *numerical aperture* A_N and this arises whenever the A_N of the transmitting fiber is greater than that of the receiving fiber (**Fig. 7a**). This must be borne in mind and, if necessary, allowed for when measuring insertion loss with the setup shown in **Fig. 4**.

Core diameter tolerances (**Fig. 7b**) have a similar effect on the insertion loss whenever the core diameter of the transmitting fiber is larger than that of the receiving fiber. Thus a core diameter variation of −5%, i.e. involving a transition to a smaller diameter fiber, such as may occur even with allegedly "identical fibers" (fibers from the same batch), will introduce an additional loss of around 0.5 dB.

The transition to a larger fiber is not in itself critical and is used selectively in certain applications, e.g. for coupling

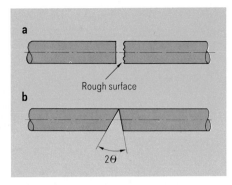

Fig. 6   Definition of surface finish on fiber endfaces
a   Rough fiber endface finish
b   Fiber endface nonperpendicularity Θ

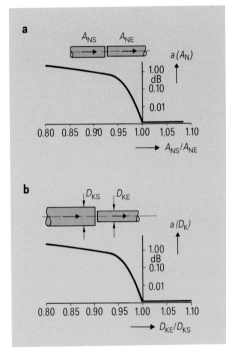

A_{NE}	Numerical aperture of receive fiber
A_{NS}	Numerical aperture of transmit fiber
D_{KE}	Core diameter of receive fiber
D_{KS}	Core diameter of transmit fiber

Fig. 7   Fiber-related factors affecting connector loss
a   Loss $a(A_N)$ due to numerical aperture tolerances
b   Loss $a(D_K)$ due to core diameter tolerances

the fiber pigtail of a laser source to the link fiber.

During fiber fabrication, particular importance is attached to minimizing *fiber tolerances*. Nevertheless, core ellipticity, index errors, eccentricities and inhomogeneities etc. may occur in step-index fibers. These defects generally only occur in small sections along the fiber and are often negligible in terms of the transmission charac-teristics. However, if a connector is inserted in one of these sections, such defects have the same effect as a (difficult to detect) area mismatch.

It should be pointed out here that the practice employed by some connector manufacturers, of specifying connector insertion losses for "ideal fibers", has little relevance to practical conditions and, consequently, should not be adopted.

Requirements on fiber-optic connectors

Generally speaking the same requirements are always placed on connectors for optical signal transmission,

- ease of assembly,
- rugged design,
- low loss,
- reproducible loss values after repeated matings,
- protection of the fiber endfaces.

The cost involved in meeting these requirements, e.g. with respect to attenuation, varies according to fiber design.

Connectors for single fibers

Single-fiber connectors should be optimized for assembly (pre-connectorization of cables), performance data and product costs. **Fig. 8** shows a plug which was developed for step-index and graded-index fibers and is already field-proven.

The ferrule diameter is 2.5 mm and conforms to the DIN 47 255 draft standard. The cable is adequately secured in the plug by crimping. A range of ferrules with different precision bores (bore diameter reduction in 3 µm decrements) is available to suit the various fiber diameters and compensate for fiber-diameter tolerances.

Fig. 9 shows a special-purpose design in which the connector contains a glass capillary for fiber support. Due to the relatively long support for the fiber in the capillary, angular misalignments can be largely eliminated. Connectors of this type are less suitable for field assembly than for producing short precision fiber pigtails connectorized at one end and subsequently spliced onto the main cable.

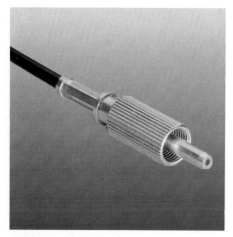

Fig. 8 Connector for step-index
and graded-index fibers (DIN 47 255)

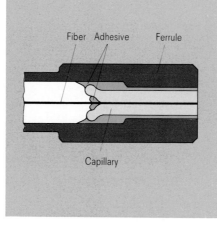

Fig. 9 Special-purpose connector

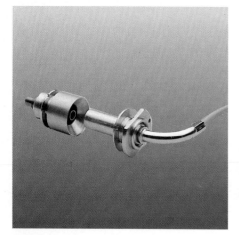

Fig. 10 Connector for style 7R
(DIN 47 255)

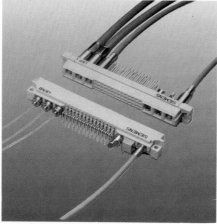

Fig. 11 Connector inserts for multi-contact
strips to DIN 41 612

The connectors shown in **Figs. 8** and **9** are screwed onto the particular optoelectronic transducer using the coupling nut located on the plug. However, for certain applications screwless solutions are preferred.

Fig. 10 shows a connector for the modular style 7R [5] mounting system. It is designed to compensate for tolerances due to misalignment between unit and rack, i.e. the connectors must "float" and provide a defined capture range.

Fig. 11 shows another design, enabling connector inserts to be mounted in a multi-contact strip conforming to DIN 41 612. In addition to AF contacts the strip can also be optionally equipped with power, RF and fiber-optic inserts. This solution is particularly advantageous if the fiber-optic transmission system, i.e. its components, is to be integrated into the familiar

mounting systems and standard housings. This underlines the advantages of connectors conforming to DIN 47 297.

Connectors for fiber bundles

The advantage of fiber bundles, usually comprising 10 to 300 single fibers, lies in their large cross section and large numerical aperture ($A_N = 0.4$ to 0.6). Fiber bundles are relatively insensitive to the failure of individual fibers and, even if a large number of fibers are broken, the operability of the overall system, if properly designed, will remain unimpaired. The condition of the fiber bundle can often be established by visual inspection as the broken fibers appears as dark points in the overall image of the fiber cross section. Insertion losses of up to 3.5 dB may occur but these only have a relatively insignificant effect on system span length due to the high attenuation of fiber bundles (50 to 700 dB/km).

Connector assembly

Disregarding lens-coupled or similar systems, connectors may be assembled onto fiber-optic cables by two main methods:

● The fiber is cleaved and secured in the ferrule such that the cleaved surface forms both the fiber endface and the entrance or exit face of the optical fiber.

● The fiber is cleaved, inserted in the ferrule and then secured with adhesive. The fiber end projecting from the endface of the ferrule is ground off and polished.

However, both methods, despite their apparent simplicity, impose a number of requirements which are crucial to the quality of a connection and therefore of the overall system. The parameters controlling the quality include:

● type of fiber
(related to fabrication process),

● fiber diameter tolerances,

● concentricity of fiber core,

● fiber diameter,

● fiber asymmetry,

● numerical aperture variations.

The significance of the individual parameters has already been discussed. The following fiber designs are commercially available:

● glass-glass (core-cladding),

● glass-plastic (core-cladding).

In the case of a glass-glass fiber the cladding is scored and then broken. If this is performed properly and the glass fiber is suitable, very clean fracture surfaces can be obtained. The advantage of a glass-glass fiber is that the fiber cladding inside the connector maintains its optical function right up to the end of the fiber.

In the case of a glass-plastic fiber it is necessary to remove the plastic cladding at the intended point of fracture; the fiber is then scored and broken. The disadvantage here is that the optical effect of the plastic cladding in the fracture zone is lost, resulting in additional loss due to transverse radiation.

Quality of the fiber endface

The quality of the cleaved surface shown in **Fig. 12** is unsatisfactory. As surface irregularities cause losses due to reflection and scattering, the cleaving

Fig. 12   Unsatisfactory cleavage
of fiber endface

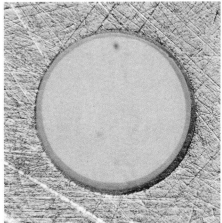

Fig. 13   Properly ground
and polished fiber endface

process must be repeated, unless subsequent grinding and polishing is envisaged. In addition to surface quality there is one further requirement, i.e. the cleaved surface must be perpendicular to the fiber axis.

Method 1 is adequate for connector assembly for certain applications and requirements. Fiber endface quality can be enhanced by grinding and polishing per method 2 (**Fig. 13**).

On fiber bundles grinding and polishing is necessary in any case. The individual fibers of the bundle must be fixed in the ferrule with adhesive.

Grinding additionally equalizes the length differences between the individual fibers.

Fiber diameter

The larger the fiber diameter the less critical become the tolerance problems and the more light can be launched into the fiber. These advantages are counter-balanced by disadvantages, e.g. the difficulty of achieving clean fracture surfaces the larger the diameter; in addition, the flexibility of the lines is lower and the costs higher.

Fiber diameter tolerances on single fib-

ers can be largely compensated by selecting the appropriate size of precision bore located in the ferrule to support the fiber.

Finishing defects

The connector insertion loss is determined not only by mechanical tolerances and fiber defects, but also by possible finishing defects. **Fig. 13** shows a well ground and polished fiber endface.

Field assembly

When long fiber-optic cables are being installed, the fiber ends are not terminated (unless already spliced to preconnectorized pigtails) until cable placement is completed and then the plugs are fitted on site. A suitably equipped case is provided (**Fig. 14**) containing all the tools required for cable and fiber preparation, micrometers for determining the fiber diameter, grinding and polishing equipment, crimping tools etc.

A further consideration is the need for repairing damaged optical fibers. In industrial applications, if the length is adequate and splicing is impossible, the approach is to fit two plugs which can be coupled in a sleeve. In telecommunications systems the usual approach to cable defects or damage is to use splices in order to minimize losses. The splice loss of a graded-index fiber with a 50/125 µm fiber diameter is around 0.1 dB.

References

[1] Knoblauch, G.: Optische Steckverbinder, Teil 1: Funktionsprinzipien. Nachr.-techn. Z. 36 (1983), pp. 26 to 29

[2] Knoblauch, G.: Optische Steckverbinder, Teil 2: Verarbeitung. Nachr.-techn. Z. 36 (1983), pp. 90 to 92

[3] Klement, E.; Rössner, K.: Principles of Optical Measurements for Communication Systems. telcom report 6 (1983) Special Issue "Optical Communications", pp. 167 to 171

[4] Cooper, R.: Connector splice loss measurements: the laboratory versus the real world. IFOC, Vol. 3, No. 3/4 (1982), pp. 38 to 46

[5] Stegmeier, A.; Trimmel, H.: A Fiber-Optic System for Transmitting 34 Mbit/s Signals. telcom report 6 (1983) Special Issue "Optical Communications", pp. 125 to 129

[6] Odemar, N.; Steinmann, P.: Jointing Techniques for Fiber-Optic Cables. telcom report 6 (1983) Special Issue "Optical Communications", pp. 50 to 54

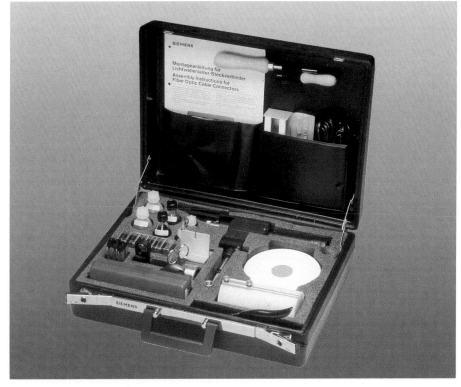

Fig. 14   Equipment case for connector assembly in the field

Hans-Norbert Toussaint and Gerhard Winzer

Technology and Applications of Couplers for Optical Communications

As long as fiber-optic transmission routes are confined to point-to-point links, i.e. connecting one transmitter to one receiver, fiber-optic couplers are of no interest. Yet, in any situation involving, for instance, bidirectional transmission of information over one fiber or incorporation of several transmitters and receivers in an optical bus structure, there is an immediate requirement for such devices. There is, however, no "standard coupler" to meet these needs, since the relevant technical and economic requirements differ too widely.

Characterization of optical couplers by the scattering matrix

Optical couplers are "multiport" devices and thus have at least two "optical ports" at which light waves can be coupled in and out. A proven aid in defining the transmission characteristics of optical multiports is the scattering matrix explained here by reference to a four-port coupler. This is shown in **Fig. 1 a** as a "black box", i.e. only its four optical ports are visible with no indication as to its physical mode of operation. A power P_{1e} coupled into port 1 is divided within the coupler between the four ports to provide the output powers P_{1a}, P_{2a}, P_{3a} and P_{4a} which can be measured at the corresponding ports.

When the output powers are measured care must be taken to ensure that termination of the individual ports is reflection-free, otherwise each emerg-

Dipl.-Ing. Dr.-Ing. Hans-Norbert Toussaint,
Siemens AG,
Safety and Security Systems Division,
Munich;
Dipl.-Ing. Dr.-Ing. Gerhard Winzer,
Siemens AG,
Research and Development Division,
Munich

ing wave would result in another wave entering by reflection. In realizing a reflection-free termination it is important to ensure that the reflection points inherent in the multiport device and unavoidable in practical application are retained. If, for instance, a four-port coupler is fitted with optical connectors, the reflection from these connectors must not be reduced or eliminated in the measurement by the possible use of an index-matching liquid. Efforts should be directed instead at eliminating reflections from the connected fiber, in particular those from the end of the fiber away from the multiport.

It has so far been assumed that power is coupled only into port 1 of the four-port device (**Fig. 1 a**). In order to characterize the device fully, however, it is necessary to couple optical powers into the other ports to establish how the powers divide between the ports (**Fig. 1 b**). The relationship between the input powers P_{ve} and the output powers $P_{\mu a}$ is as follows:

$$\begin{bmatrix} P_{1a} \\ P_{2a} \\ P_{3a} \\ P_{4a} \end{bmatrix} = \begin{bmatrix} p_{11} & p_{12} & p_{13} & p_{14} \\ p_{21} & p_{22} & p_{23} & p_{24} \\ p_{31} & p_{32} & p_{33} & p_{34} \\ p_{41} & p_{42} & p_{43} & p_{44} \end{bmatrix} \cdot \begin{bmatrix} P_{1e} \\ P_{2e} \\ P_{3e} \\ P_{4e} \end{bmatrix} \cdot$$

The scattering matrix $[p]$ applies only at the optical wavelength employed for the measurement. If the wavelength

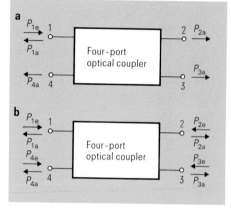

P_e Input power
P_a Output power

Fig. 1   Definition of powers coupled to and from a four-port optical coupler
a   **Input at port 1 only, output at all four ports**
b   **General case; input and output at all four ports**

dependance of the matrix elements is low, the given matrix elements will apply, for instance, over the entire wavelength range from 800 to 900 nm. Multiport devices which are strongly wavelength-dependent require a separate matrix for each wavelength of interest. In practice, however, the approach is often to specify only individual and particularly important matrix elements.

The elements of the scattering matrix are obtained from the input and output powers, so that, for instance, from **Fig. 1 b**
$p_{21} = P_{2a}/P_{1e}$
(provided that
$P_{2e} = P_{3e} = P_{4e} = 0$) and
$p_{31} = P_{3a}/P_{1e}$
(provided that
$P_{2e} = P_{3e} = P_{4e} = 0$).

The individual matrix elements are often given in decibels, i.e. numerical value in dB $= -10 \log (p_{\mu\nu})$. The elements of the scattering matrix can be used as required to describe or define other important transmission parameters of a multiport configuration.

Coupler structures

Fig. 2 shows examples of the main coupler principles. They can be divided into two groups according to the number of ports, the first group comprising *three- and four-port couplers*, the second group containing *mixers* with a larger fiber count, e.g. connecting 16 subscribers. The primary distinction drawn in terms of the coupling principle is between *end-fire couplers* and *evanescent-field couplers*. With end-fire couplers, the light guided in the incoming waveguide is coupled to the outgoing waveguide(s) according to the degree of "overlapping". By contrast, the light in the evanescent-field couplers transfers from one waveguide to another laterally through the cladding.

Figs. 2a, 2b and **2c** illustrate the principles of end-fire coupling with the light divided by the lateral *offset between the fiber axes*; **Fig. 2a** shows a mechanical fiber switch, **Fig. 2b** a symmetrical offset coupler and **Fig. 2c** an asymmetrical offset coupler. The term "asymmetrical" indicates that at least one section is of another fiber type. It is the magnitude ε of the offset that provides the offset coupler with the required power division ratio. Couplers operating on the offset principle are well suited to systems with step-index fibers and can be made with low insertion losses, provided that fiber sections are employed with particularly thin cladding (yielding maximum overlap of the core surfaces). This type of coupler is not so suitable for graded-index fibers because with increasing offset the modal spectra of the relevant fiber sections become locally mismatched, resulting in additional coupling losses.

If the symmetrical offset coupler is inserted with fiber sections 1 and 2 in a fiber link, section 3 can provide the light output. Similarly, section 4 can be used for coupling light into the link fiber. Losses p_{31} (output coupling) and p_{24} (input coupling) are equal. If just a small amount of light is to be coupled

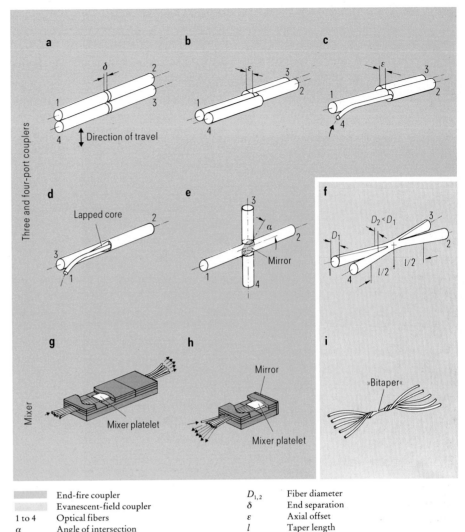

End-fire coupler
Evanescent-field coupler
1 to 4   Optical fibers
α Angle of intersection

$D_{1,2}$ Fiber diameter
δ End separation
ε Axial offset
l Taper length

Fig. 2 Fiber-optic coupler structures without imaging elements

a   **Switch**
b   **Symmetrical offset coupler (four port)**
c   **Asymmetrical offset coupler (four port)**
d   **Asymmetrical three-port coupler with lapped core**
e   **Four-port coupler with beam-splitter mirror**
f   **Four-port coupler (bitaper)**
g   **Transmissive mixer with mixer platelet**
h   **Reflective mixer with mixer platelet**
i   **Transmissive mixer (bitaper)**

out via fiber 3, this will mean that light can only be fed in via fiber 4 with high input losses.

In the asymmetrical offset coupler the rigid relationship between input and output coupling loss is eliminated. The core of fiber 4, which is relatively small compared with fibers 1, 2 and 3, is completely overlapped by the core of fiber 2, providing a low input coupling loss. If the transmission loss for the optical path from 1 to 2 is also to remain low, the core diameter of fiber 2 must be large. The asymmetrical offset coupler is therefore only of practical

importance for fiber-optic systems employing large-core fibers.

This also applies to the asymmetrical three-port coupler shown in **Fig. 2d**. The *lapped core* of fiber 3 enables this coupler to provide precise alignment of fiber axes 2 and 3 and hence low transmission loss for path $2 \rightarrow 3$ as well as path $1 \rightarrow 2$.

The precise alignment of "all" fiber sections is one of the two features of the four-port coupler shown in **Fig. 2e** with partially transmitting *beam-splitter mirror*. The axes of all four fiber sections intersect in the mirror coating applied directly to an obliquely polished fiber end, the perpendicular on the center of the mirror forming the bisector for the axis pairs 1, 3 and 2, 4. This coupler therefore shows no mode dependence apart from polarization effects and is the only lensless three or four-port coupler providing equally good performance for both step and graded-index fibers. The second feature of the coupler arises from the possibilities provided by the design of the mirror coating, which can be applied as a low-loss dielectric interference multilayer. Suitable layer design can achieve any desired light division ratio and enable the multilayer to act as a wavelength-selective filter turning the three-port structure into a *wavelength-division-multiplex coupler*.

The evanescent-field four-port coupler in **Fig. 2f** is generally referred to as a *biconical taper coupler* or *bitaper*. It is basically very easy to manufacture, a pair of fibers being twisted lightly together and drawn down (e.g. in a flame). The resultant cross-sectional changes in the fibers cause the light guided in fiber 1, for instance, to impinge on the inside of the fiber cladding at a steeper angle and – when the acceptance angle is exceeded – to transfer into the cladding glass. Then, as the cross section widens sufficiently, the light returns to the core regions of fibers 2 and 3 on the output side of the bitaper. The light splitting ratio here is a function of the diameter variation $D_2/D_1 < 1$ and the taper length l. Since the waveguide modes are characterized by their direction of propagation relative to the fiber axis, the coupling in the bitaper is largely mode-dependent.

In the two *mixers* with end-fire coupling (**Figs. 2g** and **2h**) a thin mixer platelet of quartz glass ensures that the light incoming in any fiber is equally divided between all the outgoing fibers. The thickness of the mixer platelet is selected to be about equal to the core diameter of the fiber sections coupled to it. The width of the platelet is equal to the sum of all outer diameters of the fibers coupled to each narrow side. The glass platelet – embedded in a layer of adhesive of lower refractive index – thus becomes a waveguide. If the mixer platelet is long enough, the light at the end of it will achieve a uniform spatial distribution, producing the same excitation in all the outgoing fibers regardless of the input port from which the light came.

In the *transmissive mixer* (**Fig. 2g**) the outgoing fibers are arranged opposite the incoming fibers. If the rear endface of half a transmissive mixer is mirrored, this produces a *reflective mixer* in which all the fiber sections are coupled to the same endface of the mixer platelet. Each fiber port in this device can be employed selectively or simultaneously to couple light in and out.

Fig. 2i shows a transmissive mixer made by biconically tapering and fusing a suitable number of fibers. The observations previously made in respect of the similar four-port coupler (**Fig. 2f**) also apply here. Tapering can also be used to produce a reflective mixer.

Technology and applications of wavelength-independent couplers

Switches

The mode of operation of a mechanically or electromechanically operated fiber-optic switch is explained with the aid of **Fig. 2a**. When the switch is in the "on" state, the endfaces of fiber pairs are so closely aligned that the light emerging from one endface transfers to the opposite fiber endface with no significant losses. If the coupled fibers are moved relative to each other in a plane vertical to their axes by a sufficient amount, the light transmission between fibers 1 and 2 as well as between 3 and 4 is interrupted and replaced by coupling between fibers 1 and 3 or 4 and 2, depending on the direction of the deflection.

Significant attenuation components are those due to Fresnel losses, end separation, lateral and angular misalignment. These components can be considerably reduced by careful design, precise alignment of the fibers to be coupled, and coating of the endfaces. In practice, however, these approaches are severely constrained by fabrication costs and technical factors. For instance, although angular misalignment of the fibers can be easily reduced by increasing the length of the deflected fibers this would make the switch too bulky and increase its sensitivity to vibration.

Fiber-optic switches based on the operating principle illustrated in **Fig. 2a** can be realized with step-index as well as graded-index fibers.

Fig. 3 shows schematically the prototype for an electromagnetically operated four-port by-pass switch. Opposite the two fibers 1 and 4 bonded to the fixed mount 5 are the fibers 2 and 3 which are attached to the moving reed 6. This reed presses against the stops 8 and 9 when relay winding 7 is deenergized. As soon as a sufficiently large current flows through the relay winding ("on" state), the reed is pulled down, coupling fibers 1 and 2 and fibers 3 and 4. Typical values for the "on" state of mechanically or electromechanically operated switches with graded-index fibers (core diameter 50 µm, overall diameter 125 µm, numerical aperture 0.2) are as follows [1]:

Insertion losses ≈ 1.3 dB
Isolation $\geqq 40$ dB.

The values refer to switches with pigtails. In connectorized fiber-optic switches the realizable insertion losses increase by the two additional connector losses (typical value: 2×1.5 dB = 3 dB).

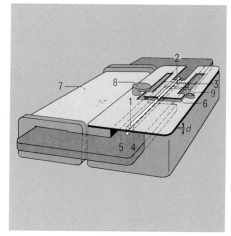

1 to 4	Glass fibers
5	Fixed mount
6	Moving reed
7	Relay winding
8, 9	Stops
d	Reed thickness

(the schematic diagram was kindly provided by Mr. B. Malorny, Siemens AG, Berlin)

Fig. 3 Electromechanically operated fiber-optic by-pass switch

Fiber offset coupler

The previously described principle on which this coupler is based is illustrated in **Figs. 2b** and **2c**. The technology and achievable characteristics are considered by reference to the asymmetrical offset coupler [2] which is particularly suitable for applications in bus systems. Fabrication involves three fibers of identical numerical aperture but differing core diameters – two thick fibers (e.g. core diameter 200 μm) and a thin one (e.g. core diameter 50 μm) – being placed and secured next to each other in one plane. They are then cleaved in a plane vertical to the axes and butted together again with lateral offset ε.

Fig. 4 shows photomicrographs of the cleaved surfaces of the mutually offset fiber groups. For the subsequent operation of the coupler only two fibers of each of the two groups are of interest and have each been photographed with illuminated core cross sections.

A typical scattering matrix for this four-port coupler (with pigtails as in the subsequent devices) using the port notation in **Fig. 2c** is as follows:

$$[p] = \begin{bmatrix} >14\,\text{dB} & 2.5\,\text{dB} & 6.5\,\text{dB} & >40\,\text{dB} \\ 2.5\,\text{dB} & >14\,\text{dB} & >40\,\text{dB} & 0.7\,\text{dB} \\ 6.5\,\text{dB} & >40\,\text{dB} & >14\,\text{dB} & >40\,\text{dB} \\ >40\,\text{dB} & 8\,\text{dB} & >40\,\text{dB} & >14\,\text{dB} \end{bmatrix}.$$

It is an inherent property of the asymmetrical offset coupler that some of the two matrix elements defining the transmission characteristics of a coupled fiber pair exhibit differing values in the two directions of transmission.

Coupler with partially transmitting mirror

The coupler shown in **Fig. 2e** is fabricated by cleaving a continuous fiber at an angle $\alpha = 45°$. After partially mirroring the interface the two fiber sections (marked 1 and 2 in **Fig. 2e**) are aligned and cemented together again. In order to pass on the light reflected at the mirrored surface, two more fibers 3 and 4, possibly identical to the others, are attached. This produces a symmetrical four-port coupler.

If only one reflective branch is provided, employing an identical fiber, the result is a symmetrical three-port coupler. A typical scattering matrix for this

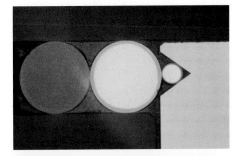

Fig. 4 Photomicrographs through the two fiber groups (with mutual lateral offset ε) forming the asymmetrical offset coupler (four port); the fibers essential to the function of the coupler are shown with illuminated cores

Top: Fibers 1 and 4 of Fig. 2c
Bottom: Fibers 2 and 3 of Fig. 2c

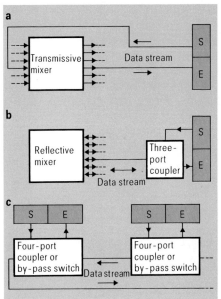

E Subscriber receiver
S Subscriber transmitter

Fig. 5 Optical bus structures for data transmission
a Star bus with transmissive mixer
b Star bus with reflective mixer
c Ring bus with four-port coupler or by-pass switch

device with graded-index fibers (50 μm core diameter, numerical aperture 0.2) and the fiber 1 input signal split in the ratio 1:1 between fibers 2 and 3, is as follows:

$$[p] = \begin{bmatrix} >14\,\text{dB} & 4\,\text{dB} & 4\,\text{dB} \\ 4\,\text{dB} & >14\,\text{dB} & >30\,\text{dB} \\ 4\,\text{dB} & >30\,\text{dB} & >14\,\text{dB} \end{bmatrix}.$$

If the reflective branch (fiber 3) employs a fiber of larger core diameter, the result is an asymmetrical three-port coupler. This reduces the losses in the transmission direction $1 \rightarrow 3$. A coupler of this type is useful for connecting fiber 3 to a receiver.

The coupler specifications can be varied over a wide range to suit differing operational requirements. It is thus possible, for instance, to realize the four-port coupler with the splitting ratio $s = p_{31}/p_{21} = p_{42}/p_{12}$ having the values 1:1, 1:2, 1:3, 1:5 and 1:10. A closer subdivision is technically feasible but would hinder efforts at standardization and rationalization.

Mixers

The complete loss matrix of a transmissive mixer with 2×30 ports contains 900 matrix elements. The element $p_{\mu\nu}$

can be considered as representative. It defines the power division from the transmitter-side port ν to the receiver-side port μ. This element can be used to define the "splitting loss" in accordance with $a_s = -10 \log (p_{\mu\nu})$. This loss for a configuration with step-index fibers (core diameter 100 μm) averages approximately 19 dB disregarding connector losses [3], and is thus about 4 dB above the ideal value obtained when power coupled into one port is split equally and without loss between the 30 outputs.

Applications for wavelength-independent couplers

Fig. 5 shows various optical bus structures in schematic form. **Fig. 5a** illustrates a bus employing a transmissive mixer, the transmitter and receiver of each subscriber being connected to the transmissive mixer by separate fibers. If a reflective mixer is employed (**Fig. 5b**), only one fiber is connected to each subscriber. Signals are coupled out to the receiver and in from the transmitter by means of a three-port coupler. The asymmetrical three-port coupler as shown in **Fig. 2d** is particularly suitable for this purpose, because the power can be coupled both in and out with relatively low losses. Assuming the transmissive and reflective mixers both cost about the same, the bus structure in **Fig. 5 b** is favorable provided that the cost of the three-port coupler is less than that of a fiber link between mixer and subscriber. **Fig. 5 c** shows a ring bus structure. This configuration allows the transmitter and receiver of each individual subscriber to be connected to the ring circuit via a four-port coupler (preferably via the asymmetrical four-port coupler in **Fig. 2 c**) or a by-pass switch [3].

Technology and applications of wavelength-selective couplers

WDM couplers

Reference was made earlier to the fact that the design of the mirror coating allows the coupler shown in **Fig. 2 e** to be configured as a *wavelength-division-multiplex three-port coupler* or WDM coupler. WDM couplers with three ports enable light of two different wavelengths from the two incoming fibers to be combined at low loss into one outgoing fiber (multiplexer) or to be separated again in a suitable coupler (demultiplexer). The selective elements considered for use in WDM couplers are the diffraction grating for large numbers of wavelength channels (five to ten) and the interference filter for smaller numbers of channels (two to four). Since a corresponding broad spectrum of source diodes to allow the use of currently available diffraction grating couplers is not so far available, consideration will be given merely to the *interference filter WDM couplers*.

These couplers are realized by making two changes to the wavelength-independent couplers with mirror coating. Firstly, the dielectric mirror is fabricated as a so-called edge filter [4] (this transmits, for instance, the shorter wavelength λ_1 to about 96% and reflects the longer wavelength λ_2 to about 99%). Secondly, the angle α indicated in **Fig. 2 e** is increased from 45 to, say, 70°. In order to achieve close channel spacing $\Delta\lambda = \lambda_2 - \lambda_1$, it is necessary to choose not only the appropriate mirror design for unpolarized light (as emitted by LEDs)

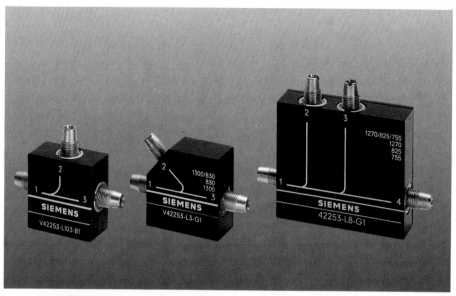

Fig. 6   Multiport couplers: wavelength-independent three-port coupler (left) and WDM couplers for two (center) and three channels (right)

but also the minimum angle of incidence $\beta = 90° - \alpha$. This is because the spectral positions of the filter edge for the light components polarized vertically and parallel to the plane of incidence will only coincide for light impinging vertically on the filter layer. The block design described in [4] allows up to 30 WDM couplers to be fabricated "en bloc" simultaneously with minimum alignment effort. Using light-emitting diodes with emission wavelengths around 800 nm and a channel separation of $\Delta\lambda = 70$ nm, the typical values measured on these couplers with pigtails are as follows (ports 1, 2, 3 assigned as in **Fig. 2 e**):

$$[p_{\lambda_1}] = \begin{bmatrix} >14\,\text{dB} & 1\,\text{dB} & 14\,\text{dB} \\ 1\,\text{dB} & >14\,\text{dB} & >40\,\text{dB} \\ 14\,\text{dB} & >40\,\text{dB} & >14\,\text{dB} \end{bmatrix},$$

$$[p_{\lambda_2}] = \begin{bmatrix} >14\,\text{dB} & 11\,\text{dB} & 2\,\text{dB} \\ 11\,\text{dB} & >14\,\text{dB} & >40\,\text{dB} \\ 2\,\text{dB} & >40\,\text{dB} & >14\,\text{dB} \end{bmatrix}.$$

For multiplexer or demultiplexer operation the two insertion losses $p_{12}(\lambda_1) = p_{21}(\lambda_1)$ and $p_{13}(\lambda_2) = p_{31}(\lambda_2)$ are important. It may be advisable to increase the so-called far-end crosstalk attenuations $p_{31}(\lambda_1)$ and $p_{21}(\lambda_2)$ by about 20 dB by adding a narrowband filter. In couplers for bidirectional operation the near-end crosstalk attenuations $p_{32}(\lambda_1)$ and $p_{23}(\lambda_2)$ are important.

A WDM coupler for the wavelengths $\lambda_1 = 850$ nm and $\lambda_2 = 1300$ nm, operating with suitable light-emitting diodes

and no additional narrowband filters, has insertion losses of $p_{13}(\lambda_2) = 1.5$ dB and $p_{12}(\lambda_2) = 0.5$ dB with increased values for the near-end crosstalk attenuations.

The position of the filter edges in the WDM couplers for two channels can be adapted in the filter design to suit user requirements. For use with light-emitting diodes, the channel separation should be selected to be at least equal to the sum of the half-intensity emission bandwidths of the two source diodes. In systems with laser diodes a closer channel spacing ($\Delta\lambda \approx 40$ to 50 nm) is possible, due to their narrower half-intensity bandwith over the entire wavelength range of interest.

Laboratory models have now successfully integrated two edge filters into a compact WDM coupler for three channels. The configuration effectively cascades two couplers for two channels each. **Fig. 6** shows this device next to a WDM coupler for two channels and a wavelength-independent three-port coupler. The insertion losses measured on the laboratory models (excluding connector losses) were

$p_{12}(\lambda_1) = p_{21}(\lambda_1) = 1.2$ dB,
$p_{13}(\lambda_2) = p_{31}(\lambda_2) = 1.6$ dB
and $p_{14}(\lambda_3) = p_{41}(\lambda_3) = 1.8$ dB
for light-emitting diodes operating at following wavelengths: $\lambda_1 = 755$ nm, $\lambda_2 = 1270$ nm, $\lambda_3 = 825$ nm. In this WDM coupler, as in those previously described, all the fiber sections consist of graded-index fibers (core diameter

50 µm, numerical aperture 0.2). However, they can also be realized with single-mode fibers using the principle described [4].

WDM applications

WDM couplers, developed primarily for use in wideband transmission systems, enable the potentially high transmission capacity of optical fibers to be better utilized. If signals can be transmitted over the same fiber independently of each other on different carrier wavelengths with close channel spacing, the resultant bandwidth-length product is multiplied. Instead of installing many fibers in parallel to meet the demand, there is the possibility of employing multiplex techniques on one or more fibers. It would even be possible to introduce what is known as service multiplexing, in which the light of the different carrier wavelengths can be modulated in different ways (in digital or analog form).

In order not to raise hopes unduly, it must be said that the additional insertion losses resulting from the use of WDM couplers shorten the potential span lengths compared with those of simple point-to-point links. Fiber cost must be balanced against coupler cost. The advantage conferred by the WDM coupler, particularly on long span lengths, may be nullified by the additional insertion losses and the consequent shorter repeater spacings. The practical significance of wavelength-division multiplexing is therefore to be found in "medium" span lengths. In TV subscriber networks, for instance, with distances typically less than 5 km it is possible to employ a WDM coupler and save the second fiber (providing the backward channel for program selection and, if required, bidirectional videotelephony).

Fig. 7 shows $N = 3$ subscribers connected to an exchange via just $2N/3 = 2$ fibers (instead of $2N = 6$ fibers) due to the use of three-channel WDM couplers of similar design to the couplers shown in **Fig. 6**.

Application areas

As has been shown, the availability of optical couplers provides the possibility of flexibly structuring the topology of fiber-optic communication networks, thus expanding the range of possible applications for optical communications. The applications diagram for fiber optics shown in **Fig. 8** identifies the possible application areas for optical couplers. The vertical axis above the plane of span length and transmission capacity indicates the degree of optical reticulation for such systems. Optical reticulation in this context refers to several transmitters and receivers being interconnected with no interposed electronics, thus eliminating multiple optical to electrical and electrical to optical signal conversion. The applications diagram indicates long-haul links and subscriber

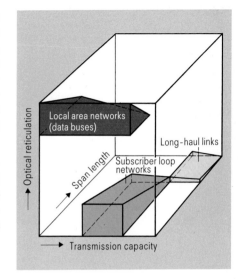

Fig. 8   Applications diagram for optical couplers

loop networks and local area networks (data buses). Long-haul links require maximum span length and transmission capacity. For extreme requirements it is necessary to avoid all-optical reticulation on account of the additional insertion losses. The only possible exceptions to this are when extremely large data rates can no longer be handled electronically. A wide application area for optical couplers are the highly-reticulated local area networks (data buses). The span lengths and data rates required in this application are not particularly large, thus allowing many subscribers to be connected to each other, e.g. on a star bus. The wavelength-division multiplexer is an example of the possible use of passive couplers in subscriber loop networks.

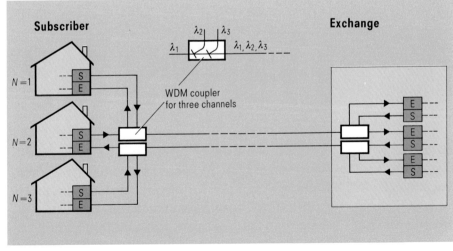

E	Receiver	N	Subscriber number
λ	Wavelength	S	Transmitter

Fig. 7   Subscriber connection to a wideband communication and distribution network by means of three-channel WDM couplers

References

[1] Stockmann, M.; Winzer, G.; Grassl, E.: Rigid reed-type routing switch for multimode optical fibers. Fiber and Integrated Opt. 3 (1980), pp. 237 to 251

[2] Witte, H.-H.; Kulich, V.: Branching elements for optical data buses. Appl. Opt. 20 (1981), pp. 715 to 718

[3] Witte, H.-H.: Optische Datenbusse für Meß- und Regelaufgaben. Elektronik 4 (1981), pp. 63 to 70

[4] Winzer, G.; Mahlein, H. F.; Reichelt, A.: Single-mode and multimode all-fiber directional couplers for WDM. Appl. Opt. 20 (1981), pp. 3128 to 3135

Optical Waveguides are Mowing into the Global Communic

Information Takes New

The future belongs to optical communications: optical waveguides, silica glass fibers fine as a hair, will progressively replace copper conductors and open up completely new possibilities. Scientists and communications engineers have found a way of using infrared light (lying next to the visible spectrum) for carrying information. Optoelectronic semiconductors convert electrical signals directly into optical signals which are sent through the optical waveguides; at the receive end the optical signal is converted back into an electrical signal. Optical cables are now produced principally for applications in telecommunications and industry. Siemens has already installed more than 30,000 km of fiber worldwide, mainly in the middle and lower network levels. A decisive stimulus to mass usage should be provided by the general introduction of digital techniques and by wideband communication, e.g. video-telephony.

telcom report 6 (1983) Special Issue "Optical Communications"

a Network...

... as Aerial Cable

... as Buried Cable

... as Submarine Cable

Paths

Optical cables are being used in many areas today, and the characteristics demanded from the cables employed vary from application to application. The conditions applying to the installation of an aerial cable (as in the case of the »alpine telephone«) are different to those valid for plowing cable into the ground, not to mention laying it under water

Optical Communications – Everything Favors the New Technology: Science, Engineering, Ecology and Practical Experience

Communication in public networks

The idea of using optical waveguides as an alternative transmission medium to copper conductors became attractive in 1970, when individual fibers with an attenuation less than 20 dB/km where successfully produced. Modern fibers have considerably lower attenuations. Optical waveguide systems from Siemens are operating successfully in the Deutsche Bundespost network. A further link in the Munich area was handed over in September 1982. It operates in the wavelength region of 880 nm with a transmission rate of 34 Mbit/s; a newly developed laser diode serves as the optical transmitter. The cut-over of the transmission equipment (below) by the Telecommunication Engineering Center of the Deutsche Bundespost was completed without a hitch. For Siemens this was the sixth project for the Deutsche Bundespost in the last four years, in which a total of about 400 fiber-km have been installed. The transmission equipment of future systems will be supplied in the standard mounting system shown at the right; the first systems of our new generation, designed for the wavelength region around 1300 nm, are currently undergoing trials in West Berlin.

Interference-free signal transmission

In close cooperation with the Austrian Power Authority, Siemens has developed an optical waveguide transmission system for communication via the high-voltage networks of electric power utility companies. This system was used for the first time on the new 110 kV line St. Peter–Ranshofen, and for the first time in Europe the optical cable was attached to the ground wire at the top of the high-voltage power line. The distance between the two portal towers amounts to 5380 m, the mast spacing is up to 320 m

Traffic – safely guided using optical waveguides

Scene of the first full-scale magnetic levitation trials in the history of German railroads was the Transrapid experimental facility in Emsland. The first construction stage of this project (sponsored by the Federal Ministry for Research and Technology) has a total of 20.6 km of track and includes two switches for the branch lines to the experimental center and the north loop. Control paths unaffected by interference from the electrical installations required for railroad operation are necessary for the reliable actuation of these switches. For enhanced safety, optical cables are used in this application

Process automation via optical cables

The first optical waveguide data bus in the world for industrial process automation was installed by Siemens in the Bruckhausen steelworks of Thyssen AG. The 28 soaking pits (in which the ingots are reheated up to more than 1200 °C and prepared for the rolling mill train) are controlled by independent microcomputer stations which are connected to the process control computer system via an optical cable. The system was developed by the Fraunhofer-Institut für Informations- und Datenverarbeitung, Karlsruhe

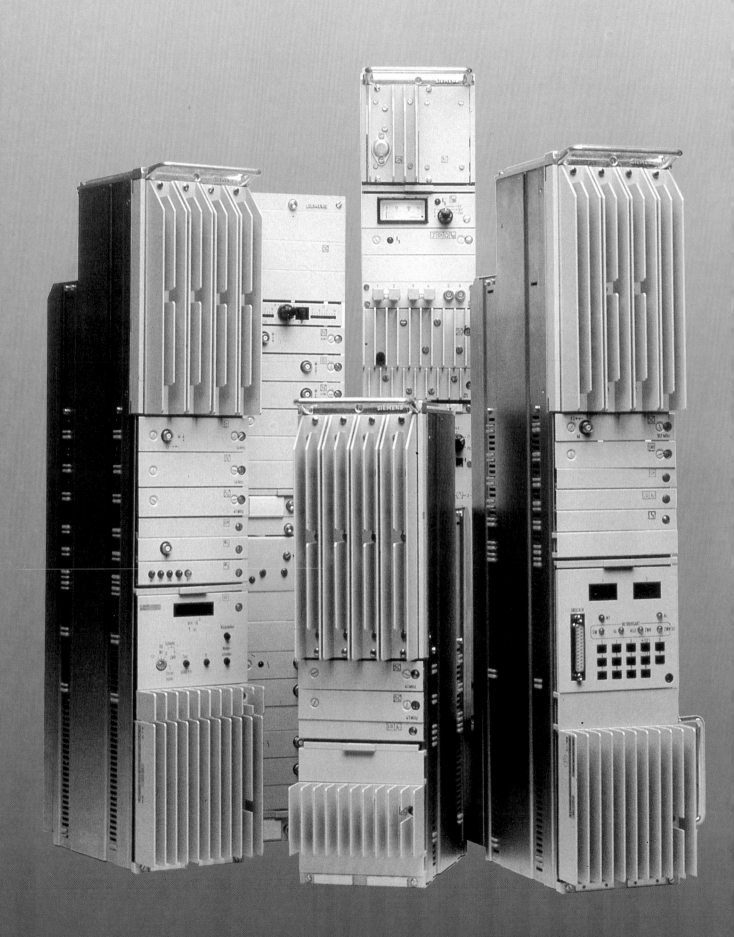

Ewald Braun and Heinrich Keil

Optical Waveguide Transmission Systems

The technical design of optical transmission systems is to a large extent dependent upon the nature of the transmitted signals (e.g. digitized voice, sound or picture signals, or analog FDM voice or video signals). They determine the way in which the optical transmitter is driven (direct intensity modulation or premodulation of an electrical subcarrier).

Depending upon the purpose for which they are employed, a distinction is made between systems for the subscriber line network, for short-haul links and for long-haul links with many repeaters. Line terminating units are the links between the multiplex equipment or other signal sources and sinks and the optical cable. The received signals are amplified or regenerated on the receive side of the line terminating units and in the repeaters.

The distances between the repeaters or the regenerators (elementary cable section or regenerator section) are dependent upon the characteristics of the optical waveguide (attenuation, dispersion), those of the optoelectronic transducers (wavelength, output power, spectral bandwidth, receiver sensitivity) and the nature of the transmitted signals (bandwidth, bit rate).

The transmission systems need facilities for supervision and fault location. Solutions have been developed for the housing and power-feeding of repeaters where these are incorporated. In all systems, but particularly those employed for telecommunications, special attention is paid to reliability and availability during equipment design, as well as during component selection and stressing.

Dipl.-Ing. (FH) Ewald Braun and
Dipl.-Ing. Heinrich Keil,
Siemens AG,
Public Communication Networks Division,
Munich

◁ Transmission systems
for optical communications

In order to transmit electrical signals via optical waveguides, use is made of optical transmission systems whose principal components are the optoelectronic transducer as the optical transmitter at the transmit end of the link, the actual optical waveguide and the optoelectronic transducer as photodetector at the receive end of the link (**Fig. 1a**). The electrical signals at the terminals of the optoelectronic transducer at the transmit end of the link are converted into optical signals and the light is launched into the fiber. The light passes through the fiber as described in [1]; at the end of the link the optical signals are converted back into electrical signals in the optoelectronic transducer and are available at the output terminals.

Since, in the simplest case, both ends of a link consist of two terminals carrying electrical signals, optical transmission systems can be measured and assessed in the same way as conventional electrical systems. Finally, for the user and the maintenance personnel the optical transmission can recede completely into the background, since the link is judged solely in terms of electrical parameters.

The transmission capacity and the maximum range between transmitter and receiver – i.e. the elementary cable section length – are generally the two system parameters of greatest importance and interest. If the distance to be bridged is greater than the maximum section length as determined by the system, repeaters or regenerators are inserted. In these units the received optical signal is converted into an electrical signal, amplified or regenerated in this form and converted back into an optical signal. As in the classical systems for metallic lines, there are line terminating units at the beginning and end of the link; the units along the intervening link are referred to as repeaters in the case of analog signal transmission and regenerators or regenerative repeaters in the case of digital signal transmission (**Fig. 1b**).

Modulation of the light

As already explained in [2], light in the wavelength region around 1000 nm is used for optical transmission; this corresponds to a frequency of about 300 THz. The fiber bandwidth of a few

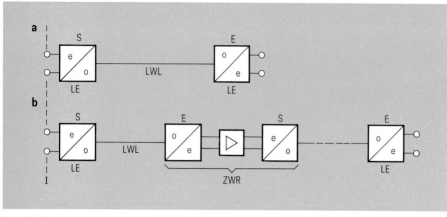

E   Receiver
e/o Optoelectronic transducer
I   Electrical interface

LWL Optical Waveguide
LE Line terminating unit
o/e Optoelectronic transducer

S   Transmitter
ZWR Regenerator

Fig. 1   Basic components for optical transmission
(a) without regenerator, (b) with regenerator

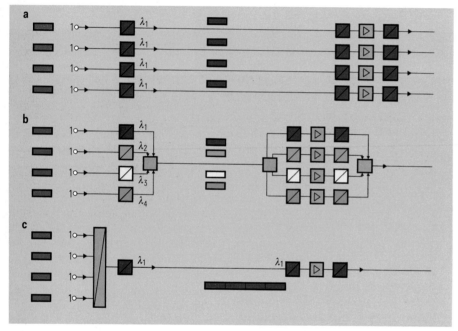

Fig. 2   Multiplexing for optical transmission in one direction (unidirectional)
a   Fiber multiplexing   b   Wavelength (λ) division multiplexing   c   Electrical (E) multiplexing

	Type of multiplex transmission		
	Fiber multiplexing	Wavelength (λ) division multiplexing	Electrical (E) multiplexing
Fibers Number Bandwidth	High Small	Low Small	Low Large
Optical transducer Number Wavelength Bandwidth	High One Small	High Various Small	Low One Large
Additional equipment At start/end In the link	None None	Optical filter Optical filter	E multiplex None
Upgrading in stages Suitable for VLSI	No No	Yes No	No Yes

Table 1   Comparison of the various types of multiplex transmission on optical waveguide links

hundred Megahertz in the case of a graded index fiber and of up to several Gigahertz in the case of a single-mode fiber, as well as the characteristics of the optoelectronic transducers permit the modulation of the light wave with frequencies up to 1 GHz and above; in comparison with the carrier frequency that is extremely narrow-band operation. However, the transmission window in which the attenuation and bandwidth of the particular fiber have favorable values has a width of more than 100 nm, corresponding to 30 THz. This enormous frequency range can be used for the transmission of several light waves. If light is transmitted from differing sources with mutually different wavelengths, each light ray can be individually modulated. The light from various sources can be combined in optical couplers at the start of the link and separated again in optically selective beam splitters at the end of a link.

This procedure offers the possibility of effectively increasing the transmission capacity of a fiber.

Transmission capacity

There are three fundamentally different ways of simultaneously transmitting several electrical signals via an optical waveguide link. This is explained below using the transmission of four television signals as an example.

In the first case there is a system with a separate fiber available for each signal (**Fig. 2 a**). All systems are of identical design; this arrangement is referred to as *fiber multiplexing*.

If in the preceding arrangement optoelectronic transducers with four differing wavelengths are used and their output optical powers are combined via an optically selective coupler, one fiber is adequate for the transmission. This arrangement is usually referred to as *wavelength (λ) division multiplexing* (**Fig. 2 b**).

In the third possible means of transmission the four input signals are first combined electrically – i.e. an electrical multiplex signal is formed – and this signal is used to drive the optoelectronic transducer. This arrangement is referred to as *electrical (E) multiplexing* (**Fig. 2 c**).

For completeness the typical circuit complexity at a repeater station is given for each of the possible solutions.

Which method is used in practice depends upon many factors and finally also on the economics. A few comparative assessments are shown in **Table 1**.

From the **table** it would appear to be advisable initially to employ electrical multiplexing of the signals to either completely utilize the bandwidth available for one optical wavelength, or at least employ it to the extent permitted by the technology of the transmission equipment. When one of the two limits is reached, the transmission capacity of each fiber can be further increased by wavelength division multiplexing.

A special role is reserved for the wavelength division multiplex transmission over short distances without repeaters (e.g. in the subscriber line network). Instead of providing a separate fiber for each transmission direction, the signals are transmitted in bidirectional WDM multiplex via a single fiber (**Fig. 3**).

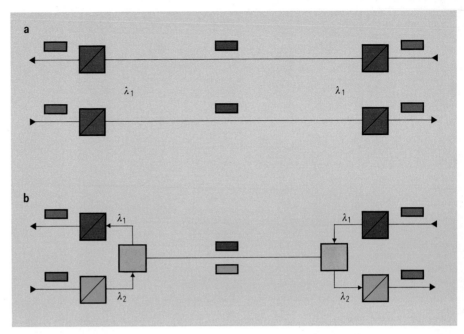

Fig. 3   Multiplexing for optical transmission in two directions (bidirectional)

a   Fiber multiplexing
b   Wavelength (λ) division multiplexing

Transmission methods

The optical transmission method actually employed depends upon the nature of the signals to be transmitted (analog or digital signals).

In the case of *direct intensity modulation* of the light, the temporal response of the optical power is directly proportional to the temporal response of the electrical signal; it is also referred to as an *analog transmission method*. Good transmission characteristics, i.e. high linearity, can only be achieved if the characteristics in the transmitter and receiver coincide. Since an adequately good coincidence can only be achieved in small sections of the characteristics, such systems have only a small dynamic range with a low bridgeable link loss. Systems with intensity modulation of the light are of very simple design; however, their use is strictly limited.

Intensity modulation can be used with advantage for simply transmitting digital signals over short distances *without* regeneration (such systems are described in [3]). The noise and linearity characteristics attainable with simple intensity modulation are frequently

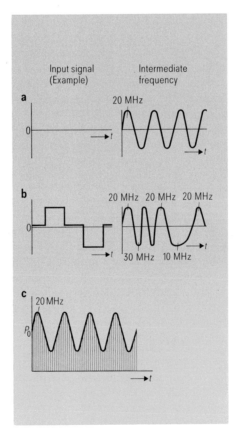

Fig. 4   Frequency modulation of a 20 MHz electrical subcarrier (intermediate frequency)

a   Without input signal
b   Pseudoternary digital signal as input signal (frequency deviation ±10 MHz)
c   Light signal P_0 launched into the fiber without an input signal to the frequency modulator

inadequate for the transmission of analog signals.

Better transmission properties are obtained by the *premodulation* of an electrical subcarrier and *subsequent intensity modulation* of the light. **Fig. 4** shows the various waveforms using frequency modulation (FM) as an example. The advantage of such a transmission method lies in the improved signal-to-noise ratio (FM gain) and in the independence of the nonlinearity of the optoelectronic transducers, since, as is well known, the information in the case of FM is contained in the temporal zero transitions of the signal.

Systems operating with FM are likewise of relatively simple design; they are particularly suitable for the transmission of TV signals in the video range over short to medium distances [4 to 6].

Digital signal transmission is most favorable for spanning large distances, for large transmission capacities, as well as for maximum demands on the transmission quality. The coded switching on and off of an optical source, as was done in earlier times, was a form of optical transmission. With modern optoelectronic semiconductors up to several hundred million

		Graded-index	Single-mode
Transmission capacity	Mbit/s	140 (spanning)	
Optical waveguide		Graded-index	Single-mode
Optical wavelength	nm	1300 (spanning)	
Optical power in the fiber			
Transmitting	dBm	−3	−4
Receiving for bit error rate 10⁻⁹	dBm	−40	−43
2 optical connectors	dB	3	4
System loss, theoretical	dB	34	35
Margin for effects which cannot be evaluated individually, such as Tolerances, temperature, aging Nominal bit error rate margin	dB	6 (spanning)	
Regenerator section loss, maximum	dB	28	29
Bandwidth of regenerator section	MHz	>120	>170
Fiber attenuation, cabled	dB/km	0.8 to 1.0	0.5
Mean pulling length	km	1 (spanning)	
Splice loss (0.2 dB per splice)	dB/km	0.1 to 0.2 (spanning)	
Margin for repair length and splices	dB/km	0 to 0.2 (spanning)	
Fiber attenuation, total	dB/km	0.9 to 1.4	0.6 to 0.9
Regenerator section length, maximum	km	31 to 20	48 to 32

Table 2   Power budget for a digital system for optical waveguides

switching operations can be performed in a second, so that large volumes of information are best transmitted digitally.

Transmission limits and interfaces

As described in [1] the transmission bandwidth on the optical waveguide link is limited by various factors. Typical per kilometer 3 dB bandwidth values for the different types of fiber are:

- step-index fiber up to about 20 MHz,
- graded-index fiber up to 2000 MHz,
- single-mode fiber up to 40 GHz.

The optoelectronic transducers employed as optical sources determine the system parameters through their modulation capability and optical power. Modern light-emitting diodes (LED) with a spectral width of about 50 nm can be modulated at over 100 MHz with about −13 dBm (50 µW) of transmitter optical power launched into the fiber. Optical powers of about 1 mW with modulation bandwidths up to 1 GHz and above can be obtained with laser diodes (LD), which usually have a spectral bandwidth of less than 5 nm. Although transmitters employing light-emitting diodes are generally sim-

pler in design and thus have a price advantage over those incorporating laser diodes, the high optical power and the resulting considerably greater attainable range with laser diodes are points in their favor. The modular laser design and suitable production methods ensure a high operating lifetime and reliability for the laser diode [2].

PIN or avalanche photodiodes, which can be used for the conversion of optical powers in the nanowatt range at frequencies up to 1 GHz and above into electrical signals, are suitable as optoelectronic transducers on the receive side. For high frequencies and high input sensitivity the PIN diodes are followed directly by an electrical amplifier (FET).

As already mentioned, the characteristics of optical transmission systems can be defined and described at electrical interfaces. For this reason the known interfaces introduced in connection with transmission systems on metallic cables can be adopted; as a consequence, the same hierarchy levels and identical interfaces are used in the digital systems.

A comparison of the regenerator section lengths or elementary cable sec-

tion lengths for the various transmission systems employed in the long-haul network with the repeater section lengths of coaxial cable systems is shown in Fig. 5.

For point-to-point connections without regenerators (e.g. for the local network), the digital systems can be of simpler design than is necessary for long-haul applications. For instance, a light-emitting diode is adequate as the optical source up to 140 Mbit/s. The outlay for supervision, line coding, scrambler and the like, can also be reduced for this special application. In spite of the simplifications, ranges from about 15 to 10 km can be bridged without regenerators at an optical wavelength of 1300 nm by systems for 2 to 140 Mbit/s, which is completely adequate for the local network.

In addition to the characteristics of the optoelectronic transducers and the intrinsic fiber attenuation, other losses, such as splice and connector losses, as well as certain necessary reserves must be taken into account when determining section lengths realizable in practice. Thus in table 2 and the associated calculations for the other systems only one optical connector at the start of the link and one at the end of the link has been allowed for. If the design principles employed for the established cable systems using metallic conductors are adopted, further disconnect points in the form of connectors, e.g. as line distributors, must be included. The realizable section lengths are thus considerably shorter than they would be if only the physical and theoretical optimum values had to be taken into account.

Table 2 shows such a system calculation – also known as a power budget – using the 140 Mbit/s system as an example.

For practical reasons optical waveguide connectors at the beginning and end of the link are defined as the optical interfaces between the equipment and the optical link. Finally, only the attenuation and the bandwidth of the regenerator section are the important and system relevant data which must be correct for the interoperation between the equipment and the cable system. It is the function of line engineering to assure these values on the basis of the specific fiber characteristics.

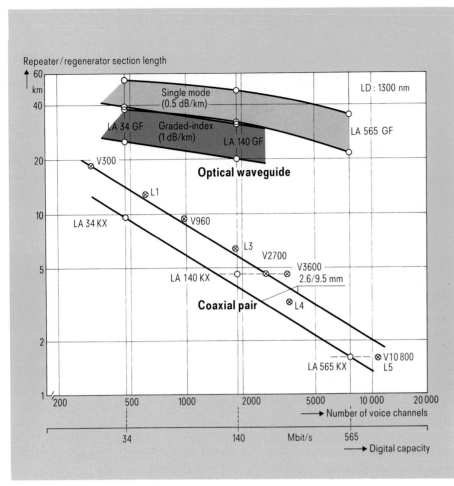

LD   Laser diode

Fig. 5   Repeater and regenerator section lengths *l* of various transmission systems on lines as a function of the transmission capacity

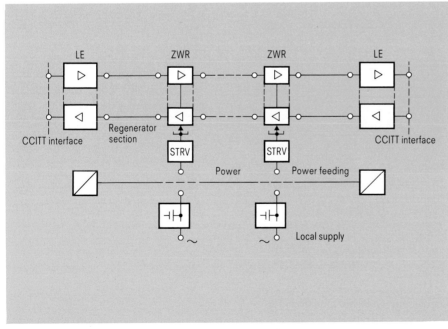

LE   Line terminating unit
STRV   Power supply
ZWR   Regenerator

Fig. 6   Schematic arrangement of an optical waveguide link with possible power supply

Peripheral systems

In addition to the actual task of optical transmission, a large number of operationally important points have to be considered in the practical design of the complete transmission system.

For instance, if repeaters are provided, details of their mechanical design and accommodation have to be determined. Since in equipment employed for optical transmission there is no high cable potential, such as occurs in the power feeding of amplifiers for coaxial cable systems, the repeaters can be of the same mechanical design as the line terminating equipment.

The regenerators can be housed above ground in telecommunication station buildings or underground in containers. Based on the experience of coaxial cable systems, the advantages should lie with housing in underground containers.

Regenerators require a preferably nobreak source of power in the order of 10 to 20 W for their operation. Whereas in systems for coaxial cable the regenerators are remotely powered directly via the inner conductor of the coaxial pair, other methods have to be employed for optical cables.

In general, the necessary power can be taken from the public network, which is available in the telecommunication station buildings. Batteries, tricklecharged from the ac power line, are available for emergency operation.

Other means must be provided for repeater stations without an ac power connection. For instance, the necessary power can be derived from solar cells, wind power or various combustion processes. If the various sources are assessed somewhat more accurately, one arrives at the classical dc series feeding as a favorable solution, apart from the special case of solar energy.

When a separate power-feeding cable in parallel with the optical cable is employed, several systems can be power-fed from a single power source (**Fig. 6**). The requirements for power feeding with redundancy, protection of personnel and fault location can be optimally met in this way.

As in the case of coaxial cable systems, fault location procedures are incorporated for the location of cable and

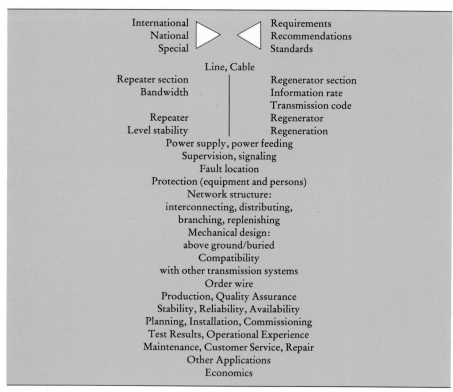

International
National
Special

Requirements
Recommendations
Standards

Line, Cable

Repeater section
Bandwidth

Regenerator section
Information rate
Transmission code

Repeater
Level stability

Regenerator
Regeneration

Power supply, power feeding
Supervision, signaling
Fault location
Protection (equipment and persons)
Network structure:
interconnecting, distributing,
branching, replenishing
Mechanical design:
above ground/buried
Compatibility
with other transmission systems
Order wire
Production, Quality Assurance
Stability, Reliability, Availability
Planning, Installation, Commissioning
Test Results, Operational Experience
Maintenance, Customer Service, Repair
Other Applications
Economics

Table 3   Principal features for line transmission systems

equipment faults on the link. Depending on the system, use is made of procedures based on loop closure or supervision during operation.

In order to exclude any possible risk to the eyes of persons in the vicinity, laser transmitters must be switched off immediately if light can escape from a broken fiber. This ensures that innocent bystanders do not suffer injury even when a broken optical cable is exposed.

The standards so far applicable do not specify binding limits for laser radiation from exposed fibers in damaged optical cables. If values are adopted from related fields, then the values associated with optical transmission lie slightly above or slightly below the critical limit, depending upon the definition. In order to exclude the possibility of any deleterious effects, the aforementioned automatic switch off is provided.

Table 3 contains a summary of the characteristics for system engineering. As in the case of the established and well-tried systems for copper cables, a large number of characteristics have to be optimized, so that, finally, technically equivalent systems for optical waveguides and coaxial cables are available to the user.

Individual systems for different application in the large field of communication are described in detail in the following papers [7 to 10].

References

[1] Geckeler, S.: Physical Principles of Optical Waveguides.
telcom report 6 (1983) Special Issue "Optical Communications", pp. 9 to 14

[2] Weyrich, C.; Zschauer, K.-H.: Principles of Optoelectronic Signal Conversion.
telcom report 6 (1983) Special Issue "Optical Communications", pp. 14 to 19

[3] Knoblauch, G.: Fiber-Optic Components and Systems for Industrial Application.
telcom report 6 (1983) Special Issue "Optical Communications", pp. 161 to 165

[4] Pichlmayer, E.; Stegmeier, A.: A Fiber-Optic Transmission System for Signal Bandwidths up to 7.5 MHz.
telcom report 6 (1983) Special Issue "Optical Communications", pp. 151 to 155

[5] Aichholz, E.; Tilly, B.: A Fiber-Optic System for FM Radio Relay Feeder Links and High-Quality TV Transmission.
telcom report 6 (1983) Special Issue "Optical Communications", pp. 147 to 150

[6] Anders, A.: A Fiber-Optic Analog System for Application in Electric Utilities.
telcom report 6 (1983) Special Issue "Optical Communications", pp. 156 to 160

[7] Fluhr, J.; Marending, P.; Trimmel, H.: A Fiber-Optic System for Transmitting 8 Mbit/s Signals.
telcom report 6 (1983) Special Issue "Optical Communications", pp. 119 to 124

[8] Stegmeier, A.; Trimmel, H.: A Fiber-Optic System for Transmitting 34 Mbit/s Signals.
telcom report 6 (1983) Special Issue "Optical Communications", pp. 125 to 129

[9] Dömer, J.; Gier, J.: A Fiber-Optic System for Transmitting 140 Mbit/s Signals.
telcom report 6 (1983) Special Issue "Optical Communications", pp. 130 to 133

[10] Kügler, E.: Development Trends in Higher Order Fiber-Optic Transmission Systems.
telcom report 6 (1983) Special Issue "Optical Communications", pp. 134 to 136

Josef Fluhr, Peter Marending and Herwig Trimmel

A Fiber-Optic System for Transmitting 8 Mbit/s Signals

Alongside the copper cable transmission systems hitherto employed in the short-haul network, fiber-optic transmission is now also playing an increasingly significant role. The system described here was first employed in the transmission network of the Swiss PTT and is designed for second-order digital transmission at 8448 kbit/s (abbreviated to 8 Mbit/s) in accordance with CCITT Recommendation G.742. As the electrical interfaces conform to CCITT Recommendation G.703, the system can interoperate with digital multiplexer DSMX2/8 or with a digital exchange for 120 telephone channels. Connection of a video-telephony codec is also possible.

System design

To ensure adequate performance of this optical transmission system, a laser diode is employed as the optical source and the optical detector is an avalanche photodiode. These are coupled to the fiber via suitable interface connectors. The *optical transmitter* and *optical receiver* modules are shown in **Fig. 1**.

The line equipment can be operated on optical fibers with differing transmission properties, though the span length will vary according to the quality of the fibers. The equipment is designed in equipment style 72 standardized by the Swiss PTT. Power supply, supervision and fault location facilities are compatible with this equipment standard, but can be adapted to suit other user requirements.

Ing. (grad.) Josef Fluhr and
Ing. (HTL) Peter Marending,
Siemens-Albis AG,
Long Range Transmission Development,
Zurich,
Dipl.-Ing. Herwig Trimmel,
Siemens AG,
Public Communication Networks Division,
Munich

Owing to the large repeater spacings possible, the intermediate repeaters are locally powered and no remote power feeding equipment is required. As a result, the power supply arrangements are the same both for the line terminating equipment and for the intermediate repeaters. The same optical transmitter and receiver modules and also the same power supply units can be used throughout the entire system.

System principles

Optical line code

When selecting a line code, a designer is usually confronted with a comprise between a code which can be easily generated and a code which enables him to overcome a large optical loss for a given bit error rate.

To assist in estimating the bandwidth requirement of the codes under consideration, **Fig. 2** shows the curves of the power density spectra for different line codes as a function of the normalized

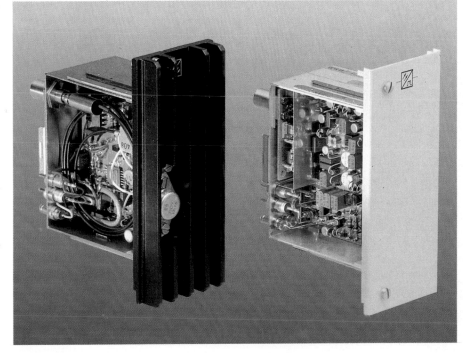

Fig. 1 Optical transmitter and optical receiver for transmitting 8 Mbit/s signals

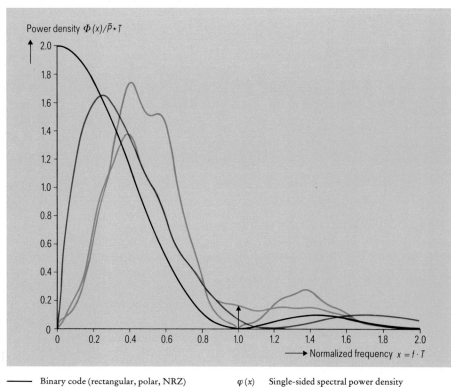

Fig. 2 Power density spectra of various codes (the codes are illustrated without the average value)

——	Binary code (rectangular, polar, NRZ)	$\varphi(x)$	Single-sided spectral power density
——	5B/6B code (rectangular, polar, NRZ)	$\bar{P}$	Mean power
——	MCMI code (rectangular, polar, NRZ, 0→01)	x	Normalized frequency ($x = f \cdot T$);
——	HDB3 code (rectangular, RZ)		$T = 1/8448$ kHz for all codes

frequency $x = f \cdot T$ ($x = 1$ for $f = 1/T$ = 8448 kHz). Unlike the nonredundant binary code, the other three codes produce only small low-frequency signal components.

An examination of the bandwidth from 0 Hz to 16 896 kHz ($x = 2$) reveals that the proportion of spectral power in this range is about 94% of the total power for the 5B/6B code, about 91% for the HDB3 code and approximately 89% for the MCMI code.

When choosing between the binary 5B/6B block code and the modified CMI code from the 1B/2B code group, preference was given to the latter on account of the following features:

● simple code conversion, hence low circuit costs and low power consumption for transmit-side conversion of the HDB3 coded 8448 kbit/s interface signal into the two-level line signal, and for receive-side decoding,

● no signal scrambling necessary and therefore no error multiplication,

● simple and reliable timing recovery owing to the high level of timing information present in the line signal,

● easy bit error detection owing to the high code redundancy.

As the symbol rate of the 2B code employed is double that of the nonredundant binary code, the cable plant is required to provide a higher bandwidth. This requirement can be met economically by present-day graded-

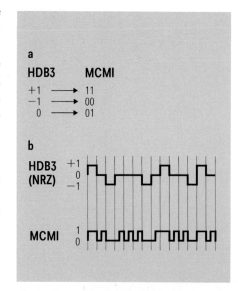

Fig. 3 Conversion law (a) and an example of conversion from HDB3 code to MCMI code (b)

index fibers. In addition, the increased transmission rate results in a loss of receiver sensitivity of about 3 dB and hence a reduction in the repeater section length. This seems acceptable for the intended application, since use of this coding considerably reduces the complexity of the equipment required.

The HDB3 coded 8448 kbit/s interface signal is converted into the MCMI coded optical line signal according to the rule shown in **Fig. 3**.

Optical transmitter and optical receiver

Transmit side

The transmit-side output unit converts the incoming electrical signal into an optical NRZ (non-return-to-zero) signal with constant modulation depth, the optoelectronic transducer used being a GaAlAs oxide-stripe laser diode module with a multimode emission spectrum. Versions with optical wavelengths of 840 and 880 nm are available to match the spectral attenuation characteristics of the various types of fiber used. The optical output power measured at the connector is 0 dBm after subtracting the power guided in the fiber cladding.

Besides the optoelectronic components (laser diode with monitor photodiode for sensing the optical power), the hermetically sealed laser module SFH 408 also incorporates a Peltier cooler and a temperature sensor. Cooling the laser diode ensures stable laser operation with an extremely low aging rate even at high operating temperatures.

Fig. 4 shows the functional circuit diagram of the optical transmitter, comprising the laser module, the drive circuit, the circuits for controlling temperature, optical power and modulation depth, and the laser protection and alarm signaling circuits.

The drive circuit regenerates the amplitude of the incoming signal (ECL level) and supplies the modulation current for the laser diode. In addition to the modulation current I_{mod}, the laser diode is fed with a bias current I_0 just below the lasing threshold. This biasing prevents the rise of the light pulse being delayed with respect to the drive current pulse.

120

Since the light-current characteristic of the laser diode is a function of temperature and aging, the optical power and modulation depth are regulated via two control loops. One control loop causes the bias current I_0 to track the mean optical power. Laser slope variations are compensated by suitably controlling the modulation current I_{mod} to ensure that the optimum operating point is maintained below the lasing threshold.

A laser protection and alarm circuit prevents the laser diode from being overloaded.

Receive side

In the receive-side input unit (**Fig. 5**), an avalanche photodiode (APD) receives the incoming optical signal and converts it into an electrical signal. The optical input sensitivity for a bit error rate of 10^{-10} is −54 dBm.

The supply voltage for the avalanche photodiode is produced via a dc converter which is incorporated in the automatic gain control circuit.

The APD circuit with an optical control range of 15 dB is followed by a gain-controlled, low-noise preamplifier (transimpedance amplifier) which converts the current pulses from the avalanche photodiode into voltage pulses. The conversion factor can be reduced automatically from 20 to 1 μV/nA. The preamplifier is followed by a dual-gate field-effect transistor whose gain can be varied by a factor of 17 via the gate bias voltage.

The entire electrical dynamic range is 50 dB, equivalent to an optical dynamic range of 25 dB. This, together with the gain control range of the avalanche photodiode, produces a total optical dynamic range of 40 dB. The receiver can, therefore, handle optical input power levels up to −14 dBm without limiting. For larger input levels, an optical attenuator is required.

A five-section maximally-flat low-pass filter at the output of the signal amplifier provides band limiting.

Repeater spacing

Optoelectronic components for the 8 Mbit/s system are available for optical wavelengths of 840 and 880 nm as standard. With further development of the optical system components, it will also be possible to employ the system at optical wavelengths around 1300 nm (second optical transmission window).

Table 1 shows the achievable repeater spacings as a function of optical wavelength and transmitter type, the fiber losses used being currently regarded as typical values. To facilitate comparison with higher-bit-rate systems, the optical transmit and receive power levels given in **Table 1** have been corrected for the finite extinction ratio of the laser.

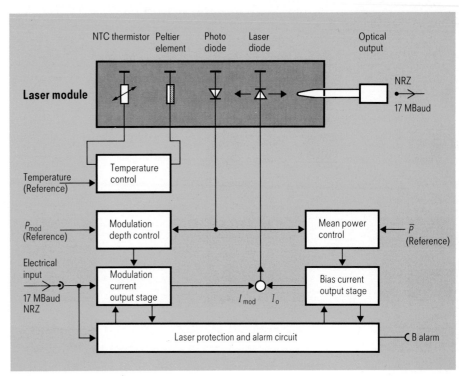

I_0 Bias current
I_{mod} Modulating current
$\bar{P}$ Mean power
P_{mod} Modulation power

Fig. 4   Functional circuit diagram of the optical transmitter

Equipment

Line terminating equipment

As shown in **Fig. 6**, the signals arriving in the transmit direction via terminal "F2 in" are equalized up to 12 dB at the 4224 kHz Nyquist frequency in an automatic equalizer to compensate the frequency-dependent station cable attenuation. They are then fed through a regenerator with a timing recovery circuit of low Q-factor to provide a high input jitter tolerance.

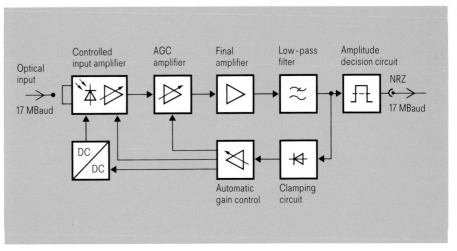

DC/DC   Voltage converter   NRZ   Signal "Non Return to Zero"

Fig. 5   Functional circuit diagram of the optical receiver

Optical waveguide		Graded-index fiber			
3 dB bandwidth		25 MHz per repeater section			
Optical wavelength	nm	840/880		1300	
Optical transmitter		IRED	Laser	IRED	Laser
Transmit power	dBm	−16	−2	−17	−2
Required receive power for a bit error rate of 10^{-10}	dBm	−56		−49	
Attenuation of two equipment connectors	dB	3			
Theoretical system loss	dB	37	51	29	44
System margin	dB	6			
Maximum repeater section loss	dB	31	45	23	38
Fiber loss	dB/km	3		1	
Splice loss with 1 km pull-in length	dB/km	0.2			
Additional loss for reserve splices	dB/km	0.3			
Cable loss	dB/km	3.5		1.5	
Repeater spacing	km	8.8	12.8	15.3	25.3

Table 1   Data for the optical link

Transmission rate	8448 kbit/s
Transmission code	HDB3
Nominal peak voltage at the output	2.37 V
Impedance	75 Ω, unbal.
Pulse shape	Rectangular, per CCITT Recommendation G.703, Fig. 17
Automatic station cable equalization, transmit-side	$\leqq 12$ dB, at 4224 kHz

Table 2   Electrical characteristics of the F2 interface

The *MCMI coder* converts the regenerated HDB3 signal into a two-level HDB3 signal better suited to optical transmission. Since this MCMI coded line signal can contain no more than three consecutive zeros, excellent timing recovery in the regenerators is achieved. The *"optical transmitter"* performs optoelectronic signal conversion and launches the light pulses into the pigtail.

In the receive direction, the optical signal is fed from the transmission route via interface "F1 in" to the *optical receiver* where the optical light pulses are converted back into electrical signals, amplified and assigned to logic level 0 or 1 in the amplitude and time decision circuit. The *MCMI decoder* converts the binary signal into an HDB3 signal which is passed through an amplifier and fed to interface "F2 out".

The electrical characteristics of the 8448 kbit/s HDB3 interfaces on the F2 side (**Table 2**) conform to CCITT Recommendation G.703, permitting interoperation with other equipment complying with this Recommendation.

Transmit-side supervision and alarm facilities

The incoming 8 Mbit/s information signal (F2 in) is supervised continuously after regeneration. If the transmit supervision circuit (SÜ) does not receive a signal within an observation interval of $\geqq 250$ μs, an urgent alarm (A alarm) is initiated and at the same time the AIS (*alarm indication signal*) generated by a dedicated crystal oscillator is applied to "F1 out" in place of the live traffic signal.

For preventive supervision of the laser, both its bias current and its modulation current are monitored. If only one of these currents rises more than 50% above the nominal value, a non-urgent alarm (B alarm) is produced. Both alarms are indicated by light-emitting diodes on the front panel of the *"transmission monitor"* unit and are available as electrical criteria.

Receive-side supervision and alarm facilities

Receive-side supervision involves establishing the presence of the signal and determining the bit error rate. If the optical input signal (F1 in) is missing or if an error rate of 10^{-3} is exceeded, an A alarm is initiated. In this event, the traffic signal is replaced by an alarm indication and the AIS is applied to the 8 Mbit/s interface (F2 out). A bit error rate of $>10^{-6}$ is signaled as a B alarm. The two receive-side alarms similarly provide visual indication by means of light-emitting diodes on the *"transmission monitor"* module.

Locally powered intermediate repeaters

The intermediate repeaters required for spanning long distances between line terminating units incorporate a regenerator and associated supervision equipment for each of the two transmission directions.

As in the line terminating equipment, the optical signals arriving at interface "F1 in" are converted by an optical receiver into electrical signals and amplified. A cascaded amplitude and time decision circuit then regenerates the signals, after which the following optical transmitter converts them from electrical into optical form and launches them into the optical fiber. The "F1 in" and "F1 out" interfaces

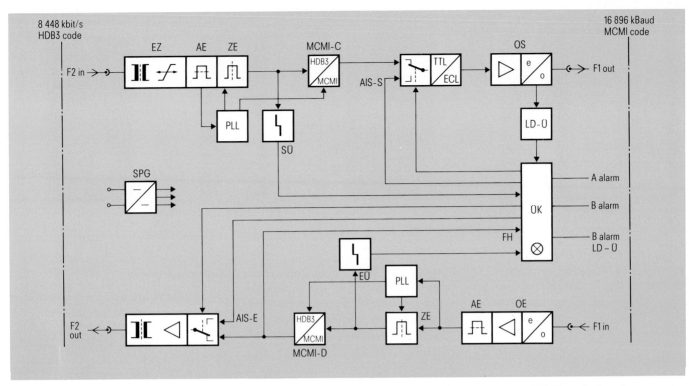

AE	Amplitude decision circuit	EÜ	Receive supervision	MCMI-C	MCMI coder	SPG	Power-feeding unit
AIS	Alarm indication signal	EZ	Equalizer	MCMI-D	MCMI decoder	SÜ	Transmit supervision
AIS-E	AIS receive	FH	Error rate (BER)	OE	Optical receiver	TTL	Transistor-transistor logic
AIS-S	AIS transmit	LD-Ü	Laser diode supervision	OS	Optical transmitter	ÜK	Transmission monitor
ECL	Emitter-coupled logic			PLL	Phase-locked loop	ZE	Time decision circuit

Fig. 6 Functional circuit diagram of the line terminating equipment

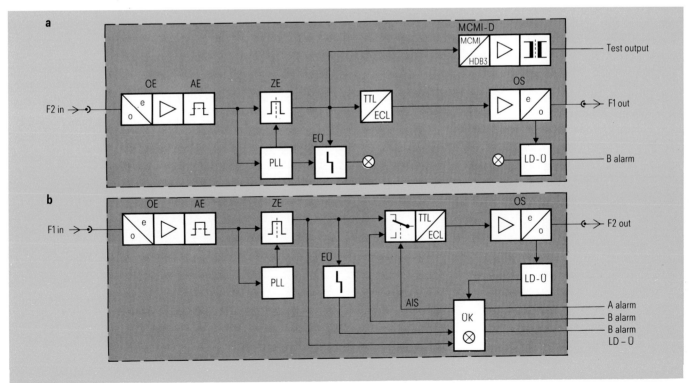

AE	Amplitude decision circuit	EÜ	Receive supervision	OE	Optical receiver	TTL	Transistor-transistor logic
AIS	Alarm indication signal	LD-Ü	Laser diode supervision	OS	Optical transmitter	ÜK	Transmission monitor
ECL	Emitter-coupled logic	MCMI-D	MCMI decoder	PLL	Phase-locked loop	ZE	Time decision circuit

Fig. 7 Functional circuit diagram of the intermediate repeaters (one-way)
a Intermediate repeater for in-service remote monitoring
b Intermediate repeater for local monitoring

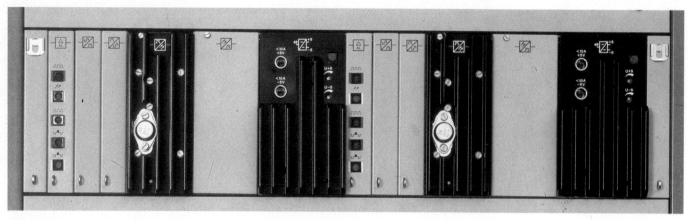

Fig. 8 · Style 72 equipment frame housing two line terminating equipments

are designed as optical connectors. As shown in **Fig. 7**, the intermediate repeater is available in two versions which differ only in their supervision circuits.

Intermediate repeaters for in-service monitoring

Since the two transmission directions are equipped with their own supervision and alarm circuits, only one direction need be considered.

The level of the 17 megabaud input signal is continuously supervised. Any loss of signal is indicated automatically by the intermediate repeater. As in the line terminating equipment, the laser diode is continuously monitored for bias current and modulation current. Excessively high currents initiate a B alarm and are indicated by a second light-emitting diode.

For locating defective intermediate repeaters and determining the bit error rate even during service, each regenerator is assigned an additional circuit. This circuit converts the MCMI signal into an HDB3 signal and has an isolated test output. These test outputs can be used to connect the units of an existing remote supervision system so that they can interoperate, for instance via a balanced copper circuit, with supervisory equipment in the terminal stations.

Intermediate repeater for local monitoring

Since the optical intermediate repeaters are intended to be housed in surface buildings, there is a possibility of employing local monitoring, thus avoiding considerable expenditure on equipment for a remote supervision system. It is clearly preferable for a local intermediate repeater supervision circuit to be identical in design to the supervision circuit in the line terminating equipment. This is achieved merely by incorporating in the one-way repeater the *transmission monitor* module as used in the line terminating equipment.

This version of the intermediate repeater can respond to an A alarm (caused by loss of the input signal or an error rate $>10^{-3}$) by transmitting the characteristic AIS.

Equipment design

The 8 Mbit/s line equipment for optical communication is manufactured in equipment style 72. The design principle uses horizontal equipment insets of uniform width, known as equipment frames. An equipment frame 462 mm wide, 122 mm high and 175 mm deep can contain either the plug-in units for two line terminating equipments or the plug-ins for a two-way intermediate repeater. A frame equipped with two line terminating equipments is illustrated in **Fig. 8**, showing from left to right the *transmission monitor, interface S, interface E, optical transmitter, optical receiver* and *power-supply units*. Alongside, in the same sequence, are the units of a second line terminating equipment.

The racks for mounting the equipment frames are available in two heights, the standard rack being 2736 mm high and the small rack for low rooms being 2196 mm high. A standard rack can house up to 16 line terminating equipments or eight two-way intermediate repeaters together with the rack power supply.

Anton Stegmeier and Herwig Trimmel

A Fiber-Optic System for Transmitting 34 Mbit/s Signals

The introduction of optical communications by the Deutsche Bundespost (DBP) started with systems operating at 34 Mbit/s. After successful trials on an experimental link in Berlin [1] from which basic experience of the new transmission medium and the necessary optoelectronic devices was gained, the first operational link with intermediate repeaters was cut over in February 1979 [2]. This 15.4 km link connects the Frankfurt-Ginnheim main exchange to the Oberursel tandem exchange. The transmission system used already has all the characteristics of a fully operational system and has since been installed elsewhere in Germany and abroad. This success is now being followed by a second generation 34 Mbit/s system, and it is this latest development which is described in this paper.

System configuration

The 34 Mbit/s fiber-optic system provides for simultaneous transmission of 480 telephone channels at 64 kbit/s each. It can, however, also be used to transmit data, sound-program or TV signals. The system is incorporated into digital networks via the 34 Mbit/s signal interfaces specified in CCITT Recommendation G.703 [3].

Apart from the line terminating unit and the intermediate repeater, the line equipment also includes power-feeding units. These units are mounted as required in style 7R racks [4] together with a terminal panel, a fiber-optic cable distributor, an optical line building-out network and an alarm signal panel. A line terminating unit rack can be equipped either with three line terminating units or two line terminating units together with a power-feeding inset (**Fig. 1**).

The line terminating units form the end points of a line section, their function being to terminate the line and provide supervision and fault-location facilities. If the system is used in the local network, power-feeding is not usually required, since the unrepeated distances which can be spanned with fiber optics are relatively large (**Table 1**).

The system can be operated in the short-haul network using one power-feeding inset to supply the necessary intermediate repeaters. Depending on the diameter of the power-feeding cable, it is possible with dc series feeding to power up to five intermediate repeaters from one end. In this way, power-feeding sections of up to some 120 km are possible. Although the copper power-feeding cable is generally kept separate from the fiber-optic cable for technical and economic reasons, the two can in fact be laid side by side.

Anton Stegmeier and
Dipl.-Ing. Herwig Trimmel,
Siemens AG,
Public Communication Networks Division,
Munich

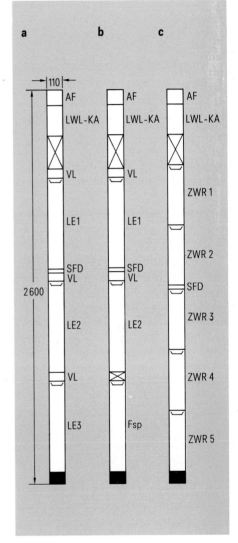

AF	Terminal panel	
Fsp	Power-feeding inset	
LE	Line terminating unit	
LWL-KA	Fiber-optic cable housing	
SFD	Alarm signal panel	
VL	Optical attenuator (line build-out)	
ZWR	Intermediate repeater	

Fig. 1   Style 7R rack 2.6 m high accommodating the line equipment

a }
b } Line terminating equipment rack 34 GF

c   Intermediate repeater rack 34 GF

System principles

Line code

The choice of line code is largely influenced by the transmission bandwidth of the fiber-optic cable used. For the 8 Mbit/s system, there are graded-index fibers available with sufficient bandwidth to present no problems in doubling the symbol rate for the 1B/2B line code used on that system [5].

For higher-order systems the transmission bandwidth required for the 1B/2B code can only be achieved at significantly higher cost in terms of cable plant. This disadvantage is particularly serious for systems operating at 1300 nm, where there is the additional factor of longer repeater spacings requiring correspondingly higher bandwidth-distance products.

The 34 Mbit/s and the 140 Mbit/s fiber-optic systems therefore employ a 5B/6B block code, which is economical in terms of transmission bandwidth. The symbol rate is increased by a factor of only 1.2 to 41.2 or 167 Mbaud. Line coding is performed by converting 5-bit words into 6-bit words according to the code table given in **Table 2**. For the 32 possible combinations of the 5B input word there are 64 possible output combinations of the 6B word. The combinations used for conversion are divided into two groups, one group containing only those combinations with word disparity "0" or "+1" (three zeros and three ones or two zeros and four ones) and the other only those with word disparity "0" or "−1" (three zeros and three ones or four zeros and two ones). Unbalanced words result in group changeover, so that the running digital sum (RDS) at the end of a 6B word is between ±1. The limits imposed on the RDS allow fault supervision to be carried out during operation.

The resulting code table has been designed for a minimal error multiplication factor, the value achieved being about 1.2. The power density spectrum of this 5B/6B code is given in [5]. The scrambling of the signal prior to encoding eliminates periodic signals and enables the 5B/6B decoder at the receive end to achieve word synchronization regardless of bit sequence. This 5B/6B line code is being introduced by

the Deutsche Bundespost as the standard for 34 and 140 Mbit/s fiber-optic systems.

Optoelectronic components

The repeater spacing of the 34 Mbit/s fiber-optic system is determined by the components of the optical link, by the optical wavelength used and by the attenuation coefficient of the cable system (see **Table 1**). The system is designed so that the optical link can be configured with the following options:

Optical wavelength	840/880 nm or 1300 nm
Optical source	Laser diode (LD) or infrared-emitting diode (IRED)
Optical detector	Avalanche photodiode (APD) for 840/880 nm or PIN-FET for 1300 nm
Fiber type	Graded-index or single-mode fibers

For transmission in the first optical window there are optical sources available at wavelengths of 840 or 880 nm to match the spectral loss characteristics of the cable system.

The transition to optical wavelengths near 1300 nm and the consequent reduction in cable attenuation ($\leq$1.5 dB/km) allows the repeater spacing to be approximately doubled. The optoelectronic components for this wavelength are already sufficiently advanced to allow their use in operational systems. IREDs emitting at 1300 nm achieve lifetimes of 10^8 h at room temperature [6]. The useful life of 1300 nm laser diodes is now comparable with the high life expectancy of Siemens 840/880 nm laser diodes.

At the receive end, there are only Ge avalanche photodiodes and PIN photodiodes currently available for operation at 1300 nm. As Germanium avalanche photodiodes are consider-

Fiber		Graded-index fiber			Single-mode fiber
3 dB bandwidth		50 MHz per repeater section			
Wavelength	nm	850	1300		
Optical transmitter		Laser diode (LD)	Infrared-emitting diode (IRED)	Laser diode (LD)	
Transmit power	dBm	−3	−19	−3	−4
Minimum receive power (bit error rate $\leq 10^{-10}$	dBm	−52	−47	−47	−47
Connector loss (2)	dB	3			4
Theoretical system loss	dB	46	25	41	39
System margins for units (inc. aging, tolerances)	dB	6			
Maximum repeater section loss	dB	40	19	35	33
Fiber loss	dB/km	3	0.8 to 1.0		0.5
Splice loss for 1 km pull-in length	dB/km	0.2	0.1 to 0.2		0.1 to 0.2
Loss reserve for repair splices	dB/km	0.3	0 to 0.3		0 to 0.3
Cable loss	dB/km	3.5	0.9 to 1.5		0.6 to 1.0
Repeater spacing	km	11.5	21 to 12.6	39 to 23	55 to 30

Table 1   Data for optical link for the 34 Mbit/s fiber-optic system

5B word		6B word			
		Group +	Following group	Group −	Following group
0	00000	50 110010	+	50 110010	−
1	00001	51 110011	−	33 100001	+
2	00010	54 110110	−	34 100010	+
3	00011	35 100011	+	35 100011	−
4	00100	53 110101	−	36 100100	+
5	00101	37 100101	+	37 100101	−
6	00110	38 100110	+	38 100110	−
7	00111	39 100111	−	7 000111	−
8	01000	43 101011	−	40 101000	+
9	01001	41 101001	+	41 101001	−
10	01010	42 101010	+	42 101010	−
11	01011	11 001011	+	11 001011	−
12	01100	44 101100	+	44 101100	−
13	01101	45 101101	−	5 000101	+
14	01110	46 101110	−	6 000110	+
15	01111	14 001110	+	14 001110	−
16	10000	49 110001	+	49 110001	−
17	10001	57 111001	−	17 010001	+
18	10010	58 111010	−	18 010010	+
19	10011	19 010011	+	19 010011	−
20	10100	52 110100	+	52 110100	−
21	10101	21 010101	+	21 010101	−
22	10110	22 010110	+	22 010110	−
23	10111	23 010111	−	20 010100	+
24	11000	56 111000	+	24 011000	+
25	11001	25 011001	+	25 011001	−
26	11010	26 011010	+	26 011010	−
27	11011	27 011011	−	10 001010	+
28	11100	28 011100	+	28 011100	−
29	11101	29 011101	−	9 001001	+
30	11110	30 011110	−	12 001100	+
31	11111	13 001101	+	13 001101	−

Table 2   Code table for 5B/6B code

loss. These factors must be incorporated in the loss budget, and include losses due to connectors, splices and repair splices, the aging of optoelectronic components, the measurement uncertainty and the required system margin.

All the essential system parameters are summarized as a loss budget in **Table 1**. This shows the requirements for spanning particular repeater spacings. The theoretical system losses given are minimum values. The kilometric loss data for the cable system are currently regarded as typical values.

In the first optical transmission window it is possible (for example, at an optical wavelength of 880 nm) to achieve fiber losses ≤ 2.5 dB/km. All other conditions being equal, this will provide a repeater spacing of 13.3 km.

Line equipment

Line terminating unit

The line terminating unit is accommodated in a 600 mm high style 7R inset, with the optical transmit and receive units and other equipment plugged vertically into the upper section of the inset (**Fig. 3**). This has advantages for both the thermal and mechanical

ably less sensitive than silicon diodes, a hybrid integrated PIN-FET module has been developed (**Fig. 2**). This provides the maximum sensitivity achievable with state-of-the-art components.

The 34 Mbit/s fiber-optic system is equipped for transmission on graded-index fibers as standard, but can be adapted for use with single-mode fibers. Although the smaller core diameter of single-mode fibers (about 10 µm) makes jointing losses more pronounced than in graded-index fibers, the lower loss of single-mode fibers enables the repeater spacing to be increased.

System range

The system range or repeater spacing is determined by the components of the optical link. When setting up an operational system there are certain factors to take into account in addition to the transmit/receive powers and the fiber

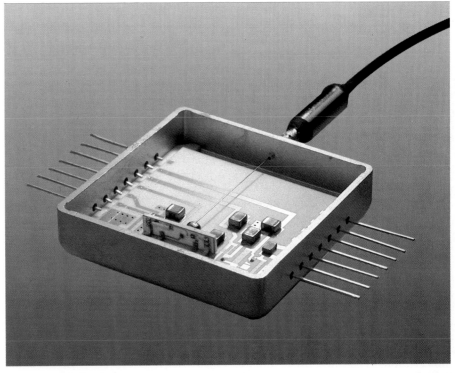

Fig. 2   PIN-FET module

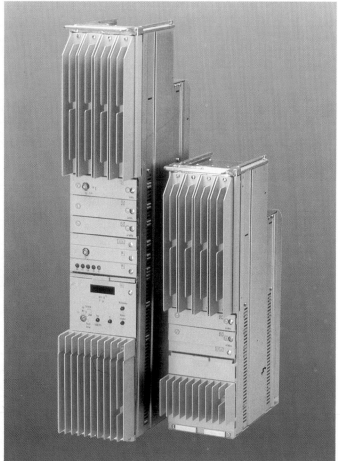

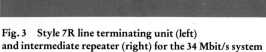

Fig. 3   Style 7R line terminating unit (left)
and intermediate repeater (right) for the 34 Mbit/s system

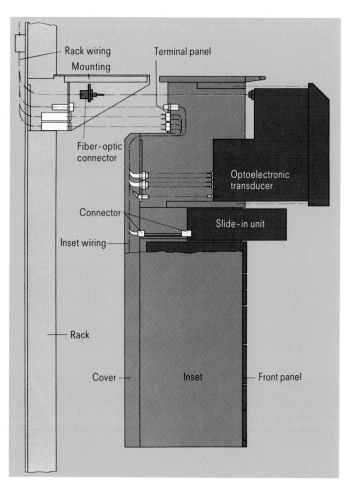

Fig. 4   Fiber-optic terminations

design. In order to minimize losses due to optical connectors, the number of connectors is reduced to a minimum. This is achieved by making the optical connection not via the inset wiring, as is usually the case, but by routing it directly from the unit to the rack (**Fig. 4**).

As shown in **Fig. 5**, the line terminating unit converts the HDB3-encoded signal from the digital multiplexer into a form suitable for optical transmission. The signal is equalized, regenerated, scrambled after binary conversion and converted to the 5B/6B line code. Subsequent optoelectronic conversion produces the binary optical transmit signal which is launched into the fiber. The incoming optical signal is converted back to an electrical signal, amplified, regenerated and decoded. The scrambling performed at the transmit end is then reversed, producing the HDB3 signal required at the interface.

The HDB3 encoder and HDB3 decoder, the scrambler and descram-

bler as well as the 5B/6B encoder and 5B/6B decoder are designed as VLSI chips. This high degree of integration enables the power loss of high-speed logic circuits to be kept within limits [7]. The design of the optical transmitter incorporating laser diodes (**Fig. 6**) corresponds to the functional circuit diagram given in [5]. The laser diode is mounted in a hermetically sealed module together with a cooler, a temperature sensor and a monitor photodiode [8]. For 1300 nm laser diodes in particular it is necessary to limit the operating temperature of the laser to a range below 30 to 40°C. If IREDs are used, no power or temperature control is necessary, owing to the extremely low aging rate of IREDs and the fact that their optical characteristics do not vary as a function of temperature.

The optical receiver for the 840/880 nm wavelength is as shown in the functional circuit diagram given in [5]. The input sensitivity is −52 dBm for a bit error rate of $\leqq 10^{-10}$. The maximum

input level is −10 dBm. For transmission at 1300 nm a hermetically sealed PIN-FET module (**Fig. 2**) with high input impedance is used. By hybrid integration of the PIN photodiode, GaAs field-effect transistors and bipolar transistors on a ceramic substrate, an input capacitance of approximately 0.7 pF is achieved. The sensitivity of the optical receiver for a bit error rate of 10^{-10} is −47 dBm. The maximum input level is −23 dBm, an optical line building-out network (optical attenuator) being provided for higher input levels.

Faults and disturbances within a line section can be detected with the aid of the supervision equipment in the line terminating unit. They are indicated by light-emitting diodes in the supervision module or passed to a central supervision point. The incoming signal and the timing recovery are therefore monitored in the transmit and receive paths, the receive end checking the signal for code rule violations and evaluat-

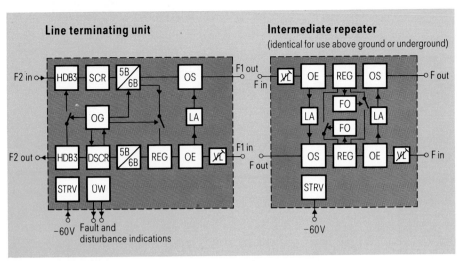

Line terminating unit   Intermediate repeater
(identical for use above ground or underground)

Abbreviation	Description
5B/6B	5B/6B encoder
DSCR	Descrambler
FO	Fault location
HDB3	HDB3 encoder
LA	Laser shutdown
OE	Optical receiver
OG	Fault locating unit
OS	Optical transmitter
REG	Signal regenerator
SCR	Scrambler
STRV	Power supply
ÜW	Supervision
VL	Optical attenuator (line building-out network)

Fig. 5 Functional circuit diagram of line equipment LA 34 GF

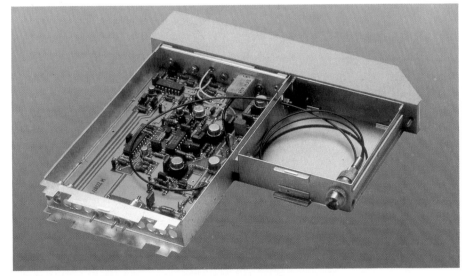

Fig. 6 Transmit module of the 34 Mbit/s fiber-optic system

ing the bit error rate (BER). If the BER is $\geqq 10^{-6}$, a B alarm (non-urgent) is initiated, and for a BER $\geqq 10^{-3}$ an A alarm (urgent).

Supervision of the 34 Mbit/s style 7R fiber-optic system conforms to Deutsche Bundespost guidelines and hence the basic principles of the CCITT maintenance philosophy [9]. The fault-locating unit enables a defective repeater section to be detected in the event of a fault on a link containing intermediate repeaters. The fault-locating procedure uses unaddressed loop-back, similar to that employed on coaxial cable system LA34 KX [10].

Intermediate repeater

The intermediate repeater for two transmission directions is accommodated in a 400 mm high style 7R inset. Apart from the power converter, the equipment largely comprises slide-in units from the line terminating unit (**Figs. 3 and 5**). The received optical signal is converted to an electrical signal, regenerated in amplitude and time and, after optoelectronic conversion, retransmitted to line.

The intermediate repeater as in **Fig. 1** is designed for mounting in style 7R racks. Containers are available for installing the repeater underground.

Voltage can be supplied locally or via a power-feeding system, a standard 60 V interface being provided for this purpose.

References

[1] Graßl, F.; Krägenow, H.: Die Lichtwellen-leiter-Kabelstrecke Berlin, ein Projekt von grundsätzlicher Bedeutung. telcom report 1 (1978), pp. 40 to 45

[2] Müller, K.; Unterlaß, W.; Weber, W.: Two Years' Experience with the First Operational Fiber-Optic Route in the Deutsche Bundespost Network. telcom report 4 (1981), No. 4, pp. 246 to 249

[3] CCITT-Yellow Book, Rec. G.703

[4] Weis, G.: Physical Design of Systems and Equipments for Digital Transmission. telcom report 2 (1979) Special Issue "Digital Transmission", pp. 29 to 33

[5] Fluhr, J.; Marending, P.; Trimmel, H.: A Fiber-Optic System for Transmitting 8 Mbit/s Signals. telcom report 6 (1983) Special Issue "Optical Communications", pp. 119 to 124

[6] Heinen, J.; Lauterbach, Ch.: High-radiance surface emitting (In, Ga)(As, P)/InP IREDs with an emission wavelength of 1.3 μm for transmission rates of 34 Mbit/s and 140 Mbit/s. Siemens Forsch.- u. Entwickl.-Ber. 11 (1982), pp. 209 to 215

[7] Dömer, J.; Eich, W.: Technological Migration in the Line Terminating Units of Digital Transmission Systems. telcom report 5 (1982), pp. 97 to 100

[8] Althaus, H. L.; Kuhn, G.: Modular Laser Source. telcom report 6 (1983) Special Issue "Optical Communications", pp. 84 to 90

Josef Dömer and Jürgen Gier

A Fiber Optic System for Transmitting 140 Mbit/s Signals

For the optical transmission of fourth-order signals at a rate of 139,264 kbit/s (140 Mbit/s for short) line equipment has been developed for use with graded-index and single-mode fibers as the transmission medium in the 1300 nm wavelength range. Using graded-index fibers, the design path length is 1200 km, while the maximum spacing between intermediate repeaters is up to 30 km depending on the optical fiber cable installation. System supervision and fault location are provided on an "in-service monitoring" basis.

System configuration

The system is designed to transmit a 140 Mbit/s signal in accordance with CCITT Recommendation G.703 [1] and is therefore suitable for transmitting various signals including digitized speech, sound and TV signals as well as data signals. Overall, this system comprises line terminating units and intermediate repeaters designed in style 7R [2] for mounting in narrow racks. Power can be supplied to intermediate repeaters locally, e.g. by means of a 48 V or 60 V battery. In addition, a power-feeding system is available with capacity for remotely feeding up to three intermediate stations, each containing five repeaters, via a separate power supply cable from a dc source. The length of the power-feeding sections is determined by the cross section of the copper conductors used, the current, and the maximum available input voltage. For example, for a wire cross section of 1.5 mm², a feeding current of 400 mA, and a feeding voltage of

± 700 V, the length of the power-feeding section will be 54 km. The spacing between main (power-feeding) stations will therefore be 126 km.

System range

The repeater spacing for the 140 Mbit/s system is determined by the optical components of the link, and the optical wavelength used. The **table** shows the repeater spacings which can be achieved in practice, as a function of the optical waveguide used and of the optical transmitter. Data for cable loss and bandwidth are currently regarded

as typical values. The equipment is designed to permit optional use of the optical components listed in the **table**.

A 140 Mbit/s digital line path (DSGL) employing a graded-index fiber and with input and output interfaces meeting the relevant CCITT recommendations may for example be up to 1200 km long (**Fig. 1**). Line terminating units are inserted after 25 repeaters to reduce the jitter on the link sufficiently to allow another digital line section (DSGLA) to be added. CCITT Recommendation G.703 specifies values for the lower limit of tolerable input jitter and for the permissible output jitter. The components of the 140 Mbit/s transmission system described here conform to the values in the CCITT recommendations.

System design

The ends of the line section are provided with *line terminating units* to process and regenerate the digital signals in the transmit and receive direc-

Dipl.-Ing. Josef Dömer and
Dipl.-Ing. Jürgen Gier,
Siemens AG,
Public Communication Networks Division,
Munich

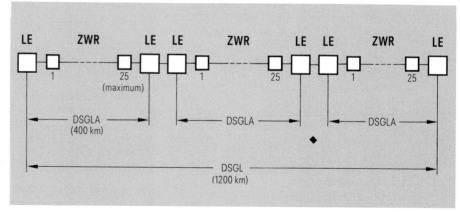

| DSGL | Digital line path | LE | Line terminating unit |
| DSGLA | Digital line section | ZWR | Intermediate repeater |

Fig. 1   Basic configuration of the 140 Mbit/s link

tions, and to perform supervisory functions. At the end of a repeater section the digital signal is regenerated in an *intermediate repeater.*

Line terminating unit

The slide-in modules in the line terminating unit, including the voltage converter which produces several internal supplies from the 48/60 V station battery, are accommodated in a 600 mm high inset (**Fig. 2**). The optoelectronic transducers and the high dissipation modules such as the scrambler with 5B/6B encoder and the descrambler with 5B/6B decoder incorporating LSI devices from the SH 100 series are equipped with vertical cooling fins and located in the upper section of the inset. In addition to good heat dissipation, this configuration provides a direct plug-in interface for the optical input and output between the slide-in module and the rack.

Intermediate repeaters

Each intermediate repeater is made up of modules from the line terminating unit and contains an optical receiver, a regenerator and an optical transmitter for each transmission direction. Provision is also made in each repeater for an optical shutdown facility activated by fiber breakage to protect personnel if a laser is employed. The repeater also contains modules for processing fault-locating signals. Two optical transmitters and two receivers are accommodated side by side in the upper section of the inset. All the slide-in modules, including the voltage converter, designed for operation from a 48/60 V source, can be accommodated in a 400 mm high inset.

Rack design

The line terminating units are generally accommodated in a style 7R rack, which can be equipped with either one or two systems (**Fig. 3 a**). A *fault-locating unit* with two fault-locating modules can also be inserted in this rack, when the modules are not housed in the line terminating units. The power dissipation in the fully equipped rack is 98 W. A rack for intermediate repeaters in style 7R contains up to five repeaters, with a maximum power consumption of 18 W each (**Fig. 3 b**).

Optical waveguide		Graded-index fiber ($d_c = 50\ \mu m$)		Single-mode fiber ($d_c = 10\ \mu m$)
Optical wavelength	nm	1300		
Optical transmitter		IRED	LD	LD
Transmit power	dBm	−20	−3	−4
Receive power (bit error rate $\geqq 10^{-10}$)	dBm	−40	−40	−43
Repeater section bandwidth (modal dispersion)	MHz	$\geqq 170$	$\geqq 120$	—
or maximum fiber dispersion	ps/nm · km	—	—	$\leqq 12$
Connector loss (two connections)	dB	3		4
Theoretical system loss	dB	17	34	35
System margin	dB	6		
Maximum section loss	dB	11	28	29
Fiber loss	dB/km	0.8 to 1.0		0.5
Splices	dB/km	0.1 to 0.2		0.1 to 0.2
Repair splices	dB/km	0 to 0.2		0 to 0.2
Cable loss	dB/km	0.9 to 1.4		0.6 to 0.9
Repeater spacing	km	7.3	31 to 20	48 to 32

Table   Design values for 140 Mbit/s operational systems

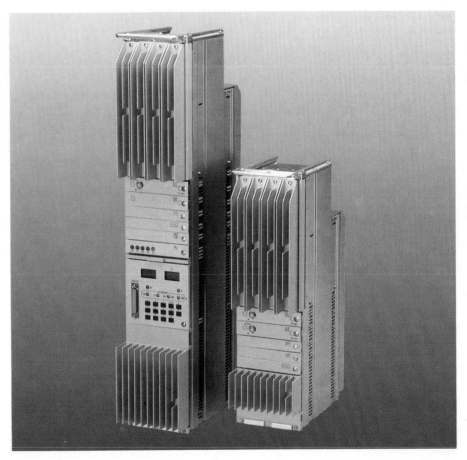

Fig. 2   Style 7R line terminating unit (left) and intermediate repeater for the 140 Mbit/s system

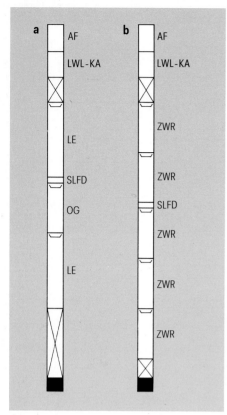

AF	Terminal panel
LE	Line terminating unit
LWL-KA	Fiber-optic cable housing
SLFD	Alarm signal panel
OG	Fault-locating unit
ZWR	Intermediate repeater

Fig. 3   Style 7R narrow racks for the 140 Mbit/s system
(Power dissipation for LE $\leq$ 40 W, for ZWR $\leq$ 18 W and 2.OG $\leq$ 18 W)
a   **Line terminating unit rack for two systems (height 2.60 m)**
b   **Intermediate repeater rack for five systems (height 2.60 m)**

Operation

The functional circuit diagram of the 140 Mbit/s operational system is shown in **Fig. 4**.

Line equipment

On the transmit side, the line terminating unit converts the digital CMI coded signal arriving from the electrical interface to a signal suitable for optical transmission. For this purpose, the electrical input signal is equalized, regenerated, decoded, scrambled, transformed into the binary 5B/6B line code [3], and converted to the optical transmit signal in the transmit module. The optoelectronic transducers are accommodated in hermetically sealed modules [4]. The design of the optical

transmitters with laser diodes is as shown in the functional circuit diagram [5]. Owing to the higher temperature-dependence of the light-current characteristic for 1300 nm laser diodes, power and temperature regulation is advisable. Light-emitting diodes, however, do not require power or temperature regulation, as the temperature dependence of their light-current characteristic is negligible and their aging rate extremely low.

On the receive side, the optical receiver – e.g. for λ = 1300 nm a PIN-FET module with high input impedance as per [3] – converts the signal from the fiber back to an electrical signal. The sensitivity of the optical receiver, assuming no bandwidth limitation by the fiber (**table**), is approximately -43 dBm for a bit error rate of 10^{-10}. The maximum permissible input level is -20 dBm; a four-section switchable optical attenuator is available for higher input levels. The electrical receive signal is equalized, regenerated, decoded, descrambled and converted to the interface code. The scrambler and the 5B/6B encoder in the transmit direction as well as the 5B/6B decoder and the descrambler in the receive direction are LSI devices from the Siemens series SH 100 [6, 7].

Apart from the modules directly

involved in signal conversion, the line terminating unit contains a shutdown facility activated by fiber breakage to protect personnel from optical radiation if a laser is employed [3]. It also contains supervision and fault-locating facilities. The frequency converters required for 5B/6B conversion are designed as narrow-band "phase-locked loop" circuits and provide jitter reduction. **Fig. 5** shows the "scrambler and 5B/6B encoder" module incorporating the LSI devices from the SH 100 series.

Supervision and fault location

Each digital line section is continuously supervised at both ends during operation. Faults and disturbances evaluated in the line terminating unit are indicated by means of light-emitting diodes in the supervision module of the line terminating unit. They are divided according to priority into A and B alarms, which are transferred to the alarm signal panel in the rack and to the central service observation point. Immediately a fault is detected by the supervision facilities of the line terminating units, an AIS (*Alarm Indication Signal*) is inserted in place of the disturbed information signal in order to suppress further fault alarms in downstream supervision units.

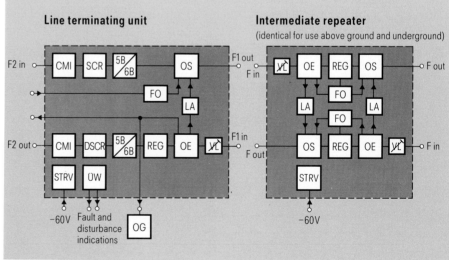

5B/6B	5B/6B encoder
CMI	Interface code per CCITT (*Coded Mark Inversion*)
DSCR	Descrambler
FO	Fault location
LA	Laser shutdown
OE	Optical receiver

OG	Fault-locating unit
OS	Optical transmitter
REG	Signal regenerator
SCR	Scrambler
STRV	Power supply
ÜW	Supervision
VL	Optical attenuator

Fig. 4   Functional circuit diagram of the line terminating unit and intermediate repeater for the 140 Mbit/s system

132

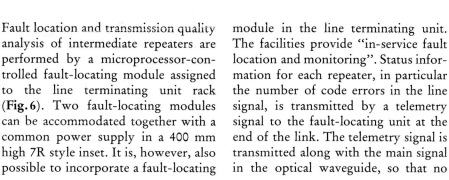

Fig. 5 "Scrambler and 5B/6B encoder" module for the 140 Mbit/s system

Fig. 6 Fault-locating unit

Fault location and transmission quality analysis of intermediate repeaters are performed by a microprocessor-controlled fault-locating module assigned to the line terminating unit rack (**Fig. 6**). Two fault-locating modules can be accommodated together with a common power supply in a 400 mm high 7R style inset. It is, however, also possible to incorporate a fault-locating module in the line terminating unit. The facilities provide "in-service fault location and monitoring". Status information for each repeater, in particular the number of code errors in the line signal, is transmitted by a telemetry signal to the fault-locating unit at the end of the link. The telemetry signal is transmitted along with the main signal in the optical waveguide, so that no additional transmission medium is required for the telemetry signal. The status information is transmitted in message blocks, which are generated in each repeater and transmitted via downstream repeaters to the end of the line. The fault location method is such that individual identification (addressing) of the intermediate repeaters is not required.

References

[1] CCITT-Yellow Book Rec. G. 703

[2] Weis, G.: Physical Design of Systems and Equipments for Digital Transmission. telcom report 2 (1979) Special Issue "Digital Transmission", pp. 29 to 33

[3] Stegmeier, A.; Trimmel, H.: A Fiber-Optic System for Transmitting 34 Mbit/s Signals. telcom report 6 (1983) Special Issue "Optical Communications", pp. 125 to 129

[4] Althaus, H.L.; Kuhn, G.: Modular Laser Source. telcom report 6 (1983) Special Issue "Optical Communications", pp. 84 to 90

[5] Fluhr, J.; Marending, P.; Trimmel, H.: A Fiber-Optic System for Transmitting 8 Mbit/s Signals. telcom report 6 (1983) Special Issue "Optical Communications", pp. 119 to 124

[6] Gonauser, E.; Müller-Glaser, K.D.; Glasl, A.: Microprocessing applications of subnanosecond masterslice arrays. Siemens Forsch.- u. Entwickl.-Ber. 8 (1979) pp. 251 to 255

[7] Dömer, J.; Eich, W.: Technological Migration in the Line Terminating Units of Digital Transmission Systems. telcom report 5 (1982), pp. 97 to 100

Eberhard Kügler

Development Trends in Higher Order Fiber-Optic Transmission Systems

Optical fibers are particularly suitable for transmitting signals at very high bit rates and, with single-mode fibers, transmission systems operating at a few Gbit/s are conceivable. The achievements possible within a foreseeable period are, however, determined by technical and economic criteria, important factors being the components and technologies available and their quality assurance. Wide-ranging and intensive efforts are therefore required if these criteria are to be met. A 565 Mbit/s system for single-mode fibers operating at a wavelength of 1300 nm is already under development, while studies are in progress into technologies for the Gbit/s range and investigations have begun into signal transmission at a wavelength near 1500 nm.

Fiber-optic systems for transmission rates up to 140 Mbit/s are available in standardized technology for commercial operation on cables with graded-index fibers [1, 2, 3]. Similar systems will soon also be available for cables with single-mode fibers [2, 3]. The main differences between these single-mode systems and those for graded-index fibers are merely that they employ a differently optimized laser transmitter (single-mode) and impose more stringent requirements on coupling the fibers to the optical components (diodes and connectors). The single-mode systems are of interest economically for their longer repeater spacing, at least for transmission rates above 140 Mbit/s and for application primarily in long-haul networks.

If higher transmission capacities are required, it appears at present, and probably for the foreseeable future, that a fiber-optic system operating at 565 Mbit/s ($\triangleq 4 \times 140$ Mbit/s) is more economical than several 140 Mbit/s

systems employing the space or the wavelength division multiplexing [4]. Owing to the dispersion characteristics of optical waveguides, the only suitable types for systems operating at 565 Mbit/s or higher are single-mode fibers, operating preferably at a wavelength of $\lambda = 1300$ nm [5].

At wavelengths between 1500 and 1600 nm, it is possible to achieve even lower losses and therefore longer repeater spacings than at 1300 nm, but, for the high-speed pulse transmission required, it is then necessary to use an optical transmitter with an extremely narrow spectral bandwidth. Optical transmitters of this type are currently being researched, though they are unlikely to be ready for commerical operating systems before the year 1990.

Another conceivable alternative for the future might be to use a single-mode fiber with its near-zero pulse dispersion shifted to long wavelengths by special profiling. Whether fiber-optic systems operating at 1500 nm are more economical for land cable links than similar systems at 1300 nm will only be revealed as development continues in the future.

Dipl.-Ing. Eberhard Kügler,
Siemens AG,
Public Communication Networks Division,
Munich

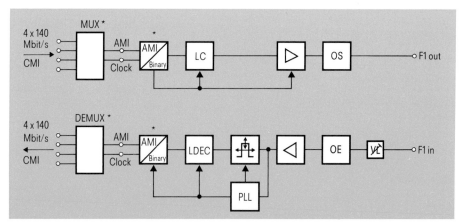

* Units are identical to the coaxial cable system of the same bit rate

AMI	Alternate mark inversion	MUX	Multiplexer
CMI	Coded mark inversion	OE	Optical receiver
DEMUX	Demultiplexer	OS	Optical transmitter
LC	Line coder	PLL	Phase-locked loop
LDEC	Line decoder	VL	Optical attenuator (line build-out)

Fig.1 **Functional circuit diagram of the line terminating unit for a 565 Mbit/s fiber-optic operating system with line multiplexer and demultiplexer**

Development of a fiber-optic system for 565 Mbit/s

A fiber-optic system for a bit rate of 565 Mbit/s is now under development for use in single-mode fiber networks in the second half of the eighties. The experience gained on prototype systems for both graded-index fibers and coaxial cables [6, 7] is providing a good basis for this work.

The principal design objectives for a 565 Mbit/s fiber-optic operating system are given in the **table**. Assuming a maximum available section loss of 21 dB, a repeater spacing of 23 km is now a realistic value for network planning. The impact of splice losses on the achievable repeater spacing is clearly apparent. Nowadays, however, the losses assumed for initial installation splices and subsequent repair splices are as given in the **table**. When lower splice losses become feasible and the repair splice loss allocation can be reduced, it will be possible to achieve repeater spacings of 26 km to 30 km and more.

The technology necessary for volume production of this high-bit-rate equipment is already available, as deliveries for the 565 Mbit/s coaxial cable system are scheduled to start from 1984. Some parts of the 565 Mbit/s fiber-optic operating system are identical to its coaxial cable counterpart in order to provide the widest possible interfacing compatibility between the line terminating units (**Fig. 1**).

The system has four ports on the receive side and four on the transmit side for four 140 Mbit/s signals conforming to the interface specifications of CCITT Recommendation G.703. The CCITT has not yet produced a recommendation for a 565 Mbit/s line interface. Designing the coaxial and fiber-optic systems with the same interface permits direct interconnections of the two systems without line multiplexers and demultiplexers.

The other modules of the line terminating unit for the 565 Mbit/s fiber-optic operating system are shown in **Fig. 1** and are essentially the same as those in the 140 Mbit/s system [3]. They differ only in being designed for higher signal speeds. A noteworthy feature is that the scrambler and descrambler functions are integrated at the 140 Mbit/s sides of the line multiplexer and demultiplexer, reducing high-speed processing functions to the minimum necessary.

The intermediate repeater (**Fig. 2**) is made up of modules from the line terminating unit. The subunits are identical and designed in style 7R. The power feeding arrangements for the repeaters are the same as for the 140 Mbit/s system (dc series feeding via a copper cable laid alongside the optical cable and powering several systems in parallel). The alarm signaling and "in service" monitoring system are also of the same design.

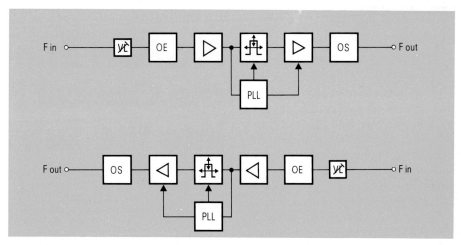

| OE | Optical receiver | PLL | Phase-locked loop |
| OS | Optical transmitter | VL | Optical attenuator (line build-out) |

Fig. 2 Functional circuit diagram of the intermediate repeater for a 565 Mbit/s fiber-optic operating system

Optical waveguide		Single-mode fiber
Optical wavelength	nm	1300
Optical transmitter		Laser diode (LD)
Transmit power	dBm	−4
Receive power (bit error rate $\geqq 10^{-10}$)	dBm	−35
Maximum fiber dispersion	ps/km · nm	$\leqq 3.5$
Optical connectors (2)	dB	4
Theoretical system loss	dB	27
System margin	dB	6
Maximum repeater section loss	dB	21
Fiber loss	dB/km	0.5
Splices	dB/km	0.1 to 0.2
Repair splices	dB/km	0 to 0.2
Cable loss	dB/km	0.6 to 0.9
Repeater spacing	km	35 to 23

Table Design objectives for a 565 Mbit/s fiber-optic operating system

Fiber-optic components for high bit rates

A very important requirement in realizing fiber-optic systems for high bit rates is the availability of suitable optical transmit and receive units. As an example, laser modules operating at a wavelength of 1300 nm are required. They must be suitable for single-mode fibers with optimum fiber coupling, while providing the highest possible operating speed and the necessary high reliability. On the receive side, PIN photodiodes are required for integrating in a suitable PIN-FET combination. However, avalanche photodiodes, preferably based on III-V components, are also of interest for the 1300 nm range.

A wide-ranging research and development program has been started to resolve all these requirements and to provide the components for bit rates into the Gbit/s range. Initial successes have already been achieved.

References

[1] Fluhr, J.; Marending, P.; Trimmel, H.: A Fiber-Optic System for Transmitting 8 Mbit/s Signals. telcom report 6 (1983) Special Issue "Optical Communications", pp. 119 to 124

[2] Stegmeier, A.; Trimmel, H.: A Fiber-Optic System for Transmitting 34 Mbit/s Signals. telcom report 6 (1983) Special Issue "Optical Communications", pp. 125 to 129

[3] Dömer, J.; Gier, J.: A Fiber-Optic System for Transmitting 140 Mbit/s Signals. telcom report 6 (1983) Special Issue "Optical Communications", pp. 130 to 133

[4] Braun, E.; Möhrmann, K.H.: Optical Communications in Short-Haul and Long-Haul Wideband Communication Networks. telcom report 6 (1983) Special Issue "Optical Communications", pp. 202 to 205

[5] Gier, J.; Panzer, K.: Principles of Optoelectronic Signal Transmission. telcom report 6 (1983) Special Issue "Optical Communications", pp. 20 to 25

[6] Burgmeier, J.; Gier, J.; Trimmel, H.: Transmitting Digital Signals at 560 Mbit/s via Optical Waveguides – An Experimental System for the Heinrich Hertz Institute. telcom report 5 (1982), pp. 27 to 32

[7] Kügler, E.: Transmission of 565 Mbit/s signals on coaxial cables and optical waveguides. Proceedings of the "3rd World Telecommunication Forum" 1979, Part 2, pp. 3221 to 3225

Ewald Braun

BIGFON Brings the Optical Waveguide into the Subscriber Area

In the BIGFON project (acronym for broadband integrated glass fiber local communication network) to be launched at the end of 1983, a possible form of future communications system will be undergoing field trials in the Federal Republic of Germany. As part of this project Siemens is setting up fiber-optic local networks in Munich and West Berlin, each serving 28 subscribers. All the existing telecommunication services, such as telephony, facsimile, teletex, videotex, as well as the new videotelephony service together with television and radio programs, will be offered to the subscriber via just one or two optical fibers.

The BIGFON project will fully utilize the large transmission bandwidth of several hundred megahertz and the low attenuation of the graded-index fiber.

With conventional technology, the subscriber loop network requires a separate copper pair for each telephone service, while television and radio programs are fed to the subscriber through distribution networks on dedicated coaxial cables incorporating many intermediate repeaters. Videotelephony would require yet another coaxial cable network.

System configuration

In the BIGFON system trial configured by Siemens, the subscriber is provided with up to 16 channels at 64 kbit/s each for telephony and other narrowband services. Each 64 kbit/s port allows for the ISDN interface (*Integrated Services Digital Network* – as of 1980) by providing an extra 8 kbit/s for signaling and another 8 kbit/s for data transmission at a later

Dipl.-Ing. (FH) Ewald Braun,
Siemens AG,
Public Communication Networks Division,
Munich

date. In addition, the subscriber and his family will receive programs over the fiber for up to four stereo receivers and four television sets. He will be able to select these programs individually from a virtually unlimited number in the switching center. A television set in conjunction with a video camera and the controlling telephone can be used together for videotelephony.

The sixteen $(64 + 8 + 8)$ kbit/s signals, which also contain the signals for program selection, are combined to form a 2.048 Mbit/s signal for transmission. With the four stereo sound signals at 2×448 kbit/s each, plus a further 2.048 Mbit/s in reserve, the resultant bit rate for transmitting what are referred to as the narrowband signals is 8.192 Mbit/s.

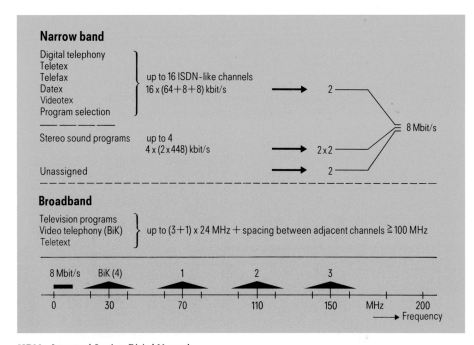

ISDN *Integrated Services Digital Network*

Fig. 1 Structure and frequency band allocation of BIGFON signals

Transmission of the video signals in television quality (5 MHz, color) can only be performed by frequency modulation or digital transmission methods. Basic coding at 140 Mbit/s produces large bandwidths and bit rates on the line. In view of the limited fiber bandwidth, the various television signals would have to be transmitted by wavelength division multiplexing, which is ultimately more expensive than electrical multiplexing. Basic coding at less than 140 Mbit/s, without using VLSI (*Very Large Scale Integrated*) technology, is also expensive. As a result of the high costs together with the lack of standards and receivers it was decided, for the purposes of the system trial, to transmit the video signals on a frequency modulated carrier with ±12 MHz deviation. This occupies a transmission band of up to about 170 MHz on the fiber (**Fig. 1**).

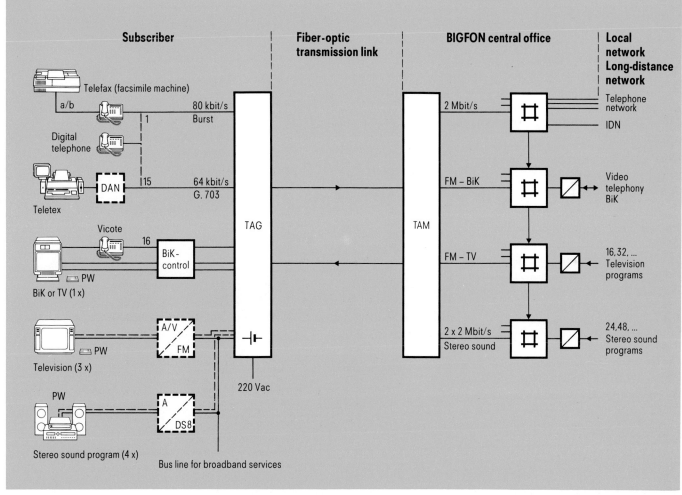

A	Audio	DS 8	Digital signal 8 Mbit/s	TAG	Subscriber line terminating unit
A/V	Audio/video	FM	Frequency modulation	TAM	Subscriber line terminating module
BiK	Videotelephony	IDN	Integrated text and data network	TV	Television
DAN	Data interface	PW	Program selection		

Fig. 2 Block diagram of the BIGFON system trial

If, at a later date, the video signals are encoded at 34 Mbit/s, the bandwidth required for their transmission on the fiber will not be any larger.

The various services to the subscriber are provided by the familiar terminals in current use. For the telephone and data signals the local office (OVSt/ BIGFON switching center) incorporates a digital exchange with connections to the public telephone network and the integrated text and data network (IDN). Broadband switching networks switch or distribute the signals for videotelephony as well as the radio and television programs.

Before they are actually distributed, the signals received from the various program sources are conditioned in central equipment (**Fig. 2**).

Line network

BIGFON is arranged like a telecommunication network, in a star configuration. Each subscriber is connected via two fibers (one for each direction) to the BIGFON switching center. Some subscribers are connected by only one fiber employing bidirectional wavelength division multiplexing (880/1300 nm) with no restriction on service.

With a fiber attenuation less than 4 dB/km, it is possible to span distances up to 5 km.

Cables with 10, 20 and 30 fibers to suit the different routes are available for pulling into ducts in lengths up to 1000 m. A thin and highly flexible cable with two fibers is available for drop and inside wiring applications. **Fig. 3** shows the structure of the BIGFON island in Munich.

Transmission

The baseband signals provided by the local office to each subscriber are combined by the subscriber line terminating module TAM to form an 8 Mbit/s signal (**Fig. 2**).

Of the four FM video signals on a 30 MHz carrier, three are translated to the final line-frequency band in the subscriber line terminating module and one is transmitted directly. Digital and FM signals drive a laser diode used as the optical transmitter.

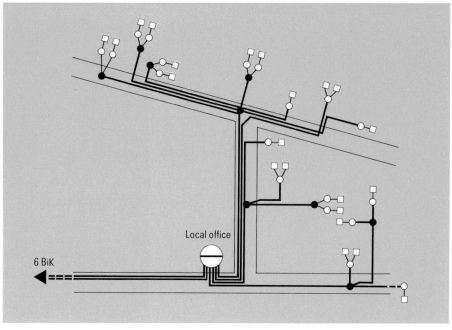

| ● | Cable distribution point | □ | Subscriber |
| ○ | On-premises distribution point | BiK | Videotelephony |

Fig. 3　Structure of the BIGFON island in Munich

Fig. 4　Digital telephone

Voice communication	Video communication	Text services
● Telephone service ● Repertory dialing ● Repeat last number ● Consultation hold ● Call transfer ● Call pickup 　Call forwarding 　Transfer of ringing ● Call waiting ● Visual displays ● Monitoring ● Hands-free speaking	● Videotelephone service 　(color), 　picture optional ● Video transmission 　of documents ● Videotex ● Remote control 　Hands-free speaking 　Self view, etc.	● Telex ● Teletex ● Facsimile ● Data transmission **Distribution services** ● Television ● Teletext ● Stereo sound programs

Table　Service features available in the BIGFON system trial

Fig. 5 Videotelephony with television set, video camera and digital telephone

The stereo receivers already in the subscriber's home are additionally provided with a stereo decoder and program selector.

Six out of each of the two groups of 28 subscribers in Munich and West Berlin receive a video camera for videotelephony (**Fig. 5**) in addition to their television set. Some will receive video telephone sets for high-quality document transmission.

Any text and data terminals already in use will also be connected.

Prospects

From the beginning of 1984 to the end of 1986, BIGFON subscribers will be testing the system under practical conditions, initially within the BIGFON islands. At the same time, the Deutsche Bundespost will be gathering experience in all aspects of this new communication system. Similar trial networks are being installed in various German cities. There are plans to interconnect some of these BIGFON islands before 1986 to provide videotelephony over long-haul routes with some sections incorporating optical fibers. The subscribers thus connected will then be able to talk to each other "face to face" anywhere in the country and at any time.

The BIGFON project is demonstrating, implementing and testing completely new approaches to communication. The field trial with all its practical aspects is an essential step in proving new ideas and concepts. They will ultimately provide the basis for the widespread introduction of this new transmission medium into the local network.

The 2 Mbit/s signals and the video signal from the subscriber are fed directly to the exchange.

At the subscriber end, the optical transmission link terminates in the subscriber line terminating unit TAG. On the receive side, the (64 + 8 + 8) kbit/s signals are recovered from the 8 Mbit/s signal and fed to the terminals via separate copper pairs. Interfaces are available for data terminals operating at less than 64 kbit/s.

The signal received in the subscriber line terminating unit is also fed into a coaxial bus line for the broadband services. As no suitable terminals are available, specially developed adapters extract the preselected program signal from the composite signal and feed it to the proprietary terminal – the television or stereo sound receiver. Facilities for program selection are provided in these adapters as well as in the modules handling the actual transmission (decoding the stereo sound signals and demodulating the FM TV signals).

Since, in contrast to copper cable systems, it is not possible to feed power to the telephone equipment in the subscriber's home, the subscriber line terminating unit (power consumption about 35 W) is powered from the public ac network. If the public supply fails, the telephone can be operated on an emergency basis for a few hours from a trickle-charged battery in the subscriber line terminating unit.

Switching and distribution

The narrowband service signals are switched in the digital exchange by electronic crosspoints using time division multiplexing. In addition to these switching functions, the digital exchange offers the subscriber a large number of new features. It controls the broadband switching networks, monitors the BIGFON network and provides the interface to the public telephone network.

The switching networks employed for switching and distributing the broadband signals were specially developed in VLSI technology.

Terminals

Each BIGFON subscriber receives a new digital telephone equipped with numerous function keys and a 16-digit alphanumeric display (**Fig. 4**). The features provided are given in the **table**.

Since FM demodulation and program selection facilities can be incorporated directly in an ordinary television set, BIGFON subscribers are provided with sets adapted in this way. These sets are also suitable for teletext and videotex.

References

[1] Braun, E.: BIGFON Heralds the Start of a New Era in Telecommunications. telcom report 5 (1982), pp. 189 to 195

[2] Braun, E.: BIGFON Points the Way to New Forms of Communication. Siemens Review L (1983), No. 1, pp. 10 to 14

Helmut Bauch and Karl Weinhardt

Communication in the Subscriber Area of Optical Broadband Networks

The large transmission capacity of the optical waveguide can be used to set up optical broadband networks capable of transmitting the signals of all current and forseeable communication services via a single subscriber line. The subscriber lines will usually consist initially of two optical waveguides. After further advances in technology it will be possible for many applications to use just one fiber to transmit in both directions with wavelength division multiplexing. For the first broadband subscriber networks to be put into service by the Deutsche Bundespost in 1983 Siemens developed a system configuration, the transmission component of which is presented in this paper.

The first wavelength region exploited for fiber-optic communication was about 800 to 900 nm. The region near 1300 nm is also currently under development, while experiments are aiming at wavelengths between 1500 and 1600 nm. These three regions within the octave between 800 and 1600 nm provide an enormous transmission capacity. The region between 800 and 900 nm alone has a bandwidth of about $4 \cdot 10^7$ MHz. This bandwidth, if it could be fully utilized in a practical system, would be enough to transmit, for instance, some $3 \cdot 10^5$ television signals at a bit rate of 140 Mbit/s each. Without doubt, fiber-optic cables once installed can satisfy any conceivable bandwidth requirement in the subscriber area for the foreseeable future. How much of this enormous transmission capacity can in fact be utilized depends on the current state of the art

Dipl.-Ing. Dr.-Ing. Helmut Bauch and
Dipl.-Phys. Dr. rer. nat. Karl Weinhardt,
Siemens AG,
Central Laboratories for Communications
Technology, Munich

in optical waveguides, optoelectronic transducers and optical filters, as well as on economic considerations. The following paragraphs will show that, for the 1983 project considered in this paper, current technology is fully capable of providing all services to the subscriber via one fiber-optic subscriber line with good quality.

Services and channels

An important aspect of designing an optical broadband network (OBN) for the subscriber area is the nature of the services to be provided. For the first projects of this type in the Deutsche Bundespost network [1] these are as follows:

● **Narrowband switched services based on 64 kbit/s channels**
This includes all the services of existing telephone networks (e.g. telephony, videotex and telefax) and the data services of the IDN (e.g. telex, teletex, facsimile etc.).

● **Broadband switched services**
These are currently available only as individually switched visual communication with moving pictures (BiK) with the option of video conferencing.

● **Distribution services**
Distribution of stereo sound programs (STT) and television programs (TV) normally provided by sound and TV broadcast services.

Since for the switched services the local area of the optical broadband network is of star configuration, it is logical to provide the distribution services on the "switched distribution" principle. The subscriber uses individual program selection channels to call up the desired programs from an OBN central office, where they are connected through to him via switching networks. One of the advantages of this approach over the conventional distribution techniques as employed in cable television (CTV) networks is that the number of distributable programs is basically unlimited.

To ensure that each service can be accessed at a subscriber outlet by several people simultaneously, an adequate number of transmission channels must be available for all services. The maximum possible number of channels is determined by the current state of the optical transmission art and by the line lengths employed in local networks.

When planning the first fiber-optic subscriber networks it was assumed at Siemens that the following maximum transmission capacity would be reasonable for both a home or business user:

● 16 narrowband channels (SB) at 64 kbit/s each for telephone or data transmission;

Two more 64 kbit/s channels are available for subscriber signaling. These include the speech and signaling channels for the BiK signals;

● 4 stereo sound channels (STT);

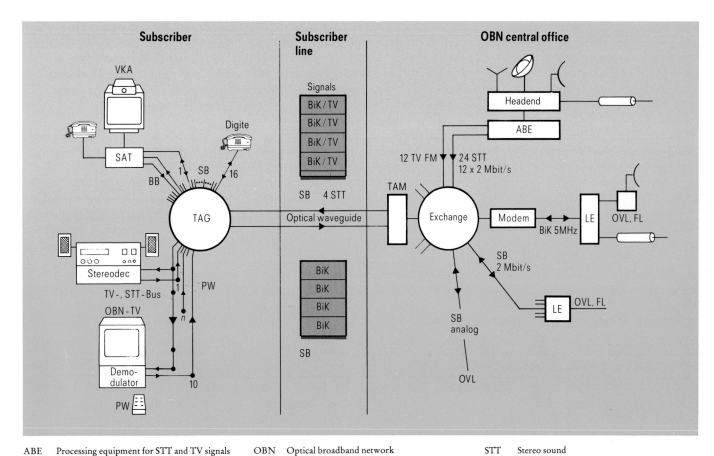

ABE	Processing equipment for STT and TV signals	
BB	Broadband	
BiK	Visual communication	
FL	Toll connecting trunk	
FM	Frequency modulation	
LE	Line-terminating equipment	
OBN	Optical broadband network	
OVL	Interoffice trunk	
PW	Program selection	
SAT	Control and terminating unit for the video communication equipment	
SB	Narrowband	
STT	Stereo sound	
TAG	Subscriber line terminating unit	
TAM	Subscriber line terminating module	
TV	Television	
VKA	Video communication equipment	

Fig. 1   Transmission system in the optical broadband network

• 4 broadband channels for visual communication (BiK) via which color TV signals and accompanying stereo sound (TV) can also be distributed.

In addition, eight program selection channels and a monitoring channel will be provided back to the OBN central office.

The equipment is of modular design so that maximum capacity can be achieved in stages and subscribers with low communication requirements are not involved in unnecessary expense. This also allows facilities to be added as communication requirements grow.

Signals and transmission paths

In **Fig. 1** an overview is provided of the transmission paths in the optical broadband network. The subscriber network has the same spatial structure as the present day telephone network. The subscriber lines will generally con-

sist of two optical fibers each. They are routed to the subscriber in a star pattern radiating from the OBN central office, which is normally collocated at the telephone exchange assigned to the subscriber. At the subscriber's premises, the line is terminated in the subscriber line terminating unit (TAG). This unit converts the electrical signals into optical format and vice versa. It also performs some of the multiplexing and demultiplexing of the signals transmitted via the indoor cabling between the TAG and the associated terminals. The terminals for the narrowband services, symbolized in **Fig. 1** by Siemens' DIGITE® digital telephone, are connected in a star configuration via balanced lines. The control and terminating unit (SAT) of the video communication equipment (VKA) is connected via a balanced line for speech and signaling information and via two coaxial lines for transmitting the video signal in both directions. The signals of the distribution services (STT and TV)

pass from the subscriber line terminating unit via coaxial bus lines to socket outlets at which the terminals can be connected (OBN-TV direct, and the stereo system via the adapter STEREODEC). The terminals incorporate the modulators and demodulators, the multiplexers for the speech and signaling information of the particular terminal in a narrowband switched service and the demultiplexers for the signals of the distribution services.

Program selection (PW) for the distribution services is effected by controlling distribution switching networks in the exchange via backward channels from the terminal. The backward channel signals from the TV receivers and STEREODECs are transmitted via star-configured balanced circuits to the subscriber line terminating unit where they are multiplexed with the narrowband signals for transmission to the central office. On BiK terminals, programs are selected via the subscriber signaling channel of the controlling telephone in the video communications equipment.

In the OBN central office, the counterpart to the subscriber line terminating unit is the subscriber line terminating module (TAM) whose primary functions are to multiplex the signals coming from the switching networks for the signals of switched and distribution services and to demultiplex the signals in the opposite direction. On the side of the exchange away from the subscriber the signals of the switched services are connected to interoffice (OVL) and toll connecting (FL) trunks via line terminating equipments (LE), in the case of BiK signals via a modem. The signals of the distribution services (STT and TV) are received via antennas or cables and demodulated in a headend. The resultant audio signals for STT and TV sound and the composite color video signals for TV are passed into the following processing equipment (ABE) to form the various line signals which are fed through the distribution switching networks to the multiplexers in the subscriber line terminating modules.

Modulation methods

The main criteria for selecting the modulation methods are – apart from attenuation and usable fiber bandwidth – the noise contributions from the optical transmitter and receiver and the nonlinear distortion due to the characteristic of the transmitter diode. As described in more detail in [2], the achievable signal-to-noise ratios of current realizable fiber-optic transmission systems are significantly worse than those of all-electric transmission systems. The same applies to the linearity of the transmitters. On the other hand, the relatively large transmission bandwidth of the optical fiber permits the use of modulation methods which reduce the effect of noise on the transmission link by expanding the signal bandwidth. The most effective method in this respect is digital transmission with a binary line signal, several signals being transmitted together by time division multiplexing. Moreover, a line signal of this type is also very insensitive to nonlinear distortion.

When service starts in 1983 it will certainly be possible for the narrowband

and stereo sound signals to be transmitted in this mode. However, the analog-digital conversion of moving picture signals would currently still require highly complex and expensive equipment with large volume and high power consumption. For this reason, an analog technique has initially been chosen for moving picture transmission. Systems providing digital transmission for the video signal will only be employed when technological advance permits very large-scale integration of the codecs. However, it will require at least a national standard for the coding technique [3] before suitable VLSI devices are developed.

For the reasons previously given, only a noise-reducing method can be considered for the analog transmission. Frequency modulation (FM) with a relatively large frequency deviation was adopted. This signal is also relatively insensitive to nonlinear distortion and can pass through limiter stages unimpaired, since the information is carried exclusively in the signal zero crossings. This latter characteristic also has a favorable impact on the complexity of the broadband switching networks in the OBN central office. The crosspoints used are logic circuits as employed for binary signals and are switched in step with the zero cross-

ings of the signal. Such circuits permit a high degree of integration, thus producing switching networks of very small size. The crosstalk problems of such a compact design are alleviated by the noise-reducing effect of the large-deviation FM.

The stereo sound signal accompanying the TV signal is also transmitted in analog form. The two audio signals modulate subcarriers at frequencies of 6 and 7.5 MHz employing a large deviation. These two FM signals are fed with the video signal to another FM modulator whose output signal is the FM broadband signal BBS1 at the carrier frequency 30 MHz (**Fig. 2**).

Transmission quality

During the planning stage it was necessary to ensure that the services would be available to the subscriber with at least equal quality to that provided by conventional transmission media. The transmission quality of digital signals is determined by the encoding law (sampling rate, number of bits per sample and eventually compander characteristic) and by the bit error rate on the transmission links. The encoding law for 64 kbit/s telephone signals is recommended by the CCITT and is employed in the codec of the DIGITE digital telephone. The coding for the

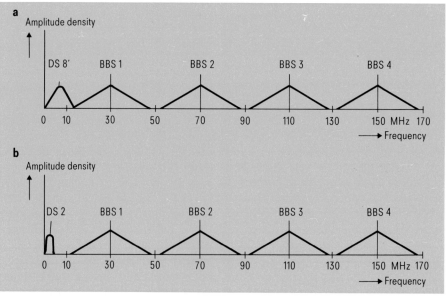

| BBS | FM broadband signal | | DS8′ | 8 Mbit/s signal from central office to subscriber |
| DS2 | 2 Mbit/s signal from subscriber to central office | | FM | Frequency modulation |

Fig. 2   Structure of the FMX frequency-division multiplex signal
a Transmission from the subscriber line terminating module (TAM) to the subscriber line terminating unit (TAG)
b Transmission from the subscriber line terminating unit (TAG) to the subscriber line terminating module (TAM)

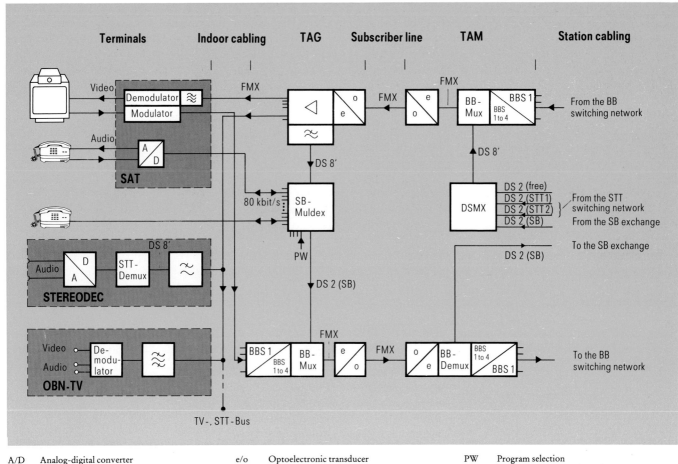

A/D	Analog-digital converter	
BB	Broadband	
BBS	FM broadband signal	
D/A	Digital-analog converter	
DS	Digital signal	
DSMX	Digital multiplex unit	

e/o	Optoelectronic transducer
FM	Frequency modulation
FMX	Frequency-division multiplex signal
MUX	Multiplex unit
OBN	Optical broadband network
o/e	Optoelectronic transducer

PW	Program selection
SAT	Control and terminating unit
SB	Narrowband
STT	Stereo sound
TAG	Subscriber line terminating unit
TAM	Subscriber line terminating module
TV	Television program

Fig. 3   Multiplex equipment and signals for the subscriber lines and terminals

STT signals is based on current work at the CCITT to standardize on a sampling rate of 32 kHz and a linear encoding of samples with 14 bits. A further bit is employed for protection against transmission errors. The overall bit rate of a stereo sound signal is thus $2 \cdot 32 \cdot 15$ kbit/s = 960 kbit/s. This coding technique provides a quality which is considerably higher than that currently achieved in CATV systems. Moreover, the bit error rate on the subscriber line, assuming correct dimensioning of the optical transmission equipment and signal levels, is a few orders of magnitude better than that recommended by CCITT for international connections. Hence, the quality of the signals to the subscriber depends almost exclusively on the quality of the signal fed into the coder.

The analog broadband signals for BiK and TV were required to provide at least the level of quality as specified for TV signals in cable TV systems by the FTZ guideline 151 R8 of the Deutsche Bundespost [4]. This requires, for instance, the weighted signal-to noise ratio at the subscriber terminal to be not less than 46 dB. On a BiK link between two subscribers connected to the same exchange a signal-to-noise ratio of 49 dB was allowed, the main noise components originating in equal parts from the two optical links. If the two BiK subscribers are connected to two different exchanges linked via an interoffice or toll connecting trunk, a signal-to-noise ratio of 52 dB has been allowed for these circuits. The signal-to-noise ratio over the entire circuit is then 47 dB and hence 1 dB better than that required for TV signals. For TV signals there is only one subscriber line to be taken into account. This results in a signal-to-noise ratio of about 52 dB, which is 6 dB higher than that required in cable television networks.

Multiplexing techniques and line code

As previously stated in the section headed "Signals and transmission paths", the SB, BiK, STT and TV signals are transmitted together via a single optical fiber from the OBN central office to the subscriber. With the current state of the art and the cost of optoelectronic transducers it is appropriate to form an electrical multiplex signal for transmission in one direction, using a single pair of transducers to perform the optoelectronic conversion.

The multiplex equipment and the associated signals passing between the exchange switching networks and the terminals are illustrated in **Fig. 3**. The signals passed to the subscriber are the digital signals for the narrowband switched services (SB) and the stereo sound programs (STT). They are based on Europe's primary PCM hierarchy level which has a bit rate of 2.048 Mbit/s (signal DS2). A DS2 (SB) signal incorporates the signals of the narrowband switched services including the associated signaling, while in the direction to the central office it additionally includes the program selection signals (PW) for selecting the STT and the TV programs, as well as the alarms for overall system supervision. Two further signals DS2 (STT1) and DS2 (STT2) each transmit two time division multiplexed STT signals. As described in the previous section, the overall bit rate of an STT signal is 960 kbit/s and for two STT signals therefore 1920 kbit/s. In addition there is the frame alignment signal at 64 kbit/s. The remaining 64 kbit/s time slot remains unassigned. A further DS2 signal is also transmitted, but not initially used for communication. The four DS2 signals are bit-interleaved to form a DS8'* time division multiplex signal at the bit rate $4 \cdot 2.048$ Mbit/s = 8.192 Mbit/s. All the tributary signals are synchronous with the clock of the associated narrowband exchange. The line signal is then formed in biphase code, increasing the symbol rate to 16.384 megabaud. This code was adopted because the biphase signal has a favorable spectrum with a zero at zero frequency, as well as a high content of timing energy. Moreover, the coding and decoding complexity is very low. The doubling of the bandwidth is unimportant in view of the bandwidth of the transmission channel.

From the subscriber to the exchange it is necessary to transmit only the DS2 (SB) signal, and this is also in biphase code.

The DS8' or DS2 digital signal and up to four FM broadband signals BB1 to BB4 are transmitted together by combining them to form a frequency division multiplex signal FMX as shown in **Fig. 2**. One broadband signal is transmitted directly at the carrier frequency F1 = 30 MHz at which it was produced in the modulator and passed through the switching network. The

---

* The signal is designated DS8' because in Deutsche Bundespost usage DS8 refers to the second-order PCM signal at the bit rate 8.448 Mbit/s [5].

other three are translated to the line frequencies F2 = 70 MHz, F3 = 110 MHz and F4 = 150 MHz before being applied to the optoelectronic transducer on their way to the subscriber, and are demodulated directly at the terminal. Signals to the central office are translated to the line frequency in the TAG and translated to the carrier frequency F1 = 30 MHz in the central office by the TAM before passing through the switching network. Owing to the large frequency deviation, the effect of intermodulation noise and other types of noise in the transmission channel is reduced in the demodulator. In the optoelectronic transducer the signal FMX modulates the intensity of the infrared light.

Transmission on the subscriber line

For technical, economic and operational reasons it must be possible, as a general rule, to operate the subscriber lines on an unrepeatered basis. The maximum repeater spacing is limited by the loss and bandwidth achievable with the type of optical fiber adopted. A justifiable choice on economic grounds is the graded-index fiber with a cutoff frequency due to modal dispersion over a length of 1 km at about 750 MHz. The line signal with the spectrum shown in **Fig. 2** requires a bandwidth of 170 MHz for the entire line. From the relationship between the bandwidth and link length given in [6], the resulting repeater spacing is 6.4 km. This spacing is only slightly reduced by the additional effect of material dispersion if laser diodes are employed as the optical transmitters. This line length is also about the maximum in terms of loss that can be accommodated by the characteristics of the optical transmitters and receivers. Allowing for a certain minimum signal-to-noise ratio at the output of the optical receiver, it is necessary to find an optimum between the effects of receiver noise on the one hand and intermodulation products on the other [2]. The systems that are described here with two optical fibers per subscriber employ receivers with avalanche photodiodes (APD) throughout. The optical wavelength is in the region 820 to 900 nm. Apart from their high sensitivity, these detec-

tors have the advantage of allowing the electrical output power to be stabilized over a relatively wide range of received optical power, i.e. of different link lengths. The maximum achievable link length increases with the sensitivity of the receiver, the average transmitted power and the transmitter modulation factor. On the other hand, the intermodulation noise increases with modulation factor. When Siemens laser module SFH408 [7] is employed at an average output power of 2 mW in a fully equipped system producing one DS8' digital signal and four BBS broadband signals, it is possible to achieve the signal-to-noise ratios given in the "transmission quality" section with a line loss of 25 dB after deducting 3 dB for the two connectors at the optoelectronic transducers. Assuming a link loss of 4 dB/km (loss introduced by fiber, splices and any other connectors), this results in a line length of 6.3 km. Since only about 2,5% of all subscriber lines in the present day telephone network of the Deutsche Bundespost are longer than 6.3 km, there will only be a very few exceptional cases requiring special action such as the installation of lower loss cables or the insertion of a repeater.

The span length can be increased somewhat by transmitting less than four broadband signals on the system and by increasing the modulation factor of the transmitter for the remaining signals.

On short lines transmitting no more than one broadband signal, it is possible to employ light-emitting diodes as the sources, producing an output power of only about 30 µW. If only one 2 Mbit/s signal is transmitted, it is possible to span a link with a loss of 25 dB. This applies to transmission to the central office by subscribers who participate in the narrowband switched and distribution services but not in the BiK service. If an additional broadband signal is transmitted, the effect of material dispersion limits the range to about 3 km.

Wavelength division multiplexing

Wavelength division multiplexing (WDM) [8], i.e. signal transmission with several optical carriers at different

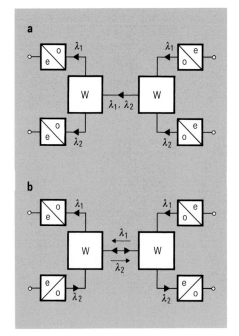

e/o   Optoelectronic transducer
o/e   Optoelectronic transducer
W   Optical combining/separating filter

Fig. 4   Wavelength-division multiplexing equipment for two wavelengths λ_1 and λ_2
a   unidirectional
b   bidirectional

wavelengths over one optical fiber, can be employed, as shown in **Fig. 4**, in one direction or in both directions (uni- or bidirectional). Unidirectional WDM is of use only in systems whose repeater spacing is limited by the bandwidth. For the maximum bandwidth of 170 MHz under consideration for this application (see **Fig. 2**), graded-index fibers are readily available from volume production (see section headed "transmission on the subscriber line"). The repeater spacing is consequently limited by the loss. The inevitable loss introduced by the combining/separating filters would only reduce the spacing even more. A further consideration is the expense of providing optoelectronic transducers for each wavelength. Although bidirectional WDM also reduces the repeater spacing as previously explained, it does nevertheless save the second optical fiber. The minimum distance beyond which it is cheaper to use WDM filters rather than the second optical fiber is thus a question of economics. On very long lines, the use of WDM techniques is limited by the reduced repeater spacing due to the loss introduced by the WDM filters.

Technical design

The subscriber line is terminated at one end by the subscriber line terminating module in the OBN central office and at the other end by the subscriber line terminating unit on the subscriber's premises. These terminating equipments each incorporate an optical transmitter and receiver as well as translators and muldex equipment to provide the necessary transmission channels on the subscriber line. The TAG additionally incorporates modules to provide suitable interfaces for the connection of subscriber terminals which are specially designed for the OBN transmission system [9]:

● The 16 SB channels can be used optionally for telephony or data transmission. Telephony is provided by connecting the DIGITE digital telephone. Transmission between TAG and DIGITE takes place using a burst mode technique on a balanced two-wire circuit. Data terminals are connected on a four-wire basis via special data circuit-terminating equipment.

● The STT channels each require that use is made of an adapter STEREODEC. It extracts one of the four digital STT signals from the DS8′ signal and recovers the audio frequency stereo pair which is then applied to a commercial stereo system and/or sound recorder. The program selection

signals are produced with the aid of a keypad in the STEREODEC.

● Television is provided by means of modified color television receivers (OBN-TV) which are equipped with a selective FM demodulator tuned in each case to one of the four broadband (BB) channels. The OBN-TV includes an additional facility to produce the program selection signals under the control of the usual remote control unit.

● The BiK service is provided by the video communication equipment VKA specially developed for OBN [9]. Each such system is permanently assigned to one of the four BB channels and incorporates the associated modulators and demodulators. The units are connected via individual coaxial pairs. The BiK voice signals are transmitted via the SB channel of the associated telephone which is connected to the subscriber line terminating unit on the same principle as the DIGITE.

The OBN-TV and the STEREODEC are connected via a common coaxial bus, as in a cable TV network. Located directly next to each TV/STT outlet there is additionally a PW jack for inserting the program selection signal. This jack is connected to the TAG via an individual balanced line. The program selection information is sent to the TAG asynchronously in serial form

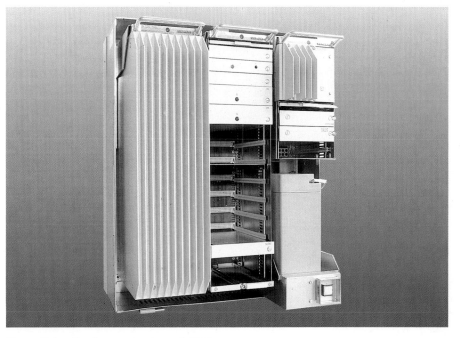

Fig. 5   Subscriber line terminating unit TAG

as a pulse message. Apart from the actual program selection information, the messages additionally include a source identifier (terminal address), i.e. the number of the STT or BB channel to which the terminal is set. It is thus possible for the user to connect the terminals to any TV/STT outlet and PW jack.

The TAG is packaged as a wall-mounted case measuring 47 cm × 38 cm × 31 cm and is therefore relatively easy to install. It incorporates its own power supply which is fed from the local 220 Vac network. The power supply incorporates a maintenance-free, sealed lead-acid battery floated across the supply in order to provide "emergency power" in the event of the public power failing. In this event, only those modules continue to be powered which are necessary for operating only one DIGITE, operation being maintained for about 8 h (6 h receive readiness and 2 h talking time). **Fig. 5** shows a TAG equipped for four telephone and two BiK connections.

Each TAM is mounted in a 400 mm high, style 7R equipment inset (**Fig. 6**). TAMs are fed in groups of four from the station battery via a common power supply. Sixteen TAMs form a TAM group which is assigned a scanning processor through which the program selection and monitoring signals are routed to the exchange.

The processing equipment (ABE) combines into one functional unit (TVA) all the facilities required for processing a TV signal. Each TVA consists of circuits for matching the interface to the headend. It also contains the modulators for the video and accompanying sound signals, as well as a module for distributing the output signal via several coaxial lines to the TV switching networks. Three TVA are mounted in one 500 mm high, style 7R equipment inset. The STT signals are digitized two at a time in a functional unit (STA) and combined to form a DS2 (STT) signal. The output signal is distributed via balanced lines to several inputs of the STT switching networks. One STA is accommodated in one 600 mm high equipment inset.

The transmission paths are monitored by several supervisory circuits installed

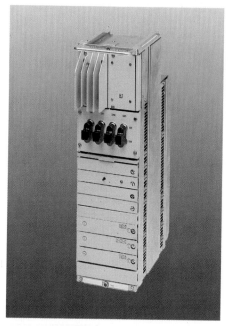

Fig. 6   Subscriber line terminating module TAM

in the units of the processing equipment and in the TAM and TAG. The outgoing 30 MHz carriers are monitored in the TVAs, while the analog-digital converters are monitored in the STAs. A scanning processor (SCP) assigned to the processing equipment receives the fault indications and transmits them to the exchange. In addition, the frame alignment signals (RKW) of the DS2 (STT) signals coming from the processing equipment are monitored at the input to the STT switching network. In the TAM the optical transmitters and all the signals coming from the exchange or the TAG are monitored. The scanning processor assigned to the relevant TAM group receives the fault indications and transmits them to the exchange.

In the TAG the optical transmitter, the RKW of the DS2 (SB) signal from the TAM and the transfer switch for emergency power are monitored. The fault indications are transmitted in the DS2 (SB) signal to the TAM and extended from there to the exchange via the assigned scanning processor. It is also possible to check each of the 16 SB channels individually on a signal from the exchange by inserting loops in the TAG and in the connected DIGITEs. The video path can be tested by establishing a loop in the video communication equipments.

As a safety precaution in the event of a fiber-optic cable breaking, the two optical transmitters are automatically shut down if either of the receivers detects no light.

Prospects

The transmission system described in this paper can be used in coming years for setting up small subscriber networks to familiarize subscribers with the services and facilities of the optical broadband network (OBN). These initial deployments will stimulate further development aimed principally at achieving further reductions in equipment size and cost, using economical quantity production techniques. An essential step in this direction will be the implementation of devices in VLSI technology to digitize the moving picture signal. This will, however, require standardization of the coding technique [3].

References

[1] Braun, E.: BIGFON Brings the Optical Waveguide into the Subscriber Area. telcom report 6 (1983) Special Issue "Optical Communications", pp. 136 to 139

[2] Gier, J.; Panzer, K.: Principles of Optoelectronic Signal Transmission. telcom report 6 (1983) Special Issue "Optical Communications", pp. 20 to 25

[3] Braun, E.; Möhrmann, K.H.: Optical Communications in Short-Haul and Long-Haul Wideband Communication Networks. telcom report 6 (1983) Special Issue "Optical Communications", pp. 202 to 205

[4] Bezugskette für die Übertragung von Ton- und Fernsehrundfunksignalen im nationalen KTV-Netz. FTZ-Richtlinie 151 R8, June 1979

[5] Draeger, R. J.; Kersten, R.; Schweizer, L.: Digital Transmission Vocabulary. telcom report 2 (1979) Special Issue "Digital Transmission", pp. 176 to 191

[6] Zeidler, G.: Designing Fiber-Optic Cable Systems. telcom report 6 (1983) Special Issue "Optical Communications", pp. 41 to 45

[7] Althaus, H. L.; Kuhn, G.: Modular Laser Source. telcom report 6 (1983) Special Issue "Optical Communications", pp. 85 to 90

[8] Toussaint, H.-N.; Winzer, G.: Technology and Applications of Couplers for Optical Communications. telcom report 6 (1983) Special Issue "Optical Communications", pp. 102 to 107

[9] Kleinke, G.: BIGFON-Leistungsangebot und Kommunikationsendgeräte im Siemens-Konzept. Sonderdruck anläßlich der Internationalen Funkausstellung Berlin 1981, Herausgeber: Siemens AG, München

Eckart Aichholz and Bodo Tilly

A Fiber-Optic System for FM Radio Relay Feeder Links and High-Quality TV Transmission

The fiber-optic analog system LA 10/70 GF is used for transmitting the frequency modulated 70 MHz intermediate frequency signal as employed in radio relay systems. Together with modem FM TV/70 A it provides a complete transmission system for a television channel in accordance with CCITT Recommendation 567. The transmission medium employed is a graded-index fiber with a 50 µm core diameter; the main element of the optical transmitter is Siemens laser module SFH408.

System configuration

The analog system LA 10/70 GF presented here employs intensity modulated light as the carrier for the traffic signal. **Fig. 1** shows an equipping option for line terminating unit LE 10/70 GF. In order to transmit an amplitude modulated video signal in accordance with CCITT Recommendation 567, it is not enough merely to convert the amplitude modulation directly into light intensity modulation. The nonlinear characteristics of the optoelectronic transducers are incompatible with the low nonlinearity requirements of the transmission channel. The video signal is therefore first converted to a frequency modulated 70 MHz signal which is then used to modulate the optical carrier.

Normally, the 70 MHz intermediate frequency (ZF) signal is already available in radio relay systems. When the same modulation parameters are used, the result is a system which will transmit these ZF signals with very good quality. A single section can be up to

Ing. (grad.) Eckart Aichholz and
Ing. (grad.) Bodo Tilly,
Siemens AG,
Public Communication Networks Division,
Munich

8 km long with a maximum optical loss of 35 dB, depending on the fiber employed.

The system is already in service with the Austrian Post Office as a radio relay feeder link on the Sonntagberg mountain. The transmission route links the radio relay station (ZF output) to the local television transmitter which is fed with the TV signal at the baseband frequency.

The system as shown in **Fig. 2** consists optionally of the following components:

TV modulator, transmit section, optical fiber, receive section and *TV demodulator*

for TV baseband transmission or

transmit section, optical fiber and *receive section*

for radio relay ZF transmission at a center frequency of 70 MHz.

The *modem* (*mo*dulator and *dem*odulator) translates the baseband signal (0 to 6 MHz) to the intermediate frequency band (70 ± 4 MHz) and vice versa.

The *transmit section* converts an intermediate frequency signal (70 ± 4 MHz) from the modulator or from a radio relay link into an intensity modulated optical signal at a wavelength in the region 820 to 880 nm.

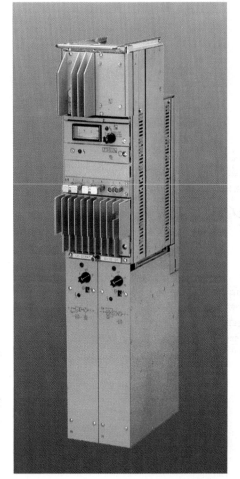

Fig. 1 Line terminating unit LE 10/70 GF

The *receive section* converts the optical signal back to an intermediate frequency signal and feeds it to a demodulator or a radio relay link.

Selected operating parameters are indicated by the *supervision unit*, which extends various alarm criteria to a central supervision facility.

Two power supply units convert the external 60 Vdc supply into the internal 24, 15 and 5 V supplies.

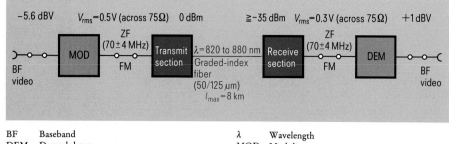

BF Baseband
DEM Demodulator
FM Frequency modulation
l Link length

λ Wavelength
MOD Modulator
ZF Intermediate frequency
$0\,\text{dBV} \triangleq V_{p\text{-}p} = 1\,\text{V}$

Fig. 2 Fiber-optic transmission link
with baseband (BF) and intermediate frequency (ZF) equipment

Optical transmitter	
Wavelength range	820 to 880 nm
Optical transmit power	0 dBm (1 mW) ± 2%
Modulation factor	80%
RMS input voltage level	0.5 V
Maximum level variation	+4/−3 (+10/−19) dB
Input impedance	75 Ω
3 dB bandwidth	500 Hz to > 500 MHz
Return loss	≧ 28 dB at 100 MHz
	≧ 20 dB at 250 MHz
Operating temperature range	−5 to +55 °C
Optical receiver	
3 dB bandwidth	10 to 200 MHz
Impedance at output	75 Ω
Return loss	≧ 28 dB
Intermediate frequency (ZF) level	
FM carrier frequency	70 MHz
FM deviation	±4 MHz
Minimum receive power	−35 dBm
Signal-to-noise ratio in 3.1 kHz test slot	> 64 dB
RMS output voltage	0.3 V
Baseband (BF) level	
Signal-to-noise ratio, weighted in video band	> 65 dB (with −15 dBm optical input level)
	> 50 dB (with −35 dBm optical input level)
Differential gain	1% at 4.3 MHz
Differential phase	1° at 4.3 MHz
Using a modem with greater deviation improves the signal-to-noise ratio correspondingly	

Table Main characteristics of the fiber-optic analog system LA 10/70 GF
used in conjunction with a graded-index fiber (50/125 μm)

The **table** contains the main characteristics of this system.

Line terminating equipment

The fiber-optic analog system LA 10/70 GF presented here is employed on fiber-optic routes with 50/125 μm graded-index fibers. As with conventional coaxial cable equipment packaged in style 7R, the fiber-optic cables are routed down into the fiber-optic cable termination, where the connection to the rack cable is established by means of a splice or connector. On short routes, an optical attenuator is inserted at this point.

The optical transmitter and optical receiver are in modules mounted directly in the top section of the inset. The fiber-optic plug mounted in the inset with a guide sleeve attached engages under spring pressure in the mating sleeve of the relevant module. This ensures that the quality of optical connections required for analog systems is achieved.

The insets are available with various equipping options to suit different applications (**Fig. 3**). An inset contains up to two transmit or receive units or can combine one transmit with one receive unit. All versions of the inset can be operated with a modulator and demodulator as well as additional co-axial cable equalizers. Baseband (BF) and intermediate frequency (ZF) connections are looped through via jacks on the front panel and can therefore be split for test purposes. Isolated BF and ZF test jacks permit in-service measurements.

Transmit section

The laser transmitter (**Fig. 4**) converts the electrical signal into optical form of correct magnitude and phase. It has a

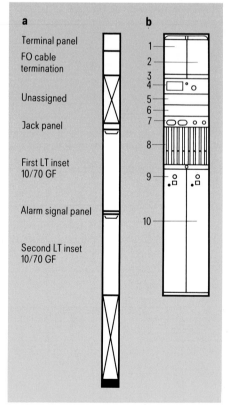

1, 2	Optical transmitter or optical receiver
3	Compartment with operating instructions
4	Supervision unit
5, 6	Receive unit
7	Jack panel
8	5 V/15 V supply
9	24 V supply
10, 11	Modulator or demodulator

Fig. 3 Equipping options for the rack (a) and inset (b)

large transmission bandwidth, making it suitable for a wide range of applications.

The semiconductor laser diode is mounted with other discrete cooling and light controlling devices in a sealed package filled with inert gas and designated Siemens laser module SFH 408 [1]. The fiber pigtail brought out of the module terminates on the fiber-optic connector which transfers the optical output signal to the outgoing fiber-optic cable. **Fig. 5** illustrates all the main functions of the laser transmitter.

The temperature of the laser chip heat sink is stabilized at 25 °C to provide the laser diode with a long life and to ensure a high-quality optical output signal. Changes in the radiation and light-current characteristics are therefore negligible.

The optical power controller stabilizes the mean optical power at the output of the pigtail at 0 dBm (1 mW). The variation in output power over the full ambient temperature range of −5 to +55 °C is ±2%. The control criterion is the optical power from the rear laser mirror. The nominal optical power can be controlled, if necessary, through the fiber monitor input. Since the optical power is the information bearer, provision is made to suppress disturbances affecting the optical control loop.

Any adjustment in input level required, for instance, by the use of long coaxial lines to feed the optical transmitter, is effected by means of a variable, plug-in attenuator preceding the wideband preamplifier. This provides equalization of level differences of up to +4/−3 dB (up to +10/−19 dB in certain cases).

A special feature is the RF input for modulating the optical carrier with the traffic signal. With this input, the optical power of the laser diode stabilized at the mean value by the regulator is modulated via a special passive circuit configuration. This passive input technique confers several advantages and acts simultaneously

- to compensate for laser modules having different slopes due to drive variations and fabrication tolerances,

- as a defined internal 75 Ω interface at a fixed voltage level of 0.5 V and

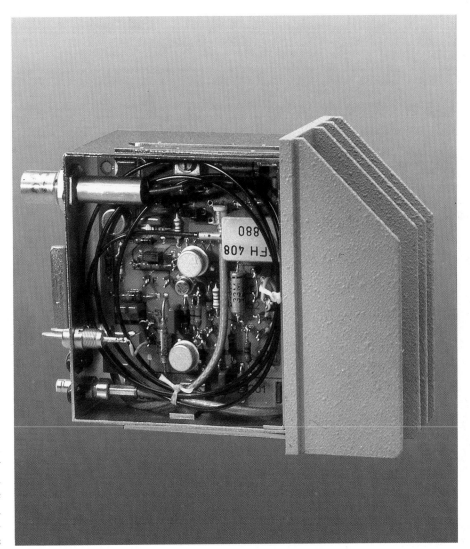

Fig. 4   Optical wideband transmitter up to 500 MHz for the wavelength range 820 to 880 nm

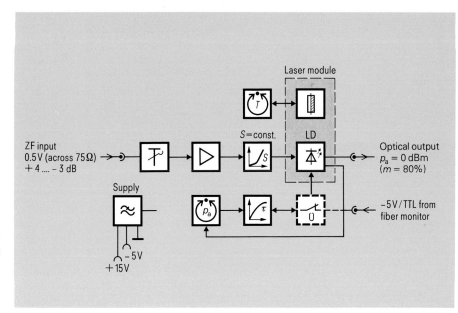

Fig. 5   Functional circuit diagram of the laser transmitter

i_{LD}	Laser diode current	τ	Turn-on time constant
m	Modulation factor	T	Temperature
p_a	Stabilized optical output power	$\ddot{U}$	Supervision
S	Slope of function (p_a/i_{LD})	ZF	Intermediate frequency

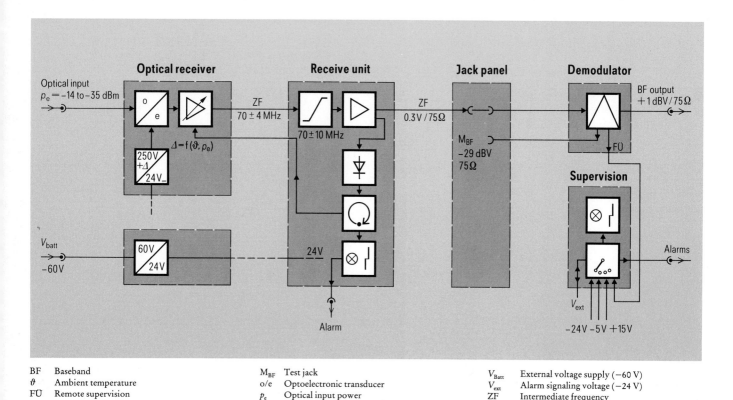

BF	Baseband	M_{BF}	Test jack
ϑ	Ambient temperature	o/e	Optoelectronic transducer
FÜ	Remote supervision	p_e	Optical input power

V_{Batt}	External voltage supply (-60 V)
V_{ext}	Alarm signaling voltage (-24 V)
ZF	Intermediate frequency

Fig. 6   Functional circuit diagram of the receive section

• as a real current source (magnitude and phase of the signal current flowing through the laser diode remain constant far outside the transmission band).

In special applications the optical transmitter is suitable for transmitting analog signals in the range extending from about 500 Hz to 500 MHz and digital signals at corresponding bit rates (transparent transmission channel).

Receive section

The units of the receive section have the following functions:

• converting the optical signal into the electrical ZF signal,

• equalizing the amplitude-frequency response of the various fiber-optic cables,

• amplifying the ZF signal to a stabilized output level.

The signal from the optical fiber is fed to an avalanche photodiode (APD). As shown in **Fig. 6** the electrical signal derived via the APD undergoes further processing in a following wideband

amplifier. This amplifier contains a control element to stabilize the ZF level appearing at the output of the receive section. The dynamic range of the input optical power is determined principally by the control range of this circuit. It was possible to expand this control range by adopting a special current-voltage characteristic in the high-voltage power supply for the APD. The hybrid design of the optical receiver provides adequate bandwidth even in special applications to 300 MHz.

The optical receiver is followed by a module which first provides precise equalization of the amplitude-frequency response in the range 70 ± 10 MHz. The distortion requiring equalization arises from the low-pass characteristic of the multimode fiber and its modal dispersion. This strap-adjustable equalizer is followed directly by a linear output amplifier. The output signal from this amplifier is rectified and fed to an integral-mode controller for output level control. The integral-mode controller sets the gain of the wideband amplifier with the aid of the previously mentioned control element in the optical receiver.

Supervision

The facilities for supervising system performance are in the form of the proven style 7R alarm signaling system. A fault indication can be sent either from the ZF transmission unit or from the modem to a central supervision facility.

Alarms are initiated by the following criteria:

• optical receive level failure and deviation outside the control range are detected indirectly via the ZF level in the receive unit (indicated by light-emitting diode on the receive unit),

• failure of the ZF level, pilot level and supply voltage in the modem (indicated by light-emitting diode on the unit),

• failure of the operating voltages.

The main system parameters are indicated on a meter in the supervision unit.

Reference

[1] Althaus, H. L.; Kuhn, G.: Modular Laser Source.
telcom report 6 (1983) Special Issue "Optical Communications", pp. 84 to 90

Erwin Pichlmayer and Anton Stegmeier

A Fiber-Optic Transmission System for Signal Bandwidths up to 7.5 MHz

In urban areas short fiber-optic links are often the only means of providing an additional transmission path in crowded cable ducts. A particular situation in which fiber-optic systems are being increasingly employed is, however, in environments where conventional copper cable systems are affected by power-line induction or electromagnetic interference. Analog transmission system A5/D10 for general applications [1, 2] has already been proven many times in such situations. System LA7/20GF has been developed from this transmission system and provides a transparent transmission channel for both analog and digital signals in the range 2 Hz to 7.5 MHz. It is therefore particularly suitable for transmitting video signals and can also be used in conjunction with interface units for transmitting 2 or 8 Mbit/s PCM signals.

System configuration

The line terminating unit of fiber-optic transmission system LA7/20GF consists of a transmitter, receiver and associated power supplies. The transmitter prepares analog or digital signals in the frequency range 2 Hz to 7.5 MHz for transmission on a graded-index fiber with a core diameter of 50 µm. This involves the baseband signal modulating a carrier frequency of 20 MHz with a maximum deviation of 10 MHz. The resultant intermediate frequency (ZF) signal is selected, amplified and limited so that it can be used to drive an infrared-emitting diode (IRED) or a laser diode (LD). The optical signal produced by the optoelectronic transducer is launched into a 50/125 µm graded-index fiber.

The receiver employs an avalanche photodiode (APD) to restore the optical signal coming via the fiber to an electrical format. This ZF signal

Fig. 1   Line terminating units LE7/20GF; insets fitted with infrared-emitting diode (IRED) transmitter and receiver (left) and laser diode (LD) transmitter and receiver (right)

Dipl.-Ing. Erwin Pichlmayer and
Anton Stegmeier,
Siemens AG,
Public Communication Networks Division,
Munich

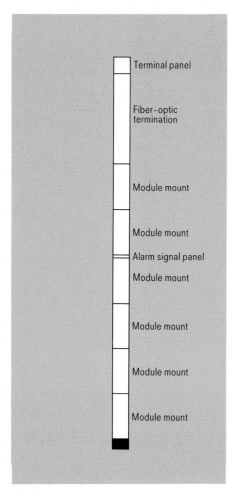

Fig. 2   Rack for accommodating line terminating unit LE7/20GF

is demodulated, filtered and then amplified. The incoming signal is monitored and a carrier failure indicated by a light-emitting diode in the receiver. At the same time, an alarm is extended to a central supervision facility.

The mechanical design of the equipment is compatible with style 7R [3]. An inset (**Fig. 1**) can accommodate the equipment for two bidirectional systems or, in unidirectional applications, three transmitters with laser diodes or five transmitters with infrared-emitting diodes or five receivers. A rack can accommodate up to six insets (**Fig. 2**).

By adapting the optical connector to the cable space available in the inset, it was possible to achieve a direct connection to the rack wiring while retaining the standard plug-in depth (**Fig. 3a**). This enabled small interchangeable units to be created at plug-in level in this instance. The required accessibility to the wiring space in the rack was achieved by adopting a hinged mechanism (**Fig. 3b**).

Transmitter

The operation of the transmitter is illustrated in **Fig. 4a**. The baseband (BF) input can be set with the aid of the attenuator (D) to the nominal level ($V_{p-p} = 1$ V for video transmission) and for levels 3 to 6 dB below the nominal. The incoming BF signal can be checked at test output M.

The preemphasis network (P) produces a frequency-dependent emphasis in the response to optimize the signal-to-noise ratio for the particular transmission mode employed. Two different preemphasis networks can be optionally inserted by means of soldered links. The following differential amplifier (V1) produces two antiphased signals to frequency-modulate the following two oscillators (VCO) (center frequencies about 140 and 160 MHz). The associated mixer (M) produces a signal centered at 20 MHz. The following low-pass filter (TP) suppresses unwanted frequency components produced in the mixer. Amplifiers V2 and V3 amplify and limit the frequency-modulated signal to a rectangular shape. In the version of the equipment employing an IRED transmitter, the diode [4] converts the electrical signal to an optical signal, which is transmitted in the optical waveguide. In the version employing an LD transmitter [5, 6], a PI controller stabilizes the laser diode to provide a constant

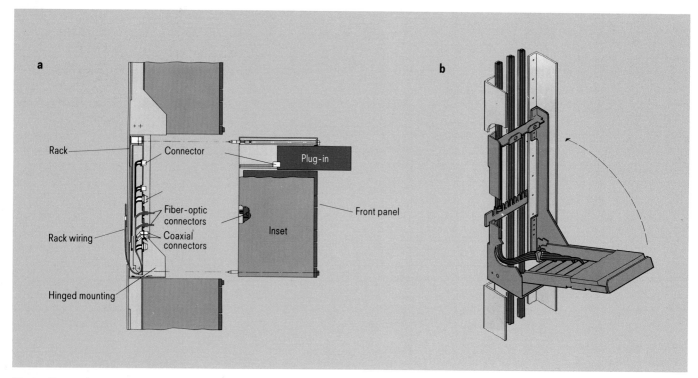

Fig. 3   Connecting arrangements (a) and hinged housing (b) on the rack

optical output power. A further PI controller limits the laser temperature in the operating temperature range to a maximum of 25 °C by means of a thermoelectric cooler.

It is possible for an externally applied frequency-modulated signal to be inserted at the ZF input. This facility can be used in conjunction with an optical receiver to form an intermediate repeater without having to demodulate the signal to the baseband. This provides improved transmission characteristics when several sections are cascaded.

Receiver

The operation of the receiver is illustrated in **Fig. 4b**. An avalanche photodiode (APD) [7] converts the optical signal received via the optical waveguide to an electrical signal, the bias voltage (150 to 300 V) for the APD being supplied by a dc-dc converter (W). The electrical signal is amplified and limited in amplifiers V1 and V2, where it is possible to extract the frequency-modulated signal at the ZF output.

The limited ZF signal from amplifier V2 is fed to the supervision circuit (Ü). If the ZF signal level falls below the set minimum, the supervisory equipment initiates either an A or a B alarm, a central indication contact is closed and a light-emitting diode lights up on the front panel of the module.

For demodulation purposes, the limited FM signal is additionally fed via a delay network (Z). The delayed and undelayed signals are both fed to a demodulator (M), which produces a pulse-frequency-modulated output containing the BF signal. The following low-pass filter (TP) suppresses the unwanted frequency components. The filter is followed by an amplifier with deemphasis network (VD) to compensate the preemphasis introduced in the optical transmitter. The final amplifier (EV) raises the BF signal to the required output level. At the test output (M), the signal can be checked with a level 20 dB below that at the main output, when terminated with 75 Ω. The principal technical data for the equipment are contained in **Table 1**.

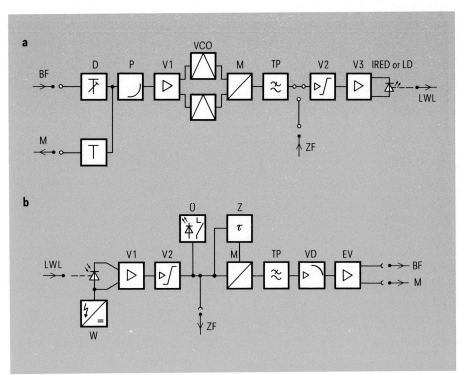

BF	Baseband	TP	Low-pass filter
D	Attenuator	Ü	Supervision circuit
EV	Final amplifier	V	Amplifier
IRED	Infrared-emitting diode	VCO	Voltage-controlled oscillator
LD	Laser diode	VD	Amplifier and deemphasis network
LWL	Optical waveguide	W	Dc-dc converter
M	Mixer	Z	Delay network
P	Preemphasis network	ZF	Intermediate frequency

Fig. 4   Functional circuit diagram of the optical transmitter (a) and optical receiver (b)

Optical parameters	
Optical wavelength for IRED in the optical transmitter	830 ± 20 nm
Spectral width	40 nm
Optical wavelength for LD in the optical transmitter	880 ± 10 nm
Spectral width	3 to 6 nm
Optical power launched into the fiber core when employing a 50/125 µm graded-index fiber, $A_N = 0.2$	
with IRED	$\geqq$ 20 µW (−17 dBm)
with LD, regulated	1 mW (0 dBm)
Electrical parameters	
Lower cutoff frequency (−3 dB)	2 Hz
Upper cutoff frequency (−3 dB)	7.5 MHz
Transmission band	10 Hz to 6 MHz
Gain/frequency response in the transmission band	$\leqq$ ±0.2 dB
Group delay/frequency response in the transmission band	$\leqq$ ±40 ns
Power supplied via dc-dc converter from battery	60 V, 48 V
Impedance at BF input/output and M output	75 Ω unbalanced
Return loss at $f \leqq$ 6 MHz	$\geqq$ 28 dB
Impedance at ZF input/ZF output	75 Ω unbalanced
Return loss at ZF input/ZF output (at 20 MHz)	$\geqq$ 26 dB
Input voltage $V_{p\text{-}p}$ at ZF input (transmitter)	0.1 to 1 V
Output voltage $V_{p\text{-}p}$ at ZF output (receiver)	0.4 V across 75 Ω

Table 1   Technical data for line terminating units LE7/20GF

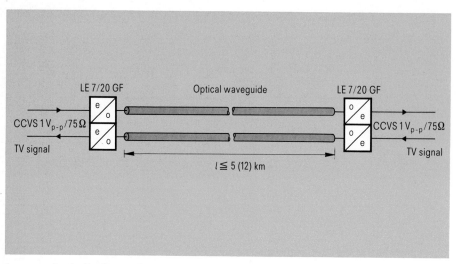

l   Section length spanned   e/o   Optoelectronic transducer
LE7/20GF   Line terminating unit   o/e   Optoelectronic transducer

Fig. 5   Transmission of video signals

Applications

The fiber-optic system LA7/20GF with its linear, unclocked operation can be used to transmit analog and digital signals in the frequency range 2 Hz to 7.5 MHz. The modulation method used (frequency modulation) is noted for good linearity and, with a favorable signal-to-noise ratio, is immune to interference of all kinds on the transmission link. It is therefore most suitable for transmitting composite color video signals in accordance with CCIR Rec. 567 (**Fig. 5**). With an IRED transmitter the system can span distances up to 5 km, while an LD transmitter provides repeater spacings up to 12 km.

When suitable interface units are used, the system can also be employed to transmit PCM signals. **Fig. 6a** shows the functional circuit diagram for the transmission of 2 Mbit/s signals together with the appropriate line terminating unit. The distances which can be spanned are 5.5 km for IRED transmitters and 13 km for LD transmitters. Interface unit DVG8 enables 8 Mbit/s signals to be transmitted (**Fig. 6b**) over section lengths of 4.5 km with IRED transmitters and 12 km with LD transmitters.

The system range for all signal types can be extended by cascading several sections. It is possible to cascade about three to four repeater sections. Connecting the ZF output of the receiver to the ZF input of the transmitter produces an intermediate repeater, processing the signal at the intermediate frequency.

Quality parameters

The quality of the system is determined chiefly by the optoelectronic components and the characteristics of the optical waveguide. The data contained in **Table 2** and **Figs. 7** to **9** are based on a 50/125 µm graded-index fiber with a numerical aperture of 0.2. When an IRED transmitter is employed, the system range is limited not only by fiber loss but also by the frequency response due to material dispersion.

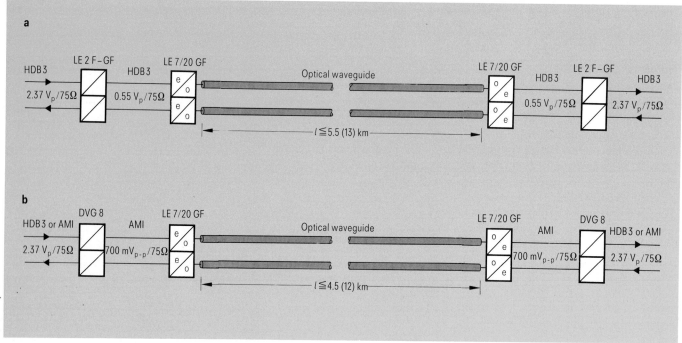

AMI   AMI code   e/o   Optoelectronic transducer   *l*   Section length spanned
            (*a*lternate *m*ark *i*nversion)   HDB3   HDB3 code   LE7/20GF   Line terminating unit
DVG8   Digital interface unit (8 Mbit/s)   (*h*igh *d*ensity *b*ipolar of order *3*)   LE2F-GF   Line terminating unit for PCM 30F-GF
                                                                          o/e   Optoelectronic transducer

Fig. 6   Transmission of 2 Mbit/s signals (a) and 8 Mbit/s signals (b)

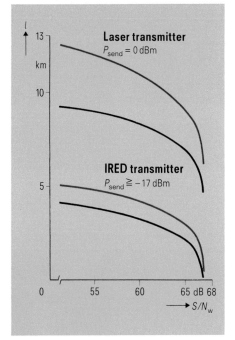

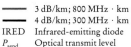

—— 3 dB/km; 800 MHz · km
—— 4 dB/km; 300 MHz · km
IRED   Infrared-emitting diode
P_{send} Optical transmit level

Fig. 7   Section length *l* as a function of the weighted video signal-to-noise ratio (S/N_{w}) (6 dB system margin included)

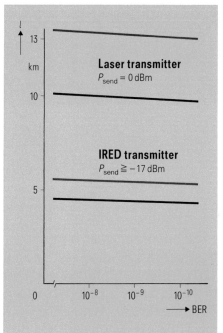

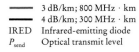

—— 3 dB/km; 800 MHz · km
—— 4 dB/km; 300 MHz · km
IRED   Infrared-emitting diode
P_{send} Optical transmit level

Fig. 8   Section length *l* as a function of the bit error rate (BER) for transmission of 2 Mbit/s signals (6 dB system margin included)

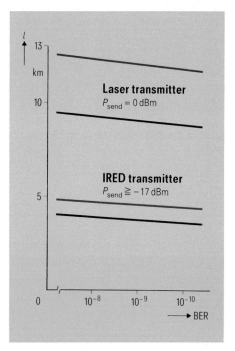

—— 3 dB/km; 800 MHz · km
—— 4 dB/km; 300 MHz · km
IRED   Infrared-emitting diode
P_{send} Optical transmit level

Fig. 9   Section length *l* as a function of the bit error rate (BER) for transmission of 8 Mbit/s signals (6 dB system margin included)

TV signal transmission	
Input voltage of composite color signal ($V_{\text{p-p}}$ selectable)	1.0/0.7/0.5 V across 75 Ω
Output voltage $V_{\text{p-p}}$	1.0 V across 75 Ω
Signal-to-noise ratio	See Fig. 7
Signal-to-periodic noise ratio	>63 dB
Signal-to-noise ratio (power frequency and harmonics)	>60 dB
Linear distortion	
50 Hz waveform distortion	≦ ± 2%
15 kHz waveform distortion	≦ ± 1%
Overshoot (rise time 200 ns)	≦ ± 1%
Nonlinear distortion at nominal level	
Differential gain at 4.43 MHz	≦ ± 2%
Differential phase at 4.43 MHz	≦ ± 2°
Intermodulation (chrominance/luminance)	≦ ± 2%
2 Mbit/s signal transmission	
LE7/20GF in conjunction with interface unit LE2F-GF	
Transmission rate	2.048 Mbit/s
Interface code	HDB3
Input voltage V_{p}	2.37 V across 75 Ω
Output voltage V_{p}	2.37 V across 75 Ω
Bit error rate	See Fig. 8
8 Mbit/s signal transmission	
LE7/20GF in conjunction with interface unit DVG8	
Transmission rate	8.448 Mbit/s
Interface code	AMI or HDB3
Input voltage V_{p}	2.37 V across 75 Ω
Output voltage V_{p}	2.37 V across 75 Ω
Bit error rate	See Fig. 9

Table 2   Quality parameters of fiber-optic transmission system LA7/20GF

References

[1] Gier, J.; Kügler, E.: Line Equipments for Optical Fiber Transmission. telcom report 2 (1979) Special Issue "Digital Transmission", pp. 111 to 117

[2] Beger, H.; Bosser, J.; Burnod, L. C.; Rossi, V.; Liertz, H.; Pichlmayer, E.: Beam Observation via an Optical Transmission System in the CERN Super Proton Synchrotron. telcom report 2 (1979), No. 3, pp. 164 to 168

[3] Weis, G.: Physical Design of Systems and Equipments for Digital Transmission. telcom report 2 (1979) Special Issue "Digital Transmission", pp. 29 to 33

[4] Clemen, Ch.; Heinen, J.; Plihal, M.: High-Radiance Light-Emitting Diodes for Optical Transmitters. telcom report 6 (1983) Special Issue "Optical Communications", pp. 73 to 78

[5] Amann, M.-Ch.; Mettler, K.; Wolf, H.-D.: Laser Diodes – High-Power Light Sources for Optical Communications. telcom report 6 (1983) Special Issue "Optical Communications", pp. 79 to 84

[6] Althaus, H. L.; Kuhn, G.: Modular Laser Source. telcom report 6 (1983) Special Issue "Optical Communications", pp. 84 to 90

[7] Plihal, M.; Späth, W.; Trommer, R.: Photodiodes as Detectors for Optical Waveguide Transmission Systems. telcom report 6 (1983) Special Issue "Optical Communications", pp. 91 to 95

Alois Anders

A Fiber-Optic Analog System for Application in Electric Utilities

Electric utilities nowadays exploit the advantages of frequency-division multiplexing wherever possible for their communication requirements. The systems most frequently employed are the TF units Z12 [1] and Z60 [2] which are two-wire systems for 12 and 60 telephone channels. These systems have hitherto employed copper-wire cables as the transmission medium, but now a new medium has emerged in the form of the optical fiber, which is totally immune to interfering fields. This immunity also means that there is no crosstalk between parallel lines. Further advantages of optical fibers are their low weight and high flexibility, allowing the cables incorporating them to be added to existing towers without these towers having to be reinforced. When suitable electrical circuits are combined with the characteristics of the optical fiber, such disadvantages of the copper circuit as cable and temperature equalization can be entirely disregarded. The electrical circuits of the system presented here are designed to enable the proven analog equipment design to be retained without modification.

System configuration

Fiber-optic systems are designed preferably for digital transmission, but the system described here is designed for transmitting analog signals. In analog transmission, the light intensity of the optical source can be controlled directly by the TF signal (intensity modulation). However, this mode of operation with its nonlinear distortion falls far short of what is required of TF transmission. This nonlinear distortion can be avoided by using angle modulation. In this approach, the TF signal to be transmitted modulates the frequency of a carrier which is then used to modulate the intensity of the light beam emitted by the optoelectronic transducer. This approach largely eliminates the nonlinearities and noise sources of the optoelectronic system by expanding the frequency band transmitted.

An established requirement in TF carrier systems is that the noise contribution due to the transmission link must not exceed 3 pW/km. An overload margin is required depending on the bandwidth of the TF system, e.g. 21 dBm0 for a 120 channel system. By contrast, digital transmission operates satisfactorily with a much smaller dynamic range. Consequently, the electrical circuits for analog transmission must be designed differently from those for digital transmission.

The optoelectronic transducers employed as transmitters are light-emitting diodes which emit light when a forward biasing voltage is applied. The wavelength of peak radiation depends on the type of semiconductor material employed for the diode. With a standard light-emitting diode it is possible to launch powers of 2 to 8 μW into a 50 μm fiber, while a Burrus diode provides launched powers of 20 to 80 μW. Owing to the optical power differences, the standard light-emitting diode can only be used for short distances. Longer distances require the Burrus diode. Other values given in this paper were obtained with the Burrus diode.

The optoelectronic transducers employed as receivers are silicon photodiodes with and without the avalanche effect. For moderate optical losses as on shorter transmission links the simple PIN photodiode is adequate. Longer links, however, need the avalanche photodiode (APD) for which the required input power is about 10 dB lower than for PIN diodes. One disadvantage of avalanche photodiodes is their high operating voltage of about 150 to 300 V and the temperature dependence of their gain. A further factor is that the amplifier circuit must be designed for extremely low noise.

In the circuits described below for the two transmission directions, the minimum optical receive power is about 10 nW. The system can accommodate link losses of about 35 dB depending on the type of fiber employed. A few more decibels must also be allowed for splices, aging etc. A 3 dB fiber can be used, for instance, in 24 channel operation to span up to 9 km without repeaters. For wider TF bands, e.g. 120 channels, the span length is restricted by the need for a higher overload margin and by the fact that the TF bandwidth is expanded from 100 to 550 kHz, the basic noise increasing with frequency.

Dipl.-Ing. Alois Anders,
Siemens AG,
Public Communication Networks Division,
Munich

156

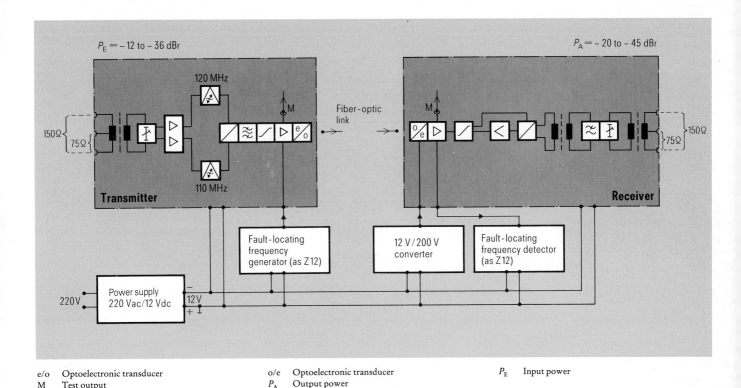

e/o   Optoelectronic transducer   o/e   Optoelectronic transducer P_E Input power
M   Test output P_A Output power

Fig. 1   Functional circuit diagram of a fiber-optic system for analog transmission of the FDM carrier systems V 12, V 24, V 60, V 72, V 120 and V 132

Line terminating unit

Fig. 1 shows the functional circuit diagram of a line terminating equipment. The transmitter has a transformer at the input for matching to the 75 and 150 Ω impedances normally employed on TF systems. The following attenuator is similarly employed for matching to the various carrier-frequency levels. This is followed by a balanced amplifier one of whose outputs varies the tuning of the associated generator via a varactor diode in accordance with the carrier frequency. The other output drives the second generator likewise via a varactor diode. The outputs of the generators are connected to the modulator inputs.

The output of the modulator produces the frequency modulated signal centered at about 10 MHz. The following filter suppresses unwanted modulation products. This is followed by a limiter which sharpens the edges of the frequency modulated signal. The limiter is followed by an amplifier which drives the current through the optoelectronic transducer.

The receiver accepts the optical signal via the optoelectronic transducer and passes the resultant electrical signal to the receive amplifier. This is followed by a limiter, one output of which applies the signal directly to the demodulator. The second output is fed to the demodulator via a delay network. The following low-pass filter selects the wanted band. The other circuits are used for matching the level and impedance to the various TF systems.

A terminal station additionally incorporates the circuits of the 12 V/200 V converter for biasing the avalanche photodiode. If the PIN photodiode is employed, this circuit section is not required. In most applications, a 12 V supply is available from the TF units so that a separate power supply is not required.

Fig. 1 additionally shows that the systems can employ the fault-locating frequency equipment normally used in TF systems. This fault-locating equipment is particularly important for longer links incorporating several intermediate repeaters. It permits continuous supervision not only of the link but also of the optoelectronic signal conversion at the terminal station.

Additional fault location facilities provided at the terminal station are test jacks which can be used to measure the frequency modulated signal and the fault-locating frequencies at the transmitter and receiver. The level setting in this system is strap-adjustable in accordance with normal telecommunication practice.

Intermediate repeater

Fig. 2 shows the functional circuit diagram for an intermediate repeater. The main path is routed via the following circuits. The optical signal from fiber 1 is fed to an APD detector which converts the signal from the electrical to optical form. This is followed by a two-stage amplifier which feeds the signal via a limiter to the transmit amplifier and then to the Burrus-type source.

The path routed in the opposite direction via fiber 2 is similar. The special feature of this circuit is that the electrical signal is amplified at the frequency modulation level only so that the original carrier frequency does not reappear at this point in the system.

This principle confers considerable advantages. It not only eliminates the modem circuits but also reduces the power consumed from the 12 V supply.

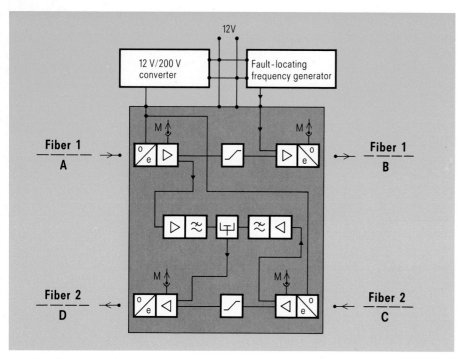

e/o Optoelectronic transducer
M   Test output
o/e Optoelectronic transducer

Fig. 2 Functional circuit diagram of an intermediate repeater

In addition, there is no attenuation distortion to accumulate over several intermediate stations as is the case with wire-line systems. The only accumulation is of the noise contributions.

In addition, the circuits are designed so that the two optoelectronic transducers can operate from a common voltage converter. The intermediate repeater always employs an avalanche photodiode as the receiver optoelectronic transducer and a Burrus diode as the transmitter optoelectronic transducer in order to maximize repeater spacings.

TF bands transmitted			
V 12	6 to 54 kHz	or	6 to 108 kHz
V 24	6 to 108 kHz	or	12 to 108 kHz
V 60	60 to 300 kHz	or	312 to 552 kHz
V 72	12 to 300 kHz		
V 120	60 to 552 kHz		
V 132	12 to 552 kHz		

Carrier frequency levels	
Optical system input Optical system output Impedances	$P_E = -12$ to -36 dBr, in steps of 1 dB $P_A = -20$ to -45 dBr, in steps of 1 dB $Z_E = Z_A = 75\ \Omega$ unbalanced or $150\ \Omega$ balanced
Supply voltage Power consumption	$V = 12$ Vdc, +ve to ground Line terminating unit with fault-locating frequency: 6 W Line terminating unit without fault-locating frequency: 5 W Intermediate repeater (two-way): 4 W

Typical system data		
Mode V 24 V 60 V 120	Link loss budget $a_L \leqq 38$ dB $a_L \leqq 25$ dB $a_L \leqq 20$ dB	Total noise <40 pW <50 pW <60 pW

Table Typical system data for line equipments LA V 24 to V 132 GF

A particular problem is the method of powering an intermediate repeater. All the circuits have been designed to minimize power consumption so that a complete intermediate repeater requires only about 4 W. With the power requirement being so low it is possible even at our latitudes to use a solar power supply floating a suitable battery if no commercial power is available on site.

The intermediate repeater, like the line terminating unit, is provided with test points preceding and following the transducers for measuring the frequency modulated signal and the fault-locating frequency.

Fault-locating frequency equipment

In wire-line transmission systems it is usual for the intermediate repeaters to be remotely supervised [2]. The fault-locating principle employed in these systems has also been adopted for use in the fiber-optic system. There was particular interest in the possibility of employing unmodified some of the fault-locating facilities available in the low-density Z 12 and Z 60 systems.

Each intermediate repeater and one of the transmitting line terminating units is each assigned a certain fault-locating frequency which, as in the Z 12 and Z 60 systems, lies above the relevant TF bands. With a TF transmission band from 6 to 108 kHz, these frequencies are spaced at 3 kHz intervals between 117 and 147 kHz, while for a transmission band of 12 to 552 kHz they are spaced between 597 and 627 kHz. It is thus possible to remotely supervise nine intermediate repeaters from one line terminating unit.

The circuit for generating the individual fault-locating frequencies is identical to that employed on the Z 12 and Z 60 systems. The fault-locating frequency (**Fig. 1**) is added to the transmission band only after the limiter, i.e. it is not frequency modulated like the TF band proper, but merely effects the intensity modulation in the optoelectronic transducer. However, this only occurs when the transmit amplifier is driven by a frequency modulated signal applied via the limiter.

Fig. 2 shows the routing of the fault-locating frequencies in an intermediate

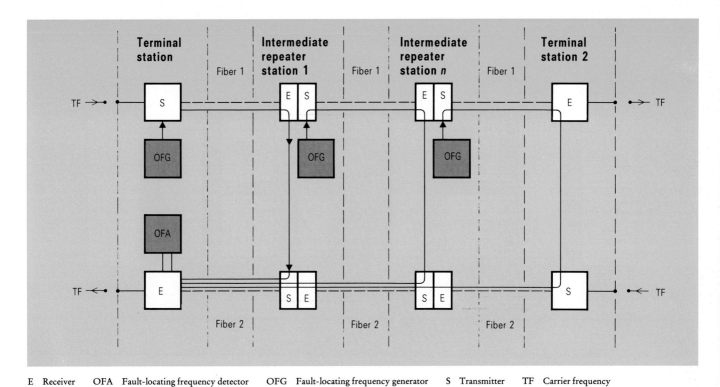

E Receiver   OFA Fault-locating frequency detector   OFG Fault-locating frequency generator   S Transmitter   TF Carrier frequency

Fig 3 Fault-locating frequency scheme

repeater. At input A the optical signal is fed to the optoelectronic transducer. The receive amplifier amplifies the frequency modulated signal and the fault-locating signal at its original frequency.

One output of the amplifier feeds both signals to the limiter which, however, passes only the frequency-modulated signal and suppresses the fault-locating signal. The other output feeds an amplifier and a low-pass filter which passes only the fault-locating frequency. This frequency is then applied via a hybrid circuit to the transmitter in the opposite direction and fed via output D together with the frequency modulated signal from input C back to the transmitting line terminating unit.

The transmit amplifier preceding output B is fed with the fault-locating frequency for the particular repeater. The fault-locating frequencies coming via input C bypass the limiter in the path C to D via an amplifier and a low-pass filter.

Fig. 3 shows the routing of fault-locating frequencies for a complete system incorporating *n* repeaters. All the fault-locating frequencies returning to the line terminating unit (**Fig. 1**) are then applied to the detector circuit (original Z 12 module).

Two-wire operation via only one optical fiber

As previously mentioned, one fiber is required for each transmission direction. However, the system also provides the facility for using only one fiber for both the go and return directions. This operating mode can be implemented with the aid of an optical splitting/combining coupler [3]. The schematic of such a system is illustrated in **Fig. 4**. A TF channel modem in the terminal station A produces at its TF transmit output a basic group in the frequency band 60 to 108 kHz which is transferred to a slightly modified Z 12 TF system incorporating no directional filter. The group band is fed at the original frequency directly to the input of the previously described fiber-optic system. The optoelectronic transducer of the transmitter is then connected to the fiber via an optical coupler. At terminal station B, the optical signal is similarly fed first to an optical coupler and only then to the optoelectronic transducer. The receive section of the fiber-optic system applies it, back in the basic group band, to the Z 12 equipment and then to the demodulator of the channel modem. Transmission in the opposite direction is similar except that, in this instance,

the basic group from the channel modem in the Z 12 equipment at terminal station B is translated to the frequency band 6 to 54 kHz before being fed to the fiber-optic circuits. At terminal station A, the Z 12 equipment translates the frequency band 6 to 54 kHz back to the basic group band.

Any overdriving of these circuits as a result of the high optical power level impinging on the much lower receive level of the same line terminating unit is prevented by the optical coupler.

The TF system Z 12 is provided with suitable filters for additional electrical protection. In this operating mode, the system can accommodate a link loss of about 20 dB.

Conclusion

The fiber-optic system presented here allows even TF systems to be operated on the new transmission medium with good characteristics, the advantages being of particular benefit when applied to electric utilities. This is due to the fact that line communication over copper wires requires considerable expenditure on components and electrical circuits to eliminate, in particular, the effects of electromagnetic interference (e.g. due to lightning strikes or short circuits in the power lines) on the TF transmission. A

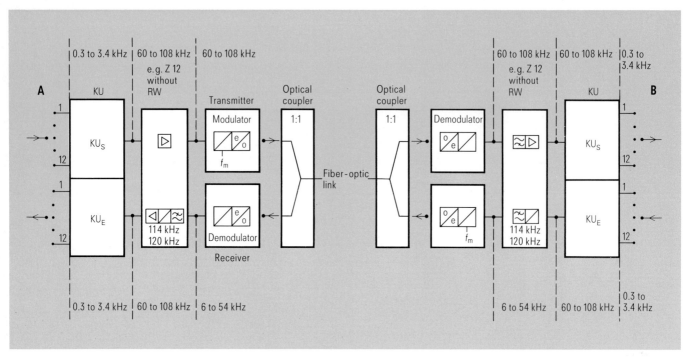

e/o   Optoelectronic transducer   KU$_E$ Channel demodulator   o/e   Optoelectronic transducer
f$_m$ Modulating frequency   KU$_S$ Channel modulator   RW   Directional filter

Fig. 4   TF carrier operation over a common optical fiber for go and return directions

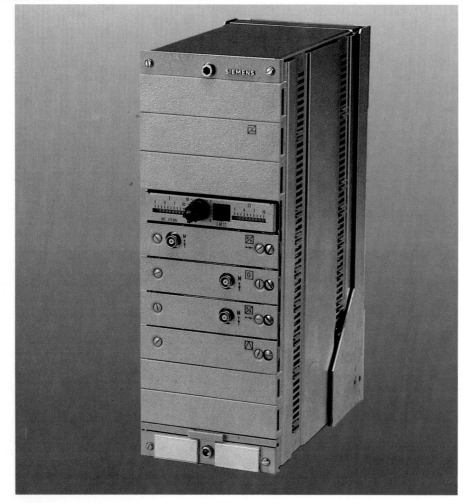

Fig. 5   Line terminating unit in a 300 mm high style 7R inset

further factor is that these systems require precise equalization of the line attenuation specific to each type of cable, as well as needing special equalizers to compensate for the effect of temperature on cable loss.

The new fiber-optic system has already undergone circuit trials in the laboratory. **Fig. 5** shows the development model of a line terminating unit. This is a 300 mm high inset in style 7R containing five slide-in units measuring 100 mm × 160 mm. The individual modules, excluding the one for detecting the fault-locating frequencies, are mounted in shielded frames in accordance with established practice for higher-density transmission systems.

References

[1] Endlich, G.; Fütterer, H.G.; Stummer, G.:
    Informationsübertragungssystem Z 12 für
    symmetrische Kabel auf Hochspannungs-
    leitungen.
    Elektr.-Wirtsch. 75 (1976), pp. 992 to 997

[2] Anders, A.; Hug, W.: Z 60 Carrier Trans-
    mission System Increases Capacity of Aerial
    Cables Fivefold.
    telcom report 3 (1980), No. 2, pp. 97 to 100

[3] Toussaint, H.-N.; Winzer, G.: Technology
    and Applications of Couplers for Optical
    Communications.
    telcom report 6 (1983) Special Issue "Optical
    Communications", pp. 102 to 107

Günter Knoblauch

Fiber-Optic Components and Systems for Industrial Applications

Source and detector diodes, fiber-optic cables, connectors, couplers and even complete transmission systems suitable for the optical transmission of information in industrial applications are now available. The advantages of optical compared with conventional wire-line transmission promise in the coming years to have a profound impact on the configuration of transmission channels through to the optical bus structure.

The introduction of microelectronics into industrial controls resulted in a significant increase in the efficacy in that field. High signaling rates at the interface, however, require low signal voltages and currents. This is where the trouble lies with conventional electrically coupled systems. Their sensitivity to electromagnetic interference, crosstalk between signal and control lines and potential equalization between transmitter and receiver are just a few of the problems which can often be very expensive to resolve. It is in such areas that fiber-optic systems provide significant advantages and facilitate new approaches.

When the configuration of an optical transmission system is compared with that of a conventional, electrically coupled transmission system, there are some common features apparent in their structures. The main functional differences, however, are found in the design of the components and in the resulting system characteristics (**Fig. 1**).

The common features in the structures consist in both systems having two interfaces both at the transmitter end and at the receiver end, namely one internal and one system interface.

The first interface (internal interface) is formed at the transition from the logic circuit technology (e.g. TTL, MOS, ECL etc.) to the interface device. The interface device can be a line driver, isolating transformer, optical coupler etc. The second interface (system interface) is usually a connector which provides electrical coupling between the interface and the electronics. This may involve the use, for instance, of DIN standardized VF or RF connectors.

The optical transmission system also has an internal interface. The signal streams at the transmit end are amplified to operate a source diode (optoelectronic transducer).

At the receive end, the signal at the detector diode (optoelectric transducer) is amplified and matched to the signal levels of the following circuits. The system interface is purely optical, employing "optical" connectors.

When comparing systems from the point of view of cost, account should also be taken of the expenditure required between the internal and external interfaces.

Features of optical information transmission

When assessing the features of information transmission via optical fibers, a mental comparison should always be made with conventional wire-line transmission systems. Some of the features of fiber-optic systems relevant to industrial application are:

Dipl.-Ing. Günter Knoblauch,
Siemens AG,
Safety and Security Systems Division,
Munich

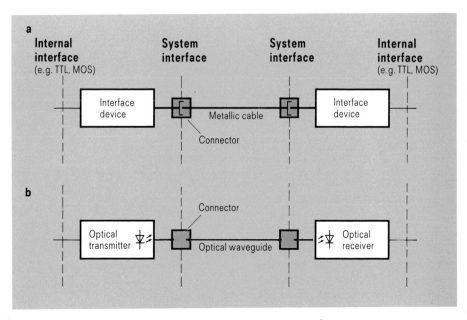

Fig. 1 Schematic of wire-line (a) and optical transmission systems (b)

- immunity to electromagnetic interference,
- electrical isolation between the transmitter and receiver,
- no signal radiation and therefore no crosstalk,
- no sparking at fiber contacts or fiber breaks,
- no ground loops.

Application areas for fiber-optic systems

The large number of features mentioned provide in themselves an indication of the wide area of application. Some of the relevant fields and branches of industry are given below.

The industry summary in the **table** indicates other applications, stating the main requirements in the transmission channel in terms of bandwidth, interference immunity and electrical isolation.

Industrial controls and process control

The emphasis here is on error-free transmission of information in a noisy electromagnetic environment (**Fig. 2**). Workshops employing process control systems are an example, with the operation and switching of sometimes heavy electrical loads on the machinery under control acting as a source of interference both to the originating process and to other processes. Similar problems exist in rolling mills, foundries with arc furnaces and in power stations.

Transportation systems

The introduction of automatic control on urban railroads and subways has placed the most stringent demands on the security of data traffic between stations. The control cables are located within the zone of influence of the power lines.

Power systems

For the transmission of direct current at high voltages up to, for example, 220 kV, the ac voltage is rectified by thyristors. The problem here is to provide an isolated link across the voltage drop between the control at the low voltage level and that at the high voltage level. This is achieved with an infrared-emitting diode (IRED) on the low voltage level operating as a source

Industry	Band-width	Inter-ference immunity	Electrical isolation
Computer systems			
Process control			
Instrumentation			
Signaling			
Broadband communication			
Medicine			
Power station			
Refineries			
Mines			
Chemical			
Military systems			

Table   Application areas for fiber-optic systems

via a fiber-optic cable only a few meters long to activate the thyristor control on the 220 kV level or to fire the thyristor directly.

Hazardous areas

Refineries, the chemical industry, mining and shipbuilding (tankers) are prone to explosions due to sparking. Sparks can be caused when connecting live cables, but especially when metallic cables are damaged or shorted.

Fig. 2   Fiber-optic transmission systems in railroad installations

Components for fiber-optic transmission systems

The requirements placed on individual components vary greatly according to the task performed and the operating conditions. This article, therefore, is confined to a selection of the fiber-optic components developed especially for industrial applications, such as connectors, transducers, systems and couplers.

Connectors

The optical connector is a key component in optical systems, as it must provide mutual mechanical compatibility between the various system components. There are a large number of designs and processes [1, 2, 3].

Optoelectronic transducers

Transducers for transmitters based on standard and high-power IREDs (Burrus diodes), laser modules with pigtails and connectors, and transducers for receivers with PIN or avalanche photodiodes are the basic components (**Fig. 3**) used in the construction of transmitters and receivers. They usually incorporate only the source and detector diodes necessary for optical transmission and form the mechanical interface and break point to the fiber-optic cable. The transducers can also be employed to construct transmitters and receivers to suit user-specific applications.

Transmitter and receiver systems

The transmission rates for industrial monitoring and process control are in

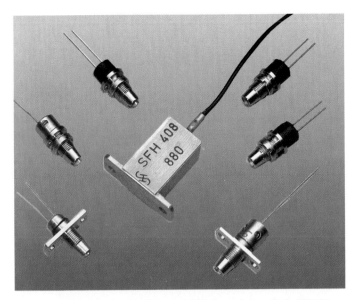

Fig. 3 Optoelectronic transducers with light-emitting diode (IRED), PIN or avalanche photodiode and laser module

Fig. 4 Standard fiber-optic system, consisting of transmitter, fiber-optic cable and receiver, as well as transmitter and receiver modules for data rates up to 10 Mbit/s

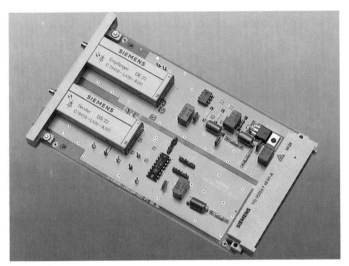

Fig. 5 Fiber-optic system for transmitting data in TTL and V.24 formats

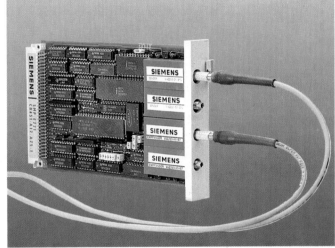

Fig. 6 Microprocessor module (SMP E221) as an optical interface

most cases less than 1 Mbit/s. Fiber-optic systems as in **Fig. 4** are most suitable for these applications. Since they have a TTL interface, they can be easily inserted into existing controls.

In industrial controls, the distances to be spanned can range from just a few meters to hundreds of meters. It is convenient for the user if he can use the same system for any route length. By providing several transmit power settings and a high dynamic range in the receiver, it is possible to cover spans of up to 4 km, depending on the type of fiber.

If, however, data are transmitted in byte format (e.g. 8, 16 or 32 bits), i.e. when bus structures exist, it is not usually possible to transmit the data in

parallel for reasons of cost. The data (including the timing) are, therefore, converted into a serial structure and transmitted serially via a single channel [3]. Converting the data format from parallel to serial increases the transmission rate by the factor of the format width and additional bandwidth is required for the timing.

Complete transmission systems

Fig. 5 illustrates a system module incorporating transmitter and receiver with TTL and V.24 interface circuits for full duplex data transmission via two fibers. The system is designed as a plug-in module for the ES902 packaging system, handling data rates of 250 kbit/s (TTL) or 100 kbit/s (V.24) and suitable for links up to 3500 m,

depending on the type of fiber-optic cable.

When configuring controls with the proven SMP modules (Siemens microcomputer PC boards), an optical interface can be provided using board SMP E221 (**Fig. 6**). It permits direct connection to the internal SMP bus instead of the standard interface module.

Distributed multiprocessing systems require high-speed and interference-immune transmission channels. **Fig. 7** shows the data transmission control (DUST 3962L) for "Siemens System 300" process control computers, providing bit-serial transmission using a full duplex procedure. The data rate on the optical interface is 1.5 Mbit/s – this is equivalent to a net data rate of

Fig. 7 Data transmission control (DUST 3962 L) for multiprocessing systems

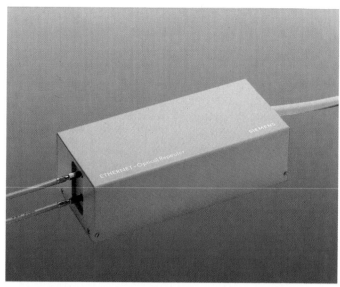

Fig. 8 Fiber-optic remote repeater for use in EMS bus networks (ETHERNET)

around 170 kbyte/s on the electrical interface. For data integrity, this transmission system employs block checking in accordance with DIN 66 221. Version of the system are available for transmission links up to 500 m or up 2000 m.

Fig. 8 shows a remote repeater with optical interface for application in *local area networks* (LANs).

This technology has also become known as the EMS bus network (Siemens "EMS 5800 DOCUMENT") system concept, in which the transmission procedures are designated CSMA/CD (*carrier sense multiple access with collision detection*) or ETHERNET. The fiber-optic remote repeater shown in **Fig. 8** allows two LAN segments up to 2.8 km apart to be connected. It can, however, also be implemented as a fiber-optic terminal for remote subscribers.

Systems for difficult operating conditions

The system components described so far have been developed for applications in systems and plant providing a certain degree of protection against direct exposure to such environmental influences as moisture and dirt. If, however, use in particularly harsh conditions is proposed (e.g. in mining, energy supply or shipbuilding), special measures are required to protect the relatively sensitive connector faces with their small, optical cross-sections

of 50 or 100 μm. **Fig. 9** shows a system component incorporating the entire transmitter and receiver electronics as well as an optical and mechanical interface. The optical interface remains closed except during installation of the system or when carrying out cabling modifications. Once in service, disconnection would normally occur only at the electrical interface. Since this interface has rugged, solid electrical contacts, it is easy to handle even, for example, wearing gloves (in winter).

Optical relay

The fiber-optic relay shown in **Fig. 10** was developed for applications requiring low-loss switching of optical transmission channels. Other possible applications include situations where a system failure within an optical bus or network structure must not result in the entire system breaking down. A defective system can be bypassed easily by means of an optical relay.

Optical couplers

The components described so far enable links to be established from point to point. There are other applications, however, either requiring the signal to be branched and fed to several receivers, or involving several transmitters sending to a single receiver. In practice, both possibilities often occur together. The systems communicate freely with each other and are known as interactive systems. Examples include centralized process monitoring

systems and multiprocessing structures.

The significance of these bus structures is growing continually. This trend is being reinforced by the advance of integrated circuits and in particular of microprocessors. Simple optical branches and complex optical bus structures can be established using couplers as shown in **Figs. 11** and **12**.

The type of coupler (three-port tee, four-port or star) best suited to the particular system depends on the system structure and redundancy requirements (system availability). This means that, apart from the simple ring or data bus, there will be many situations favoring hybrid network configurations (using star and tee couplers) [3, 4].

Introduction of fiber-optics to industrial practice

The introduction of fiber-optic transmission systems to industrial environments is best carried out in two stages.

Stage 1

A standard fiber-optic system is used to evaluate the system characteristics under operating conditions. Siemens has put together a transmitter, optical fiber and receiver to form a user's evaluation kit for this purpose (**Fig. 4**). The standard TTL interface has the advantage that no circuitry needs to be developed at this stage, so that the system can be integrated directly into an existing system configuration and

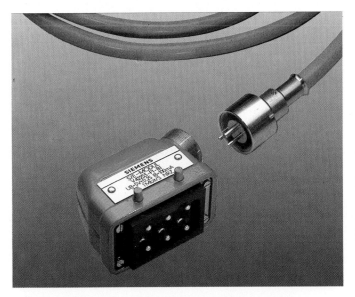

Fig. 9   Transmit-receive module with an optical and an electrical interface for applications with difficult operating conditions

Fig. 10   Fiber-optic relay

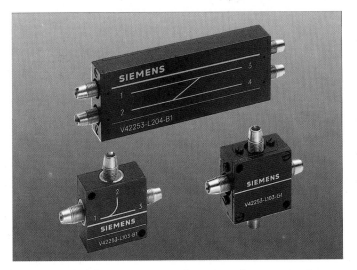

Fig. 11   Optical three-port (tee) coupler and two four-port couplers for fibers with a core diameter of 50 and 100 µm

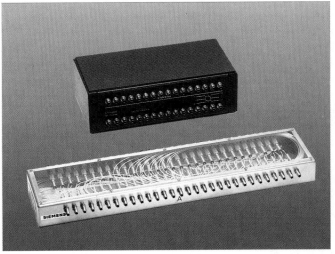

Fig. 12   Star couplers for 16 and 62 subscribers

effort can be concentrated entirely on evaluating its performance on optical fibers.

Stage 2

After successful evaluation, it is necessary to find the right balance between system performance and system cost, i.e. the process of establishing which optical components are suitable for volume application begins. Some applications may be suitable for the use of complete systems off-the-shelf, while others may require a circuit to be developed for a specific problem using the optoelectronic transducers shown in **Fig. 3**.

When selecting the connectors, such criteria as standardization can be important. Siemens fiber-optic connec-

tors conform to the German draft standard.

Prospects

A comparison of market analyses over past years shows that the demand for fiber-optic systems is growing more quickly than originally anticipated. A contributory factor in this is that most of the components now available or announced have already reached volume production status and are suitable for industrial applications. Fiber-optic systems employing principally digital techniques will penetrate all areas of industry. They will, initially, take the form of single links between systems, developing later as optical data buses for complex process control systems.

References

[1] Knoblauch, G.: Optische Steckverbinder; Teil 1: Funktionsprinzipien, Teil 2: Verarbeitung. Nachr.-techn. Z. 36 (1983), pp. 26 to 29 (Part 1), pp. 90 to 92 (Part 2)

[2] Knoblauch, G.; Toussaint, H.-N.: Connectors for Fiber-Optic Components and Systems. telcom report 6 (1983) Special Issue "Optical Communications" pp. 96 to 101

[3] Knoblauch, G.: Informationsübertragung über Lichtwellenleiter im industriellen Bereich. Siemens Components 18 (1980), pp. 1 to 7 (Part 1) and pp. 144 to 150 (Part 2)

[4] Toussaint, H.-N.; Winzer, G.: Technology and Applications of Couplers for Optical Communications. telcom report 6 (1983) Special Issue "Optical Communications" pp. 102 to 107

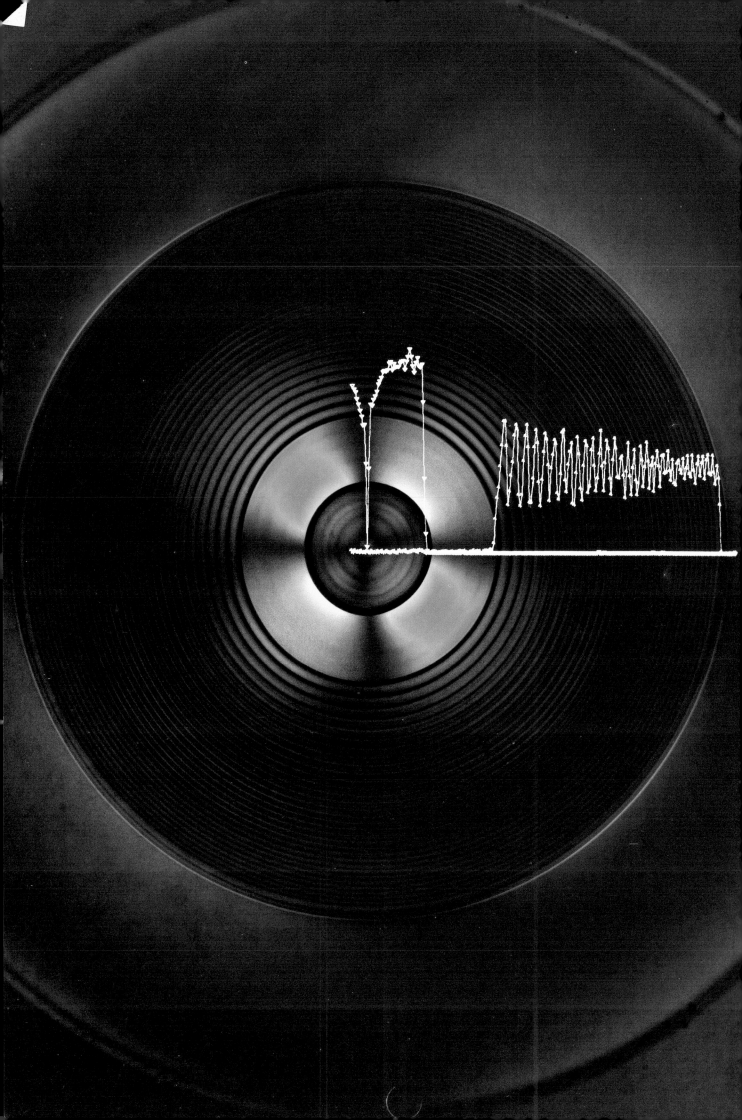

Ekkehard Klement and Karl Rössner

Principles of Optical Measurements for Communication Systems

Such great advances have been made in optical-fiber communication systems in recent times that communication administrations throughout the world are beginning to set up transmission facilities employing this new medium: the optical waveguide. Measurements of the transmission characteristics of these optical communication paths are necessary both for the manufacturer as well as for the user. Above all, the test results must be reproducible, and this with a reasonable investment in technology and time. In order to achieve this, the test methods and test conditions for optical waveguide systems must be agreed both nationally and internationally. Among other bodies, the CCITT is actively engaged in producing recommendations for test methods, including the associated limits. The results of work carried out by the IEC are used as a basis for this purpose.

Many problems currently arise when measuring the parameters relevant to the transmission properties of optical waveguides. A consequence of this is that the test results are frequently not comparable and reproducible to the extent that one is nowadays accustomed in the case of conventional communication links via radio and copper cable.

In order to attain this objective in the case of optical communications, it is necessary for the responsible committees to establish standards at the earliest possible date. **Table 1** gives an overview of the committees and of the relevant state of work of those parts dealing with transmission measurement. It should be mentioned that there is close cooperation between the working groups of IEC and CCITT, and that these groups are endeavoring to issue proposals for test methods which are identical in content and, in part, also in text. The various national standards committees – in the Federal Republic of Germany the VDE – align their national standards with these proposals. Such "standards" are intended to ensure that, when measuring the parameters, the same conditions prevail and identical interpretations ensue, e. g.

Dipl.-Phys. Dr. rer. nat. Ekkehard Klement,
Siemens AG,
Research and Development Division,
Munich;
Dipl.-Ing. (FH) Karl Rössner,
Siemens AG,
Measuring Devices Manufacturing Plant,
West Berlin

◁ The photomicrograph shows the cross section of a preform for single-mode fibers (developed by Siemens and produced by the MCVD process). Superimposed are the microprobe analyses of the radial concentration profile of germanium in the silica glass core and of phosphorous in the cladding. It can be seen that refractive index variations (they cause the dark rings in the sample illuminated with polarized light) and stress differences are closely correlated with the composition

Standards	Attenuation	Bandwidth	Backscatter	Numerical aperture	Notes
DIN	DIN 57 472 Part 252	DIN 57 472 Part 253	DIN 57 472 Part 251	DIN 57 472 Part 254	The DIN specifications listed here will be issued in draft form in 1983
IEC VDE	Described in 46 (Central Office) 11, November 1982				The consultative documents will shortly be sent to the national committees and will be finally adopted in October 1983
CCITT	"Yellow book 81" Vol. 3 Rec. G. 651	"Yellow book 81" Vol. 3 Rec. G. 651	"Yellow book 81" Vol. 3 Rec. G. 651	"Yellow book 81" Vol. 3 Rec. G. 651	"Yellow book 81" is available. In the current study period (four years) the texts will be improved and aligned with IEC

Table 1   Standardization of test methods

through identical conditions for coupling light into the optical waveguide. When measuring multimode fibers (step-index and graded-index fibers), these coupling conditions determine the mode distribution of the light at the launch point. In contrast, temporally stable coupling into the very thin core of a few micrometers diameter is a problem in the case of single-mode fibers. Other factors influencing the result arise from the shape and condition of the glass surface (cleaved surface) at the launch point.

For both the supplier and the user, the solution of the problems described is of great importance in the assessment of the condition of optical transmission facilities. The principal parameters for the various interest groups concerned with the measurement of optical waveguides are listed in **Table 2**.

Attenuation measurement

The attenuation is a very important quality characteristic for the assessment of an optical waveguide. Its dependence upon the wavelength is of particular interest to the fiber manufacturer. The attenuation measurement at the operating wavelength or wavelengths is adequate for the cable and system manufacturers, and also for the user. Optical waveguides have now such a low attenuation that the measurement of splice and connector losses is of great significance in the planning and realization of optical transmission systems. A maximum measurement uncertainty of 0.1 dB is aimed for. The distance between the two ends of the cable makes the attenuation measurement difficult in the case of installed optical cables.

Three measurement methods are described in IEC documents and are also being adopted by CCITT: the cut-back method, the insertion-loss method and the backscatter method [1].

In the *cut-back method* an optical power, which is constant over the measuring period, is fed to the input of the fiber to be tested and the optical power at the fiber output (P_2) is measured. The fiber is then cut off approximately 2 m from the input end and the optical power (P_1) present there is mea-

sured. The attenuation a (in dB) can be calculated from the equation

$$a = 10 \lg (P_1/P_2). \tag{1}$$

Although the cut-back method is being discussed by CCITT as a reference test method, reproducible test results are difficult to obtain even with careful handling. With improving fabrication techniques, the danger arises that the measurement errors will become inadmissibly large unless extreme care is taken with the test conditions; in addition, the fiber is reduced in length by about 2 m at each measurement. Consequently, this type of measurement cannot be employed for installed cable systems with cables containing several fibers [2].

In the *insertion-loss method* the optical source and the optical receiver are interconnected via a short reference fiber, and the optical power P_1 is measured. The fiber to be measured is then inserted in place of the reference fiber and the optical power P_2 is measured. The attenuation can be calculated from (1).

As mentioned earlier, the coupling into the test item during measurement of multimode fiber attenuation has a considerable effect on the test result and on the measuring accuracy. For this

reason a mode scrambler – also known as a mode mixer – (e.g. input fiber of adequate length) must be used to produce an almost stable mode distribution. Stable means that the light distribution is determined only by the differential attenuation of the modes and not by the light distribution at the launch point. A very similar effect can be achieved, however, if the light beam is so shaped by a suitable lens-aperture-stop system that about 70% of the core diameter and 70% of the numerical aperture are illuminated. These coupling conditions are shown in dashed line in the "phase-space-diagram" (**Fig. 1**), where it should be noted that, due to the quadratic scales, 70% excitation corresponds to the point (0.5, 0.5) [3]. This method also yields an approximately stable mode distribution after a few meters only [4].

The *backscatter method* utilizes the light scattered along the fiber by Rayleigh scattering. A small proportion of this scattered light (determined by the acceptance angle) returns to the launch end and can be measured there. From this scattered optical power and the time delay in the fiber, a diagram can be produced from which the attenuation coefficient over the entire length of the fiber can be seen (**Fig. 2**).

Optical waveguide measurement	Fiber manufacturer	Cable manufacturer	Cable installer	Cable operator
Attenuation as function of wavelength	××	×	–	×
Attenuation as function of fiber length	×	××	××	×
Reflection and backscatter as function of fiber length	××	××	××	×
Transmission bandwidth (design and wavelength dependent)	××	××	–	×
Transmission bandwidth (fiber length dependent)	×	××	–	××
Numerical aperture (launch angle)	××	×	–	–
Fiber dimensions (noncircularity, concentricity error, core diameter)	××	×	–	–

Table 2   Important parameters for the various groups

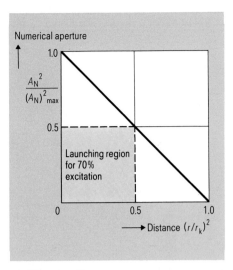

r_K Fiber core radius

Fig. 1 Numerical aperture A_N
of a graded-index fiber as a function
of the radial distance r from the fiber axis

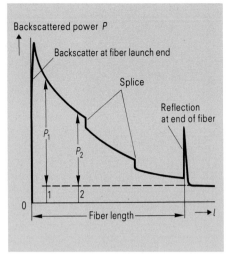

$P_{1,2}$ Optical power at fiber points 1 and 2, respectively

Fig. 2 Backscatter diagram
of a fiber consisting of three spliced sections

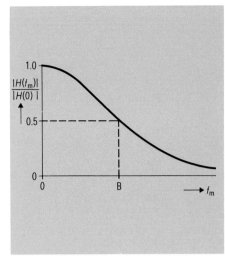

B Bandwidth f_m Modulation frequency

Fig. 3 Typical transfer function $|H(f_m)|$
of a glass fiber (response similar to a
Gaussian low-pass filter)

The attenuation a (in dB) of an arbitrary section can then be obtained from the equation

$$a = 5 \lg (P_1/P_2). \qquad (2)$$

P_1 and P_2 are the optical powers at points 1 and 2 of the fiber; due to the double traverse of the light, a factor 5 is employed here in contrast to (1).

The advantage of this method is that only one end of the fiber must be accessible for the measurement, which makes things much simpler in an operational system. However, the method has a few disadvantages, the principal of which are:

● The backscatter signal is very weak, which means that optical pulse powers up to a few watts are necessary to bridge large fiber attenuations or lengths. In order to achieve an adequate measuring accuracy, the receiver sensitivity must be operated at the noise limit of the photodetector and, in addition, averaging must be carried out, which at each doubling of the number of measurements improves the signal-to-noise ratio by 3 dB.

● Equation (2) is valid under the assumption that the scattering coefficient, the numerical aperture and the core diameter are constant along the fiber. If this assumption is not met with sufficient accuracy, the resulting measurement errors can be averaged by making measurements from the two ends [5].

Bandwidth measurement

After the attenuation, the bandwidth is the second most important parameter determining the transmission characteristics of an optical waveguide. It is described by the complex transfer function $H(f_m)$, where f_m is the modulation frequency. Its magnitude has a response similar to that of a Gaussian low-pass filter (**Fig. 3**). The frequency at which

$$\frac{|H(f_m)|}{|H(0)|} = 0.5 \qquad (3)$$

is referred to as the bandwidth B of the optical waveguide.

The transfer function can be measured either in the frequency domain or the time domain. In both cases modulated light from a suitable source is launched into an optical waveguide of known length, received at the far end and evaluated. Both measuring methods conform to standards. The measured values should be quoted for 1 km length. It is assumed that the bandwidth of a fiber decreases linearly with the length, which is only true for relatively short lengths of fiber [4].

The magnitude of the transfer function is given by

$$|H(f_m)| = \frac{P_2(f_m)}{P_1(f_m)} \qquad (4)$$

where P_1 and P_2 are the amplitude-modulated powers at the beginning and

end of the test section respectively. From this is derived directly the most important measuring technique in the frequency domain: the optical power P of the source is modulated with a continually increasing frequency and $|H(f_m)|$ is determined in accordance with (4).

For the measurement in the time domain, a short light pulse (e.g. with 0.1 ns half-power width) is launched into the optical waveguide. Due to the differential delay between the various modes as well as to the material dispersion, a broader pulse appears at the end with the response $s(t)$, from which the following quantities can be derived:

the pulse area

$$A = \int_{-\infty}^{\infty} s(t)\, dt, \qquad (5)$$

the pulse center

$$t_c = (1/A) \cdot \int_{-\infty}^{\infty} t\, s(t)\, dt, \qquad (6)$$

the second central moment

$$M = (1/A) \cdot \int_{-\infty}^{\infty} (t-t_c)^2 \cdot s(t)\, dt = \sigma^2 \qquad (7)$$

and the rms pulse width

$$t_{rms} = 2 \cdot \sigma. \qquad (8)$$

If the first three quantities are determined for the pulse launched at the input to the test fiber and for the pulse emerging at the end, they can be used for the calculation of several parameters relating to the optical waveguide:

the fiber attenuation

$$a = \alpha \cdot L = 10 \lg (A_1/A_2), \qquad (9)$$

the fiber length

$$L = \frac{c}{n_\mathrm{g}}(t_{c2} - t_{c1}) \qquad (10)$$

(n_g group refractive index [3])

and an approximate value for the bandwidth

$$B = (5\sqrt{\sigma_2^2 - \sigma_1^2})^{-1}. \qquad (11)$$

The exact value for the bandwidth can be obtained by determining the signal spectrum $S(f_\mathrm{m})$ for both pulses by Fourier transformation

$$S(f_\mathrm{m}) = \frac{1}{A} \cdot \int_{-\infty}^{\infty} s(t) \exp(-j2\pi ft)\,dt. \qquad (12)$$

This yields the transfer function

$$H(f_\mathrm{m}) = \frac{S_2}{S_1}. \qquad (13)$$

Since the pulse broadening in a graded-index fiber largely results from the differential delay between the various modes, the excitation condition referred to in connection with the attenuation measurement must be observed for the bandwidth measurement, in order to obtain reliable test results.

Measuring the numerical aperture and the near field

Two optical waveguides can only be spliced together with low loss if there is close agreement between their numerical apertures [5]. The measurement of the numerical aperture is consequently important for the manufacturer of optical waveguides and cables.

The schematic of an arrangement for determining the *numerical aperture A_N* by measuring the far field is shown in **Fig. 4a**. It consists of launching optics, which permit the setting of a defined spot size and acceptance angle, and a detector which can receive light from a small angular range only, and which is scanned over the output end of the fiber. The optical power is thus measured as a function of the angle Θ.

Both ends of the fiber are inserted into index-matching cells, which strip the modes in the cladding and simultane-

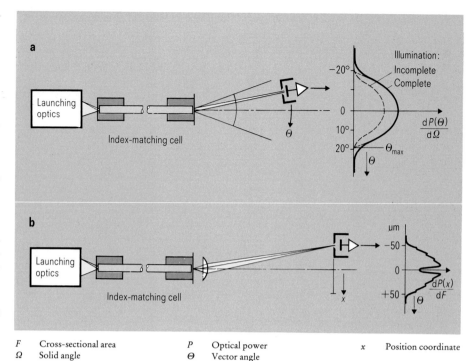

| F | Cross-sectional area | | P | Optical power | | x | Position coordinate |
| Ω | Solid angle | | Θ | Vector angle | | | |

Fig. 4 Measuring the far field (a) and the near field (b) of a graded-index fiber

ously reduce the demands made on the quality of the end surfaces.

Fig. 4a also shows typical field distributions of a graded-index fiber. It can be seen that, with complete illumination of the fiber input end, the angle

$$\Theta_\mathrm{max} = \arc \sin A_\mathrm{N} \qquad (14)$$

can be determined from the curve $dP/d\Omega$ by mathematical extrapolation to $dP/d\Omega = 0$ with a very small error.

With the aid of the arrangement shown in **Fig. 4b** the *optically effective core diameter* can be determined from the near field. For this purpose, an enlarged image of the end of the fiber is produced and scanned by a small-area photodiode. With complete excitation of all modes, this near field has practically the same shape as the index profile. The intersections of $dP/dF = 0$ give the core diameter.

Determining the fiber dimensions

In order to produce low-loss demountable connections and splices, it is important for the core to be as near to the center of the optical waveguide as possible, and for there to be good agreement between near field and far field. In addition, the outside diameter

of the fiber should be known. The CCITT recommendation (so far submitted for optical waveguides with 125 µm outside diameter and 50 µm core diameter [1] only) allows tolerances of a few percent for diameter deviations, noncircularity and concentricity errors.

Whereas the outside diameter is relatively easy to measure, the core diameter can only be measured with adequate accuracy using optoelectronic methods (an example was given in the preceding section). Measurement of the *concentricity error* and the *noncircularity* necessitate the recording of the entire enlarged image of a fiber end and its evaluation with the aid of a computer.

The simplest optical method for determining the length of an optical waveguide is to calculate it from the time delay of a short light pulse, measured either by the transmission or backscatter method. However, the group index must be known for this purpose, and this must be established by a time delay measurement on a section of fiber of the same type, whose length has been determined mechanically. Due to the unavoidable fluctuations in the group index, errors of a few percent cannot be prevented.

Outlook

A series of parameters must be measured for the characterization and quality control of optical waveguides. The fact that various manufacturers are already offering test equipment [6], even though standardization of the test methods has by no means been completed, indicates the significance of these measurements. The optical communication scene is characterized by continuing turbulent developments. In the forefront of these developments are the transition to longer wavelengths and the use of single-mode fibers, resulting in fresh problems for testing and standardization of test methods [7], which will have to be dealt with before the old problems have been finally resolved.

References

[1] CCITT Rec. G. 651

[2] Kaiser, M.: Messung der Übertragungseigenschaften von Multimode-Lichtwellenleitern. Nachr.-tech. Z. 34 (1981), pp. 418 to 422

[3] Geckeler, S.: Physical Principles of Optical Waveguides.
telcom report 6 (1983) Special Issue "Optical Communications", pp. 9 to 14

[4] Zeidler, G.: Planung von LWL-Kabelanlagen. Nachr.-tech. Z. 34 (1981), pp. 848 to 852

[5] Schicketanz, D.: Anwendung des Rückstreumeßplatzes in der Lichtwellenleitertechnik. Siemens-Forsch. u. Entwickl. Ber. 10 (1981), pp. 53 to 59

[6] Eibl-Vogt, A.; Permien, J.: System Test Equipment for Optical Waveguides and Optical Cable Links.
telcom report 6 (1983) Special Issue "Optical Communications", pp. 171 to 175

[7] Deserno, U.; Schicketanz, D.: Test Methods for Future Fiber-Optic Applications.
telcom report 6 (1983) Special Issue "Optical Communications", pp. 176 to 182

Further literature

- Midwinter, J.E.: Optical Fibers for Transmission. New York, J. Wiley & Sons 1979
- Marcuse, D.: Principles of Optical Fiber Measurement. New York, Academic Press 1981

Alfred Eibl-Vogt and Joachim Permien

System Test Equipment for Optical Waveguides and Optical Cable Links

Optical waveguide transmission facilities are now coming into widespread use. It is therefore necessary to make available to both the manufacturer and the user of optical transmission systems suitable test equipment which is adapted to this new situation. This was only partly true of the test equipment used hitherto, since these instruments have to be operated by specialists. When using them the test results of interest can only be determined by graphical or numerical evaluation of the test signals. In addition to the rapid and reproducible determination of the test results, the new generation of test equipment is characterized principally by simplicity of use and generally by computer-aided presentation of test results in digital or graphical form.

Attenuation measurement

If the optical power P_0 is coupled into an optical waveguide with homogeneous attenuation coefficient, the optical power after a distance x is a function of the attenuation coefficient α and is given by

$$P(x) = P_0 \cdot e^{-\alpha x} \qquad (1)$$

This wavelength-dependent attenuation is caused by absorption and scattering [1].

Several methods are available for the measurement of optical waveguide attenuation. They differ principally in the way in which they are employed and in the attainable measuring accuracy. The *backscatter method* [2] is a so-called single-ended method, in which the attenuation is measured from one end of the fiber. The *insertion-loss* and *cut-back methods* [3] are two-ended methods in which determination of the measured value is somewhat more complicated than in the case of the single-ended method, but which permit reduction of the measurement error. However, the cut-back method cannot be used for measurements on connectorized fibers, i.e. those with fitted connectors, since with this method a section of fiber must be cut off each time. For this reason the attenuation test set described below is based on the insertion method. The use of the cut-back method in the case of fibers without connectors is also possible.

The way in which the light is coupled into the test item is of fundamental importance in the attenuation measurement, since the excited modes are subject to differing attenuations. In order to prevent measurement errors, it is necessary to ensure a quasi-stable mode distribution at the beginning of the fiber. This condition is considered to have been achieved if, after a fiber length of 2 m and with a Gaussian distribution of the near and far fields, a light spot diameter of $26 \pm 2\,\mu m$ is measured in the near field and a numer-

Ing. (grad.) Alfred Eibl-Vogt,
Siemens AG,
Measuring Devices Manufacturing Plant,
West Berlin;
Dipl.-Ing. Joachim Permien,
Siemens AG,
Public Communication Networks Division,
West Berlin

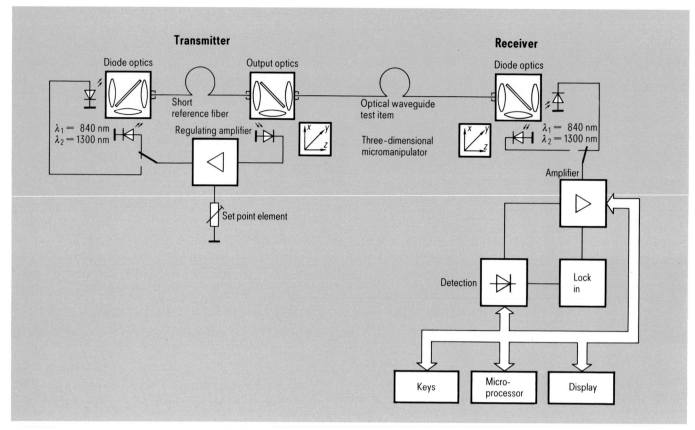

λ   Optical wavelength

Fig. 1   Functional diagram of the attenuation test set

ical aperture A_N of 0.11 ± 0.02 is measured in the far field (for graded-index fibers with a core diameter of 50 μm and a numerical aperture of 0.2). This corresponds to the proposed international and national standards. There are several ways of achieving this, including the use of

- a long launching fiber, or
- a mode filter (scrambler), or
- a lens-aperture-stop system.

The aforementioned prerequisites for the equilibrium condition are attained with an approximately 70% excitation of the numerical aperture and the core area of a 50 μm graded-index fiber. Unfavorable excitation conditions, e.g. caused by too large a light spot from the optical source and/or too large a numerical aperture, generate cladding modes and leaky modes which are subject to strong attenuation. This results in the measurement of a false value for the attenuation [4]. With correct launching, the value of the attenuation derived by adding the losses of the discrete cable sections forming a transmission link must not differ from the value subsequently measured on the com-

pleted transmission link. Obviously, the splice losses must then be taken into account.

Attenuation test set

Fig. 1 shows the functional diagram of the attenuation test set. The test item is coupled via a three-dimensional micromanipulator, permitting measurements to be carried out on all important types of fibers (50 μm graded-index fiber, 100 μm step-index fiber, 200 μm large-core fiber and monomode fiber). The wavelength of the emitted light can be switched between 840 and 1300 nm. Output optics ensure that the excitation conditions are maintained with differing test items. A fraction of the light is coupled out as an actual value, a control circuit ensuring that this actual value corresponds to the set point value. The optical output power is maintained at a constant level in this way. The transmitter signal is modulated with 1 kHz in order to permit selective, and consequently low-noise, signal processing with a wide dynamic range in the receiver.

In the receiver the test signal passes via receiving optics to an optoelectronic

transducer corresponding to the optical wavelength in use. The gain of the subsequent amplifier can be switched in six steps (in the case of 840 nm) or four steps (in the case of 1300 nm) each of 10 dB. After phase-sensitive detection, the signal is digitized. The built-in microprocessor automatically carries out measurement range selection and forms the logarithm of the measured value. The result is displayed in three digits with 0.1 dB resolution (**Fig. 2**). Further signal processing can take place via the IEC interface. Automatic line-voltage selection, battery operation, relative test level transmission and an intercom system, for alignment purposes, make this a test set which can be used everywhere.

Attenuation tester

The attenuation tester is used for simpler and quicker measurements on optical waveguides. It consists of two small handy units (transmitter and receiver) which are battery powered and, consequently, can be used practically anywhere (**Fig. 3**).

A light-emitting diode generates the transmitter optical signal. Pulse modulation of the transmitter signal at a frequency of 1 kHz suppresses extraneous light components and the photodiode dark current at the receive end.

As optoelectronic transducer the receiver contains a PIN photodiode which produces a photocurrent proportional to the optical power. The detected signal is fed via a logarithmic amplifier, which permits display of the measured value in decibels, to an integrated analog-to-digital converter which simultaneously drives the liquid crystal display.

Short-circuit calibration with a reference fiber of about 1 m length should be carried out at the start of the measurement. After replacing the reference fiber by the test item, the attenuation can be read directly in decibels on the receiver; the measurement range of 31 dB is adequate for almost all measurements occurring in practice.

The short-circuit calibration is carried out with a fiber of the same type as the test item, so that the largely type-dependent launching and extraction losses of the fiber are equalized. Using the level control, the transmitter output power is adjusted so that the receiver indicates an attenuation of 0 dB; possible measurement errors due to temperature and aging-dependent changes of the test setup are practically excluded by this means. In addition to the equipment specification, factors affecting the measurement uncertainty include the effect of the concentricity error between the fiber and the connector and the excitation of cladding modes.

Eccentricities of a few micrometers relative to the connector axis can arise during the fitting of connectors to the fibers. Such concentricity errors cause a coupling error of up to about 1 dB. Due to the simple method of launching employed, leaky modes are also excited in the fiber and, although these are subject to high attenuation in the direction of propagation, they influence the result of the short-circuit calibration. Consequently a higher attenuation is measured than would be the case with a stable mode distribution. However, both effects can only be excluded by means such as are employed in the attenuation test set. Nevertheless the

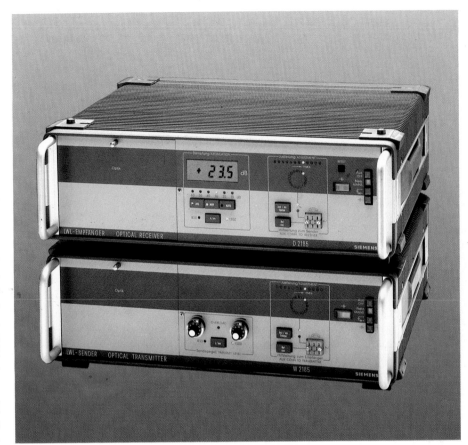

Fig. 2   Attenuation test set

Fig. 3   Using the attenuation tester

results are generally acceptable for an operability test.

Optical time-domain reflectometer

The backscatter method permits investigation of the local attenuation profile of optical waveguide transmission facilities, measurement of connector and splice losses, location and analysis of discontinuities, as well as determination of the total loss. These investigations are carried out from one end of the fiber. Due to its versatility, the optical time-domain reflectometer has become one of the most important measuring instruments in the field of optical waveguide systems.

In the backscatter method a light pulse is launched into the fiber and, as a result of Rayleigh scattering, a small fraction of the light is scattered back. The optical power scattered back from each length element of the fiber and detected at the fiber input is proportional to the optical power in the length element concerned. In addition, discontinuities and joints in the fiber cause reflections which have a strong influence on the optical power measured at the input to the fiber. The temporal response of the backscatter sig-

nal consequently contains information relating to the local attenuation characteristic of the fiber under investigation [2].

The light pulses are produced by a high-power semiconductor injection laser (**Fig. 4**), which emits light at a wavelength of 850 nm. The light is focused onto the end face of the coupled fiber via a lens system and a beam splitter.

A test fixture, which is adjustable in all three dimensions, is used for coupling the fiber. Since a whole range of differing connector systems is in use and it is frequently necessary to measure unconnectorized fibers, this type of coupling ensures maximum flexibility for the user.

The backscattered light is reflected via the beam splitter onto an avalanche photodiode (APD), whose photocurrent signal is converted into a voltage signal by a matching amplifier. The following amplifier, with gain switchable in steps, raises the signal level to a value suitable for the analog-to-digital converter. A synthesizer generates the sampling rate for the converter from the input propagation velocity; a fixed fiber length is thus assigned to the individual samples. Since the start signal

for the laser pulse and the sampling signal are synchronized via the sequencer, precise location is possible during signal evaluation.

In order to obtain a large dynamic range, the backscatter signal is multiple-sampled to suppress noise and the samples are averaged. This results in an improvement in the signal-to-noise ratio due to the statistical distribution of the noise amplitudes. The selectable number of averagings can therefore be used to choose between a rapid display refresh for adjustment operations and a slow display generation for precise evaluation.

Rapid and reliable test signal evaluation is ensured by the computer-aided digital signal processing, together with the display in the form of text and graphics. In addition, the interactive operation makes the varied possibilities of the measuring instrument available to the user in an easily mastered way.

The result of a measurement on a fiber with splices is shown in **Fig. 5**. Due to the logarithmic display, a straight line results for the fiber without fault while a step in level occurs at the discontinuity. The superimposed values for the attenuation coefficient D_F and

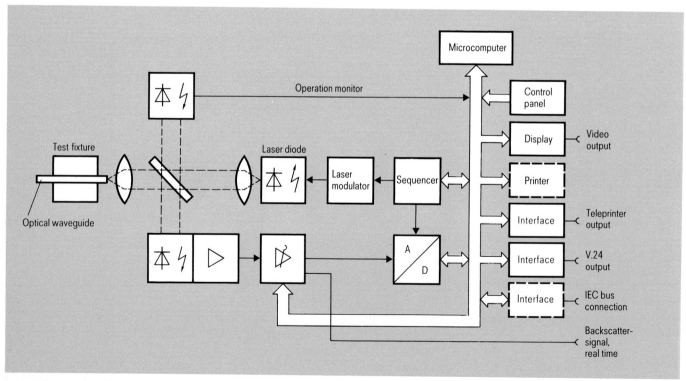

A/D   Analog-to-digital converter

Fig. 4   **Functional diagram of the optical time-domain reflectometer**

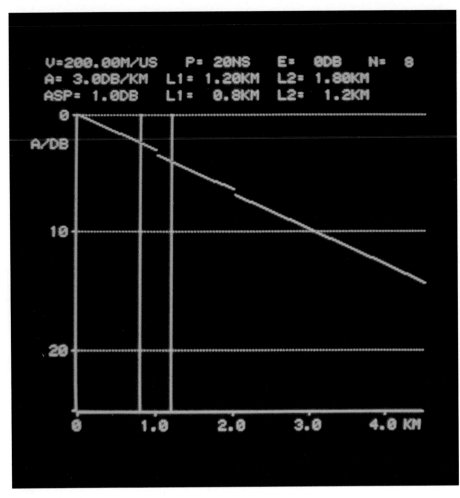

V=200.00M/US   P= 20NS   E=   0DB   N=   8
A= 3.0DB/KM   L1= 1.20KM   L2= 1.80KM
ASP= 1.0DB   L1= 0.8KM   L2= 1.2KM

Fig. 5   Optical time-domain reflectometer display

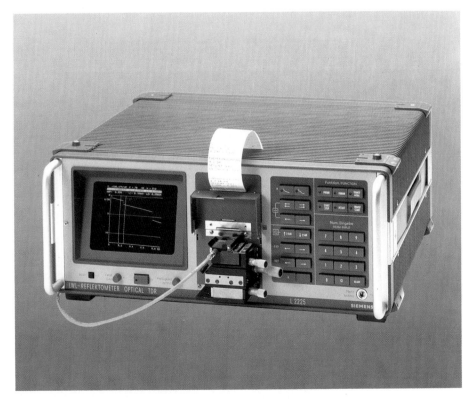

Fig. 6   Optical time-domain reflectometer with integrated printer

the attenuation step D_S are derived from the following equations [2]:

$$D_F = \frac{5 \lg \dfrac{P_1}{P_2}}{(t_2 - t_1)\dfrac{v}{2}} \ \mathrm{dB}; \qquad (2)$$

$$D_S = 5 \lg \frac{P_1}{P_2} - D_F \cdot (t_2 - t_1) \cdot \frac{v}{2} \ \mathrm{dB}. \qquad (3)$$

Since the light traverses the fiber twice, the factor 5 is employed in the expression for the level, and half the propagation velocity v of the light in the fiber for locating purposes.

A choice can be made between linear and logarithmic display for the signal presentation. In addition, display of the attenuation coefficient is also possible. The computer automatically generates the associated coordinates. The displayed range, with a maximum measurement range of 16 km, can be expanded to a section of 200 m for particularly accurate signal evaluation. Two cursors, which are freely movable over the screen, and superimposed range data permit exact location of faults. The evaluation permits the determination of both the attenuation coefficient as well as the attenuation of individual discontinuities or splices.

The results of the measurement can be recorded in various ways. A built-in printer produces a record without additional devices (**Fig. 6**). The entire screen content can be copied with the aid of a video printer via the video output. The IEC and V.24 interfaces permit the measured values to be transmitted to a remote point for further processing.

References

[1] Unger, H.-G.: Optische Nachrichtentechnik. Berlin: Elitera-Verlag 1976

[2] Schicketanz, D.: Theorie der Rückstreumessung bei Glasfasern. Siemens Forsch.- u. Entwickl.-Ber. 3 (1980), pp. 242 to 248

[3] Kaiser, M.; Zwick, U.: Vergleich verschiedener Meßverfahren für die Faserdämpfung. NTG-Fachber. 75 (1980), pp. 139 to 141

[4] Charlton, D.; Reitz, P.R.: Making fiber measurements. Laser Focus 15 (1979) No. 9, pp. 52 to 64

Ulrich Deserno and Dieter Schicketanz

Measurement Methods for Future Fiber-Optic Applications

Measurement techniques for optical communications will continue in the future to present a challenge which should not be underestimated. The dramatic developments in this field would be inconceivable without an effective system of measurements to support manufacturing technology, quality assurance in fiber and cable production, and systems development. This paper outlines a number of important future measuring tasks and describes state-of-the-art laboratory methods with the aid of such examples as measuring the radiation pattern and bandwidth of multimode fibers, the time-domain spectra of laser transmitters and the principal parameters of single-mode fibers.

Developments in optical communications can be broadly characterized by the following trends:

● improvements in glass and fiber drawing technology (reduction in OH-content, attenuation values, geometric and physical tolerances, improved strength),
● advances in the manufacture and handling of single-mode fibers (controlled counterbalancing of waveguide and material dispersions, development of low-loss splicing techniques),
● as a consequence optical transmission over longer distances and at transmission rates into the gigabit range,
● accompanied by the search for low-cost manufacturing technologies in the wake of increasing demand for fiber-optic systems.

Dipl.-Ing. Dr. phil. Ulrich Deserno and Ing. Civ. Elec. Dr. phil. Dieter Schicketanz, Siemens AG, Research and Development Division, Munich

Systems employing *graded-index fibers* are already in operation at up to 140 Mbit/s. In many respects both the methods and equipment for testing these systems are already highly sophisticated, e.g. for measuring the attenuation and bandwidth of optical fibers by transmission and backscatter methods. An important task currently arises from the need to specify realistic standard test conditions for these measurements as soon as possible, since the results of the measurements are influenced by the light distribution in the optical fiber [1, 2]. Existing proposals recommend using the equilibrium mode distribution which develops in long fibers as a standard measurement condition [3]. However, it is still unclear as to how this standard distribution can be established simply and reproducibly without excessive cost (e.g. by using a long input fiber). The use of a *radiation pattern method* can considerably simplify the investigation of steady states and the development of excitation methods. A second important task is to improve bandwidth prediction for long transmission links on the basis of individual measurements.

Systems based on *single-mode fibers*, which are likely to be used in future because of their exceptional performance, impose special test requirements for the transmitter and optical fiber. At transmission rates above about 500 Mbit/s, for instance, the dynamic variation in the optical spectrum of the laser source must be measured and taken into account. Measurements on single-mode fibers are simpler than on multimode fibers as regards the *distribution* of launched light. On the other hand, greater complexity is generally necessary for single-mode fibers because of the lower available power levels, the much higher bandwidths and the factors affecting the polarization of the guided light [4]. New measurements required specially for single-mode fibers relate to parameters of the "equivalent step-index profile" and the cutoff wavelength of the second mode.

Radiation pattern of multimode fibers

It is generally known that the attenuation and bandwidth of multimode fibers depend on which mode groups, identified e.g. by propagation constant and leakage, contribute to the light propagation. The distribution of optical power in the mode volume is determined by the launched power distribution, the differing attenuation of the individual modes and the exchange of power between them. This distribution varies as a function of the stated effects along the length of the transmission link, producing a corresponding variation in transmission characteristics.

It is therefore important to quantify the distribution of power in the mode volume inside the fiber and this raises the following questions:

- In what way are attenuation and bandwidth a function of mode distribution?

- Over what length and in which form does equilibrium mode distribution occur?

- How does this distribution vary on spliced links?

- What form does equilibrium mode distribution take for various fiber types?

- How widely does equilibrium mode distribution vary between specimens of a given fiber type?

- How can the equilibrium mode condition for a given fiber type be simulated using simple methods (e.g. special excitation conditions, launching fibers and mode mixers) on short lengths of fiber?

The distribution of power among *individual modes* can be determined only by coherent optical methods, e.g. holographic filters. However, this involves an unjustifiably high experimental cost. It must also be realized that in practice the individual mode numbers fluctuate locally along the fiber. For practical purposes, therefore, it is advisable to manage with the distribution information for the important *mode groups*. This information can be obtained using incoherent methods.

Near-field and *far-field* measurements were initially used for this purpose. However, these alone do not always provide the complete distribution information. This can only be provided by a two-dimensional *raster-scan method* [5]. The various methods are shown in **Fig. 1**. The parameter measured for the *far field* is the "radiant intensity" $\partial P/\partial \Omega$ as a function of the polar angle Θ and for the *near field* the parameter is the "intensity" $\partial P/\partial A$ as a function of the position coordinate x on a fiber diameter, where P is the optical power, $\Omega \approx \pi \Theta^2$ is the solid angle coordinate and $A = \pi x^2$ is the area coordinate. The raster-scan method detects both parameters. Using a large aperture microscope objective, position and angle coordinates can be scanned by traversable aperture stop and detector. This is used in a first step to

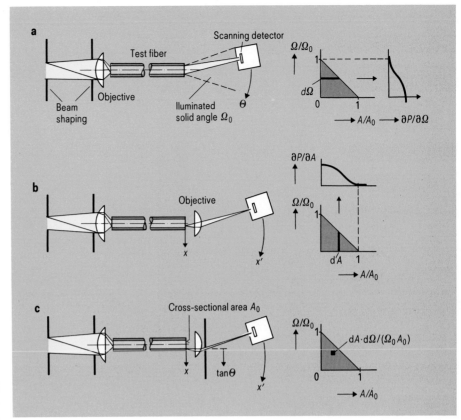

$$
\begin{array}{ll}
A, A_0 & \text{Normalized cross-sectional area} \\
\Omega, \Omega_0 & \text{Normalized solid angle} \\
\partial P/\partial A & \text{Intensity}
\end{array}
\qquad
\begin{array}{ll}
\partial P/\partial \Omega & \text{Radiant intensity} \\
\Theta & \text{Polar angle} \\
x, x' & \text{Radial coordinates}
\end{array}
$$

Fig. 1 Comparison of far field (a), near field (b) and radiation pattern (c) of an optical fiber (left, measurement schematic; right, representation in phase space)

measure the radiance $\partial^2 P/(\partial A \partial \Omega)$ at the fiber end as a function of Θ and x. For evaluation it is convenient to transform the measured radiance distribution mathematically to a "phase space" spanned by Ω and A. It is proposed to designate the thus transformed optical power distribution $P'(\Omega, A)$ as the "radiation pattern".

By virtue of the coordinate system selected, the phase space concept [6] is particularly suitable for the interpretation and quantitative description of cylindrically symmetric transformations. The phase space can be uniquely mapped region by region on the mode volume of a circular cylindrical optical waveguide [7]. The radiation pattern defined above thus contains the complete distribution information within the mode volume.

The scanning method as described is relatively complicated to use. For practical purposes the modified arrangement after Stewart [8] is therefore recommended which, despite its equip-

ment complexity, is extremely rapid, simple and reliable (**Fig. 2**).

The method is basically as follows. Using a special optical arrangement consisting of two slotted aperture stops, spherical and cylindrical lenses and a video camera, the polar angular distribution of the light emerging from the test fiber is first recorded as a function of radial coordinate x. This distribution may be termed the "local far field". The radiation pattern is then computed from the video camera data and outputted. The computer is additionally used for quadrant averaging (exploiting the trefoil symmetry of the local far field) as well as for correcting, normalizing and finally storing and displaying the test data. **Fig. 3** shows a color graphic with the local far field recorded by the video camera and the computed radiation pattern.

The resolution of both the basic scanning method and the modified scanning method is limited by diffraction at the aperture stops. The inherent

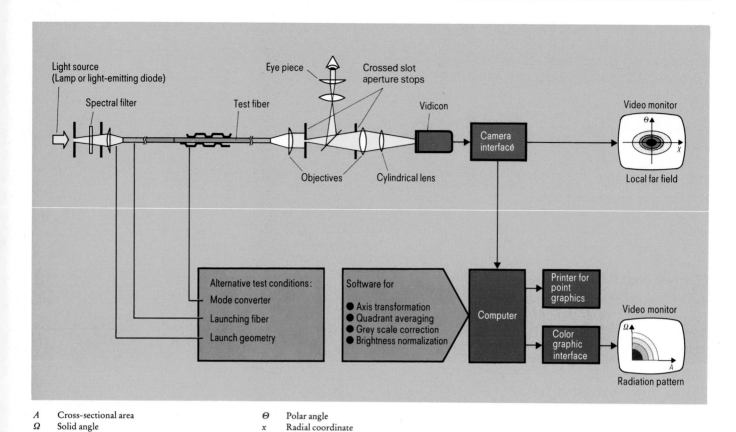

A	Cross-sectional area
Ω	Solid angle

Θ	Polar angle
x	Radial coordinate

Fig. 2 Test arrangement for video scanning method per [8]. Computer evaluation of the local far field yields radiation pattern in phase space

residual uncertainty is determined by the diffraction limit $\Delta\Theta \cdot \Delta x = 0.61\,\lambda$. From this, it is possible to state a minimum resolvable phase space element, e.g. for graded-index fibers, as $(\partial A/A_0) \cdot (\partial\Omega/\Omega_0) = 16/N$ where the fiber-specific normalization parameters A_0 and Ω_0 can be obtained from **Fig. 1** and N is the number of modes. With a typical mode number of $N = 500$, there are therefore approximately $N/16 \approx 30$ picture elements. Two power distributions which cannot be differentiated within this resolution limit can be treated the same as regards all in-coherent influences (e.g. statistical bending).

Measurements for single-mode systems

In communication transmission systems employing single-mode fibers particular attention must be paid to the short-term spectral variations in the emission of the laser source, the transmission characteristics of the fiber (attenuation and bandwidth), the coupling between optical source and fiber as well as the losses introduced by cabling and splices.

Time-domain spectroscopy of optical sources

In a fiber-optic transmission link, it is necessary to consider the optical spectrum of the source at high bit rates on account of the chromatic dispersion of the fiber, since variations in the spectrum produce unwanted noise. This spectrum can be investigated in the time domain using a test setup as shown in **Fig. 4**. With this arrangement the light from the source under test is guided through a high-resolution monochromator to a video camera or a wideband receiver. The video camera enables the integral spectrum to be observed and recorded. **Fig. 5** shows the spectrum of a laser diode for $\lambda = 1300\,\text{nm}$ during continuous wave and pulsed operation. Direct comparison reveals that during pulsed operation the overall spectrum broadens and the linewidth of the individual modes increases. The spectrum broadens because the laser cannot respond to short light pulses in the nanosecond range, while the individual modes broaden because the refractive index of the laser material is a function of the drive current.

The wideband optical receiver of the test setup shown in **Fig. 4** is used to record the spectrum of the optical transmitter in the time domain. **Fig. 6** shows the result of this measurement on a 560 Mbit/s system operating at 850 nm. The spectrum varies during the pulse and is also dependent on the bit pattern. A binary one following several zeros is particularly critical. As a result of the spectral shift in the source emission, the pulses will arrive at the end of the fiber at different times due to delay dispersion, thus producing additional phase noise.

Measurements on single-mode fibers

Attenuation

Attenuation measurement on single-mode fibers presents no problems as regards the geometric excitation conditions. However, a factor which must be taken into account with these fibers is their polarization response. A technique employed in many instances is the *cut-back method.* In order to measure the attenuation over a wide spectral range a photometer as shown in **Fig. 7** is used. The comparatively low spectral radiance of the incoherent thermal light

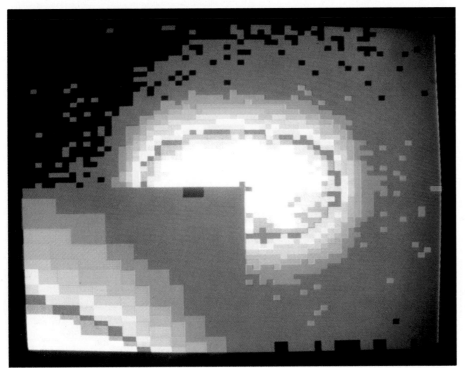

Fig. 3   Video scanning method
The computer-generated color graphics show the local far field recorded in the X-Θ-space on a short graded-index fiber under overfilled launch conditions. At bottom left is the computed radiation pattern in the A-Ω-space. The computer evaluation employs 256 brightness values. These are displayed on the screen using a twelve-point color scale

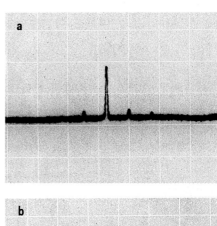

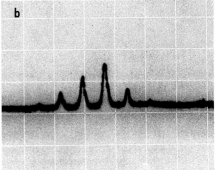

Fig. 5   Spectrum of a laser diode at 1300 nm for identical optical power but different drives

a   continuous operation
b   modulated at 20 Mbit/s

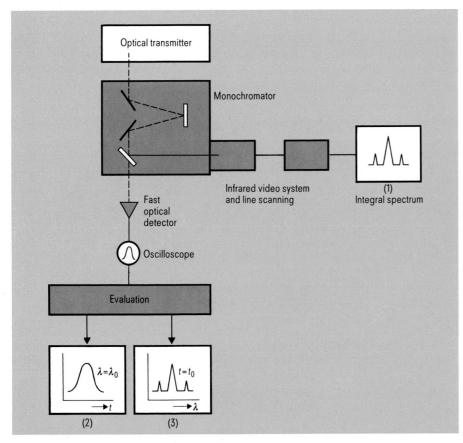

Fig. 4   Arrangement for measuring time-domain spectra.
The results obtained are the integral spectrum (1), the pulse shape at a certain wavelength λ_0 (2) or the spectrum at a certain instant t_0 of the pulse (3)

source necessitates greater sophistication particularly at the detector, since the spectral radiance of a halogen lamp is about 1 $\mu W/(\mu m^3\,sr)$ or about 1 nW per mode and nanometer at maximum.

Owing to the greater alignment sensitivity, it is not advisable to preshape the fundamental mode of the fiber in the launch microscope (**Fig. 7**). Instead the input end of the fiber should be overfilled so that the guided modes are excited in the fiber with maximum intensity, *independently of geometry*. Weakly guided modes and cladding modes are then stripped by means of index-matching cells.

A typical response curve is shown in **Fig. 8**. The fiber is single-mode for wavelengths above the wide attenuation band between 950 and 1100 nm due to cutoff of the LP_{11} mode. The other absorption maxima are due to residual OH in the silica material.

The achievable resolution is typically 0.1 dB/km in the range 1000 to 1500 nm, the attainable dynamic range about 20 dB. Apart from the attenuation maxima, it is possible to record usable spectra on fibers up to 10 km long.

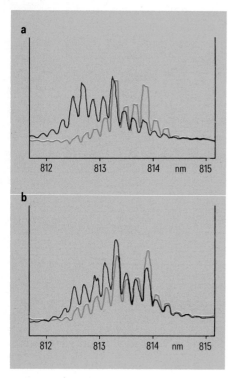

Fig. 6 Time-domain spectrum of a 560 Mbit/s transmitter at 850 nm. The spectrum of a one following zeros (a) is radically different from that of a one following a one (b). The spectrum is recorded for the start (red) and end (blue) of the pulse in each case

For attenuation measurement at a single wavelength only, the *backscatter method* is also frequently used [10]. At present the test sets operate only in the 850 nm region, as powerful pulsed lasers and highly sensitive photodiodes are available at this wavelength. With *multimode fibers* it is possible to use this method to measure splice losses and locate faults even on routes designed for 1300 nm, since these imperfections are wavelength-independent. This does not apply to *single-mode fibers* because if the fiber is operated at below the cutoff wavelength the next higher mode is also guided. In addition, the spot size is wavelength-dependent. Nevertheless, the properties of single-mode fibers can be measured with sufficient precision at 850 nm if the fiber is measured from both ends and the two measurements averaged.

However, as there are no sensitive avalanche photodiodes currently available at 1300 nm, the output power must be suitably increased in order to be able to measure long sections. In the laboratory a Q-switched Nd laser is

used for this purpose, producing pulse powers up to 100 kW at 1064 nm (and also at 1320 nm using special mirrors). Owing to the considerable amount of equipment involved (water cooling, power supplies) and the necessary laser safety precautions, a device of this kind is difficult to use outside a laboratory. However, it is particularly suitable for measuring test splices and connectors on single-mode fibers, as well as for investigating the polarization in these fibers [10].

In order to make the setup insensitive to polarization, it is preferable to deflect the backscattered light onto the photodetector acousto-optically rather than using a beamsplitter. This prevents the initial reflection from destroying the detector photodiode and allows a smaller dynamic range at the receiver. 35 km of a single-mode fiber link have already been measured using this method [11].

Bandwidth and impulse response

The bandwidth-length product of single-mode fibers is currently in the range 10 to 100 GHz · km. The upper limit can be attained if, at the given transmission wavelength, the material dispersion is exactly balanced by the profile-related waveguide dispersion. Direct measurement of such high bandwidths requires a sophisticated

measuring technique in the picosecond range.

An easier approach is to determine the wavelength of maximum bandwidth, since the group delay due to the fiber exhibits a minimum at this wavelength. This minimum can be found with the aid of a light source pulsed in the nanosecond range and spectrally tunable between 1000 and 1850 nm, e.g. an Nd laser with Raman converter (**Fig. 9**) [12].

On short fibers it is possible to use an impulse response measurement to determine whether the fiber guides one mode only. If the fiber contains two or more modes, the higher-order mode can be identified by bending the fiber, as this mode has greater radiation losses (**Fig. 10**). This measurement is useful for quality assurance because it eliminates the possibility of confusion between fibers with different transmission wavelengths.

Guidance properties for polarized light

Measurements on single-mode fibers must take account of the polarization of the guided light. In order to understand the polarization response, the mode guided in the fiber may be regarded as being split into two orthogonal components having slightly different propagation constants β_x and β_y

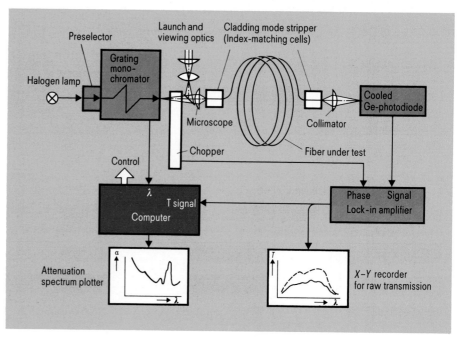

α Spectral attenuation $\qquad\qquad\qquad$ λ Optical wavelength

Fig. 7 Schematic of a microspectrometer for single-mode fibers

depending on azimuthal waveguide geometry. The polarization response of a fiber is characterized by the *beat length* $L_s = 2\pi/(\beta_x - \beta_y)$ caused by birefrigence, and the *coupling length* L_k, defining the energy exchange between the two polarization components such as occurs e.g. at waveguide discontinuities [4].

The beat length L_s can be measured on short fiber lengths by the spectrometer used for the attenuation measurement with the addition of a polarizer and analyzer. A periodic variation in fiber transmission is then observed. With period Δ and fiber length L the beat length L_s for the nominal wavelength λ is

$$L_s = L \cdot \Delta/\lambda.$$

For attenuation measurements over a wide spectral range it is hardly possible to avoid residual polarization of the test ray at the input end of the fiber. It is therefore particularly important for the optics employed at the detector end to have no analyzer effect (**Fig. 7**). If this cannot be avoided, the length L_f of the section of fiber remaining after cutting back must not be substantially shorter than the coherence length of the birefrigence, i.e. $L_f \gtrless L_s \cdot \lambda/\Delta\lambda$, where $\Delta\lambda$ is the spectral resolution of the monochromator. Using the typical values $L_s = 20$ cm, $\lambda = 1000$ nm, $\Delta\lambda = 2$ nm produces $L_f = 100$ m. The selected value of $\Delta\lambda$ should therefore not be smaller than necessary.

Characteristic parameters

The main parameter determining the coupling, bending, microbending and splice losses of single-mode fibers is the *spot size w*, defined as the $1/e$ radius of the radial distribution of the field amplitude of the fundamental mode in the Gaussian approximation. Actual fibers must be optimized with respect to spot size to suit the given application. For example, the bending losses increase at w^6, while the splice losses for a given offset decrease at $1/w^2$.

The parameter w, referred to the core radius a, is a function only of the *normalized frequency* $v = (2\pi a/\lambda) A_N$, which relates to the physical fiber parameters at a given wavelength λ and numerical aperture $A_N = \sqrt{n_1^2 - n_2^2}$. This is expressed as

$$w/a = G(v). \qquad (1)$$

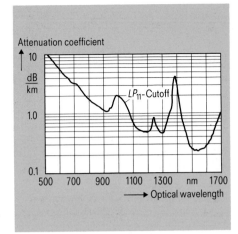

Fig. 8 Spectral loss of a single-mode fiber, measured on a 3 km length of fiber using the cut-back method

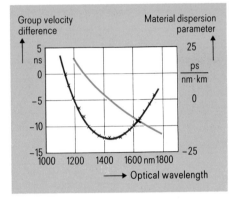

Fig. 9 Measured group velocity difference for a 3.2 km long single-mode fiber (red). The material dispersion parameter (blue) is calculated from a fitted curve

For the rectangular profile in the single-mode region this function approximates to:

$$G(v) \approx 2.7/v. \qquad (2)$$

Parameter v thus defines the spatial concentration of the field in the fiber core. In detail, the function $G(v)$ depends on the shape of the refractive index profile $n(r)$ [13].

However, the actual core radius, the precise numerical aperture and the complete refractive index profile in single-mode fibers are more difficult to determine than in multimode fibers, due to the small geometry and diffraction effects.

A helpful concept at this point is the *equivalent step index* (ESI) profile. The idealized ESI profile can be completely defined using only two parameters (a', A'_N), and is characterized by having exactly the same spot size w' as the actual fiber with its complex refractive

index profile $n(r)$, i.e. $w' = w$. It has been shown that an ESI profile can be found for arbitrary profiles and that it can be used in conjunction with known relationships to predict with sufficient accuracy the characteristics of actual fibers, e.g. as regards bending and microbending losses, for most commonly encountered fiber profiles (such as graded-index profiles) [13].

This gives rise to the need for a measurement to determine the ESI parameters a' and A'_N. This task is synonymous with determining the spot size w and the cutoff wavelength λ_c for the first higher-order mode; w and λ_c can be directly converted to the ESI parameters, since for the ideal *step-index profile* the function $G(v)$ in (1) is known and $v_c = 2.405$ is given exactly [13]. Consequently

$$\lambda_c = \frac{2\pi}{2.405} \cdot a' \cdot A'_N. \qquad (3)$$

The spot size w can be derived by definition from the $1/e^2$ *width* of the nearfield, but also by measuring the coupling efficiency. For this purpose a single-mode fiber is broken and the fracture faces are removed along the fiber axis. The spot size w can be simply calculated from the resultant light transfer, the optical wavelength and the separation between the fiber end faces [14]. If this measurement is performed at two different wavelengths with constant separation, it is possible to establish the ESI parameters completely.

In a variant of the method the light transfer is recorded as a function of the radial misalignment of the fiber ends [15]. The $1/e$ *width* of the response curve yields the spot size w almost exactly. The method could probably be simplified further if one of the fibers were replaced by a microscopically produced light spot.

Cutoff wavelength

Measurement techniques for the cutoff wavelength λ_c require a spectrally tunable light source. They utilize various effects which occur when λ_c is exceeded. These effects include a sudden reduction in spot size [16], disappearance of the dip in the nearfield pattern [17] or a steep drop in the excess bending or microbending losses [18].

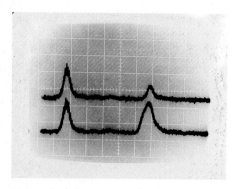

Fig. 10 Impulse response of a single-mode fiber operated below the cutoff wavelength and therefore propagating two modes (lower trace). In the upper trace part of the fiber is tightly bent causing the higher-order mode to decrease in amplitude as a result of the increased radiation losses

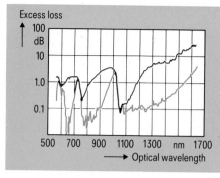

Fig. 11 Excess loss of a single-mode fiber looped once round a mandrel 20 mm (red) and 30 mm (blue) in diameter. The measurement gives the effective cutoff wavelengths of the lowest-order modes (here 1050 nm, 760 nm, ...) as well as an estimate of the bending losses of the fundamental mode

The last method is attractive because it can be performed using the previously described *fiber spectrometer* without modification. It involves forming a loop of 1 to 3 cm diameter in, for instance, the center of a short fiber section and determining the spectral response of the excess loss compared with the fiber laid out straight. The response shows (**Fig. 11**) several pronounced peaks, with steep long-wavelength edges marking the effective cutoff wavelengths of the lowest fiber modes in a way which is largely independent of the test conditions. Above about 1100 nm, as in the example of **Fig. 11**, only the fundamental mode LP_{01} propagates. Its bending loss increases towards longer wavelengths because the field spreads out further.

It has been shown that the effective cutoff wavelength obtained by this method is about 50 to 100 nm shorter than the "true" cutoff wavelength determined by the waveguide characteristics [19]. The reason for this is that in the vicinity of the waveguide cutoff the next higher order mode is so strongly attenuated, in fact, that it practically disappears within a few centimeters. As a result, it is no longer excited at the point of additional bending and so does not contribute to the bending loss. The *effective cutoff* is important for transmission engineering, while the *true cutoff* is important for coupling purposes.

References

[1] Gloge, D.; Marcatili, E.: Multimode theory of graded core fibers. Bell Syst. Techn. J. 52 (1973), pp. 1563 to 1578

[2] Olshansky, R.; Keck, D. B.: Pulse broadening in graded index optical fibers. Appl. Opt. 15 (1976), pp. 483 to 491

[3] CCITT Recommendation G. 651: Fibre test methods, Genf 1980

[4] Kaminow, I.: Polarization in optical fibers. IEEE J. of Quantum Electron. 17 (1981), pp. 15 to 22

[5] Olshansky, R.; Oaks, S. H.; Keck, D. B.: Measurement of different mode attenuation in GRIN optical waveguides. Digest of Topical Meeting on Optical Fiber Trans. II, OSA, Washington, D. C. (1977) Paper TuE 5

[6] Klement, E.; Rössner, K.: Principles of Optical Measurements for Communication Systems. telcom report 6 (1983) Special Issue "Optical Communications", pp. 167 to 171

[7] Geckeler, S.: Das Phasenraumdiagramm, ein vielseitiges Hilfsmittel zur Beschreibung der Lichtausbreitung in Lichtwellenleitern. Siemens Forsch.- u. Entwickl.-Ber. 10 (1981), pp. 163 to 171

[8] Stewart, W. J.: Method for measuring power distributions in graded and step index fibers. Topical Meeting on Optical Fiber Commun., Washington, D. C., (1979) Paper ThG 1

[9] Schicketanz, D.: Theorie der Rückstreumessung bei Glasfasern. Siemens Forsch.- u. Entwickl.-Ber. 9 (1980), pp. 242 to 248

[10] Kim, B. Y.; Choi, S. S.: Analysis and measurement of birefringence in single mode fibers using the backscatter method. Opt. Let. 6 (1981), pp. 578 to 580

[11] Nakazuwa, M. u. a.: Marked extension of diagnosis length in optical time domain reflectometry using 1.32 μm YAG lasers. Electron. Let. 17 (1981), pp. 783 and 784

[12] Cohen, L. G.; Lin, C.: Pulse delay measurements in the zero material dispersion wavelength region for optical fibers. Appl. Opt. 16 (1977), pp. 3163 to 3169

[13] Matsumura, H.1 Suganuma, T.: Normalization of single mode fibers having an arbitrary index profile. Appl. Opt. 19 (1980), pp. 3151 to 3158

[14] Masuda, S.; Iwama, T.; Daido, Y.: Nondestructive measurement of core radius, numerical aperture and cut off wavelength for SM fibers. Appl. Opt. 20 (1981), pp. 4035 to 4038

[15] Streckert, J.: New method for measuring the spot size of SM fibers. Opt. Let. 5 (1980), pp. 505 and 506

[16] Cannel, G. J. et al.: Measurement repeatability and comparison of real and ESI profiles. Cannes 1982, Paper A IV-5

[17] Murakami, Y.; Kawana, A.; Tsuchija, H.: Cutoff Wavelength Measurement for Single-Mode Optical Fibers. Appl. Opt. 18 (1979), pp. 1101 to 1105

[18] Katsuyama, Y. et al.: New method for measuring v-value of a SM optical fiber. Electron. Let. 12 (1976), pp. 669 and 670

[19] Gambling, W. A.; Payne, D. N.; Matsumura, H.; Norman, S. R.: Measurement of normalized frequency in SM optical fibers. Electron. Let. 13 (1977), pp. 133 and 134

Norbert Sutor

Testing the Mechanical and Thermal Characteristics of Optical Cables

Optical cables are nowadays employed for the most diverse applications, and extensive demands are made on the transmission and environmental characteristics of the cable. Whereas the transmission property is principally dependent upon the fiber, the environmental characteristics are largely influenced by the cable design. Differing characteristics are always emphasized in the multiplicity of cable designs, but the principal parameters can still be determined with the aid of mechanical and thermal test procedures. On the basis of such investigations it is then possible to predict, with a high probability of accuracy, how an optical cable will perform under the anticipated operating conditions.

Optical cables have a range of advantages over conventional cables. However, the disadvantages are the general sensitivity of the fibers to microbending, which causes additional attenuation, and the limited long-term tensile strength of the silica glasses employed. In the extreme case fiber strain can lead to breakage of the optical waveguide as a result of propagating microdefects.

The increase in attenuation due to microbending results from the fact that the critical angle for total internal reflection is exceeded and, as a consequence, light escapes from the fiber core. Microbending can arise either directly due to external mechanical stress applied to the cable, such as tensile stress, lateral force, pressure, bending and twisting, or indirectly due to temperature variation which, depending on the type of installation, can lead to contraction of the cable material with decrease in temperature and expansion in the case of increase in temperature.

Generally speaking, optical cables must be so constructed that they completely satisfy the prescribed operating conditions. Extensive tests are necessary in order to assure compliance with the specified characteristics for the various types of cable [1].

Test methods

The most important investigations carried out on optical cables are consequently temperature cycling and tensile stress tests. Depending upon the application, a series of other characteristics, such as behavior when subject to lateral pressure, flexing, impacts, vibration, the effects of lightning and chemicals, fire, etc. is also important. For all these qualification tests, as well as for the regular 100% inspection, it is primarily the attenuation or change in attenuation of the fibers that is measured (**Fig. 1**).

Temperature cycling

Optical cables can be subjected to widely differing temperatures during storage and operation. Whereas in the

Dipl.-Ing. Norbert Sutor,
Siemens AG,
Public Communication Networks Division,
Munich

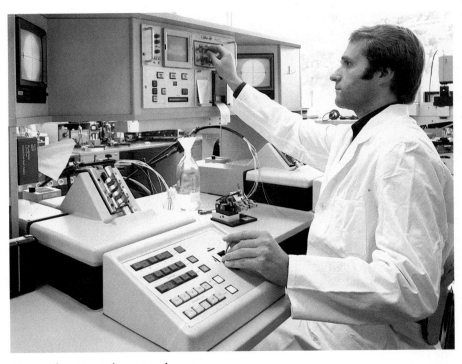

Fig. 1   Fiber attenuation test equipment

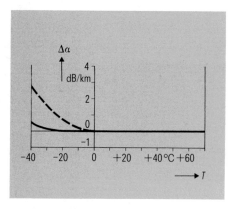

– – – Single-fiber cable without
antibuckling member for indoor use
——— Stranded minibundle cable
with a steel antibuckling
member for outdoor use

Fig. 2 **Change in attenuation $\Delta \alpha$ in optical cables as a function of the temperature T**

case of buried and underground cables only modest variations in the ambient temperature are to be anticipated, a wide temperature range must be reckoned with in the case of aerial cables.

Within the specified temperature range the transmission property is only permitted to change within a defined tolerance band.

Measurement of the change in attenuation as a function of the temperature is performed using a computer-controlled climatic test chamber. For this purpose the cable is mounted on a collapsible drum in the chamber and both ends are connected to a multiple attenuation test set for a maximum of eight fibers. A defined temperature profile, consisting of the limit temperatures, the times that they are effective, the rate of change of temperature as well as the number of cycles, is fed into the computer. At preset intervals the changes in the fiber attenuations are scanned and stored, and the intermediate results are displayed on the screen.

The evaluation of the results is effected by the computer; a connected plotter records the changes in attenuation as a function of the temperature, as well as the changes in attenuation and temperature as a function of time. In addition, the maximum values of attenuation measured on the group of fibers are printed out numerically at preset temperatures.

Fig. 2 shows the temperature response of two cables for differing applications.

One is a stranded mini-bundle cable with steel antibuckling member for outdoor use, while the other is a single-fiber cable without an antibuckling member for indoor use. The first cable shows an appreciably better characteristic in the negative temperature range, since, on the one hand, the antibuckling member opposes the contraction forces resulting from the contraction of the jacket and, on the other, due to the stranding the fiber has additional room for movement in the fiber buffer. Due to the tensile load members (predominantly made of Kevlar) no changes in attenuation are anticipated for either cable in the positive temperature range up to about 70 °C.

Tensile Stress

Considerable tensile forces can arise during cable installation and these must not impare the operability of the optical waveguides. After the cable has been installed, the residual tensile forces must not cause permanent fiber stress and thus an increase in attenuation. This applies in particular to aerial cables.

These tensile characteristics can be checked with a tensile test equipment (**Figs. 3** and **4**) specially developed for this purpose. It consists of a cable-holder resembling a block and tackle, with a maximum capacity of 132 m of cable, and the actual tensile testing

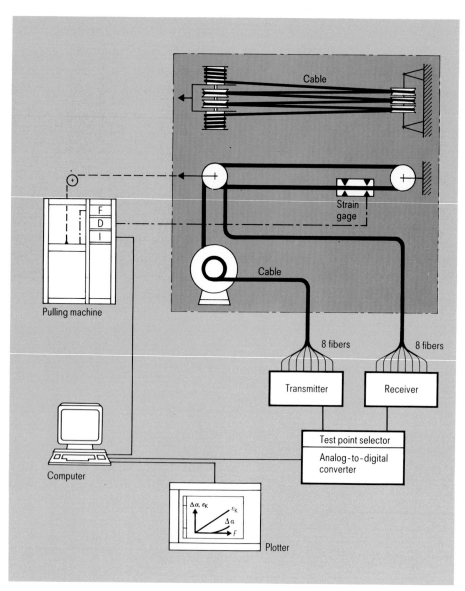

$\Delta \alpha$ Change in attenuation
ε_K Cable strain
F Tensile force

Fig. 3 **Tensile test equipment (principle)**

machine which produces the tensile force. The cable holder contains five movable and two fixed rollers which hold the cable in two to six strands. With the cable attached by several loops around the fixed rollers, the cable strain can be measured with the aid of a strain gage attached to the cable. In order to determine the attenuation, the ends of the cable are attached to a multiple attenuation test set (complete with computer and plotter) in such a way that the change in attenuation $\Delta\alpha$ of up to eight fibers, as well as the cable strain ε_K, can be recorded simultaneously as function of the tensile force F. All important test parameters, such as pulling speed, maximum tensile force, number of strands, as well as the individual fiber designations, are polled in succession by the computer. In addition to the tensile response curves, the maximum changes in attenuation, the residual attenuation changes at the end of the tensile test, as well as the maximum cable strain are recorded numerically (**Fig. 5**).

In order to determine the fiber strain ε_F as a function of the cable strain or the tensile force, the fiber in question is connected to a pulse delay test set and the pulse shift as a function of the tensile force is determined with an oscilloscope.

The fiber strain can be calculated from

$$\varepsilon_F = \frac{\Delta l}{l} = \frac{c}{n} \cdot \frac{1}{l} \cdot \Delta t - \frac{\Delta n}{n}.$$

$$\frac{\Delta n}{n} = k \cdot \frac{c}{n} \cdot \frac{1}{l} \cdot \Delta t,$$

ε_F Fiber strain,
Δl Fiber elongation,
l Fiber length in the testing machine,
Δt Delay difference between pulses,
n Mean refractive index of the core glass,
Δn Change in the mean refractive index due to tensile stress,
c Velocity of light in vacuum,
k Proportionality factor [2, 3].

Optical cables are differentiated by two principal design characteristics: one type contains tightly-buffered fibers and is mainly used for special applications (e.g. in the industrial field), whereas the other type contains loose buffers each containing one or more

Fig. 4   Tensile test equipment

fibers per buffer tube [4]. The latter type is designed to provide the fiber in the cable with the best possible transmission characteristics and can be used for all applications.

The two types are compared in **Fig. 6**. Due to the loose fiber buffer and the associated freedom of movement for the fiber in the buffer, the minibundle cable (**Fig. 6 a**) exhibits no fiber strain and increase in attenuation under tensile stress; in the case of the cable with tightly-buffered fibers (**Fig. 6 b**) both values rise almost linearly with the ten-

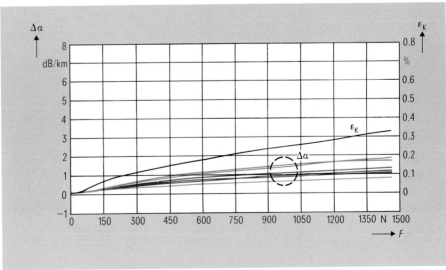

Gage length	$6 \times 22 = 132$ m
Pulling speed	100 mm/min
Wavelength	875 nm

Cable and fiber strain
ε_K ($F = 0.5\ F_{max}$): 0.202 %
ε_K ($F = 1.0\ F_{max}$): 0.331 %

Fiber	$\Delta\alpha_{max}$	$\Delta\alpha_{F=0}$
White	1.8	0.2 dB/km
Green	1.1	0.2 dB/km
Blue	1.1	0.2 dB/km
Yellow	1.7	0.3 dB/km
Orange	0.7	0.1 dB/km
Brown	1.2	0.3 dB/km

Fig. 5   Tensile test record

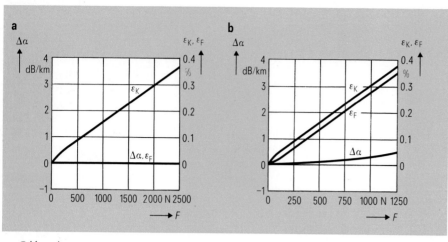

ε_K Cable strain

ε_F Fiber strain

Fig. 6 Change in attenuation $\Delta\alpha$ and cable/fiber strain ε_K ε_F as a function of the tensile force F
a Unit construction cable
b Cable with tightly-buffered fibers

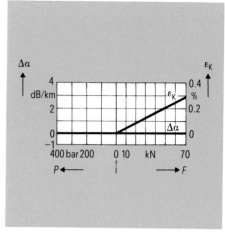

ε_K Cable strain

Fig. 7 Change in attenuation $\Delta\alpha$ of a submarine cable as a function of the tensile force F and the hydrostatic pressure P

sile force [5]. The magnitude of the increase in attenuation can be influenced by the type of fiber coating or fiber buffer. Soft materials lead to reduced sensitivity of the fiber to mechanical stress and, consequently, to smaller increases in attenuation.

High-pressure stress

Submarine cable can be subjected to high hydrostatic pressures. In order to investigate the pressure characteristics, the cable is placed in a special high-pressure chamber with the two ends fed out via sealing plugs to an attenuation test set or a time-domain reflectometer, and the changes in attenuation are recorded as a function of the pressure (**Fig. 7**).

Crush resistance

The cable is subjected to particular and usually localized stress when it is run over by vehicles or squeezed in any other way. In order to assess the crush resistance, the cable is pressed between two flat parallel plates and the change in attenuation is measured (test per IEC 46 E Method IEC XXE 3). Two stress limits are defined:

● a stress A up to which no change in attenuation occurs, and
● a stress B up to which the change in attenuation is fully reversible when the stress is removed.

The crush resistance characteristic can be strongly influenced by the cable design. For instance, the limit A is a factor of 2 higher in the case of filled loosely-buffered fibers than in the case of unfilled loosely-buffered fibers. The results are strongly influenced by the nature and thickness of the fiber coating, the buffering of the fiber, the type of stranding and the cable jacket design.

Flex resistance

High demands are placed on the flex resistance of cables for use in mobile applications, as well as for cables in moving equipment. These characteristics can be tested with a suitable test equipment in accordance with IEC 46 E Method IEC XXE 6, the cable being clamped between two jaws and repeatedly bent through an angle of $\pm 90°$ (**Fig. 8**). The test parameters

Fig. 8 Test setup for determining the flex resistance

bending radius and test weight are a function of the cable diameter. The number of flexure cycles to fiber fracture is recorded. Some test results are given in the **table**.

Impact strength

Cables can be subjected to impact stresses during installation or operation; for instance, falling tools, stones or other heavy items can cause dangerous deformation due to their shock energy. The resistance of the cable to such stresses can be determined with the aid of impact strength equipment in accordance with IEC 46 E Method IEC XXE 4. With this arrangement the hammer weight as well as the height of the drop and, consequently, the impact energy can be varied; the peen (radius and thus contact area) is fixed. The test criterion is the number of impacts necessary to cause fiber fracture. Some results obtained using this test method are likewise included in the **table**.

Operating range of optical cables

The thermal and tensile tests are the most important of all the previously mentioned qualification and screening tests, since they provide information on the principal cable characteristics. These are largely determined by the range of fiber free movement provided in the cable by the designer. A combined diagram (**Fig. 9**) shows the contraction range at temperatures below normal ambient temperature (RT) as

Cable characteristics			Indoor cable		Outdoor cable		
			I-V	I-W	A-WF	A-WS	A-DSF
Number of fibers			1	1	8	12	66
Cable diameter		mm	3.6	5.2	8.5	10.2	18.0
Maximum permissible tensile stress	continuous	N	30	100	250	250	500
	temporary	N	400	500	1000	1200	2500
Lateral force	$\Delta \alpha = 0$	N/cm	50	60	150	150	150
	$\Delta \alpha$ = reversible	N/cm	>1000	>1000	>1000	>1000	>1000
Impact strength	Impact energy	Nm	1.0	1.5	1.5	1.5	3.0
	Impacts to fiber fracture		>5	>10	>100	>100	>100
Smallest permissible bending radius		mm	30	30	175	200	250
Flex resistance	Radius / Weight	mm / N	100 / 5	100 / 5	200 / 20	200 / 20	200 / 20
	Cycles to fiber fracture		>10000	>10000	>10000	>10000	>10000
Temperature range		°C	−30 to +60	−30 to +70	−30 to +60	−30 to +70	−30 to +70

Table   Characteristics of a few selected cable designs

individual tests, particular attention being paid to the installation or pulling characteristic and the thermal characteristic of the optical cable. Valuable experience can also be gained with special cables, e.g. the installation and operation of a self-supporting, solid-dielectric aerial cable, or the installation and use of a submarine cable.

With all this experience it is possible nowadays to offer an extensive range of mature products; the characteristics of a few standard designs are listed in the table. It is true to say that, by suitable design, optical cables can be adapted to any special requirements and thus can be supplied for the most diverse applications.

well as the strain range under tensile stress, and thus provides information on the possible operation range of a cable. The fiber elongation, resulting from an increase in temperature in the normal range (up to about 70°C), is usually negligible. After establishing the permissible changes in attenuation at the two limits, the allowed tensile

and thermal stresses can be read directly from the diagram.

In order to be able to correctly interpret the results obtained in laboratory experiments, it is essential to carry out field trials [1] as well as to evaluate results from completed installations [6 to 8] and to correlate them with the

References

[1] Mayr, E.; Schöber, G.; Sutor, N.: Properties of Fiber-Optic Cables. telcom report 4 (1981), pp. 236 to 240

[2] Philen, D. L.; Patel, P. D.: Measurement of strain in optical fibre cables using a commercial distance meter. 8. ECOC, Cannes, Sept. 21 to 24, 1982, Conf. Proceed., pp. 256 to 259

[3] Nagano, K.; Kawakami, S.; Nishida, S.: Change of the refractive index in an optical fibre due to external forces. Appl. Opt., Vol. 17, No. 13, July 1, 1978

[4] Oestreich, U.: Design of Fiber-Optic Cables. telcom report 4 (1981), pp. 231 to 236

[5] Bark, P. R.; Oestreich, U,; Zeidler, G.: Stress-strain behaviour of optical fiber cables. 28th Wire + Cable Symposium, Cherry Hill, Nov. 1979, pp. 385 to 390

[6] Graßl, F.; Krägenow, H.: Die Lichtwellen-leiter-Kabelstrecke Berlin, ein Projekt von grundsätzlicher Bedeutung. telcom report 1 (1978), pp. 40 to 45

[7] Kahl, P.; Köstler, G.; Laufer, A.; Wartmann, H.: First Optical Cable Link of the Deutsche Bundespost. telcom report 2 (1979), pp. 169 to 173

[8] Goldmann, H.; Köstler, G.; Krägenow, H.; Reibnitz, H. P.; Schöber, G.; Steinmann, P.: Die erste LWL-Ortskabelanlage für die Deutsche Bundespost. Nachr.-tech. Z. 33 (1980), pp. 608 to 610

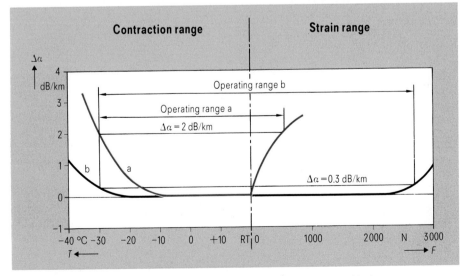

Fig. 9   Operating ranges of optical cables: indoor cable (a) and outdoor cable (b)

Gerhard Völkel and Erich Wallner

Quality Assurance Methods for Optoelectronic Semiconductors

In fiber-optic transmission links the optoelectronic interfaces are of critical importance and place correspondingly stringent demands on the mechanical, electrical and optical quality of the emitter and detector devices. Apart from quality in terms of the as-supplied condition, the user also requires reliability, i.e. quality over a period of time, to withstand electrical stresses or environmental influences in the particular application.

Backed by years of experience fabricating a wide range of optoelectronic semiconductors and equipped with the most modern technical and scientific facilities, Siemens can meet the stringent demands placed on fiber-optic components, young as this technology still is. The departments involved in fundamental research, product development, production and quality assurance contribute by working hand in hand to supply products conforming to the high technical quality standards of the communications industry.

Modern technology aids inspection

Comprehensive checking of materials, parts and the resultant components through the various production stages involves the use of a large amount of equipment, ranging from conventional inspection aids, such as sliding calipers and gages, through optical or infrared microscopes and high-grade electronic instruments to computer-controlled test setups, automatic testers, electron and measuring microscopes (**Fig. 1**).

To ensure that the results are at all times reproducible, all test equipment is regularly checked for correct functioning and calibration. Since the determination of optical and radiative quantities is particularly demanding on the instrumentation, special care is taken in calibrating all instruments.

Idea – design – qualification

The path from an idea to the mature product is generally a long one. The concepts and processes developed at the research laboratories are reviewed and refined again and again in the step-by-step approach to achieving defined objectives. Even at this early stage the embryonic product is subjected to extensive high-stress testing in order to

Dipl.-Phys. Dr. rer. nat. Gerhard Völkel,
Siemens AG,
Components Group, Regensburg;
Dipl.-Ing. Erich Wallner,
Siemens AG,
Components Group, Munich

Fig. 1   Computer-based measuring microscope in receiving inspection

predict the technological limits. If weaknesses appear, attempts are made to improve the design.

It is only when all tests have been satisfactorily completed that the product data are handed over to the relevant development department. Here, the component is tailored, i.e. undergoes further development to meet production and user requirements. It is designed to incorporate all the technical and quality related characteristics defined in a type and quality specification drawn up before the development work was started. This specification is oriented primarily to the market and competition but also to special customer requirements. National and international standards and regulations must also be taken into account.

It is at this stage of development that the subsequent operating conditions (electrical, mechanical and environmental stresses, specified useful life, etc.) are taken fully into account. A laser chip from the research laboratory, for instance, may fulfill the function of a laser in every respect but is of no use in a fiber-optic system without a package and optical coupling to the transmission link.

In the initial phase the development department performs its own investigative tests to determine the current state of development and the direction which future development should take. Even at this stage the quality assurance department is involved in an advisory capacity, reporting directly to the general management and thus remaining independent of the development and manufacturing departments.

Some of the new ideas must, however, be rejected early on because they are incapable of meeting the high requirements. It is only when the development engineer himself is satisfied with the quality of his product that it is passed to the quality assurance department for qualification testing. If the product passes this test it is authorized for pilot production.

Qualification testing involves extensive investigations accompanied by numerous measurements (**table**). In addition to electrical, climatic and mechanical tests they include, for instance, tests for package sealing, solderability and sol-

Test	Conditions	Standard
Cold (low-temp. storage)	96 h at Ts_{min}	IEC 68-2-1 Test Aa or Test Ad*
Dry heat (high-temp. storage)	96 h at Ts_{max}	IEC 68-2-2 Test Ba or Test Bc*
Damp heat, steady state	21 days at $T_a = 40\,°C$ and 93% rel. humidity or $T_a = 85\,°C$ and 85% rel. humidity	IEC 68-2-3 Test Ca if appropriate* analogous to IEC 68-2-3
Temperature change	10 cycles $Ts_{min} \leftrightarrow Ts_{max}$ dwell time: 30 min Transfer <30s or dwell time: 30 min Rate of temp. change: $5\,°C \cdot min^{-1}$	IEC 68-2-14 Test Na (two chamber method) Test Nb (one chamber method)
Temperature shock	10 cycles $-10\,°C/+90\,°C$ Severity 2	Test Nc (bath method)
Solderability	Solder bath 235 °C	IEC 68-2-20 Test Ta (possibly after aging)
Resistance to soldering heat	Solder bath 260 °C Immersion time: 10 s	IEC 68-2-20 Test Tb
Robustness of terminations	Per standard	IEC 68-2-21 Test Ua1 (tensile) Test Ub (bending)
Sealing (where applicable)	Per standard	IEC 68-2-17 Test Qc (gross leak, gas leakage) Test Qk (fine leak, tracer gas detected with mass spectrometer)
Shock (depending on application)	Per standard	IEC 68-2-27 Test Ea or IEC 68-2-29 Test Eb (repetitive shocks)
Vibration (depending on application	Per standard	IEC 68-2-6 Test Fc (sinusoidal) or IEC 68-2-34 Test Fd (random vibration)
Acceleration, steady state (depending on application)	Per standard	IEC 68-2-7 Test Ga
Corrosive atmospheres	Per standard	Depending on application: IEC 68-2-11 Test Ka (salt mist) and/or IEC 68-2-42 Test Kc (SO_2) and/or IEC 68-2-43 Test Kd (H_2S)

* Components under electrical stress

Table   Environmental tests on optoelectronic components

Fig. 2 Facilities for long-term testing

Fig.3 Computer-assisted test data acquisition and evaluation

dering heat resistance in accordance with the relevant standards (IEC, DIN and MIL).

Accelerated tests (overstress, e.g. electrical and thermal overloading) are used to assess early on the long-term behavior of important characteristics or parameters. The relevant literature quotes experimentally backed conversion methods for this purpose. The investigations are concluded by user-oriented long-term trials (**Fig. 2**), the results after 1000 to 2000 hours being required for the decision on type and fabrication authorization. Nevertheless, tests are extended where possible beyond 10,000 hours to provide a reliable prediction of the long-term behavior and to confirm the extrapolations.

Tests over long periods of time and/or with a large quantity of test items enable statistical predictions to be made about the reliability and aging of all optoelectronic components. Aging, for instance, as applied to optical transmitters refers to the gradual reduction in the radiant power emitted by the semiconductor.

The voluminous data obtained from many intermediate measurements are acquired, evaluated and concentrated in powerful EDP systems (**Fig. 3**). This is the only way in which reliable information about the quality of a component can be obtained in a short period of time.

If the results of qualification testing are not satisfactory, the product presented is not authorized and is returned to the development department for redesign. The repetitive testing required in this instance is error-specific and aimed at such characteristics and parameters which may have been affected by new materials or processes.

Qualification testing is applied to a suitable number of samples from the development laboratory to prove that they achieve the objectives in the type and quality specification. These tests are repeated on the initial quantities from pilot production employing all the processes later to be used in volume manufacture. The inclusion of application-related tests provides evidence that the new type will meet all practical requirements. If all the results prove

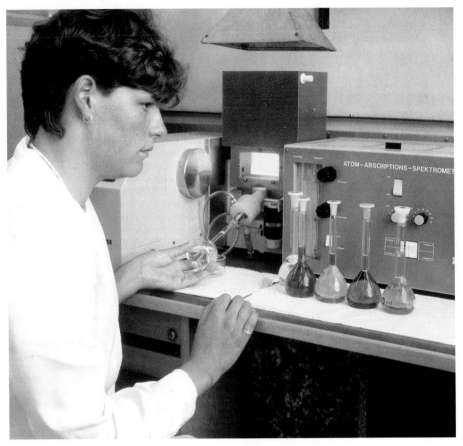

Fig. 4   Material analysis using an atom absorption spectrometer

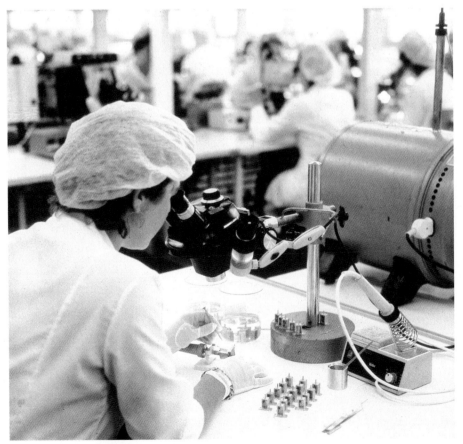

Fig. 5   In-process inspection during laser module fabrication

satisfactory, production is released, and volume manufacture can then begin.

If the technology or an individual process is changed, the entire release test procedure must be repeated. Partial repetition of the relevant tests is acceptable only for modifications whose impact can be reliably predicted and confined.

Controlled manufacture

Suitable controls are applied as soon as the necessary materials and parts are procured for production. Stringent selection and continuous inspection using the most modern test facilities are standard practice (**Fig. 4**).

The incoming inspection department checks each supplied batch to inspection plans based on international standards, the resultant data being concentrated with computer assistance to permit objective appraisal and selection of potential vendors. The extent and stringency of the inspection are flexibly determined by the results of preceding inspections, thus limiting the not inconsiderable inspection cost while ensuring that the uncompromisingly high quality of supplies is maintained at all times. The procurement of raw materials and prefabricated items from internal departments or other Siemens groups is also controlled by this procedure.

On this basis, production can start to fabricate components with the characteristics stated in the specifications. The manufacturing specifications, which should ensure that as uniform a quality as possible is maintained throughout production, have by then been finalized.

The materials and parts passed by incoming inspection are processed step by step and assembled into the final product, with each production step assigned an in-process inspection (**Fig. 5**). Preliminary batch inspections, also carried out in the production department, are employed to prevent possibly expensive operations being undertaken unnecessarily. The flowchart in **Fig. 6** shows the main process steps and inspection stations.

The quality assurance department audits these controls and actively

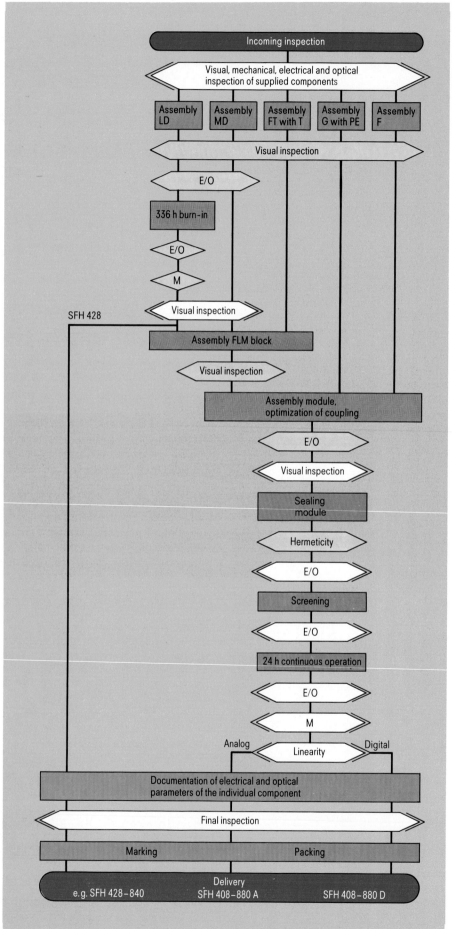

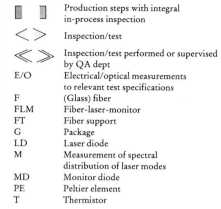

Fig. 6 Simplified flowchart of laser module fabrication

		Production steps with integral in-process inspection
$<$ $>$		Inspection/test
$\ll$ $\gg$		Inspection/test performed or supervised by QA dept
E/O		Electrical/optical measurements to relevant test specifications
F		(Glass) fiber
FLM		Fiber-laser-monitor
FT		Fiber support
G		Package
LD		Laser diode
M		Measurement of spectral distribution of laser modes
MD		Monitor diode
PE		Peltier element
T		Thermistor

involves itself in critical manufacturing stages. On completion, all components are submitted to the test department for final testing, involving "100% inspection" of all essential parameters to nationally or internationally standardized procedures and specifications. Non-standard inspection requirements can be agreed with customers individually for special applications. Additional batch sampling inspections are carried out in the quality assurance department to prevent errors of organization, instrumentation or method resulting in defective or incorrect components being delivered.

Particularly critical characteristics are subjected to extremely stringent screening in the production sequence. Laser diodes, for instance, are subjected to electrical and optical tests as well as a two-week burn-in at high ambient temperature (**Fig. 7**), as soon as they have been mounted on the chip carrier. Only those lasers showing no changes are passed for final assembly. This screening process prevents time and money being spent on packaging components which prove to be defective in the short or medium term. This approach raises the production yield, while eliminating early failures.

Before the module package is sealed the quality of the laser module is again subjected to a 100% visual inspection. Defect-free packages are sealed and passed to final testing. They are then subjected to a 24 h continuous operation test to the limits of the data sheet or the customer specifications.

Fig. 7   Laser diodes being burned in

Burrus diodes, for example, are subjected to such screening. After a 168 h burn-in they are examined for dark spots or dark lines. The spot of each individual Burrus diode is magnified on a display with the aid of a vidicon. Only Burrus diodes with no significant aging, dark spots or lines are passed for final testing.

Feedback of application experience

The real touchstone for the effectiveness and suitability of the quality assurance methods applied is customer use. No matter how careful and far-sighted the planning, it is not possible in commercial manufacture to prevent occasional defects in use attributable to technical weaknesses or gaps in the quality assurance system.

For this reason, the responsibility of the quality assurance department does not end at delivery of the components, but extends to providing the interface for the application experience fed back from the user. It is here, too, that customer complaints are checked and analyzed in detail. This feedback often includes useful suggestions for further improvement.

Any failure attributable to the manufacturer is followed by a review of the technological concepts, the manufacturing methods and the quality assurance activities. If the fault is attributable to the application, the customer receives detailed advice regarding the problem.

The complexity of many components and of the factors relating to their application generally make it impossible to take account of every quality aspect. The optical components for fiber-optic systems are therefore no exception in requiring a helpful interchange of information between manufacturer and customer to achieve demanding objectives.

Consistent application of the quality assurance concepts described in this paper can help to limit the risks involved in introducing innovative technology, such as that associated with optical communications.

High-way   Time stage   Space stage

Franz Auracher and Rudolf Keil

Integrated Optics for Single-Mode Transmission Systems

Due to the increasing demand for high-capacity transmission links, the importance of single-mode systems continues to grow. These systems – as well as the multimode systems already in service – are currently realized in hybrid form using discrete components. However, a gradual integration of optical and electronic components (analogous to that which has already occurred in electronics) is to be expected in future optical communication systems. The level of integration achievable in optical integration, however, will be orders of magnitude lower than that already attained in electronics. The anticipated advantages are compact, robust and reliable components, fewer interconnections and, not least, economic production. In optoelectronic integration, for instance, an attempt is being made to integrate lasers with the driver stage, signal-power monitor and control electronics at the transmit end, as well as repeaters or detectors with a preamplifier at the receive end [1]. In the case of integrated optics, optical components (directional couplers, filters, switches and modulators) are being developed in planar technology and attempts are being made to integrate them on a common substrate [2, 3].

The border line between optoelectronic and optical integration is formed by the source diode at the transmit end and the detector diode at the receive end. The advantage of the separation of optoelectronic and optical integration is that in each case the most favorable material system – e.g. GaAlAs or InGaAsP for the optoelectronic integration and LiNbO₃ or glass for the optical integration – can be chosen. Even with this design philosophy one still has to accept a hybrid structure. In order to reduce the number of interconnections between components, an attempt is being made to realize optoelectronic and optical integration on a common substrate (monolithic integration). This is possible both in the material systems GaAlAs and InGaAsP, even though less favorable performance parameters than in the case of LiNbO₃ have to be accepted for the optical components. Numerous attempts at monolithic integration have already been made [4, 5], even though this path is still associated with considerable difficulties.

Optical waveguides

The basis of all integrated optical components is the optical waveguide produced on or in a flat substrate by planar technology. **Fig. 1** shows the light propagation in the simplest waveguide (homogeneous planar waveguide). The waveguide is usually of the single-mode type and consists of a thin film (0.1 µm to a few microns thick) with a refractive index typically 0.1 to 1%

Dipl.-Ing. Dr. Franz Auracher and
Dipl.-Ing. Dr.-Ing. Rudolf Keil,
Siemens AG,
Research and Development Division,
Munich

◁ Integrated optics will provide a further innovative stimulus to future optical waveguide technology. Optical amplifiers and broadband couplers will then permit direct regeneration and through-connection of the signals

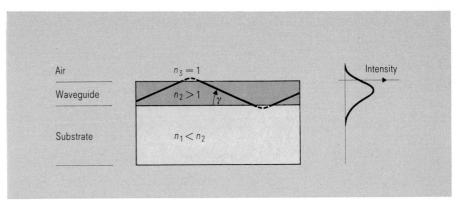

n Refractive index

Fig. 1   Structure, ray trajectory and intensity distribution in a planar optical waveguide

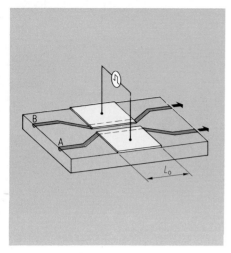

A, B   Strip waveguide
L_o Coupling length

Fig. 2   Controllable (electrooptic) directional coupler as waveguide switch

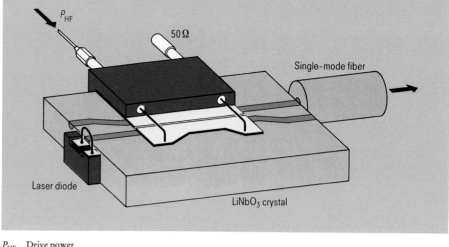

P_{HF} Drive power

Fig. 3   Laser source with external directional coupler modulator

higher than that of the substrate. The film with the higher refractive index forms the core region, the surroundings (substrate, air or coating) the cladding region of the waveguide. In terms of ray optics the light in the waveguide core propagates in a way similar to that in optical fibers, i.e. in a zigzag path due to total internal reflection at the boundaries between the core and the cladding region, provided the angle of incidence of the rays to the substrate does not exceed the critical angle for total reflection γ_G. Most of the integrated optic components are intended to be coupled to single-mode fibers; instead of planar waveguides, therefore, strip waveguides (similar to printed circuit conductor tracks) are produced, in which the light is also guided laterally.

The width of the strip (a few microns) and the increase in the refractive index of the waveguide region (0.1 to 1%) compared with the substrate are so chosen that only the fundamental mode can propagate and the intensity distribution of the guided light is well matched to that of the single-mode fiber, in order to permit efficient coupling to single-mode fibers. When viewed more critically from a wave optics standpoint, it can be seen that the light also penetrates slightly into the cladding region of the waveguide (evanescent wave), as a result of which interaction of the guided light with adjacent waveguides becomes possible.

Integrated optical devices

A particular interest attaches to components in which the light can be modulated, deflected or switched between two waveguides. In these devices, for instance, use is made of the fact that the refractive index of electrooptical crystals can be slightly varied by the application of electric fields.

As an example a controllable directional coupler is shown in **Fig. 2**. Two identical strip waveguides A and B are arranged so close to each other (typical spacing 3 μm) over a certain length that the electromagnetic fields of the evanescent waves overlap and, as a result, the desired interaction between the two light waves occurs. If light is coupled into waveguide A, a periodic energy interchange between the two waveguides takes place so that, for instance, after the length L_o the light has been completely transfered to waveguide B. This interchange is only complete when the velocities of propagation of the light in both waveguides are identical.

With differing refractive indices and, consequently, differing velocities of propagation for the light in the two waveguides, there is only a partial interchange which, in addition, occurs over a shorter length. The refractive index difference is produced by electric fields in opposing directions excited in the two waveguides via electrodes. At a

certain voltage at the electrodes the small fraction of light coupled from A to B is coupled back into waveguide A after a length L_o. Thus with voltage applied the light emerges from A and without applied voltage from B, and consequently an optical switch has been realized. Such switches have already been operated at over 3 Gbit/s with a switching voltage of only 4 V [6], and have also been integrated to form a 4 × 4 matrix with which light from four inputs can be switched in any combination to four outputs [7]. By suitable design of the coupled waveguides it can be arranged that the light transfer is strongly dependent upon the wavelength, so that a wavelength-dependent filter with electrically tuneable pass band results.

Such or similar filters in integrated form could be used for the multiple utilization of optical fiber transmission lines by wavelength-division multiplexing. The use of gratings is a further possible way of producing wavelength-dependent components. If, for instance, two gratings are etched in an optical waveguide at a certain distance from each other, an optical resonator is produced. Very narrow-linewidth semiconductor lasers have already been realized using such resonator structures. Since the resonator can be produced using planar technology, it can be integrated with other optical components on a common substrate. The integration of six lasers of this type

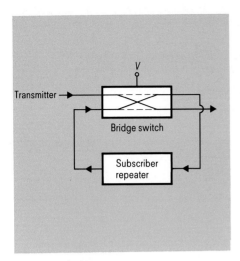

V Control voltage

Fig.4 Controllable directional coupler as bridge switch

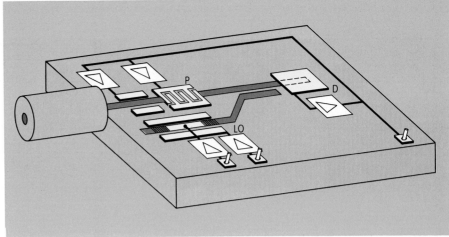

D Detector
LO Local oscillator
P Polarization converter

Fig.5 Integrated optical heterodyne receiver

with differing emission wavelengths has already been demonstrated in principle [8].

Use of integrated optical components

If required, electrooptic intensity modulators for very high bit rates could come into use in the next few years, in order to avoid the problems arising in connection with the direct modulation of laser diodes at high bit rates. **Fig.3** shows a possible design for a laser transmitter with external modulator based on the directional coupler principle. The laser diode is operated CW, which results in a very clean spectral characteristic; intensity modulation is performed by the following electrooptic modulator. The design shown in **Fig.3** is still hybrid; monolithic integration with the source diode could be carried out at a later date. It should also be possible in the near future to produce components (quasi-isolators) in planar technology for reducing the effect of reflected signals on the laser diode. These could then be integrated with the external modulator or, even better, with the laser diode at a later date.

Bridge switches, e.g. in the form of the previously mentioned directional coupler switch, are also suitable for early implementation. **Fig.4** shows the use of a bridge switch in a transmission link: the signal is normally transmitted via the repeater; if the repeater fails, the bridge switch connects the signal straight through.

In the more distant future considerably more complex components are conceivable, such as, for instance, the optical heterodyne receiver with a tuneable local oscillator shown schematically in **Fig.5**. On the input side can be seen an automatic control circuit for reestablishing the desired light polarization, the heterodyne section with the tunable laser as local oscillator, the detection of the heterodyned signal, as well as subsequent signal level regeneration and pulse shaping devices. Whereas the realization of such complex circuits lies in the future, the functions of all necessary optical and electronic components have already been demonstrated in planar technology. However, the difficulties associated with the integration of these functions are still considerable.

Problems and limits of integrated optics

One of the greatest problems associated with single-mode technology, and thus also with integrated optics, lies in coupling, e.g. between laser diode, strip waveguide and glass fiber. Since the cross sectional dimensions of the strip waveguide and the single-mode fiber only amount to a few microns, the demands placed on the alignment accuracy are very high. In addition to that, the core cross sections of the optical waveguides to be connected must be matched to each other, in order to ensure high coupling efficiency.

If one wishes to integrate several components on a common substrate, additional problems arise. In contrast to electronics, no sharp kinks, (e.g. angular changes in the waveguide of more than 1°) or tight curves (e.g. with radii below 20 mm [9]) must occur in the waveguide layout, which is why the components are arranged geometrically one behind the other for integration. In addition, the effects employed (e.g. electro-optic effect) are relatively weak, so that interaction lengths of, typically, 0.5 to 10 mm arise. As a consequence, relatively large lengths result (a few centimeters) even at a low level of integration, while the transverse dimensions can be very small due to the small waveguide cross sections (e.g. 10 to 100 μm including electrodes). This extreme length-to-width ratio of the components is very unfavorable for production.

Further technological difficulties arise in connection with monolithic integration, since differing functions require differing band gaps in the semiconductor material (e.g. small band gap for laser diodes and detectors, large band gap for waveguides). This means that structures of differing alloys (e.g. $Ga_xAl_{1-x}As$ or $In_xGa_{1-x}As_yP_{1-y}$) will have to be grown on a common substrate (e.g. GaAs or InP) in several masking steps. This masked growth still presents great difficulties, but here too the first signs of solutions are discernible in the research laboratories [10], so that in the distant future a multiplicity of integrated optic circuits can be expected. However, for the reasons given, the level of integration of these circuits will be orders of magnitude lower than in the case of electronics.

References

[1] Melchior, H.: Semiconductor materials: perspectives of optoelectronic integration in integrated optics.
J. of non-cryst. Sol. 47 (1982), pp. 179 to 190

[2] Alferness, R.C.: Guided-wave devices for optical communication.
IEEE J. of Quantum Electron. QE 17 (1981), pp. 946 to 959

[3] Auracher, F.: Optische Nachrichtentechnik – heute und morgen.
Naturwiss. 67 (1980), pp. 347 to 351

[4] Carter, A.C.; Forbes, N.; Goodfellow, R.C.: Monolithic integration of optoelectronic, electronic and passive components in GaAlAs/GaAs multilayers.
Electron. Let. 18 (1982), pp. 72 to 74

[5] Wright, Ph.D.; Nelson, R.J.; Wilson, R.B.: Monolithic integration of InGaAsP heterostructure lasers and electrooptical devices.
IEEE J. of Quantum Electron. QE 18 (1982), pp. 249 to 258

[6] Kubota, K.; Noda, J.; Mikami, O.: Traveling wave optical modulator using a directional coupler $LiNbO_3$, waveguide.
IEEE J. of Quant. Electron. QE 16 (1980), pp. 754 to 760

[7] Schmidt, R.V.; Buhl, L.L.: Experimental 4 × 4 optical switching network.
Electron. Let. 12 (1976), pp. 575 to 577

[8] Aiki, K.; Nakamura, M.; Umeda, J.: Frequency multiplexing light source with monolithically integrated distributed-feedback diode lasers.
Appl. Phys. Let. 29 (1976), pp. 506 to 508

[9] White, I.A.; Hutcheson, L.D.; Burke, J.J.: Modal fields and curvature losses in Ti-diffused $LiNbO_3$, waveguides.
Proc. of the Soc. photo-optical Instrum. Eng. (SPIE) 239 (1980), pp. 74 to 79

[10] Shelton, J.C.; Reinhart, F.K.; Logan, R.A.: Rib waveguide switches with MOS electrooptic control for monolithic integrated optics in $GaAs-Al_xGa_{1-x}As$.
Appl. Opt. (1978), pp. 2548 to 2555

Ulrich Oestreich and Günter Zeidler

Development Trends in Fiber and Cable

Although only ten years have passed since low-loss optical waveguides were first fabricated, their place in communication engineering is already assured. Graded-index fibers are being employed primarily in the trunk and long-haul network and on a trial basis in the local network at wavelengths of 850 to 1300 nm. The first applications of single-mode fibers operating at 1300 nm are already on the way. Continuing development of fiber-optic cable systems is expected to produce advances in fiber technology and innovations in cable applications. This paper is an attempt to outline these areas of activity.

An initial review reveals activity concentrating in the following areas:

● extension of the wavelength range of the doped silica glass fiber (the single-mode fiber in particular) from 1300 to 1600 nm,

● investigation of new material systems (non-oxide glasses, possibly even polymers) suitable for optical waveguides,

● development of fiber-optic submarine cables for long repeater spacings,

● development of high-strength cable structures for extreme operating conditions.

Dipl.-Ing. Ulrich Oestreich and
Dipl.-Ing. Dr. phil. Günter Zeidler,
Siemens AG,
Public Communication Networks
Division, Munich

Characteristics of optical waveguides in the 1600 nm wavelength range

The transmission window for dielectric waveguides is delineated

● at its short-wavelength end, by light absorption due to electron transitions in the atomic structure (in the UV wavelength region in silica glass) and

● at its long-wavelength end. by light absorption due to molecular vibrations (e.g. the vibrations of the SiO_4 tetrahedron in the wavelength range 3000 to 22,000 nm result in attenuation increasing from 10^4 to 10^{10} dB/km).

These absorption bands have attenuation tails falling off exponentially into the transmission window, forcing the operating wavelength to be located some distance away from the attenuation skirts (e.g. the infrared absorption of the silica glass produces attenuation of about 10 dB/km at 2000 nm but at 1600 nm it is less than 0.1 dB/km).

In the window region the attenuation due to light scattering falls away towards longer wavelengths (decreasing as the fourth power of the wavelength in accordance with Rayleigh). The attenuation minimum is thus located at the long-wavelength end of the window.

In silica glass this physically based attenuation has a minimum at a wavelength of about 1600 nm. Single-mode fibers have already been fabricated with an attenuation at 1600 nm of slightly less than 0.2 dB/km [1], making repeater spacings possible which are 30 to 50% longer than those at 1300 nm. This advantage can be utilized directly on systems at transmission rates under 50 Mbit/s. At higher transmission rates additional account must be taken of material dispersion whose minimum in silica is known to be in the 1300 nm wavelength range. In this minimum dispersion region, a single-mode fiber is expected to yield a bandwidth-length product of about 100 GHz · km (referred to 1 nm of source linewidth), whereas at 1600 nm it is only likely to be about 20 GHz · km. There are two ways of resolving this difficulty. The first is to use laser diodes with a restricted spectral bandwidth. The second is to develop a single-mode fiber whose refractive index distribution is designed such that the material dispersion is compensated by waveguide dispersion.

Which of the two approaches, i.e.

● laser with broad spectrum and fiber with compensated dispersion, or

● laser with limited spectrum and fiber with material dispersion,

is finally adopted or whether a combination of the two will be favored is still open to discussion. Both approaches are technically feasible and have been realized experimentally in the laboratory [2 to 4].

The low fiber attenuation at 1600 nm can, of course, be fully exploited only if all the added losses in the actual cable installation are reduced and splice losses in particular, are kept on average below 0.1 dB. Even the cable construction requires care to avoid any increase in attenuation however slight. This can be achieved by consistently isolating the fiber from the cable structure, having regard to the permissible bending radius for the single-mode fiber ($R > 80$ mm). The often described filled, loose tube design providing sym-metrical clearance for longitudinal fiber movement in the stranded structure will therefore assume even greater importance in this application than in all others.

Optical fiber materials for the wavelength range above 1800 nm

Whenever optical waveguides are required with attenuation below the best values achieved by doped silica glass fibers, it is necessary to move to longer wavelengths due to light scattering [5, 6]. This calls for materials in which absorption due to molecular vibrations occurs only at long wavelengths, a requirement which can be met by reducing the binding force and (or) increasing the vibrating masses. The periodic table of the elements allows some general conclusions to be drawn leading to longer wavelength ranges of operation:

● Replacement of silicon by heavier atoms (Ge, Sn, Pb also As, Sb and possibly heavy alkali and alkaline-earth atoms Ca, Sr, Ba).

● Replacement of oxygen by the elements below it in the periodic table, the chalkogens S, Se and Te.

● Changing to the halogenides, but although the infrared bands in the F, Cl, Br, J group move further into the long-wavelength range with increasing atomic weight, the resistance to moisture diminishes in each case.

It is generally true that a reduction in the binding forces is accompanied by an increase in chemical reactivity. As a result the glass becomes more sensitive to aging processes. A compromise will therefore have to be found between transmission and stability.

There is wide scope here for fundamental research, with many additional factors affecting materials selection (glass forming capability, availability of the pure input materials, etc.). A further requirement is the ability to produce a clean core-cladding structure free of scattering centers.

The attendant technological problems are not likely to be solved immediately. It is nevertheless possible that optical waveguides will be available in the next decade providing losses well below 0.1 dB/km in the wavelength range 2000 to 5000 nm.

Plastic optical waveguides

Optical waveguides of polymer materials have had quite a high loss hitherto, caused by their high degree of scattering compared with silica glass and by the numerous molecular vibration bands (particularly C-H). There are further problems associated with synthesizing the plastic from high purity starting materials and in controlling the melting and fiber drawing processes to achieve the necessary cleanliness. Although laboratory experiments have already been successfully performed achieving losses of around 20 dB/km at about 660 nm with high purity acrylic glasses, it is still impossible to tell at this stage whether large-scale fabrication of plastic optical waveguides with attenuation and bandwidth values suitable for telecommunications will be possible in this decade. The advantages of this polymer material, such as large elongation capability and easy fusibility, will however make it suitable for some special applications in the industrial field.

Use of optical waveguides in submarine cables

The transmission capacity of more than 100 Mbit/s per fiber and a 50 km repeater spacing makes a multifiber submarine cable once again an economically and technically (owing to the interference immunity of the link) attractive proposition. The design principle of the loose fiber in a filled tube, being insensitive to pressure, is superior to all others.

If the cable core is filled as completely as the buffer tube there is no prospect of the cable being deformed by high water pressure or highly stressed armoring. This leaves volume compressions on the order of 1 to 2% per 100 bar which can easily be absorbed by a suitable core structure. The usual metallic tubes required for tightly buffered and loosely packed fibers are unnecessary and, in view of the need for cable flexibility, could never in any event be made thick enough not to deform under sufficient pressure. Designs with completely fil-

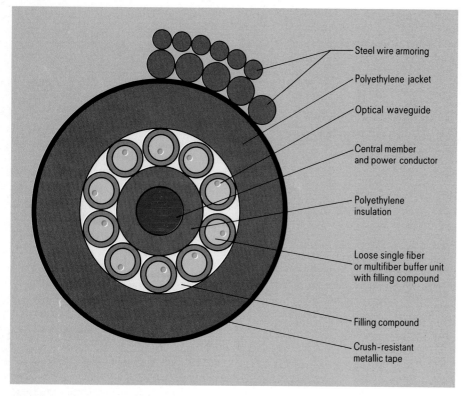

Submarine cable of loose tube design

Labels in figure:
- Steel wire armoring
- Polyethylene jacket
- Optical waveguide
- Central member and power conductor
- Polyethylene insulation
- Loose single fiber or multifiber buffer unit with filling compound
- Filling compound
- Crush-resistant metallic tape

led buffer tubes and core have been tested up to 400 bar and there appears to be no problem in withstanding even higher pressures.

Whether such cables should have a continuous metallic sheath or not depends merely on the assessed effect of such a sheath on the mechanical fatigue of the fibers. If the fibers are held in a condition in which the only stress is that of bending due to stranding there is not likely to be any effect from indiffusion of moisture. Conversely, even a continuous metallic sheath does not provide reliable protection against fatigue for fibers under constant mechanical stress. As always, prevention is better than cure.

The **figure** shows a submarine cable of filled, loose tube design.

Fiber-optic aerial cable for high tensile loads

Similar, if somewhat less severe, conditions apply to aerial cables. Provided that the ice and wind loadings are not unusually high, standard cables can be used directly for lashed installation because the length variations of in-situ messenger wires are mainly elastic in nature and seldom exceed $\pm 4 \cdot 10^{-3}$.

Cables for the communication network can be installed using the wire lashing technique normally employed in the USA. Cables on high-voltage lines generally need to be all-dielectric and must not be lashed with wires which could hang down loosely if broken. The only exception are aerial cables encased in ground conductors, but these should also have an all-dielectric core to permit freedom of routing down the tower. The discontinuous clamping technique used on ground or phase conductors (in medium-voltage networks) provides a particularly economical method of installing all-dielectric standard cables [7].

In extra-high-voltage lines it is preferable to employ self-supporting all-dielectric cables for maximum freedom of installation (not on phase conductors owing to corona damage). There are two designs available for this application, having similar core designs with loose tubes, of course, for extra high elongation capability, but having quite different characteristics:

● Figure-8-cables with aramid yarn messenger

Advantages
highly flexible,

extremely resistant to breakage, vibration damped, experience over years with no setbacks [8].

Disadvantages
larger in one axis hence somewhat larger ice loads, the aramid yarn messenger creeps and this must be allowed for in the elongation capability of the core.

● Cable with glass-epoxy supporting element

Advantages
size and weight advantages, no creepage.

Disadvantages
flex resistant, tensile and bending stresses added, susceptible to fatigue even under normal loading, not vibration damped, no previous experience.

It remains to be seen whether in future one of these two designs or a combination of both or simply lashing the cable to the ground conductor will become the standard.

Fiber-optic cables for special applications

As a result of efforts to improve efficiency and extend surveillance of the technical situation underground, interest is focusing on fiber-optic cables for mines. As in high-voltage installations, the attraction is the complete isolation from electromagnetic interference. Mining applications call for rugged cable designs resistant to impact, abrasion and buckling, suitable for suspension in the shaft as well as providing a high degree of flame resistance. Thick jackets made of flame-retardant polyurethane or flame resistant noncorrosive PE-compounds with good mechanical coupling to strength and antibuckling members are the main feature of these cables.

Cables with buffer tubes individually protected against tension and buckling are of interest when the buffer units are required to be routed like independent cables from the distribution or branch point into buildings. Impregnated glass yarns as tensile and antibuckling members or combinations of impregnated and unimpregnated glass or aramid yarns with normal or flame-retardant jacketing make the buffer units of these fan-out cables sufficiently rugged for the purpose. Whether the increased expenditure on the cables is compensated by reduced installation cost is a matter for decision in the individual case.

There is an increasing requirement for cables operable at intermittently or continuously high temperatures. Shipbuilding and aircraft construction, industrial and military users require designs withstanding 150°C and more. Aramid yarns provide only limited application here because the Young's modulus and strength begin to decline at these temperatures. Glass fibers impregnated with high temperature resistant lacquers, and using high strength glasses in special applications, have proved suitable. Buffer tubes and cable jackets consist of fluoropolymers, while buffer and core fillings are made of extremely soft silicone rubber. These elements can also be incorporated in power-feeder cables (excavator, crane, X-ray and elevator cables) which must undergo vulcanization.

If diameter restrictions on low fiber-count cables prevent the use of the short-lay, loose tube design, it must be accepted that the elongation of the fiber will be proportional to that of the cable but it is nevertheless possible to avoid or reduce added loss by using loose tubes. If these tubes are also of elastic, impact and crush resistant design and protected with the previously mentioned impregnated glass yarns, they produce extremely rugged structures for normal or high temperatures.

If, for installation reasons, the user is seeking to combine small buffer diameters with high mechanical strength, a suitable solution is a hybrid buffer unit having the dimensions (diameter $\leqq 1$ mm) and the external behavior of a fiber with the usual silicone rubber, polyamide buffering. This unit comprises the fiber buffer made of UV cross-linked acrylate or silicone rubber surrounded by an extremely hard shell made of extruded aramid or similar highly molecular molding material and has a thin layer of Newtonian fluid in between. This coating makes the fiber superior to any tightly buffered fiber as regards tube deformation and enables

the fiber to absorb limited longitudinal movement in the shell.

This element can be handled almost like an insulated copper conductor and fills the gap in applications for which the proper loose buffer tube is too bulky or not crush resistant enough, but for which the normal tightly buffered unit is undesirable owing to its sensitive reaction to mechanical deformation.

A new type of loose buffer for single or multi-fiber applications is on the way. It is a large and very rugged tube which may be used unstranded, containing several fibers in approximately regular helices. The nondraining filling compound places no restriction on movement of the fibers. In some cases this element may be used in place of stranded loose buffers, either for economic reasons or for applications where the central position of the fiber-containing element is inevitable, e.g. self-supporting aerial cables with external supporting structures. The tube will be rugged enough to allow direct clamping on the jacket, even without resin impregnation of the supporting structure.

References

[1] Schneider, H.; Zeidler, G.: Manufacturing Processes and Designs of Optical Waveguides.
telcom report 6 (1983) Special Issue "Optical Communications", pp. 27 to 33

[2] Ainslie, B.J.; Beales, K.J.; Cooper, D.M.; Day, C.R.; Rush, J.D.: The simultaneous achievement of ultra low loss and minimum dispersion at 1.55 microns.
8th Europ. Conf. on Opt. Commun. Cannes, September 1982

[3] Ainslie, B.J.; Beales, K.J.; Cooper, D.M.; Day, C.R.; Rush, J.D.: Monomode fibre with ultra-low loss and minimum dispersion at 1.55 µm. Electron. Lett. 18 (1982), pp. 842 to 843

[4] Ikegami, T.; Kuroiwa, K.; Itaya, Y.; Shinohara, S.; Hagimoto, K.; Inagaki, N.: 1.5-µm transmission experiment with distributed feed-back laser. 8th Europ. Conf. on Opt. Commun. Cannes, September 1982

[5] Gentile, A.L.; Braunstein, M.; Pinnow, D.A.; Harrington, J.A.; Henderson, D.M.; Hobrock, L.M.; Myer, J.; Pastor, R.C.; Turk, R.R.: Infrared fiber optical materials. Fiber Optics – Advances in Research and Development. Ed. by B. Bendow and S.S. Mitra, Plenum Press, New York (1979), pp. 105 to 118

[6] Gannon, J.R.: Optical fiber materials for operating wavelength longer than 2 µm. J. Non-Cryst. Solids 42 (1980), pp. 239 to 246

[7] Goldmann, H.: Installation of Fiber-Optic Cables.
telcom report 6 (1983) Special Issue "Optical Communications", pp. 46 to 49

[8] Köstler, G.: Fiber-Optic Projects for the Deutsche Bundespost and other Users in Europe.
telcom report 6 (1983) Special Issue "Optical Communications", pp. 59 to 65

Ewald Braun and Karl Heinz Moehrmann

Optical Communications in Short-Haul and Long-Haul Wideband Communication Networks

Scarcely a decade has passed since the first experiments involving transmission via optical waveguides. If one compares this period of time with that employed for the introduction of transmission systems using metallic lines, the time appears relatively short and this could lead to the assumption that the technology is not yet suitable for widespread introduction. However, experience shows that, in the end, a new technology gains acceptance if it is more economic than the existing one. This position has now being attained – optical waveguide transmission is ready for widespread introduction.

A series of optical waveguide transmission systems is currently being developed on a broad basis, and their introduction into practical service is imminent. The introduction of such systems after the fundamental work of past years is also the impetus for standardization, which has been rather neglected hitherto, and for the consideration of operational matters, such as has been normal for decades with established systems using metallic lines. For the immediate future there is thus a requirement to build and operate systems. Experience will show how developments, which are now only faintly discernible, will be introduced into future system generations.

Dipl.-Ing. (FH) Ewald Braun,
Siemens AG,
Public Communication Networks
Division, Munich;
Dipl.-Ing. Karl Heinz Moehrmann,
Siemens AG,
Central Laboratories for Communications
Technology, Munich

Optical wavelength

Starting from the wavelength region around 850 nm, the attenuation of the optical waveguide at first decreases with increasing wavelength. Systems with the maximum possible spacings between optical transmitter and receiver will utilize these regions of longer wavelength, in which simultaneously the uncertainty regarding the risk of eye damage due to laser light is somewhat alleviated.

As already indicated in [1], optical transmission makes possible the use of wavelength division multiplexing. *However,* as long as the optical waveguide and the circuitry are suitable for electrical multiplex transmission at a single optical wavelength, electrical multiplexing is more economic and considerably less complex than wavelength division multiplexing on normal telecommunication links for the transmission of digital signals with line terminating units and regenerators. In addition, electrical multiplexing of digital signals enables cost-effective VLSI (*very large scale integration*) circuits to be used.

On the other hand, if one considers the use of wavelength division multiplexing as a "hidden reserve" for a possible increase in transmission capacity at a later date, it appears to be completely sensible to plan for a single optical wavelength with the maximum possible system loss currently experienced and to assume that, on subsequent expansion with wavelength division multiplexing, the additional attenuation of the WDM components will be approximately compensated by the improved performance of the optical transmitters and receivers. In the course of this expansion it may be necessary to replace the system originally used.

However, it may be advisable to use wavelength division multiplexing instead of electrical multiplexing in the subscriber line network, due to the greater flexibility provided for gradual expansion (cf. section "Gradual expansion of the subscriber line network").

Range and transmission capacity

Whereas with transmission systems on metallic lines (e.g. coaxial cables) repeater section lengths and transmission capacities (historically influenced by the performance of electron tubes) have assumed standard values in the course of the preceding decades, all is basically wide open in the case of optical transmission.

The principal system parameters, such as transmission capacity, characteristics and design of the optoelectronic transducers, determine both the maximum *bridgeable* optical attenuation and the bandwidth required of the optical waveguide.

The *bridgeable* loss results in differing section lengths, depending upon the characteristics of the optical waveguide. This represents an important starting point for standardization, in order to sensibly limit a possible variety of types.

The practical limit is reached for digital links via graded-index fibers at a transmission rate of 140 Mbit/s per optical wavelength and with a regenerator section length of about 20 km. It is true that even larger section lengths would be possible with particularly good fibers, however an increase in the speed of transmission above 140 Mbit/s for each optical wavelength is not feasible in practice due to the limited bandwidth. In contrast, higher bit rates can be transmitted and longer section lengths achieved using single-mode fibers, but, as in the case of coaxial cable systems, the circuit technology will no doubt limit the transmission rate to 565 ($\approx 4 \cdot 140$) Mbit/s, at least in the near future. For the longer term, transmission rates >1 Gbit/s are being considered.

Integrated networks

The optical waveguide, with its large bandwidth and low attenuation, is an excellent transmission medium for use in the subscriber line network to transmit a multitude of narrow-band and wideband signals to the subscriber without electronics on the link [2, 3].

If, for any reason (usually not technical), the number of services is limited, it is only in the minority of cases that an optical wideband network is competitive with conventional copper cable networks. This applies, for instance, to the provision of narrow-band ISDN services with $[(2 \cdot 64) + 16]$ kbit/s per subscriber line and for the extensive distribution of television and radio programs.

The technical and economic advantages will not be realized until the introduction of subscriber-oriented wideband communication services, such as video telephony with normal TV quality, and the joint transmission of the established services together with signals of these new services in an integrated network (wideband ISDN), and this would not be possible without a wideband optical network. The system trial BIGFON is indicating the technical

possibilities for the first time [2]. Due to the limited number of subscribers and because there are still no standards for digital picture signal transmission, the TV video signals and, correspondingly, the video telephony picture signal are transmitted as frequency modulated signals in the Siemens concept.

In the long term, transmission of all signals in digital form is logical, in order to have a uniform signal format for all services in the short-haul and long-haul areas, and in order to fully utilize the advantages of an economic realization of all components in VLSI technology. Wideband visual communication including full motion, i.e. video telephony with a resolution corresponding to that of the 625 line standard, will only become economically possible over large distances with digital transmission. In addition, the switching of analog signals on a large scale is technically difficult (crosstalk problems). Due to the uniformity, compatibility and technical advantages, the TV program transmission should also be digitized when the distribution services are included. In the case of visual communication, the TV video signals appear in digital form at the connector panel of the video camera or, in the case of TV program distribution, from the processing equipment at the head end, or directly over the lines from the studio; they pass unchanged (save perhaps for a modified bit rate) through the network with all switching and distribution functions and are directly processed in the terminal equipment [4].

The joint transmission of several different signals over a subscriber line is of particular significance for future integrated services networks. From the relevant local exchange the services for the long-haul network can be systematically combined and transferred to the established and standardized digital systems. These already form integrated transmission paths.

Structure of the subscriber line network

The tree structure, as used in large cable television systems, is unsuitable for a network with subscriber-oriented bidirectional narrow-band and wide-

band communication, since switchable channels cannot be realized. As in the case of BIGFON, an integrated optical waveguide network of this type will be star-shaped, and the subscriber will be offered individual communication services at various basic bit rates at suitable interfaces.

Since moving-picture transmission will require by far the greatest transmission capacity, the choice of a suitable encoding bit rate, taking into account the economic consequences and the desired signal quality, is of primary importance in the design of such systems.

At a bit rate of 34 Mbit/s per wideband signal, for instance, considerable advantages result [4]: electrical multiplexing can be employed cost-effectively for the simultaneous transmission of several signals via an optical waveguide. For low levels of network development, light-emitting diodes can be used instead of laser diodes as optical transmitters; the bit rate of the data streams to be switched amounts to only 34 Mbit/s. The know-how for producing the codecs and multiplexers in cost-effective VLSI technology is available. If the sum bit rates are not too high, in-house distribution can take place using a coaxial bus structure.

In contrast, at 140 Mbit/s per wideband signal, for instance, laser transmitters are necessary in many cases, electrical multiplexing is only possible under certain stringent conditions and the in-house distribution of the wideband signals must be on a star-shaped basis.

Gradual expansion of the subscriber line network

The transmission of all signals via an optical waveguide permits gradual expansion of the network to be realized in various ways. For instance, in an initial stage all signals of the narrow-band services, such as telephone and data transmission, can be transmitted via a single fiber to the subscriber using bidirectional wavelength division multiplexing, e.g. in the range from 800 to 900 nm (**Fig.** 1). If visual communication is to be offered at a later date, these signals are transmitted at two

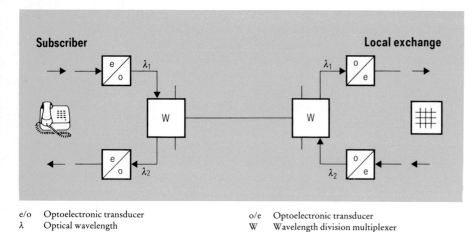

e/o   Optoelectronic transducer
λ   Optical wavelength

o/e   Optoelectronic transducer
W   Wavelength division multiplexer

Fig. 1   Transmission of narrow-band signals using optical waveguides

further optical wavelengths, e.g. in the 1300 nm region; the optical waveguide link is merely supplemented by additional optoelectronic transducers (**Fig. 2**). If required, television and stereo sound programs can be transmitted in time-division multiplex or by wavelength division multiplexing via the same fiber or via an additional fiber (which could be installed at the same time as the first fiber). In this way one obtains a structure which is adaptable to the requirements, and separates telephone and distribution services as long as this is appropriate to the normal practices. However, the ultimate objective can only be an integrated network, as is already being anticipated by the BIGFON concept.

Wideband signals – bit rate and quality

Visual communication

Since the transmission of arbitrary picture sequences (e.g. video recordings, text, graphics) is intended to be possible, it would be advisable to have a suitably high resolution in area and movement, as well as color transmission. In addition, compatibility (identical or easily interconvertible standards for both services) between visual communication and TV program distribution is desirable in order to facilitate, for instance, both "passive video telephony" [4], and also a uniform technology for the codecs and terminal

equipment and thus minimize cost. A requirement could thus be that the signal received by the subscriber should exhibit the same characteristics as those associated with present television reception (i.e. bandwidth at least corresponding to PAL quality, 625 lines per frame, in accordance with CCIR standard B, G). This requirement can be well met by suitable encoding at a bit rate of 34 Mbit/s.

Within the framework of the COST 211 program [5] a 2 Mbit/s video telephony system was developed jointly in Europe by several administrations. The bit rate of 2 Mbit/s was recommended by CEPT study group TR/SG1 for the international transmission of video conference signals [6]. In principle, this low transmission rate also permits the connection of video terminals via balanced copper lines, and transmission via satellite. In the longer term, the use of a system with higher quality and, consequently, a higher bit rate at least in the subscriber line network or at a national level would appear to be wise in an optical waveguide network, due to the high transmission capacity available there.

Composite or component encoding?

Composite encoding of a color TV signal has so many disadvantages compared with the separate encoding of the components (luminance signal Y and chrominance signals U, V) [4] that in the longer term the systems should be designed with only component encoding. This results in the advantage of continuous uniform encoding from the camera to the receiving monitor, without the disadvantages of a particular color TV standard (PAL, SECAM).

TV program distribution

CCIR recommends a standard with component encoding for the digitized television signal in the studio sector [7]. Every proposal for encoding TV signals in the subscriber sector should be compatible with this CCIR standard, i.e. the selected sampling rates should be readily derivable from this standard. A few examples of possible sampling rate (and bandwidth) combinations are given in the **table**. In this case also, the quality achievable with 34 Mbit/s is higher than that of present PAL television.

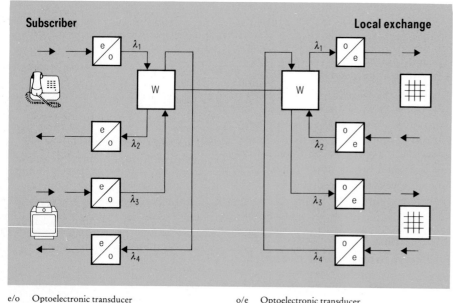

e/o   Optoelectronic transducer
λ   Optical wavelength

o/e   Optoelectronic transducer
W   Wavelength division multiplexer

Fig. 2   Transmission of wideband signals using optical waveguides

Luminance signal (sampling frequency $f_{T\,Lum}$, Bandwidth B)	Chrominance signals (separately or line sequentially)		
	$f_T = f_{T\,Lum/2}$	$f_T = f_{T\,Lum/3}$	$f_T = f_{T\,Lum/4}$
Studio standard $\quad f_T = 13.5$ MHz $\;\; B = 6$ MHz	$f_T = 6.75$ MHz $\;\; B = 3$ MHz		
(5/6) $\qquad\qquad f_T = 11.25$ MHz $\;\; B = 5$ MHz	$f_T = 5.625$ MHz $\;\; B = 2.5$ MHz		
(3/4) $\qquad\qquad f_T = 10.125$ MHz $\;\; B = 4.5$ MHz		$f_T = 3.375$ MHz $\;\; B = 1.5$ MHz	$f_T = 2.53$ MHz $\;\; B = 1.1$ MHz
(2/3) $\qquad\qquad f_T = 9$ MHz $\;\; B = 4$ MHz		$f_T = 3$ MHz $\;\; B = 1.3$ MHz	$f_T = 2.25$ MHz $\;\; B = 1$ MHz
(Assumption: usable bandwidth $f_T/2.25$)			

Table Sampling rates and signal bandwidths derived from the CCIR studio standard

For the future "digital" TV program distribution, demands are frequently made these days for bandwidths lying considerably above those of the decoded PAL signal and which, consequently, necessitate a higher sampling rate as well as a higher transmission rate (70 or 140 Mbit/s) [8]. It is open to debate as to what extent the previously mentioned increased expense for transmission is justified by the increase in quality, which is hardly perceptible subjectively to the subscriber.

Combination of switched and distribution services

If all services are combined in an integrated network, then, due to the partly contradictory requirements, the following paths can be followed:

- encoding of visual communication and TV distribution signals at differing bit rates,

- encoding of visual communication and TV distribution signals at identical, possibly higher bit rates in the subscriber network; reduction of the bit rate for visual communication signals in the long-haul network (disadvantage: differing visual communication signal qualities for short-haul and long-haul links),

- encoding of picture signals in the entire network at the same bit rate.

In none of the assessments made so far concerning visual communications do the possible savings in the codec, as a result of using a bit rate higher than 34 Mbit/s, offset the increased cost for the transmission of the visual communication signals in the long-haul network at the higher bit rate. Uniform encoding of all picture signals at 34 Mbit/s, corresponding to a sampling rate for the luminance signal of 9 (maximum 10.125) MHz and, for example, a third or a quarter of this sampling rate for the (line-sequentially transmitted) chrominance components, therefore appears to be a qualitatively justifiable and economically favorable compromise [4].

High definition TV

High definition television (HDTV) will require a bit rate of at least 140 Mbit/s for digital transmission.

As already mentioned, a system can be planned today for one (or two) optical wavelengths and can be subsequently extended using wavelength division multiplexing. There is thus no obstacle to retrofitting available optical waveguides for HDTV transmission, if this is subsequently required.

Realization

Economic realization of the electrical equipment for picture encoding and for the optical transmission is only possible using VLSI technology – and in the long term in the form of only a few modules. However, this expensive development can only be carried out when standards are available, both for the bit rate as well as for the encoding, multiplex and transmission methods.

References

[1] Braun, E.; Keil, H.: Optical Waveguide Transmission Systems. telcom report 6 (1983) Special Issue "Optical Communications", pp. 113 to 118

[2] Braun, E.: BIGFON Brings the Optical Waveguide into the Subscriber Area. telcom report 6 (1983) Special Issue "Optical Communications", pp. 136 to 139

[3] Bauch, H.; Weinhardt, K.: Communication in the Subscriber Area of Optical Broadband Networks. telcom report 6 (1983) Special Issue "Optical Communications", pp. 140 to 146

[4] Bauch, H.; Christiansen, H.M.; Möhrmann, K.H.; Starck, A.R.: Encoding and transmission of signals for visual communication and program distribution in future optical fiber networks. Internat. Conference on Communications (ICC '82), Philadelphia, 14.–17. 6. 82, Conf. Record, pp. 2G. 4–1 to 2G. 4–6

[5] Wendt, H.: Stand der Ergebnisse der Arbeiten des COST 211-Ausschusses zu einer europäischen digitalen Bildfernsprechnorm. NTG-Fachber. Bd. 74: Text- und Bildkommunikation. Berlin: VDE-Verlag 1980, pp. 362 to 369

[6] Thompson, J.E.: Visual services trial – the british telcom system for teleconferencing and new visual services. British Telecommunications Eng. 1 (1982) pp. 28 to 33

[7] CCIR Rec. 601: Encoding parameters of digital television for studios

[8] Wengenroth, G.: Die Codierung von Farbfernseh- und Bildfernsprechsignalen in einem digitalen optischen Teilnehmeranschlußnetz. ntz Arch. 4 (1982) pp. 103 to 107

Edwin Wolf

Worldwide Introduction of Fiber-Optic Systems

Optical fibers are already being applied in a great many fields. Most applications are currently in telecommunication systems and this will continue to be the case, though of course the existing spare capacity available in copper cables will be utilized first. In addition there are now complete fiber-optic systems available for new installations. From the mid-eighties onward, the dramatic rate of development in this new technology will make field-proven, economical systems increasingly available in a number of wavelength ranges, providing very large transmission capacities particularly in the long-distance network. As further developments are made, fiber-optic technology will for the first time allow individual subscribers to be connected directly to broadband communication networks via a single fiber.

Of all the transmission media that have been introduced in telecommunications over the years, there has probably been none that has raised as many hopes as the optical fiber, and there is no doubt that the possibilities offered by this new medium – whether they be technical, economic or application-related – are far from being exhausted. Recognizing the known advantages, there is a discussion currently on the application of fiber-optic technology to computers, aircraft, vehicles, power plants, industry, office equipment and instrumentation to name but a few of the possible areas. One area that is seen to be of particular significance is that of government projects, but without doubt by far the greatest field of application is and will continue to be telecommunications, accounting for around 50% of total volume (**Fig. 1**).

It is due to the use of fiber-optic systems that *moving picture communication* is entering the bounds of technical and above all economic feasibility for the first time. As a result, communication services such as high-quality videoconferencing and videotelephony will become an increasingly common part of the range of services offered by PTTs. For high-quality digital video and sound signal transmission, with its greater bandwidth requirements, the optical fiber is eminently suitable as a distribution medium. Moreover, the transition to "digitized" communication networks brings with it the possibility of freely combining bit streams from a very wide variety of sources. For these applications, fiber-optic systems provide an ideal "pipeline" of virtually unlimited bandwidth for all network levels down to the individual subscriber, although the weighting may differ at the various levels in such networks and for the various services. The essential advantages which characterize fiber-optic technology are dependent on certain system parameters. The main characteristics include:

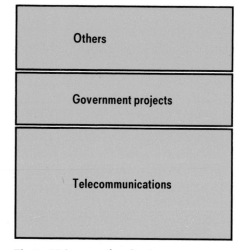

Fig. 1   Main areas of application for fiber-optic systems

- low attenuation,
- large bandwidth,
- multiple utilization by wavelength division multiplexing,
- no electromagnetic interference, no external electromagnetic field,
- considerably thinner and lighter cable.

Fig. 2 shows the present and future use of optical fibers in four selected countries; the curves provide impressive indications of the starting phase in this area. Most systems currently operate at 850 nm on graded-index fibers and employ light-emitting diodes as the optical source with short repeater spacings. The systems are employed in the local and short-haul networks providing capacities equivalent to 500 to 1000 voice channels.

More and more routes are being set up to operate at longer wavelengths (1300 nm) with laser sources, though still predominantly on graded-index fibers. These installations must of

Dipl.-Ing. Edwin Wolf,
Siemens AG,
Public Communication Networks
Division, Munich

course be viewed as experimental, since there are as yet no proven long-haul systems in operation, although many PTTs already have plans for such systems.

Characteristic features of fiber-optic technology are its high rate of innovation, coupled with its transition from 850 to 1300 nm (or possibly 1600 nm), and its primary importance for *long-haul applications*. These features will permit even *higher bit rates* and *longer repeater spacings* for these applications, thus reducing the need for intermediate repeaters housed in underground containers at all network levels.

In the *local area* it is anticipated that even the lower-density fiber-optic systems will become economical in the next few years – particularly when this coincides with the exchanges going digital.

In the case of systems based on single-mode fibers, however, there are still some problems to be solved over the

Optical transmitter		Light-emitting diode		Laser diode	
Repeater spacing limited by		Attenuation	Bandwidth*	Attenuation	Bandwidth*
Graded-index fiber for 850 nm (400 MHz · km)					
Transmission rate (Mbit/s)	2	8 to 12 km		12 to 16 km	
	8		≈ 11 km	10 to 15 km	
	34		≈ 5 km	10 to 13 km	
Graded-index fiber for 1300 nm (1300 MHz · km)					
Transmission rate (Mbit/s)	34		≈ 12 km	17 to 30 km	
	140		≈ 7 km		≈ 17 km
Single-mode fiber for 1300 nm (20 GHz · km)					
Transmission rate (Mbit/s)	140			20 to 40 km	
	565			16 to 30 km	

* Full required bandwidth with no allowance for equalization or power

Table 1   Regenerator spacings

next two or three years before the widescale introduction of proven systems into the long-haul network can be started towards the middle of the eighties.

The *optical fibers* currently available for *single-mode cables* are experimental lengths. Attenuation values of ≤ 0.5 dB/km have been reported by various manufacturers but the guaranteed values still lie between 0.5 and 0.8 dB/km. As the core diameter of a single-mode fiber is considerably smaller than that of a graded-index fiber, it is more difficult to achieve low losses on connectors and particularly on cable splices in the field. In addition, the coupling losses are higher (core diameter ≤ 10 µm compared with 50 µm for graded-index fibers).

Long-haul systems operating at high bit rates and with large repeater spacings require not only single-mode fibers but also laser diodes as the *optical transmitters*. The AlGaAs lasers employed for this purpose at 850 nm are not suitable for 1300 nm. The materials employed at this wavelength are significantly more critical in terms of temperature stability [1].

For *optical receivers*, the best solution at 1300 nm is currently regarded to be PIN FET amplifiers, though these do not achieve the sensitivities of the

avalanche photodiodes (APD) used at 850 nm.

Another problem area is the fiber-optic *single subscriber loop*. It is not so much the availability and reliability of fiber-optic systems as the costs involved (new installation, cable costs) and thus the economic viability of the systems (subscriber charges) which will control their introduction into the subscriber network.

Parameters for system planning

The most important planning parameters for a *long-haul link* (with a transmission rate, for example, of 140 Mbit/s) are given in [2 to 7]. **Table 1** is a simplified summary of the examples given in **Figs. 3** and **4**. The colored areas indicate whether the repeater spacings are limited by attenuation or bandwidth, the figures given being the achievable repeater spacings in kilometers.

The conclusions to be drawn are:

● *Fiber-optic systems with graded-index fibers for 850 nm* are well suited to applications at bit rates of 2, 8 and possibly 34 Mbit/s. If *light-emitting diodes* are used, the achievable repeater spacings are limited to between 8 and 12 km. Fibers with bandwidth-distance products of about 400 MHz · km are

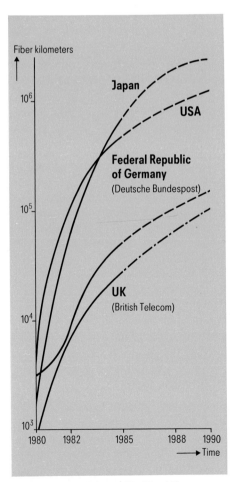

Fig. 2   Predicted demand in fiber kilometers for fiber-optic systems (cumulative curve)

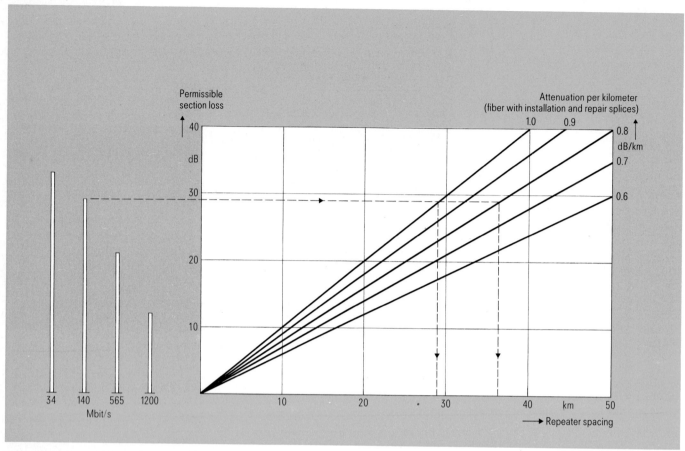

Fig. 3 Repeater spacing as a function of attenuation coefficient
(single-mode fiber, laser diode, $\lambda = 1300$ nm)

perfectly adequate; there is no point in using wider bandwidth fibers. With *laser diodes,* the bandwidth limiting in the required repeater spacing range ceases to affect fibers with bandwidths of 400 MHz · km and more for all practical applications. The repeater spacing is then only determined by the permissible link loss and increases to between 12 and 16 km. Here, again, there is no advantage in using fibers with larger bandwidths.

● *Fiber-optic systems with graded-index fibers for 1300 nm* are suitable for applications at transmission rates of 34 and 140 Mbit/s. Optical transmitters with currently available *light-emitting diodes* are suitable only for short distances, as the repeater spacing in this case is largely determined by material dispersion. With *laser diodes* as optical transmitters, the repeater spacing in 34 Mbit/s systems is determined only by link loss. In 140 Mbit/s systems, however, the repeater spacing is limited by modal distortion.

● *Fiber-optic systems with single-mode*

fibers for 1300 nm are suitable primarily for high bit rates ($\geqq$ 140 Mbit/s), and up to 565 Mbit/s are limited almost only by link loss. The extent to which the quoted repeater spacings can be further increased particularly in the long-distance network, is dependent mainly on the guaranteed fiber losses, the factory lengths of the fiber-optic cables and the total number of splices required throughout the lifetime of the system.

The repeater spacing in 1300 nm fiber-optic systems employing *single-mode fibers* is shown in **Fig. 3** as a function of the attenuation coefficient. The permissible link loss is calculated from the average received optical power at the receiver circuit for a bit error rate of 10^{-10}, minus connector losses (3 dB) and system margin (6 dB), and the optical power launched into the fiber (−3 dBm). The family of curves for the attenuation coefficient contains not only fiber attenuation, but also losses for installation and repair splices. It can be seen that inclusion of all the

splice losses, which must be allowed for over the lifetime of the system, has a considerable bearing on the achievable repeater spacing.

In fiber-optic systems with *graded-index fibers,* unlike those with single-mode fibers, the bandwidth may limit the achievable repeater spacing even at medium transmission rates. These correlations are described in detail in [8]. In determining the achievable repeater spacing, therefore, both bandwidth *and* attenuation must be taken into account. **Fig. 4** elaborates the illustration in [8] by showing the repeater spacing achievable for graded-index fibers as a function of the attenuation coefficient.

Economic aspects

● The large repeater spacings that can be achieved with fiber-optic systems, particularly in the long-distance network, reduce the number of regenerators needed to such an extent that, as far as *new installations* are concerned, optical fibers are more

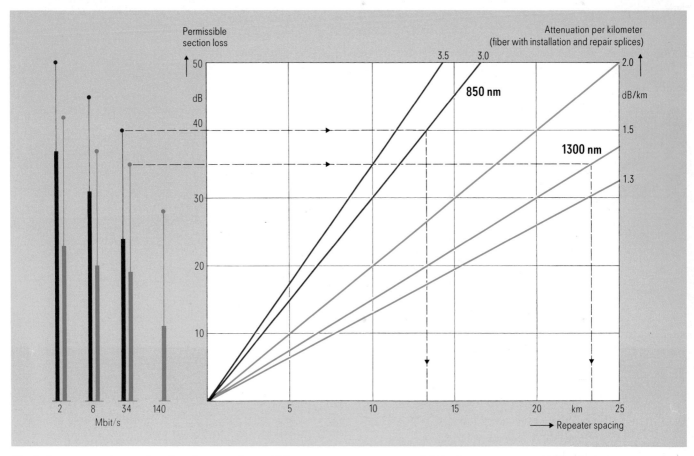

Fig. 4 Repeater spacing as a function of attenuation coefficient
(graded-index fiber, λ = 850 nm and 1300 nm)

LD } λ = 850 nm   LD } λ = 1300 nm
LED   LED

economic than coaxial lines. **Fig. 5** shows a comparison between coaxial and fiber-optic systems for a transmission rate of 565 Mbit/s. As soon as proven and reliable fiber-optic systems become available – which will be an increasingly frequent occurrence over the next few years – it is likely that optical cable will completely replace copper cable in new installations throughout the long-distance network.

• As regards *system expansion*, it is generally more economical to utilize any free capacity on existing coaxial or symmetric pair cables before installing new optical cable.

• With the long-term move towards complete digitization of the long-distance networks and the consequent *modification* of analog into digital voice channels, it will generally be more economical for the *long-distance network* to use the existing copper cables.

This will also apply at the *local level* initially. Later, however, it is expected that as digital exchanges become increasingly common at one or both ends, so lower-density (repeaterless) systems (34, 8 or even 2 Mbit/s) will become more economical than the balanced systems on existing copper cable. **Fig. 6** shows for the local network a comparison of voice frequency or 2 Mbit/s transmission on balanced cables and 8 Mbit/s transmission on optical fibers at current costs. For the purposes of this comparison it is assumed that there is an exchange with 2 Mbit/s inputs at one end and an exchange with VF inputs at the other. The model also assumes an initial capacity of 120 voice channels, expanding every 2 years by 120 channels to give a total of 720 voice channels after 10 years. The existence of ducts (or copper cable) was taken as a further parameter. The comparison shows that after only a few kilometers PCM transmission is more economical than VF transmission. Even a newly installed 8 Mbit/s fiber-optic system shows a slight cost advantage over a PCM30 system operating on existing copper cable.

Possible applications in telecommunication networks

Assuming that the most important system parameters currently finding their first applications will in a few years be state-of-the-art in proven and commercially viable systems, and applying the above-mentioned results of a current cost comparison, it is then possible to list the potential applications for fiber-optic systems in mature telecommunication networks as in **Table 2**. One can accordingly expect:

• *Graded-index fibers operating at 850 nm* only at the local and subscriber levels (even at these levels, however, 850 nm fibers are likely to be replaced in the long term by 1300 nm fibers).

• *Graded-index fibers operating at 1300 nm* at all network levels up to short-haul provided that broadband services are not required.

• *Single-mode fibers* for broadband services and bit rates ≧ 140 Mbit/s in the long-distance network.

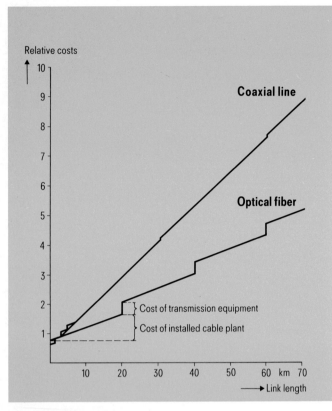

Fig. 5 Cost comparison between coaxial and fiber-optic cable systems
for a transmission rate of 565 Mbit/s

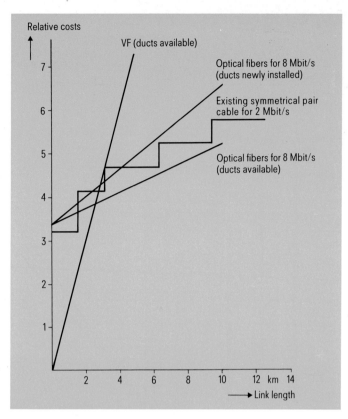

Fig. 6 Cost comparison
for PCM transmission in the local network

● *LEDs* as the optical transmitters in the local and short-haul networks.

● *Laser diodes* as the optical transmitters for broadband transmission in the long-distance and local networks and for all single-mode systems. For the BIGFON project (broadband integrated glass-fiber local communication network) laser diodes are provided for the "exchange → subscriber" direction and LEDs for the "subscriber → exchange" direction.

● *Photodiodes* as optical receivers;

at λ = 850 nm: avalanche
                photodiodes (APD),
at $\lambda \geqq$ 1300 nm: diodes in
                PIN FET technology.

"Third window" applications at 1500 to 1600 nm and the additional possibilities offered by "integrated optics" [9] have not been included in this illustration.

Special advantages for the user

Assuming success in further reducing the *attenuation* of the single-mode fibers aimed primarily at the long-distance network, it will be possible to achieve longer repeater spacings with suitable *bandwidth*. Even though in the present introductory phase remotely powered repeaters (known as regenerators in the digital context) housed predominantly in underground containers are still widely employed, this will soon be the exception in all terrestrial links, but not as regards submarine cables. Users anticipate that eliminating the "electronics" on the link will not only save expenditure but, more particularly, will yield major technical and economic benefits as regards system operation, e.g.

● elimination of power-feeding equipment,

● elimination of the risk of interference from the copper conductors of the power-feeding system,

● elimination of fault location for the repeater equipment in the outside plant, and

● considerably less time and money will be spent on fault clearance.

The large bandwidth of fiber-optic cables, ranging from "only" a few hundred MHz · km to around 1.5 GHz · km in current graded-index fibers, will greatly exceed 10 GHz · km in the single-mode fibers now coming into production. This will enable transmission rates of more than 1 Gbit/s to be achieved, a performance which no other transmission medium – not even coaxial cable – can match, irrespective of technical sophistication.

Further scope for expanding capacity will come from multiple utilization by *wavelength division multiplexing* which will in future allow several bit streams to be accommodated in only one wavelength range. Wavelength division multiplexing also allows information to be transmitted in *both* directions on *one* fiber – a welcome solution to the problem of connecting individual subscribers to future bidirectional broadband communication services.

The *immunity to electromagnetic interference* eliminates the effects of lightning strikes and power disturbances in railroad and high-voltage networks. Fiber-optic cables also have no external electromagnetic field and are therefore

Network level	Private network	Subscriber network	Local network		Long-distance network		
			without BC	with BC	Short-haul		Long-haul
					without BC	with BC	
Application (service)	High-speed data	BC	ISDN + high-speed data	ISDN + high-speed data + BC	ISDN + high-speed data	ISDN + high-speed data + BC	ISDN + high-speed data + BC
System parameters							
System capacity Mbit/s	$\geqq 10$	$n\,(64 + x)$ kbit + TV	8	$\geqq 140$	$\geqq 34$	$\geqq 140$	$\geqq 140$
Wavelength nm	850				1300		
Repeater spacing km		3 to 5	5 to 15		15 to 30		20 to 40
Cable parameters							
Type of fiber	Graded-index fiber						Single-mode fiber
Bandwidth MHz · km	$\leqq 400$			$\geqq 1300$			> 10 000
Attenuation dB/km	4 to 2.5			$\leqq 1$			0.8 to 0.5

BC   Broadband communication   ISDN   Integrated Services Digital Network

Table 2   Use of fiber-optic systems

difficult to "tap" and immune to jamming from outside.

Significantly *thinner* and *lighter cables* provide benefits in the local area, with easier installation. The ducts generally available in this area can accommodate considerably more fiber-optic cables and hence a correspondingly greater number of transmission channels. In many cases, therefore, there is no need to install the new ducts that would be required for conventional cables. Lighter cables are of particular interest for applications in aircraft and mobile service.

References

[1] Amann, M.-Ch.; Mettler, K.; Wolf, H.-D.: Laser Diodes – High-Power Light Sources for Optical Communications. telcom report 6 (1983) Special Issue "Optical Communications", pp. 79 to 84

[2] Gier, J.; Panzer, K.: Principles of Opto-electronic Signal Transmission. telcom report 6 (1983) Special Issue "Optical Communications", pp. 20 to 25

[3] Braun, E.; Keil, H.: Optical Waveguide Transmission Systems. telcom report 6 (1983) Special Issue "Optical Communications", pp. 113 to 118

[4] Fluhr, J.; Marending, P.; Trimmel, H.: A Fiber-Optic System for Transmitting 8 Mbit/s Signals. telcom report 6 (1983) Special Issue "Optical Communications", pp. 119 to 124

[5] Stegmeier, A.; Trimmel, H.: A Fiber-Optic System for Transmitting 34 Mbit/s Signals. telcom report 6 (1983) Special Issue "Optical Communications", pp. 125 to 129

[6] Dömer, J.; Gier, J.: A Fiber-Optic System for Transmitting 140 Mbit/s Signals. telcom report 6 (1983) Special Issue "Optical Communications", pp. 130 to 133

[7] Kügler, E.: Development Trends in Higher Order Fiber-Optic Transmission Systems. telcom report 6 (1983) Special Issue "Optical Communications", pp. 134 to 136

[8] Zeidler, G.: Designing Fiber-Optic Cable Systems. telcom report 6 (1983) Special Issue "Optical Communications", pp. 41 to 45

[9] Auracher, F.; Keil, R.: Integrated Optics for Single-Mode Transmission Systems. telcom report 6 (1983) Special Issue "Optical Communications", pp. 195 to 198

Siegfried Geckeler

Optical Waveguide Communications Terminology

Optical waveguide communications is still a very young field in which within a few years a host of new terms has emerged, the principal of which are explained in the following. It is in the nature of things that the linguistic usage for many of these terms is not yet uniform, so that some of them are synonyms. Among the first attempts at standardization are NBS Handbook 140, "Temporary Document 7-E" of Study Group XV of CCITT/IEC and VDE specification DIN 57888/VDE 0888 "Optical Waveguides for Telecommunication Systems, Part 1: Definitions". Terms from the field of general digital transmission were not included, since they have already been adequately dealt with in the special issue "Digital Transmission" of telcom report 2 (1979).

The emphasis is on optical waveguides as used for communication purposes, in contrast to fibers or fiber bundles used for illumination purposes or image transmission.

Terms arising in the individual explanations which are themselves explained elsewhere in the present compilation are marked by index arrows ($\rightarrow$).

Absorption

Together with $\rightarrow$ scattering this forms the principal cause of the $\rightarrow$ attenuation of an optical waveguide. It results from unwanted impurities in the waveguide material and has an effect only at certain wavelengths.

In the case of $\rightarrow$ photodiodes, absorption is the process by which the energy of an incident photon raises an electron

Dipl.-Ing. Dr.-Ing. Siegfried Geckeler,
Siemens AG,
Research and Development Division,
Munich

◁ When new technologies are introduced it is advisable to establish the specialized vocabulary at an early date, since the more accurately the terms are defined, the less ambiguous will be the interpretation of equivalent statements

from the valence band to the conduction band ($\rightarrow$ band gap).

Antonym: $\rightarrow$ emission.

Acceptance angle

Half the vertex angle of the cone within which the power coupled into an optical waveguide with uniform illumination is equal to a specified fraction of the total power coupled in. Geometric optics yield the maximum theoretical acceptance angle

$$\Theta = \arcsin \sqrt{n_1^2 - n_2^2}$$

where n_1 is the largest $\rightarrow$ refractive index in the $\rightarrow$ core and n_2 is the refractive index in the $\rightarrow$ cladding.

The sine of the acceptance angle is referred to as the $\rightarrow$ numerical aperture.

Analog transmission

Transmission of continuously varying signals, either by direct modulation of the optical power or by using an electrical subcarrier with which the optical power is then modulated.

Attenuation

Reduction in the optical power between two cross sections of an optical waveguide. The main causes are $\rightarrow$ scattering and $\rightarrow$ absorption, as well as optical losses in $\rightarrow$ connectors and $\rightarrow$ splices. It is expressed by the logarithmic quantity $- 10 \lg (P_2/P_1)$ dB, where $P_2 < P_1$.

More accurate term: CW attenuation ($\rightarrow$ transfer function).

Attenuation coefficient

The attenuation coefficient α is the $\rightarrow$ attenuation with respect to length of a uniform optical waveguide with $\rightarrow$ equilibrium mode distribution (normal unit: dB/km).

Avalanche noise

Although the photocurrent amplification in an $\rightarrow$ avalanche photodiode contributes little noise, it is not noise-free. The resulting additional noise is referred to as avalanche noise.

Avalanche photodiode (APD)

$\rightarrow$ Photodiode in which the photocurrent is amplified with low additional noise by carrier multiplication in an electric field (avalanche effect).

Band gap

The difference in energy between the valence and conduction bands of a semiconductor. This energy interval cannot be occupied by electrons (energy gap). The band gap of opto-electronic semiconductor components determines their operating wavelengths.

Bandwidth

→ Fiber bandwidth

Backscattering

A small fraction of the light that is deflected out of the original direction of propagation by → scattering suffers a reversal of direction, i.e. it propagates in the optical waveguide towards the → transmitter. By examining the temporal response of the backscattered light with the aid of a beam splitter at the transmitter, it is not only possible to measure the length and → attenuation of an installed optical waveguide from one end, but also local irregularities, e.g. optical power loss at → splices.

Branching element

→ star coupler, → tee coupler

Chromatic dispersion

Combination of the two related effects → material dispersion and → waveguide dispersion.

Cladding

All optically transparent material comprising an optical waveguide excluding the → core.

Cladding diameter

Diameter of the smallest circle that encloses the surface of the cladding.

Coating

→ Primary coating

Connector

→ Optical waveguide connector

Core

In an optical waveguide the central region provided for light transmission. It is defined by the smallest cross section enclosed by a line for which the → refractive index $n = n_2 + k \cdot (n_1 - n_2)$, where n_1 is the largest refractive index in the core, n_2 is the refractive index in the cladding and k is a constant $(0 \leqq k \leqq 0.1)$. Any central dip in the refractive index at the center of the core is not taken into account.

Core diameter

Diameter of the smallest circle that encloses the core area. The core radius is the radius of this circle.

Coupler

→ Optical waveguide coupler

Cutback method

→ Cutback technique

Cutback technique

In order to determine the → attenuation of an optical waveguide it is necessary to know the optical power at the input end (P_1) and at the output end (P_2) as accurately as possible. For precision measurements a → transmitter is first coupled to the optical waveguide and P_2 is measured. The waveguide is then cut at a distance of about 1 m from the transmitter without changing the launching conditions and the power at the end of the short fiber is measured. It is equal to the power P_1 previously fed into the long waveguide. This avoids the problem of making the launching conditions reproducible.

Cutoff wavelength

The shortest wavelength at which only the → fundamental mode of an optical waveguide is capable of propagation. For → single-mode fibers the cutoff wavelength must be smaller than the wavelength of the light to be transmitted.

Dark current noise

The noise component in a → photodiode resulting from the shot noise of the current flowing in the unilluminated photodiode.

Digital transmission

Transmission of a discrete signal (generally obtained by digitizing an analog signal) preferably by means of binary light pulses in a periodic time pattern.

Dispersion

Spread of the signal delay in an optical waveguide. It consists of various components: → modal dispersion, → material dispersion, → waveguide dispersion. As a result of its dispersion an optical waveguide acts as a low pass filter for the transmitted signals (→ transfer function).

Double heterostructure

Layer sequence in an optoelectronic semiconductor device in which the active semiconductor layer is bounded by two cladding layers with higher → band gaps. In the → laser diode the double heterostructure performs a dual function: confinement of the charge carriers and dielectric waveguiding.

Emission

→ Spontaneous emission, → stimulated emission

Energy gap

→ Band gap

Equilibrium mode distribution

The distribution of optical power among the individual → modes of → multimode optical waveguides that develops in long fibers regardless of the method of excitation. Fibers are excited with an approximation of this light distribution with the aid of → mode scramblers in order to obtain reproducible results when measuring the → attenuation coefficient or the → transmission bandwidth.

Equivalent step-index profile (ESI)

Description of → single-mode fibers with arbitrary → index profile by means of the characteristics of a → step-index fiber, whose two parameters → core diameter and → refractive index difference are so chosen that the field distributions (→ near field radiation pattern) are almost identical in both fibers.

Far-field radiation pattern

Distribution of the optical power radiated from an optical source or from an optical waveguide as a function of the angle relative to the optical axis ($\rightarrow$ radiant intensity). It determines the field distribution at a large distance from the light source and, in the case of optical waveguides, it is dependent upon the waveguide length and excitation as well as upon the optical wavelength.

Fiber

$\rightarrow$ Optical waveguide.

Fiber bandwidth

The frequency at which the magnitude of the $\rightarrow$ transfer function of an optical waveguide has fallen to half the zero frequency value, i.e. the frequency at which the signal attenuation has increased by 3 dB. Since the bandwidth of an optical waveguide is approximately reciprocal to its length ($\rightarrow$ mode mixing), the bandwidth-length product is often quoted as a quality characteristic.

Fiber buffer

It consists of one or more materials and serves to mechanically isolate the $\rightarrow$ fiber (prevention of $\rightarrow$ microbending) and to protect against damage.

Fiber cladding

$\rightarrow$ Cladding

Fiber core

$\rightarrow$ Core

Fiber tail

$\rightarrow$ Pigtail

Fundamental mode

The lowest order mode of an optical waveguide ($\rightarrow$ modes). It usually has a bell shaped (Gauss-like) field distribution and its compass in the near field is characterized by the $\rightarrow$ spot size. It is the only mode capable of propagation in $\rightarrow$ single-mode fibers.

Graded-index fiber

Optical waveguide with a graded-index profile, i.e. with a $\rightarrow$ refractive index profile which varies continuously over the waveguide cross section. The profile of normal graded-index fibers can be approximated by a $\rightarrow$ power-law index profile with $1 < g < 3$.

Group index

The velocity of propagation of light pulses in optical media is determined by the (usually somewhat larger) group index $n_g = n - \lambda \cdot dn/d\lambda$ and not by the $\rightarrow$ refractive index n.

Index of refraction

$\rightarrow$ Refractive index

Index profile

Curve of the $\rightarrow$ refractive index over the cross section of an optical waveguide ($\rightarrow$ step-index fiber, $\rightarrow$ graded-index fiber).

Induced emission

$\rightarrow$ Stimulated emission

Injection fiber

$\rightarrow$ Launching fiber

Injection laser diode (ILD)

$\rightarrow$ Laser diode

Insertion loss

The $\rightarrow$ attenuation caused by the insertion of an optical component, e.g. a $\rightarrow$ connector or a $\rightarrow$ coupler, in an optical transmission system.

Intensity

$\rightarrow$ Irradiance

Intermodal distortion

$\rightarrow$ Multimode distortion

Irradiance

Power density at a surface through which radiation passes, e.g. at the radiating surface of a light source or at the cross section of an optical waveguide (normal unit: W/cm^2).

Laser diode (LD)

Semiconductor diode which emits coherent light above a $\rightarrow$ threshold current ($\rightarrow$ stimulated emission). Continuous operation is only possible with $\rightarrow$ double heterostructure laser diodes. A distinction is made between gain-guided and index-guided laser diodes whose characteristics, e.g. the spectral width of their radiation or their noise characteristics, can differ quite considerably.

Launch angle

Angle between the propagation direction of the incident light and the optical axis of an optical waveguide. For the incident light to be coupled into the waveguide this angle must lie between zero and a maximum value which depends upon the position on the fiber end surface, more particularly upon the local $\rightarrow$ refractive index difference relative to the $\rightarrow$ cladding ($\rightarrow$ numerical aperture, $\rightarrow$ phase-space diagram).

Launching fiber

A $\rightarrow$ fiber which is inserted between an optical source and another fiber in order to excite the modes in the fiber in a particular way. It can also consist of several fibers connected in cascade and finds its principal application in measuring setups ($\rightarrow$ mode scrambler).

Leaky modes

In the boundary region between the guided $\rightarrow$ modes of an optical waveguide and the light waves which are not capable of propagation there are the so-called leaky modes which, strictly speaking, are not guided but are capable of limited propagation with increased attenuation. Leaky modes are a possible source of error in the measurement of fiber $\rightarrow$ attenuation, but their effect can be reduced by mode strippers.

Light-emitting diode (LED)

Semiconductor diode which emits incoherent light when forward biased (→ spontaneous emission). Special high radiance LEDs of → double heterostructure design are available for operation with optical waveguides.

Lightguide

→ Optical waveguide

Light waves

Electromagnetic waves in the region of optical frequencies. The term "light" was originally restricted to radiation visible to the human eye with a wavelength λ between 400 and 700 nm. However, it has become customary to refer to radiation in the spectral regions adjacent to visible light (e.g. in the near infrared from 700 to about 2000 nm) as light in order to emphasize the physical and technical characteristics they have in common with visible light. As an example, the names of both the radiation sources LED and laser contain the word "light". "Optic" and "photo" are two words related to "light" which have been derived from Greek and occur in many compounds. They too have experienced the same extension of meaning as light.

Macrobending

Macroscopic axial deviations of a fiber from a straight line, in contrast to → microbending.

Material dispersion

The → dispersion associated with a non-monochromatic light source due to the wavelength dependence of the → refractive index n of a material or of the light velocity in this material. It is characterized by the material dispersion parameter

$$M(\lambda) = \frac{-1}{c} \cdot \frac{dn_g}{d\lambda} = \frac{\lambda}{c} \cdot \frac{d^2n}{d\lambda^2}$$

where n_g is the → group index and n is the phase refractive index of the material. For the majority of optical waveguide materials M becomes zero at a certain wavelength λ_0 in the vicinity of 1300 nm. The usual unit for M is ns/nm · km; the sign has been so chosen that M is positive for $\lambda < \lambda_0$. The delay spread is obtained by multiplying M by the spectral width $\Delta\lambda$ of the light employed and by the length L of the optical waveguide, provided λ_0 does not lie within the spectrum of the light source.

Microbending

Curvatures of the fiber which involve axial displacements of a few micrometers and spatial wavelengths of a few millimeters. Microbends cause loss of light and consequently increase the → attenuation of the fiber.

Modal dispersion

→ Multimode distortion

Modal distortion

→ Multimode distortion

Modal noise

Disturbance in → multimode fibers fed by → laser diodes. It occurs when the fibers contain elements with mode-dependent attenuation (e.g. imperfect → splices), and it is the more severe the better the coherence of the laser light, i.e. the more pronounced its granulation is. A cure is provided by improvements in connector and splicing techniques, as well as by the use of → light-emitting diodes or multimode laser diodes with a broad spectrum, or by the use of → single-mode fibers.

Modes

Discrete optical waves that can propagate in optical waveguides. They are eigenvalue solutions to the differential equations which characterize the waveguide. Whereas in a → single-mode fiber only one mode, the → fundamental mode, can propagate, there are several hundred modes in a → multimode fiber which differ in field pattern and propagation velocity (→ multimode distortion). The upper limit to the number of modes is determined by the → core diameter and → numerical aperture of the waveguide (→ mode volume, → phase-space diagram).

Mode distortion

→ Multimode distortion

Mode mixer

→ Mode scrambler

Mode mixing

The numerous → modes of a → multimode fiber differ inter alia in their propagation velocities. As long as they propagate independently of each other, the → fiber bandwidth varies inversely as the fiber length due to → multimode distortion. As a result of inhomogeneities of the fiber geometry and of the → index profile, a gradual energy exchange occurs between modes with differing velocities. Due to this mode mixing, the bandwidth of long multimode fibers is greater than the value obtained by linear extrapolation from measurements on short fibers.

Mode scrambler

Optical component that is inserted between → transmitter and → multimode fiber for test purposes in order to excite the fiber with an approximation of the → equilibrium mode distribution.

Mode volume

The product of cross sectional area and solid angle available in an optical waveguide for light propagation. It is proportional to the number of → modes capable of propagation (→ phase-space diagram). In practice the guided optical power is generally not uniformly distributed among all modes capable of propagation, e.g. because the modes were not uniformly excited or because some modes are subject to above average attenuation, in particular those near the acceptance limit. This results in a reduction in the utilized mode volume as well as in the extent of the → near field and → far field radiation patterns of the optical waveguide.

Monomode optical waveguide

→ Single-mode fiber

Multimode distortion

The signal distortion in an optical waveguide resulting from the superposition of modes with differing delays. ($\to$ Dispersion)

Multimode fiber

Optical waveguide whose $\to$ core diameter is large compared with the optical wavelength and in which, consequently, a large number of $\to$ modes are capable of propagation. The $\to$ multimode distortion can be kept small by means of a graded-index profile ($\to$ graded-index fiber) so that large $\to$ fiber bandwidths are attainable, which, however, are still exceeded by those of $\to$ single-mode fibers.

Multimode optical waveguide

$\to$ Multimode fiber

Near-field radiation pattern

Distribution of the $\to$ irradiance over an emitting surface, e.g. over the cross section of an optical waveguide.

Numerical aperture

Sine of the maximum possible $\to$ launch angle of an optical waveguide ($\to$ phase-space diagram). Geometric optics yield the theoretical value $A_N = \sqrt{n_1^2 - n_2^2}$, where n_1 is the largest $\to$ refractive index in the $\to$ core and n_2 is the refractive index in the $\to$ cladding. Measured values are usually smaller, since the $\to$ far field radiation pattern of the optical waveguide is not sharply limited at large angles. In practice, therefore, the sine of a suitably defined $\to$ acceptance angle is referred to as the numerical aperture.

Operating lifetime

Period of time during which the principal parameters of a continuously operated component, e.g. a laser diode, remain within a prescribed range.

Optical fiber waveguide

$\to$ Optical waveguide

Optical receiver

Unit for converting optical signals into electrical signals. It consists of a $\to$ photodiode with $\to$ pigtail and $\to$ connector, as well as a low-noise amplifier and electronic circuits for signal processing. Where possible the principal components of the receiver are combined to form a compact subassembly, the receiver module.

Optical transmitter

Unit for converting electrical signals into optical signals. It consists of an optical source ($\to$ laser diode or $\to$ light-emitting diode) with $\to$ pigtail, $\to$ connector and driver amplifier, as well as further electronic circuits. In the case of laser diodes in particular, a $\to$ photodiode with regulating amplifier to monitor and stabilize the radiant power are necessary, as well as frequently a temperature sensor and a Peltier cooler for stabilizing the operating temperature. Where possible the principal components of the transmitter are combined to form a compact subassembly, the transmitter module.

Optical waveguide

Dielectric waveguide with a $\to$ core consisting of optically transparent material of low $\to$ attenuation (usually silica glass) and with $\to$ cladding consisting of optically transparent material of lower $\to$ refractive index than that of the core. It is used for the transmission of signals with $\to$ light waves and is frequently referred to as a fiber, particularly in compound words.

In addition, there are planar dielectric waveguide structures in some optical components, e.g. $\to$ laser diodes, which are also referred to as optical waveguides.

Optical waveguide connector

Component for the easy disconnection and reconnection of two optical waveguides. In general the $\to$ insertion loss of a connector is higher than that of a $\to$ splice.

Optical waveguide coupler

A passive optical device whose purpose is to couple light between a source and a waveguide or between several optical waveguides. A particular importance attaches to couplers which facilitate the establishment of optical fiber networks for interconnecting several transmitters and receivers ($\to$ tee coupler, $\to$ star coupler).

Optical waveguide splice

$\to$ Splice

Phase-space diagram

Representation of the light guiding properties of an optical waveguide in a coordinate system particularly suitable for this purpose. The coordinates are the area $A = \pi r^2$ of a circle with radius r and the solid angle

$$\Omega = 2\pi \cdot (1 - \cos \Theta) \approx \pi \cdot \sin^2 \Theta$$

of a cylindrical cone with a vertex angle $\pm \Theta$. The phase-space diagram shows the acceptance limit curve for guided $\to$ modes determined by the $\to$ numerical aperture, $\to$ core diameter or core radius and $\to$ index profile of an optical waveguide, as well as the distribution of the $\to$ radiance over the cross section and solid angle ($\to$ mode volume). The geometric area under the acceptance limit curve is proportional to the number of guided modes.

Photodiode

Semiconductor diode which absorbs light and feeds the released charge carriers to an external circuit in the form of photocurrent. A distinction is made between $\to$ PIN photodiodes and $\to$ avalanche photodiodes.

Photon noise

$\to$ Quantum noise

Pigtail

A short length of optical fiber for coupling optical components, e.g. a laser diode to a connector. It is usually permanently fixed to the components.

PIN-FET receiver

$\to$ Optical receiver with a $\to$ PIN photodiode and a low-noise amplifier with a high impedance input, whose first stage incorporates a field-effect transistor (FET).

PIN photodiode

→ Photodiode with → absorption primarily in a depletion layer (i-region) within its pn-junction. Such a diode has a high quantum efficiency but no internal current gain, in contrast to the → avalanche photodiode.

Power density

→ Irradiance

Power-law index profile

A class of rotationally symmetrical → index profiles characterized by

$$n(r) = n_1 \cdot \sqrt{1 - 2\,\Delta\,(r/a)^g} \quad (\text{where } r < a)$$

or by

$$n(r) = n_2 = n_1 \cdot \sqrt{1 - 2\,\Delta} \quad (\text{where } r \geqq a)$$

where $n(r)$ is the → refractive index as a function of the radius r and n_1 is the largest refractive index in the → core, n_2 is the refractive index in the → cladding, a is the core radius and g the parameter defining the shape of the profile. The cases of particular interest in practice are $g \approx 2$ (→ graded-index fiber) and $g \to \infty$ (→ step-index fiber). The parameter Δ, the normalized → refractive index difference, is always small compared with unity (e.g. 0.01).

Power-law profile

→ Power-law index profile

Primary coating

The plastic coating applied directly to the cladding surface of the optical waveguide during manufacture to preserve the integrity of the surface.

Profile dispersion

The → refractive index of glass depends upon the optical wavelength, however, not in exactly the same way for all of the glasses incorporated in an optical waveguide. The → index profile of → graded-index fibers (above all the → refractive index difference) is, consequently, likewise wavelength dependent. For this reason it is only possible to approach the optimum profile in a narrow wavelength region which permits minimum → multimode distortion, i.e. maximum → transmission bandwidth. At other wavelengths the index profile is not optimum and the bandwidth is correspondingly small.

Quantum noise

The → absorption of light and its conversion into photocurrent in a → photodiode is not a continuous process. On the contrary, the light and current are quantized (photons, electrons), and the conversion process is subject to statistical fluctuations. The resulting signal-dependent noise component in the photodiode is referred to as quantum noise or photocurrent shot noise.

Radiance

Density of the radiant power in phase-space i.e. relative to emitting area and solid angle (normal unit: W/cm²sr). By integration over the coordinates of the → phase-space diagram the distributions of → irradiance and → radiant intensity, i.e. → near-field radiation pattern and → far-field radiation pattern of a light source or an optical waveguide, can be calculated from the radiance.

Radiant intensity

Power density in the far field of an optical source, i.e. the optical power referred to the solid angle (normal unit: W/sr).

Receiver

→ Optical receiver

Receiver module

→ Optical receiver

Receiver sensitivity

The optical power required by a receiver for low-error signal transmission. In the case of → digital signal transmission, the mean optical power is usually quoted (in W or dBm) at which a bit error rate of 10^{-9} is attained.

Refractive index

The ratio n of the velocity of light in vacuum to that in an optically dense medium (e.g. glass).

More accurate term: phase refractive index

Refractive index contrast

→ Refractive index difference

Refractive index difference

Difference between the maximum → refractive index n_1 occurring in the → core of an optical waveguide and the refractive index n_2 in the → cladding. The refractive index difference determines the magnitude of the → numerical aperture and the level of the additional attenuation caused by → microbending. The normalized refractive index difference, or refractive index contrast,

$$\Delta = (n_1^2 - n_2^2)/2n_1^2 \approx (n_1 - n_2)/n_1$$

is generally used for calculations.

Refractive index profile

→ Index profile

Scattering

Principle cause of the → attenuation of an optical waveguide. It results from microscopic density fluctuations in the glass which deflect part of the guided light so far out of its original direction that it escapes from the waveguide. This effect is very weak at wavelengths above 1600 nm; towards shorter wavelengths, however, it increases as the fourth power of the wavelength (Rayleigh scattering).

Single-mode fiber

Optical waveguide with a small → core diameter, in which only a single mode, the → fundamental mode, is capable of propagation. This type of fiber is particularly suitable for wideband transmission over large distances, since its → bandwidth is limited only by → chromatic dispersion.

Single-mode optical waveguide

→ Single-mode fiber

Speckle noise

→ Modal noise

Splice

A permanent joint between two optical waveguides. A distinction is made between bonded and fusion splices.

Spontaneous emission

This occurs when there are too many electrons in the conduction band of a semiconductor. These electrons drop spontaneously into vacant locations in the valence band, a photon being emitted for each electron. The emitted light is incoherent.

Spot size

Only part of the optical power is guided in the → core of → single-mode fibers, since its → near-field radiation pattern is bell shaped and extends into the → cladding. This field distribution depends upon the → refractive index profile and the optical wavelength and determines the splice and bending losses of the fiber. It can, for instance, be characterized by the radius at which the → irradiance in the near field has fallen to $1/e^2$ of its maximum value. However, there are many more definitions in use.

Star coupler

Central component for optical fiber networks with passive star configurations. It interconnects numerous → transmitters and → receivers and distributes the optical signal power supplied by a connected transmitter uniformly to all connected receivers.

Steady-state mode distribution

→ Equilibrium mode distribution

Step-index fiber

Optical waveguide with a step-index profile, i.e. with a → refractive index profile characterized by a constant → refractive index within the → core and a steep drop in the refractive index at the boundary between the core and the → cladding. This profile can be approximated by a → power-law index profile with g > 10.

Step index optical waveguide

→ Step-index fiber

Stimulated emission

This occurs when photons in a semiconductor stimulate available excess charge carriers to radiative recombination, i.e. to the emission of photons. The emitted light is identical in wavelength and phase with the incident light (coherent).

Tapping element

→ Tee coupler

Tee coupler

Optical component for dividing the power in an optical waveguide between two outgoing optical waveguides. Conversely, it can also be used for combining the light of two optical waveguides.

Threshold current

The driving current above which the amplification of the light wave in a → laser diode becomes greater than the optical losses, so that → stimulated emission commences. The threshold current is strongly temperature dependent.

Transfer function

An optical waveguide acts as a low pass filter for the transmitted signals. Whereas at low signal frequencies only the CW attenuation affects the signal level (→ attenuation), higher frequencies are subject to additional attenuation due to the → dispersion of the waveguide. This additional attenuation is characterized by the transfer function, which has a maximum value at zero frequency and slowly approaches zero with increasing frequency. The shape of the transfer function is approximately Gaussian. Strictly speaking the transfer function of an optical waveguide is complex; however, the phase distortion is usually so small that it is sufficient to quote the magnitude of the function.

Transmission bandwidth

→ Fiber bandwidth

Transmitter

→ Optical transmitter

Transmitter module

→ Optical transmitter

Tunnelling mode

→ Leaky modes

Wavelength division multiplexing (WDM)

Simultaneous transmission of several signals in an optical waveguide at differing wavelengths.

Waveguide dispersion

The → dispersion associated with a non-monochromatic light source resulting from the fact that the ratio a/λ and consequently the field distributions and group velocities of the modes of an optical waveguide are wavelength dependent (a is the core radius, λ the optical wavelength). In practice waveguide dispersion always acts in combination with → material dispersion; the combined effect is referred to as chromatic dispersion.

MCI Fiber Optic Network

"MCI" – a company which owns and operates the second largest broadband microwave network in the world, utilizing both analog and digital systems in order to keep pace with the rapidly changing telecommunications environment in the USA, has decided to implement major large capacity fiber-optic routes.

Because of the large distances involved, these will employ single-mode fibers with the related optoelectronic equipment operating at 1300 nm.
All digital switching will be employed in the new network structure shown below, while the existing analog network will be integrated via transmultiplexers.

The first sections of this network, scheduled to be implemented between 1984 and 1985, will give a sizeable majority of U.S. telephone subscribers access to the MCI network for the widest possible range of telecommunications services.

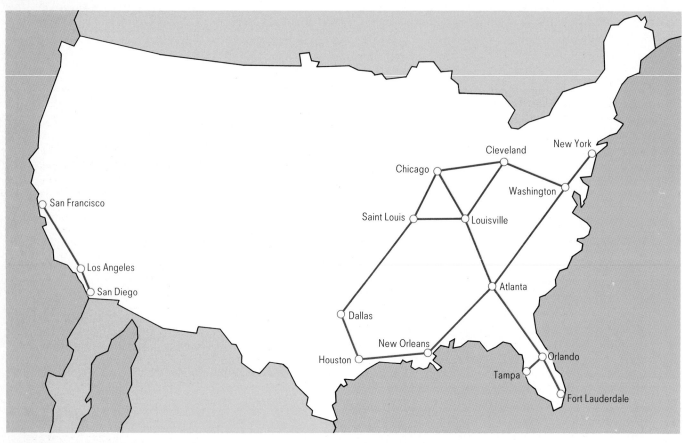

The new MCI fiber-optic network for which Siecor Optical Cable is a major cable supplier (red marked).
Most of the cables are of the Siecor minibundle design, containing approximately 20 to 100 single-mode fibers

telcom report

Published and issued by:
Siemens Aktiengesellschaft,
Berlin and Munich
© 1983 by Siemens Aktiengesellschaft,
Berlin and Munich
All rights reserved

Responsible for the contents:
D. Rost, Munich, Erlangen
Publishing director:
E. Pollak, Erlangen, Munich
Engineering periodicals:
G. Hübner, Erlangen, Munich
Editors: P. Sprenar, Munich
          H. Addicks, Munich

Professional Adviser
in the Public Communication
Networks Division:
W. Maletz, Munich

Printed by: Passavia Druckerei GmbH,
D-8390 Passau
Printed in the Federal Republic of Germany

Individual articles may be photocopied, also for use within readers' own companies, and extracts may be reprinted, provided that the author and source are acknowledged. However, articles may not be reprinted in full without express permission from the editor. Summaries of individual articles appearing in this journal may be reproduced for reference purposes and circulated free of charge, provided that the author and source are acknowledged.

The English edition of "telcom report" is published six times a year.
Special issues are not included in the subscription.
Available from bookstores and news agents.

Inquiries relating to the contents of this journal should be addressed to:
Siemens Aktiengesellschaft,
Redaktion von "telcom report",
Hellabrunner Str. 1, Postfach 103
D-8000 Munich 90,
Federal Republic of Germany.
Telephone (089) 234-3751,
Telefax (089) 234-3090,
Telex 52 10033

For information on where to obtain Siemens technical publications, periodicals, textbooks and instruction aids, please write to:
Siemens Aktiengesellschaft, ZVW 50,
Postfach 32 40.
D-8520 Erlangen 2,
Federal Republic of Germany.
Telephone (091 31) 7-6566,
Telefax (09131) 7-24349,
Telex 6 29825-5

Keil, H.; Pascher, H.   **SIEMENS**

Communications Enter a New Era with Fiber Optics

4 figures

telcom report 6 (1983)

Special Issue "Optical Communications", pp. 4 to 7

The technology for communication via optical fibers is now ready for practical application. All the requirements have now been met: complete systems for optical communications, i.e. optical cable with the necessary connectors and couplers, as well as multiplex and line equipment, are available. Such systems have already found applications in telecommunications and industry.

Descriptors: optical communications; optical waveguide systems; optoelectronic transducer; transmission system; integrated optics

---

Geckeler, S.   **SIEMENS**

Physical Principles of Optical Waveguides

10 figures, 12 references

telcom report 6 (1983)

Special Issue "Optical Communications", pp. 9 to 14

This article summarizes the physical principles involved and the methods of describing the propagation of light in optical waveguides, and defines terms such as the velocity of light, refractive index, refraction, total internal reflection, step-index fiber, acceptance angle, numerical aperture, launched power, attenuation, differential mode delay, low-pass characteristic, graded-index fiber, refractive index profile, phase space diagram, the fiber as an optical waveguide, modes, wave vector, mode designation, single-mode fibers and material dispersion.

Descriptors: step-index fiber; graded-index fiber; single-mode fiber; attenuation; material dispersion; mode

---

Weyrich, C.; Zschauer, K.-H.   **SIEMENS**

Principles of Optoelectronic Signal Conversion

9 figures, 7 references

telcom report 6 (1983)

Special Issue "Optical Communications", pp. 14 to 19

Starting with the elementary interactions between photons and electrons in a solid, the authors describe the generation and detection of optical radiation with pn junction semiconductors. These phenomena give rise to the basic requirements placed on the semiconductor material employed. For transmitters, heterostructures of GaAlAs on GaAs and InGaAsP on InP are favored. In the case of receivers, InGaAsP on InP is used in addition to Si and Ge as material for photodiodes.

Descriptors: optical transition in semiconductors; spontaneous emission; induced emission; absorption; III-V compound semiconductor; heterostructure; LED; laser diode; photodiode

---

Gier, J.; Panzer, K.   **SIEMENS**

Principles of Optoelectronic Signal Transmission

7 figures, 1 table, 13 references

telcom report 6 (1983)

Special Issue "Optical Communications", pp. 20 to 25

The properties of optoelectronic transducers and optical waveguides are of particular significance in the design of optical communication systems. The available output power, the linearity and spectral properties of the optical transmitters and the signal-to-noise ratios and sensitivity of the optical receivers are particularly important parameters of active components.

Descriptors: optoelectronic transducer; linearity; noise; receiver sensitivity; bandwidth; modulation; analog signal transmission; digital signal transmission; regenerator spacing

---

Schneider, H.; Zeidler, G.   **SIEMENS**

Manufacturing Processes and Designs of Optical Waveguides

15 figures, 14 references

telcom report 6 (1983)

Special Issue "Optical Communications", pp. 27 to 33

Low-loss optical waveguides are manufactured by converting gaseous starting materials into high-purity glass. The glass is first deposited in the form of rods (preforms) and these are then drawn to form a glass fiber. The article describes the design (core, cladding, coating) and properties (attenuation, bandwidth) of graded-index and single-mode fibers.

Descriptors: manufacture of optical waveguides; inside vapour deposition; outside vapour deposition; graded-index fiber; single-mode fiber

---

Oestreich, U.   **SIEMENS**

Fiber-Optic Cables for Long-Haul Communication Links

7 figures

telcom report 6 (1983)

Special Issue "Optical Communications", pp. 33 to 37

The demand for minimum loss without temporal variations and for maximum service life in long-haul fiber-optic cables has led in the Federal Republic of Germany to the concept of the loose, filled buffer tube with one or more (preferably 10) fibers. The author describes tried and tested cable designs and introduces a configuration consisting of a new high-tensile jacket over the cable core combining the filling compound, barrier layer, strength members and jacket in one unit. Local and long-haul cables follow the same concept.

Descriptors: fiber-optic cable; long-haul cable; cable design; high-tensile jacket

---

Mayr, E.; Schinko, H.; Schöber, G.   **SIEMENS**

Fiber-Optic Unit-Based Cables in the Local Network

6 figures, 2 tables, 4 references

telcom report 6 (1983)

Special Issue "Optical Communications", pp. 37 to 40

The large bandwidth of optical fibers enables a wide range of information and communication services to be provided in the local network. The basic module of high fiber-count optical cables is the multifiber unit, consisting of a tube with a filling compound and up to ten fibers. In terms of mechanical strength, these cables are as rugged as conventional copper cables and in view of their non-metallic design are considerably lighter, at no risk from lightning and immune to external electromagnetic interference.

Descriptors: local network; fiber-optic unit-based cable; unit; design of high fiber-count cables; non-metallic design

---

Zeidler, G.   **SIEMENS**

Designing Fiber-Optic Cable Systems

3 figures, 1 table, 13 references

telcom report 6 (1983)

Special Issue "Optical Communications", pp. 41 to 45

Starting with the attenuation and bandwidth parameters measured by various methods, the author goes on to provide design equations for planning cable systems to specified transmission characteristics.

Descriptors: attenuation and bandwidth of optical waveguides; transmission plan of optical cable systems; allowances and reserves; length dependence of bandwidth

data report

Information on the application of data technology in industry and administration. Special subjects: commercial data processing, office communication and process control computer systems.

Order No. L-11/x83-101
ISSN 0341-6526

data report

Volume XVIII, 1983, A4
44 pages per issue, 6 issues per year
Annual subscription: 69 DM
Price per copy: 12.70 DM

"data report" provides information on the manifold uses of and extensive range of openings for state-of-the-art data technology in administration, industry and science. It has as its main subjects the hardware, software and application of data processing systems, as well as market and development activities in the fields of data and information systems, communications and process control computer systems. The subject spectrum goes beyond this too, stretching from efficient communication in the professional and private sectors using data, voice, text and image/video transmission to automation systems with process control computers and microprocessors.
This journal is written for readers with commercial or industrial management qualifications. It is aimed at people who organize and use data systems in the following sectors: trade, credit banks, insurances, industry, public authorities, universities, colleges, associations, technical and industrial organizations and advisory agencies. People addressed in these areas are predominantly ones who take decisions and mold opinions.

Goldmann, H.   **SIEMENS**

Installation of Fiber-Optic Cables

6 figures, 2 references

telcom report 6 (1983)

Special Issue "Optical Communications", pp. 46 to 49

Fiber-optic cables can be easily installed using all known methods. The subjects covered by this article include the installation of long cable lengths, installation by hand, *"injection"* of cables into ducts with the aid of compressed air, multiple utilization of ducts and the "lashing" of fiber-optic cables to high-voltage open-wire lines. In this connection, the author describes an intermediate take-up unit and a clip-fitting device, which are used during installation.

Descriptors: installation; multiple utilization of ducts; cap-sealing; lashing to messengers or high-voltage lines; installation by hand; cable *injection;* cable roller guide; intermediate take-up unit; clip-fitting device

---

Bark, P.R.; Szentesi, O.I.   **SIEMENS**

Fiber-Optic Projects in the USA

5 figures, 1 table, 11 references

telcom report 6 (1983)

Special Issue "Optical Communications", pp. 66 to 71

The authors describe the activities of Siecor Optical Cable in the field of optical cable systems in the USA. The article discusses typical cable plant and the installation techniques usually employed in the USA. The authors describe installation outdoors (duct, buried and aerial cable), in buildings and underwater. In most cases, the operating data gathered showed improvements over comparable copper cable plant.

Descriptors: fiber-optic cable plant in the USA; installation and splicing techniques; duct cable; buried cable; aerial cable; in-house cable; submarine cable; reliability; emergency operation

---

Odemar, N.; Steinmann, P.   **SIEMENS**

Jointing Techniques for Fiber-Optic Cables

8 figures, 4 references

telcom report 6 (1983)

Special Issue "Optical Communications", pp. 50 to 54

The use of optical cables calls for techniques for jointing the fibers quickly and easily and for connecting these fibers to peripheral equipment. The authors describe jointing requirements, the techniques developed on the basis of those requirements and the fusion splicers and assembly equipment suitable for field applications. The connectors and splicers have already been used successfully in many locations both in Germany and abroad.

Descriptors: optical waveguide; mechanical splicer; fusion splicer; groove connector; single-fiber connector

---

Clemen, Ch.; Heinen, J.; Plihal, M.   **SIEMENS**

High-Radiance Light-Emitting Diodes for Optical Transmitters

12 figures, 15 references

telcom report 6 (1983)

Special Issue "Optical Communications", pp. 73 to 78

This article deals with light-emitting diodes as optical transmitters for fiber-optic systems. The authors describe three selected devices made from GaAs, GaAlAs and InGaAsP with emission wavelengths of 900, 830 and 1300 nm for system applications covering transmission rates from a few Mbit/s over a few meters to more than 100 Mbit/s over 10 km. Details of the design, manufacture and properties of the diodes are given.

Descriptors: optical signal transmission; optical transmitter; light-emitting diode; double heterostructure; GaAs, AlGaAs, InP and InGaAsP material systems

---

Witt, G.   **SIEMENS**

Closures and Containers for Fiber-Optic Cables

7 figures, 1 table, 2 references

telcom report 6 (1983)

Special Issue "Optical Communications", pp. 55 to 58

Closures and containers are also required on the transmission links employing optical cables. With the backing of many years' experience with conventional telecommunication cable systems, designers have adapted the well-tested universal closures and regenerator containers to the special requirements of the new transmission medium. In this way, an entire range of closures and containers was developed for this new technology.

Descriptors: optical cable; straight closure; branch closure; universal closure; optical pack; vault closure; regenerator container

---

Amann, M.-Ch.; Mettler, K.; Wolf, H.D.   **SIEMENS**

Laser Diodes – High-Power Light Sources for Optical Communications

10 figures, 12 references

telcom report 6 (1983)

Special Issue "Optical Communications", pp. 79 to 84

Laser diodes are virtually the only light sources currently available for transmitting signals over optical waveguides at high bit rates. The important system requirements can be fulfilled by the two laser structure families and with technologically controllable semiconductor materials. However, the performance and limits of optical communication systems are to a large extent defined by the characteristics of the laser employed.

Descriptors: laser diode structure family; GaAlAs/GaAs laser; InGaAsP/InP laser; temperature sensitivity; spectral characteristic; system aspects

---

Köstler, G.   **SIEMENS**

Fiber-Optic Projects for the Deutsche Bundespost and Other Users in Europe

7 figures, 1 table, 14 references

telcom report 6 (1983)

Special Issue "Optical Communications", pp. 59 to 65

This article aims to provide an overview of the fiber-optic cable systems installed by Siemens in Europe; the author discusses the seven projects for the Deutsche Bundespost – covering all levels of the telephone network. Fiber-optic cable systems of "other users" – categorized according to PTT and industry – are described with the aid of selected typical examples.

Descriptors: fiber-optic project; fiber-optic cable; operational experience; network level; development of fiber-optic cable technology

---

Althaus, H.L.; Kuhn, G.   **SIEMENS**

Modular Laser Source

10 figures, 16 references

telcom report 6 (1983)

Special Issue "Optical Communications", pp. 84 to 90

This article describes the design of a laser module for use in optical communications. The module contains the laser diode, with pigtail, optical power and temperature sensors, as well as a thermoelectric cooler. Specific laser characteristics, the modular design principle, as well as practical qualification and test methods employed for this module are described.

Descriptors: optical waveguide systems; laser source; laser characteristic; modular design; active cooling; test methods; operating life

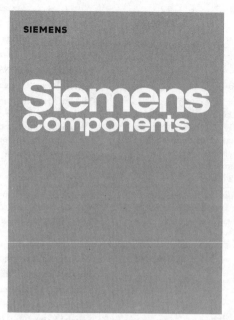

Siemens Components

For users of electronic and electro-mechanical components, including microcomputers; circuitry and applications.

Order No. L-07/x83-101
ISSN 0173-1734

Siemens Components

Volume XXI, 1983, A4,
36 pages per issue, 6 issues per year
Annual subscription: 25 DM
Price per copy: 4.20 DM

This journal is of help to everyone who wants information on the broad field of electronic and electromechanical components and who wishes to broaden his knowledge. The main aim of the specialist articles is to provide details and ideas concerning the utilization of components, their technologies and their structure. The use of components in specific applications is also dealt with, while articles indicating trends and interviews afford an overview of the development of particular product groups. Several pages are devoted to describing new products and providing their technical data.

Siemens Components is written for engineers and technicians in development departments, designers, applications engineers and specialized staff in purchasing departments.

Branches of trade: electrical and electronics industry, fine mechanics, optics, mechanical engineering, chemical industry, broadcasting stations (radio, TV), public authorities, science and education in the electronics sector, advisory agencies.

Plihal, M.; Späth, W.; Trommer, R. **SIEMENS**

Photodiodes as Detectors for Optical Fiber Transmission Systems

12 figures, 10 references

telcom report 6 (1983)

Special Issue "Optical Communications", pp. 91 to 95

Simple silicon PIN photodiodes and avalanche photodiodes with complex doping structures are used in the transmission window around 850 nm. Photodiodes for the longwave transmission windows around 1300 and 1500 nm consist of Ge or III-V semiconductor alloys, in particular InGaAsP material systems which can be deposited epitaxially on an InP substrate. The design, fabrication and characteristics of the diodes are described.

Descriptors: optical signal transmission; detector; PIN photodiode; avalanche photodiode; Si, Ge, InP and InGaAs material systems

---

Braun, E.; Keil, H. **SIEMENS**

Optical Waveguide Transmission Systems

6 figures, 3 tables, 10 references

telcom report 6 (1983)

Special Issue "Optical Communications", pp. 113 to 118

The technical design of systems for optical communications is principally dependent upon the nature of the signals to be transmitted, since it determines the way in which the optoelectronic transducer is driven. Depending upon the application, a distinction is made between transmission systems for the subscriber line network, for short-haul links and for long-haul links. In addition, the effect of the selection and stressing of components on reliability and availability are particularly important.

Descriptors: optical communications; transmission system; optoelectronic transducer; optical waveguide, line equipment; supervision and fault location; power-feeding

---

Knoblauch, G.; Toussaint: H.-N. **SIEMENS**

Connectors for Fiber-Optic Components and Systems

14 figures, 6 references

telcom report 6 (1983)

Special Issue "Optical Communications", pp. 96 to 101

The authors begin by outlining the principles of a separable fiber-to-fiber connection and go on to discuss the tolerance problems of such connections. They also consider the tolerances both of the fibers and the individual precision connectors, and the factors involved in processing the fiber end faces. The tools required for field assembly are also presented.

Descriptors: optical signal transmission; optical waveguide; connector; measurement and definition of connector loss; tolerance effect: connector assembly

---

Fluhr, J.; Marending, P.; Trimmel, H. **SIEMENS**

A Fiber-Optic System for Transmitting 8 Mbit/s Signals

8 figures, 2 tables

telcom report 6 (1983)

Special Issue "Optical Communications", pp. 119 to 124

The article describes a second-order digital transmission system with regenerators; the electrical interfaces correspond to CCITT Recommendation G.703. The supervision equipment is designed for in-service monitoring or local monitoring; the optical components are designed for transmission at optical wavelengths around 850 nm on graded-index fibers. For a cable attenuation of 3.5 dB/km a distance of approximately 13 km can -be spanned between regenerators.

Descriptors: optical communications; 8 Mbit/s system; MCMI line code; line terminating unit LA8GF

Toussaint, H.-N.; Winzer, G. **SIEMENS**

Technology and Applications of Couplers for Optical Communications

8 figures, 4 references

telcom report 6 (1983)

Special Issue "Optical Communications", pp. 102 to 107

Optical couplers are "multiport" devices, whose behavior is described by a scattering matrix. A basic distinction is made between end-fire and evanescent-field couplers. The article deals with the technology of various types of coupler and describes some typical applications (for example in optical bus systems) in addition to technical data.

Descriptors: optical communications; scattering matrix; optical multiport; optical coupler; optical switch

---

Stegmeier, A.; Trimmel, H. **SIEMENS**

A Fiber-Optic System for Transmitting 34 Mbit/s Signals

6 figures, 2 tables, 8 references

telcom report 6 (1983)

Special Issue "Optical Communications", pp. 125 to 129

The article describes a third-order digital transmission system with regenerators; the interface conditions correspond to CCITT Recommendation G.703. The system is designed for optical wavelengths of 850 and 1300 nm. Graded-index or single-mode fibers can be used as the transmission medium. The components used on the optical transmission path allow regenerator spacings to be as much as 55 km.

Descriptors: optical communications; 34 Mbit/s systems; 5B/6B line code; line equipment LA34GF

Photoreport **SIEMENS**

Information Takes New Paths

9 figures

telcom report 6 (1983)

Special Issue "Optical Communications", pp. 108 to 111

Optical waveguides, silica-glass fibers with a thickness of about 0.1 mm, will be used in the global communication network. This alternative to the copper conductor will open up completely new possibilities for future communications. The available bandwidth would permit the moving picture to be added to the forms of communication employed hitherto. Siemens has already used this new technology in many areas; more than 30,000 km of fiber have been installed so far.

Descriptors: optical communications; optical waveguide; completed project; cable system; transmission system

---

Dömer, J.; Gier, J. **SIEMENS**

A Fiber-Optic System for Transmitting 140 Mbit/s Signals

6 figures, 1 table, 7 references

telcom report 6 (1983)

Special Issue "Optical Communications", pp. 130 to 133

The authors describe the line equipment for the optical transmission of 140 Mbit/s digital signals. Both graded-index and single-mode fibers in the 1300 nm wavelength region are suitable as the transmission medium. If graded-index fibers are used, the maximum spacing between two regenerators is 18 km, while the length of a digital line path may be up to 1200 km.

Descriptors: optical communications; digital signal transmission; digital line path; 140 Mbit/s operating system; line terminating unit; regenerator; fault location

Siemens Power Engineering

Volume V, 1983, A4, 44 pages per issue,
6 issues per year,
1 being a double issue
Price per copy: 20.40 DM
Double issue: 40.80 DM

Through up-to-the-minute articles and brief news items this journal informs the reader about the generation, transmission, distribution and application of electrical energy and about installation systems and equipment. Since in almost all these sectors there is an increasing tendency for instrumentation and control equipment to incorporate computer components, regular reports are provided on the state of the computer art, including process control computers. This journal gives an insight into development, planning, production and operation.

Readership: power supply and transport companies, all branches of trade and industry, public authorities, administrations and associations, technical and technical/trade organizations, advisory agencies, universities and colleges, institutes and libraries.

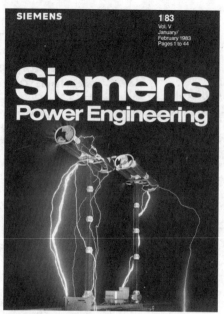

Order No. L-04/x83-101
ISSN 0170-950X

Siemens Power Engineering

with

Siemens Power Engineering PRODUCT NEWS

(These two journals are covered by one subscription) a total of 10 issues,
1 being a double issue
Price of annual subscription: 158 DM

Order No. L-21/x83-101
ISSN 0721-5681

Siemens Power Engineering PRODUCT NEWS

Volume III, 1983, A4,
24 pages per issue,
4 issues per year
Price per copy: 6.80 DM

Siemens Power Engineering PRODUCT NEWS reports on products from the fields of drive and control systems, automation and instrumentation systems and standard power engineering products.

The structure and basic applications of the products described are largely not dependent on the branch of industry they are required for.

Readership: licenced electricians, technical staff, engineers and managers in the fields of industry, trade and crafts, in small firms and in the power production and distribution sectors.

Main areas of activity: development, planning and design, production, test department, purchasing department, maintenance.

Kügler, E. **SIEMENS**

Development Trends in Higher Order Fiber-Optic Transmission Systems

2 figures, 1 table, 7 references

telcom report 6 (1983)

Special Issue "Optical Communications", pp. 134 to 136

Optical waveguides are suitable for transmitting signals at very high bit rates; for example, transmission systems employing single-mode fibers operating at a few Gbit/s are conceivable. The components and technologies available – and their quality assurance – are important factors. A 565 Mbit/s system for single-mode fibers operating at $\lambda = 1300$ nm is under development, while current studies are investigating technologies for the Gbit/s range.

Descriptors: optical waveguide; single-mode fiber; digital signal transmission; 565 Mbit/s system; 1300 nm transmission window

---

Pichlmayer, E.; Stegmeier, A. **SIEMENS**

A Fiber-Optic Transmission System for Signal Bandwidths up to 7.5 MHz

9 figures, 2 tables, 7 references

telcom report 6 (1983)

Special Issue "Optical Communications", pp. 151 to 155

The LA7/20GF system offers a transparent transmission channel for both analog and digital signals in the 1 Hz to 7.5 MHz range. The signal modulates the frequency of a 20 MHz carrier which drives an infrared-emitting diode or a laser diode. An avalanche photodiode at the receiver restores the optical signal to an electrical signal; it is then demodulated and amplified. The system transmits video signals and PCM signals up to 8 Mbit/s.

Descriptors: fiber-optic transmission system LA7/20GF; frequency modulation; transparent transmission channel; video signal transmission; PCM signal transmission

---

Braun, E. **SIEMENS**

BIGFON Brings the Optical Waveguide into the Subscriber Area

5 figures, 1 table, 2 references

telcom report 6 (1983)

Special Issue "Optical Communications", pp. 136 to 139

With BIGFON the Deutsche Bundespost has taken a decisive step towards further improving telecommunications of the future. The article describes the system concept for the establishment of "BIGFON islands" which will soon appear in West Berlin and Munich once the range of services on offer and the timetable have been finalized. In the context of this Special Issue, this article is more concerned with the problems of transmission in the BIGFON system trials.

Descriptors: fiber-optic transmission; broadband communication; local communication network; subscriber terminal

---

Anders, A. **SIEMENS**

A Fiber-Optic Analog System for Application in Electric Utilities

5 figures, 1 table, 3 references

telcom report 6 (1983)

Special Issue "Optical Communications", pp. 156 to 160

The article describes an analog system which can transmit up to 132 FDM telephone channels on optical fibers. The system is particularly suitable for electric utilities to provide communication links running parallel to high voltage lines. Repeaters are provided for spanning long distances. In addition, the advantages of the optical transmission of analog signals over transmission via metallic lines are discussed.

Descriptors: optical communication in electric utilities; FDM analog system; frequency range 6 to 550 kHz; fault-locating equipment; two-fiber/single-fiber operation

---

Bauch, H.; Weinhardt, K. **SIEMENS**

Communication in the Subscriber Area of Optical Broadband Networks

6 figures, 9 references

telcom report 6 (1983)

Special Issue "Optical Communications" pp. 140 to 146

The following are provided on one subscriber line, consisting of two optical fibers: 16 channels at 64 kbit/s each for telephone or data transmission, 4 channels at 960 kbit/s each for stereo sound transmission and 4 FM channels for video telephony or TV transmission. The TDM digital signals are combined with the analog signals to form a 170 MHz FDM signal with which the intensity of an 880 nm carrier is modulated.

Descriptors: subscriber line; switched and distribution services; frequency modulation; frequency division multiplex and wavelength division multiplex

---

Knoblauch, G. **SIEMENS**

Fiber-Optic Components and Systems for Industrial Applications

12 figures, 1 table, 4 references

telcom report 6 (1983)

Special Issue "Optical Communications", pp. 161 to 165

The advantages of transmitting information via optical waveguides has led to the development of a wide range of components specially for industrial applications. Connectors, optoelectronic transducers, simple transmitters and receivers, complete systems for standard interfaces and couplers for establishing complex optical bus structures for future process control systems are all described in this article.

Descriptors: optical information transmission; fiber-optic components; fiber-optic systems; connector; optoelectronic transducer; coupler

---

Aichholz, E.; Tilly, B. **SIEMENS**

A Fiber-Optic System for FM Radio Relay Feeder Links and High-Quality TV Transmission

6 figures, 1 table, 1 reference

telcom report 6 (1983)

Special Issue "Optical Communications", pp. 147 to 150

The article describes fiber-optic analog system LA10/70GF as a feeder for radio relay equipment with the standard FM/IF interface of 70 MHz. The most important components of the optoelectronic transducer are the laser diode with its regulated cooling and optical power on the transmit side, and the avalanche photodiode on the receive side. The transmission medium is a graded-index fiber with a core diameter of 50 μm.

Descriptors: fiber-optic analog system LA10/70GF; TV signal transmission; radio relay feeder; broadband laser source; laser module; optical receiver; avalanche photodiode

---

Klement, E.; Rössner, K. **SIEMENS**

Principles of Optical Measurements for Communications Systems

4 figures, 2 tables, 9 references

telcom report 6 (1983)

Special Issue "Optical Communications", pp. 167 to 171

The transmission characteristics of optical waveguides are described by several parameters with differing importances for manufacturer and user. Test methods for the principal parameters are described in this article. Standardization of the test methods is necessary to facilitate comparison, but this has not yet been completed. The current status is outlined.

Descriptors: optical communications; standardization of test methods; attenuation, bandwidth, transfer function; equilibrium mode distribution; numerical aperture; index profile

Order No. L-02/x83-101
ISSN 0302-2528

Siemens Review

Volume L, 1983, A4,
32 pages per issue, 6 issues per year
Annual subscription: 60 DM
Price per copy: 10 DM

Siemens Review provides information on the aims and achievements of the company as a whole, including the consolidated holding companies, and above all on innovations, development trends, customized approaches to solving problems and the position of Siemens AG with regard to economic and social questions. The topics are dealt with in an easily understandable manner, emphasis being placed on the higher economic and social aspects. This magazine is aimed at people who take decisions in economic, administrative and public sectors and those who mold opinions in state and society.

Siemens Review

Reports on the company's technical, economic and social aims and achievements. Comments on topics under public discussion.

Eibl-Vogt, A.; Permien, J.　　　　**SIEMENS**

**System Test Equipment for Optical Waveguides
and Optical Cable Links**

6 figures, 4 references

telcom report 6 (1983)

Special Issue "Optical Communications", pp. 171 to 175

The new generation of system test equipment is easy to use and permits rapid measurement and display of the results. The way in which light is coupled into the test item in the attenuation test set is so arranged that a quasi-stable mode distribution is ensured at the beginning of the fiber. The handy attenuation testers are battery powered and can be used practically anywhere. The fiber characteristics can be investigated from one end of the fiber using the reflectometer.

Descriptors: optical waveguide test equipment; attenuation test set; attenuation tester; reflectometer

---

Auracher, F.; Keil, R.　　　　**SIEMENS**

Integrated Optics for Single-Mode Transmission Systems

5 figures, 10 references

telcom report 6 (1983)

Special Issue "Optical Communications", pp. 195 to 198

After a short introduction to integrated optics, a few examples of modules already realized and of some conceivable in the future are given. The advantages of this new technology are principally the compact structure, robust and reliable components, fewer interconnections and, not least, cost-effective production. The problems and limits of integrated optics are also indicated.

Descriptors: integrated optics; optical waveguide; optical modulator; switch, single-mode technology

---

Deserno, U.; Schicketanz, D.　　　　**SIEMENS**

Measurement Methods for Future Fiber-Optic Applications

11 figures, 19 references

telcom report 6 (1983)

Special Issue "Optical Communications", pp. 176 to 182

This paper considers as yet unresolved aspects of the measurements required for future applications. The effect of excitation conditions on the attenuation of multimode fibers is discussed with particular reference to measuring the radiation pattern. The difficulties associated with single-mode system measurement are in determining attenuation, spot size, cutoff wavelength and minimum dispersion.

Descriptors: radiation pattern; dynamic spectrum; single-mode fiber; attenuation; spot size; cutoff wavelength; minimum dispersion; polarization

---

Oestreich, U.; Zeidler, G.　　　　**SIEMENS**

Development Trends in Fiber and Cable

1 figure, 8 references

telcom report 6 (1983)

Special Issue "Optical communications", pp. 198 to 201

Continuing development of optical cable systems is expected to produce advances in fiber materials and innovations in cable applications. In the case of fiber, there are signs that the usable wavelength range will continue to be extended into the infrared region, giving even smaller overall attenuation values. As far as cable is concerned, we can expect special cable designs to open up new applications involving extreme stresses (e.g. aerial or submarine cable).

Descriptors: optical waveguides in the wavelength range around 1600 nm and above 2000 nm; non-oxide glass; submarine cable; aerial cable

---

Sutor, N.　　　　**SIEMENS**

**Testing the Mechanical and Thermal Characteristics
of Optical Cables**

9 figures, 1 table, 8 references

telcom report 6 (1983)

Special Issue "Optical Communications", pp. 183 to 187

Extensive demands are made on the transmission and environmental characteristics of optical cables. Whereas the transmission property is principally dependant upon the fiber, the environmental characteristics are primarily influenced by the cable design. A series of mechanical and thermal test methods is employed to determine the environmental characteristics.

Descriptors: testing optical cables; thermal cycle; tensile strength; fiber and cable strain; crush resistance; flex resistance; hammer test; operating range

---

Braun, E.; Möhrmann, K.H.　　　　**SIEMENS**

**Optical Communications in Short-Haul and Long-Haul
Wideband Communication Networks**

2 figures, 1 table, 8 references

telcom report 6 (1983)

Special Issue "Optical Communications", pp. 202 to 205

The introduction of optical waveguides into the short-haul and long-haul networks permits, on the one hand, subscriber-oriented wideband communication with normal television quality and, on the other, the realization of integrated networks in which all switched and distribution services are offered simultaneously. The choice of a suitable encoding bit rate is of primary importance for moving picture transmission. Picture signal encoding with a bit rate of 34 Mbit/s is considered to be a favorable compromise.

Descriptors: optical communications; wideband communication; integrated network; BIGFON; moving-picture encoding

---

Völkel, G.; Wallner, E.　　　　**SIEMENS**

Quality Assurance Methods for Optoelectronic Semiconductors

7 figures, 1 table

telcom report 6 (1983)

Special Issue "Optical Communications", pp. 188 to 193

The article deals with quality assurance methods for optoelectronic semiconductors. Detailed descriptions are given of concepts, methods and activities involved in development, testing and manufacture, with examples taken from optical waveguide systems.

Descriptors: quality assurance; test equipment; testing; components; optoelectronic semiconductor

---

Wolf, E.　　　　**SIEMENS**

Worldwide Introduction of Fiber-Optic Systems

6 figures, 2 tables, 9 references

telcom report 6 (1983)

Special Issue "Optical Communications", pp. 206 to 211

To an increasing extent optical cables are replacing traditional copper cables; the major field of application is and will continue to be telecommunications. The use of this new technology in the subscriber network will open up completely new horizons: it will allow, for the first time, broadband services with bidirectional moving picture communication on a single cable to be provided on an economic basis alongside the digital services, such as teletex, already available via copper cable.

Descriptors: market chances for optical waveguide systems; parameters for system planning; economics; use in future telecommunication networks; broadband communication

telcom report

Volume VI, 1983, A4,
approx. 48 pages per issue,
6 issues per year,
2 being double issues
Annual subscription: 90 DM
Price per copy: 14 DM
Double issue: 22.80 DM

telcom report provides information on the entire spectrum of communications technology and on applications for data technology in the telecommunications sector. This information ranges from discussions about new ideas and descriptions of exchanges and systems to customers' reports on their practical experience. Trends in the communications sector are dealt with, and views on cost-effectiveness are given. Each of the issues is designed to illustrate the activities in the fields of communications terminals, private and special communications networks, public communications networks, security systems, research and development, data processing and components for communications and data systems. This journal shows how Siemens is able to offer complex solutions to all communications-oriented problems. It is written for people who take decisions in the spheres of technology and industrial management and for those who mold opinions.
Readership: PTTs, other operators of communications facilities, government departments, public authorities, local authorities, railroad administrations, police, military departments, customers in trade and industry and power supply companies, specialist circles such as universities and colleges, associations, technical and technical/trade organizations, advisory agencies, operating companies.

Order No. L-13/3816-101
ISBN 3-8009-3816-2

telcom report
Special Issue
"Digital Transmission"

Overview of the entire field of Siemens digital transmission, modulators and multiplexers, line equipment for symmetrical and coaxial cables.
1979, 191 pages, 201 figures, 22 tables, A4, hardback, 55 DM

Order No. L-13/x83-101
ISSN 0344-4880

telcom report

State of the art and development trends in voice, text, image and data communications. Specialist articles on switching and transmission systems, terminals, networks for public and private use, security systems and data teleprocessing.